W9-AZJ-624

REGIONAL
DYNAMICS
OF THE
INDONESIAN
REVOLUTION

REGIONAL DYNAMICS OF THE INDONESIAN REVOLUTION

UNITY FROM DIVERSITY

EDITED BY

Audrey R. Kahin

UNIVERSITY OF HAWAII PRESS

HONOLULU

Library of Congress Cataloging in Publication Data

Main entry under title:

Regional dynamics of the Indonesian Revolution.

  Includes index.
  1. Indonesia—History—Revolution, 1945–1949.
  2. Indonesia—History, Local. I. Kahin, Audrey.
DS644.R36   1985   959.8'035   85–8532
ISBN 0-8248-0982-3

CONTENTS

Maps	vii
Preface	ix
Introduction	1
PART 1 REGIONS FREE OF EXTERNAL AUTHORITY	21
The Tiga Daerah Affair: Social Revolution or Rebellion? Anton Lucas	23
Banten: "Rice Debts Will Be Repaid with Rice, Blood *Debts with Blood"* Michael C. Williams	55
Aceh: Social Revolution and the Islamic Vision Eric Morris	83
PART 2 BATTLEGROUNDS FOR COMPETING STATES	111
East Sumatra: Accommodating an Indonesian Nation within *a Sumatran Residency* Michael van Langenberg	113
West Sumatra: Outpost of the Republic Audrey R. Kahin	145
PART 3 REGIONS OF DUTCH DOMINANCE	177
Jakarta: Cooperation and Resistance in an Occupied City Robert Cribb	179
South Sulawesi: Puppets and Patriots Barbara S. Harvey	207
Ambon: Not a Revolution but a Counterrevolution Richard Chauvel	237

Overview 265
Glossary 285
Contributors 293
Index 295

MAPS

Indonesian Archipelago	xii
Tiga Daerah	22
Banten	54
Aceh	82
East Sumatra	112
West Sumatra	144
Jakarta	178
South Sulawesi	206
Ambon	236

PREFACE

It is now forty years since Indonesia's independence was proclaimed, and soon it will be impossible to hear the story of the revolution from those who actually participated. Already this is true of most of the national leaders who headed the independence movement. Fortunately, before their deaths several wrote down their reminiscences or responded to interviewers' questions, so that their perspective on the struggle has been recorded.

The idea for the present book grew initially out of my own research in West Sumatra on the nature of the 1945–1950 revolution there. From this research I had come to realize that many of the generalizations being drawn on the basis of national-level histories of the revolution and the accounts of leaders in the Republic of Indonesia's central government gave an unbalanced picture of the revolutionary experience. Often, it was clear to me, these generalizations did not accord with the nature of events in the Minangkabau region of West Sumatra. Assuming that this was probably also true for other areas, and aware that several scholars had recently been focusing their attention on writing histories of various regions of the archipelago, I attempted to bring together a group of scholars who had established themselves as specialists on the revolutionary history of a particular region, in the hope that the presentation of a diverse cross-section embracing a variety of local perspectives might further illuminate the nature of the struggle waged in Indonesia during the 1940s. Earlier efforts, of course, have been made to shift the angle of vision from which to view the revolutionary years. The most important of these were, first, John Smail's *Bandung in the Early Revolution, 1945–1946* (1964) and more recently Anthony Reid's *Blood of the People: Revolution and the End of Traditional Rule in Northern Sumatra* (1979), but these two studies present the viewpoint of single regions.

A history such as the present one is long overdue, but it would have been extremely difficult to accomplish until a few years ago as scholars began to have access to, and draw on, the military and political records of the Dutch administration for the 1945–1950 period. As will be seen from the notes, all the contributors relied heavily on these archives to supplement and balance the information received from Indonesian participants in the areas where they conducted their research. The following are the major Dutch archives to which frequent references appear throughout the book. On political and economic affairs, the General State Archives (Algemeen Rijksarchief, ARA) in The Hague (where the principal collections concerning the events of 1945–1950 are those of the General Secretariat [Algemene Secretarie, Eerste en Tweede Zending, ASB I and II] and the Attorney General [Procureur-Generaal bij het Hoogerrechtshof van Nederlandsch-Indië, *Proc. Gen.*]) and the archives of the former Ministry of the Colonies (Ministerie van Overzeese Gebiedsdelen [Minog]), now under the Ministry of Internal Affairs (Ministerie van Binnenlandse Zaken), also in The Hague. Military records are found in two principal locations, the Central Archives (Centraal Archieven Depot) of the Ministry of Defense (Ministerie van Defensie, MvD) and the Historical Section (Sectie Krijgsgeschiedenis, SK) of the Staff of the Commander of Land Forces (Staf van de bevelhebber der Landstrijdkrachten), both in The Hague.

Other repositories contain materials on the period of Japanese and British influence during the early 1940s. Most of the British records are held in the Public Record Office (PRO) in Kew, London, particularly in the files of the Cabinet Office (CAB), Foreign Office (FO), and War Office (WO). Two major sources of materials on the Japanese occupation are the State Institute for War Documentation (Rijksinstituut voor Oorlogsdocumentatie) in Amsterdam and the Nishijima Collection at Waseda University in Tokyo. Among the many other archives and libraries where relevant materials are housed are the National Library (Perpustakaan Nasional) and National Archives

(Arsip Nasional) in Jakarta, the Royal Institute of Linguistics and Ethnography (Koninklijk Instituut voor Taal-, Land- en Volkenkunde) in Leiden, and the John M. Echols Collection at Cornell University Library, in Ithaca, New York.

Indonesian orthography always presents problems. For the sake of consistency, the spelling of Indonesian words throughout the book follows the new system introduced in 1972, with the exception of quotations from documents and personal names, which have been spelled according to individual preference insofar as this could be determined. This attempt at consistency has resulted in some anomalies, in that organizations and parties that had ceased to exist before the new spelling was introduced appear as they never did during their lifetime (e.g., Masyumi rather than Masjumi). However, in the long run the procedure should avert some confusion.

This book has been more than four years in the making, and during this period I have incurred many debts of gratitude. I wish to thank in particular Tsuyoshi Kato, Takashi Shiraishi, Benedict Anderson, and George McT. Kahin, who all contributed in different ways through their comments and criticisms, and Susan Osborne Rogers, who helped in editing earlier draft chapters and made me realize that the project might in fact eventually be completed. I wish also to thank Ann Wicks, Roberta Ludgate, and Trudy Calvert, all of whom aided at different stages in typing the manuscript. The University of Hawaii Press has been most encouraging and supportive, and I would particularly like to thank Damaris Kirchhofer and the editorial staff who have given me many useful suggestions. I wish also to thank the two readers whose constructive criticisms enabled me to revise and improve some parts of the manuscript.

No editor could wish for a more cooperative and patient group of contributors than I have had the good fortune to work with; and I wish to acknowledge my appreciation to them for these qualities as well as for the value of their contributions.

AUDREY R. KAHIN

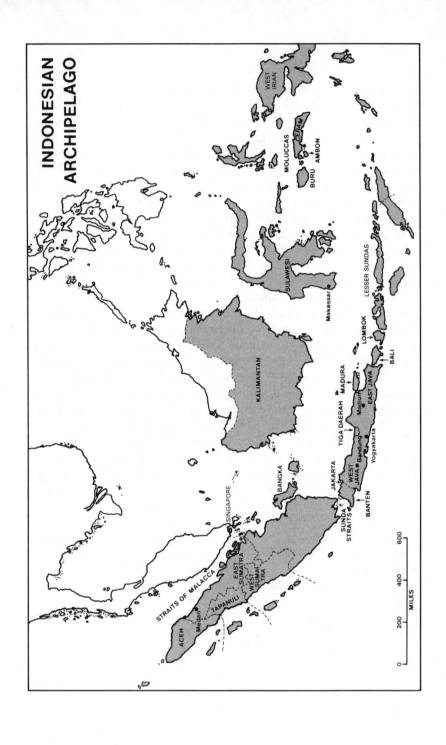

INDONESIAN ARCHIPELAGO

WEST IRIAN

MOLUCCAS
CERAM
BURU
AMBON

SULAWESI

Makassar

LESSER SUNDAS

LOMBOK

BALI

KALIMANTAN

TIGA DAERAH
MADURA
Madiun
EAST JAVA
Yogyakarta

JAKARTA
WEST JAVA
Bandung
BANTEN
SUNDA STRAITS

BANGKA

SINGAPORE

EAST SUMATRA
WEST SUMATRA

STRAITS OF MALACCA

TAPANULI

ACEH
Medan

MILES

0   200   400   600

INTRODUCTION

Audrey R. Kahin

The views and perspective of Indonesia's national leaders have dominated studies of the country's independence struggle. Most histories of the revolution have looked outward from the center of the revolutionary Republic to the country's own regions as well as to the international world. In a nation whose extensive territories incorporate diverse ethnic, religious, and cultural groups, and where the record of events and attitudes in outlying areas has not been easily accessible, the dominance of such a perspective is perhaps inevitable. However, the men leading the Republic from its capital on Java were basing their claims to leadership of the country and its revolution on an assumption of popular support in the *daerah* (regions), and without the strength provided by that military, political, and moral backing, they would have been unable to compel the Dutch to acknowledge the independence of the new nation state. Thus the course of events in Indonesia's regions is an integral and decisive part of the struggle through which the country gained its independence.

Recognizing this fact, this book endeavors to shift the perspective usually adopted in histories of this period and view the revolutionary process from the local level rather than from the center. It presents a series of studies of the revolutionary period in eight regions of Indonesia. Three of these lie in Sumatra (Aceh, East Sumatra, and West Sumatra), three in Java (Banten, Jakarta, and the "Tiga Daerah" ["Three Regions" on the north coast of Central Java]), and two in eastern Indonesia (South Sulawesi and Ambon). Each of the contributors views the events of the revolutionary years essentially through the eyes of the local participants (all the authors having drawn on the memories of survivors and on local records as well as on material available in Indonesian and Dutch national archives). No such study could, of course, embrace the whole of the archipelago, but the areas covered are sufficiently diverse to give some indication of the range of revolutionary experiences making up the Indonesian independence struggle as well as of the diversity of groups, cultures, and attitudes in the country to whose peoples the Dutch finally yielded sovereignty. It is hoped that, by providing this regional context of the revolution, these accounts will provide new insights into its structure and into the nature of the Indonesian national state that emerged from the conflict.

The boundaries of that new Indonesian state were arbitrarily determined by the degree of Dutch success during the previous centuries in establishing control over an archipelago stretching approximately three thousand miles and embracing widely differing societies and peoples. Colonial rule had come first to a number of small islands in the eastern archipelago, including Ambon, where in the early 1600s the Dutch East India Company (VOC) dislodged earlier Portuguese colonialists. In 1619 it took over the town that was to become the capital of the Netherlands East Indies—Batavia (now Jakarta) on the north coast of Java. Thereafter Dutch expansion through the archipelago was slow and spasmodic. Although nationalist slogans later referred to three hundred years of colonial rule, even a hundred and fifty years ago the Netherlands Indies administration, which superseded the Company at the end of the eighteenth century, ruled over relatively small, scattered areas of what was to become Indonesia. It was not until the mid- and late nineteenth century that the rapid expansion of colonial control took place. From 1825 to 1830 the Dutch confronted major indigenous opposition in Central Java, and in 1837 they subdued long religious-led resistance in the uplands of central Sumatra. By 1850 they dominated all of Java and much of Sumatra. Only after thirty years of bitter warfare, from 1874 to 1904, however, were they able to overcome opposition in the Islamic Sultanate of Aceh, and only in the first decade of the twentieth century were the last independent areas both of Aceh and South Sulawesi brought under colonial control.

From early in this century, then, the Dutch exerted varying degrees of authority over virtually all of the territories that would later constitute an independent Indonesia. From that time on, events in the outlying areas were intertwined with those occurring at the center, first of Dutch and then of Republican power. During the first four decades of this century the growth of an Indonesian consciousness spread widely and deeply through the archipelago. It was never confined, as most Dutch believed, to just a few small groups of Western-educated leaders in the towns and cities. Frequently married with long-nurtured local opposition to colonial rule, the concept of the Indonesian entity held in many of the regions, however, generally diverged from that in the major urban centers of Dutch power. The envisaged shape and character of "Indonesia" were in part determined by each region's own traditions, culture, and history, and by the orientations of the local groups that spearheaded opposition to the colonial power there.

In depicting the struggle in the regions, the histories brought together here assume some understanding of the national and international context of the Indonesian revolution and of some of the basic divisions within the Republic proclaimed in August 1945. To help explain these and provide guidance to references made in the regionally focused chapters that make up this book, the following few pages will sketch in some of this background.

The Prewar Nationalist Movement

The first Indonesia-wide vehicle for the anti-Dutch nationalist movement was the Sarekat Islam (SI, Islamic Union), established in Surakarta in 1912 as a protective association for indigenous batik merchants. Attracting support from a broad spectrum of society, it grew rapidly, claiming more than two million members throughout the archipelago by 1918 and calling in its program for complete independence for the Netherlands Indies. Although the SI embraced a wide range of political ideologies, Islamic leaders dominated the association in its early years. Increasingly, however, this dominance was challenged by Marxist and non-Marxist radicals among its members. Their ISDV (Indies Social Democratic Association) founded in 1914 was transformed in 1920 into the Indonesian Communist Party (PKI, Partai Komunis Indonesia). Apprehensive of the Communist success in many of the SI's local branches, its Islamic leaders passed a resolution at the 1921 Congress of the Sarekat Islam prohibiting members from belonging to other organizations—a resolution which in effect expelled the Communists. Subsequent struggles between Moslems and Communists for control at the local level further weakened the SI. At the same time, Dutch repression of the PKI in the early 1920s prevented it too from developing a cohesive organization throughout Indonesia, and the Communists also suffered from internal dissension over how to counter government restrictions against them. The PKI central committee's decision to mount a revolution in 1926 against Dutch rule finally split the party. Tan Malaka, then the Comintern's representative in Southeast Asia, believed that such an uprising would be premature and doomed to failure, so he actively campaigned against it. Ultimately the revolt, rather than breaking out in all regions of Indonesia, occurred only in Banten and West Sumatra and was easily suppressed by the Dutch. The outcome was not only destructive of the Communist organization but resulted in an enduring schism within Indonesian communism between the remnants of the PKI and the followers of Tan Malaka, who in 1927 in Bangkok founded a national Communist party, Pari (Partai Republik Indonesia). After the decline of the Sarekat Islam in the early 1920s and the crushing of the PKI in 1926 to 1927, neither religious- nor Communist-led movements were again to achieve major national prominence in the prewar period. They yielded place to a nationalist movement based in the major urban centers of Indonesia, largely dominated by that small number of Indonesians who had received tertiary-level Western education either in the Netherlands or at advanced institutions in Indonesia, chiefly in Jakarta and Bandung.

Sukarno, a young graduate in engineering of mixed Balinese/Javanese parentage, emerged as the paramount leader of the new nationalist movement, founding the Partai Nasional Indonesia (PNI) in 1927 and leading it until his arrest in December 1929. During his imprisonment the PNI split into the Partai Indonesia (Partindo), which Sukarno joined after his release in December 1931, and the Pendidikan Nasional Indonesia (Indonesian National Education) or PNI Baru (New PNI) headed by Mohammad Hatta and Sutan Sjahrir, two West Sumatrans who had received advanced education in the Netherlands.

The split between them and Sukarno was based on broad differences of strategy, with Sukarno favoring mass mobilization, while Hatta and Sjahrir sought to develop a cadre organization which they thought would be more resistant against Dutch repression and better able to spread deep understanding of nationalist ideas. In the event, neither approach was successful, for in a further crackdown in 1933 the Dutch arrested and interned until World War II not only Sukarno but also Hatta and Sjahrir, and banned both organizations. From then until the Japanese occupation in 1942, nationalist activity had to take place within the strict parameters laid down by the colonial authorities and through the controlled and powerless representative institutions they permitted to be established.

The dramatic break in the character of the nationalist movement that occurred in the 1920s, when religious and Communist organizations at the national level were virtually excluded from its mainstream, was much less evident in the areas of Indonesia outside Jakarta and other large urban centers. In the regions, charismatic leaders such as Sukarno and gestures such as the Youth Oath of 1928, in which a Congress of young Indonesians pledged allegiance to one land, one people, and one language, had an appeal that reached down to the lowest levels of society, giving a more strongly nationalist stamp to existing resistance. But the nationalism which these new leaders offered did not supplant existing anticolonial movements in the regions. In many areas, despite a consciousness of the events and leadership of the Jakarta-based nationalist movement, the major vehicles of Indonesian nationalism remained traditional and religious. As is evident in the regional histories that follow, much of the actual opposition to colonial rule in rural and outlying areas during the 1920s and 1930s was in fact still nurtured in traditional and religious associations and educational institutions, where the influence of Western thought was scarcely felt and where the Dutch could rarely penetrate effectively. Communist organizations, however, were a direct target of Dutch security forces, and they were less successful in maintaining their influence in rural areas. Both the PKI and the followers of Tan Malaka could generally continue at best a holding action, maintaining skeletal structures usually through personal contacts within villages and rural areas, or in cooperation with religious organizations.

The Coming of Independence

The Japanese occupied Indonesia from March 1942 to August 1945 and in their administration divided the country into three military territories: the 16th Army was responsible for Java; initially Sumatra formed part of the Malaya military administration, but from April 1943 it was governed as a separate unit by the 25th Army; and the Japanese Navy's Southwestern Fleet administered the whole of eastern Indonesia. Intending to annex the eastern archipelago as a permanent part of their empire, and having similar plans for Sumatra (in union with Malaya), the Japanese granted little latitude to Indonesian nationalist aspirations in either of these territories. In Java, however, the situation was different. Ambivalent regarding that island's future status, the Japanese granted Sukarno, Hatta, and other prewar nationalists considerable freedom to promote the idea of Indonesian independence in return for their help in mobilizing local support behind the Japanese war effort.

It was with the aim of utilizing indigenous support against a future Allied invasion that the Japanese also provided military training to large numbers of Indonesians on both Java and Sumatra, first in the auxiliary Heihō and later in the Peta (Pembela Tanah Air, Defenders of the Fatherland) on Java and the Giyūgun (People's Militia) on Sumatra. As Allied success multiplied and the Japanese position became more precarious, however, they increased their demands for forced labor and rice deliveries from the Indonesian people. Combined with the virtually complete cessation of consumer imports into Indonesia, this created widespread suffering throughout all regions of the country, which deepened during the final year of the occupation to a point unparalleled in recent Indonesian history.

Even before the Japanese capitulation, international priorities dictated by events in other parts of the world influenced the way in which Indonesia was to achieve independence. In July 1945 the Allied leaders at Potsdam reached strategic decisions shifting responsiblity for operations in most of the Netherlands East Indies from General MacArthur's command to the South East Asia Command (SEAC) of Admiral Louis Mountbatten, whose authority had previously extended from mainland Southeast Asia only to Sumatra. Because of insufficient manpower, transport, and military intelligence, Mountbatten's British and Indian forces were unable to embark on their task of repatriating the Japanese and liberating Allied prisoners of war on Java and Sumatra until at least late September. In much of Java and Sumatra, nationalists had by then seized on the opportunity presented by this absence of outside power. Nationalists in east Indonesia, however, had no such chance, for before the end of the war Australian forces were already strongly established in Kalimantan and New Guinea, and immediately after the Japanese surrender they moved both to disarm and repatriate the Japanese and restore Dutch authority to much of the eastern archipelago.

On August 17, 1945, in Jakarta, Sukarno and Hatta jointly proclaimed Indonesia's independence. This was followed by a series of hasty measures in the capital to create a Republican state. The Committee for the Preparation of Indonesian Independence, convened by the Japanese shortly before their surrender and attended by representatives from several parts of the archipelago, adopted a constitution, elected Sukarno and Hatta as president and vice-president, respectively, and transformed itself into the Central Indonesian National Committee (KNIP, Komite Nasional Indonesia Pusat). The new government appointed a governor for each of the eight provinces into which it had divided the country. Despite its inability to back up its claim to leadership by force of arms, the Republican government on Java issued directives—administrative, political, and social—to the regions by radio and telegraph. But in those areas of the archipelago where nationalists seized power, it was usually the local leaders who took the initiative and gave substance to the very vague and general guidelines emanating from Jakarta.

For most of Indonesia, the proclamation was followed by a period of transition. The Allies charged the Japanese with maintaining law and order until British or Australian forces could take over from them, but, despite this, in many of the towns and rural areas both on Java and Sumatra during these weeks, Republicans were able to assume control. The Australians were officially in command of most of the eastern archipelago by September, and the British took over from the Japanese in the rest of the country in early October. The British, however, made little effort to extend their control beyond a few scattered enclaves, usually journeying inland only to prisoner-of-war camps and for brief reconnaissance missions. Even within their restricted base areas, they faced far greater opposition than they had bargained for, and, in the face of de facto Republican control of the surrounding areas, they felt it necessary to compromise to an extent that the outraged Dutch charged was a virtual recognition of the Republic. Sporadic clashes sometimes escalated into heavy sustained fighting, and the British were frequently so hard pressed that they had to rearm Japanese troops and send them to fight against the Indonesians. The fiercest battle occurred in Surabaya, where in October to November 1945 it was only after more than three weeks of savage fighting that British air, naval, and ground forces were able to wrest the town from its Indonesian defenders.

The War against the Dutch

For at least the first year of the Republic's existence, its adherents controlled most of Java and Sumatra and faced little military opposition from the Dutch. The Netherlands' devastated condition at the end of the war made it immensely difficult for her government to mobilize sufficient forces to mount a major campaign to regain her former East Indies possessions, and so Dutch officials did their utmost to prolong the stay of the Allied troops to maintain control of key areas until Netherlands forces were strong enough to replace them. In view of their military weakness and the extent of support within Indonesia for the independence declaration, the Dutch felt obliged to make some concessions to the resurgent forces of nationalism and attempted to establish a new relationship, one which would preserve important aspects of the old colonial tie, but in a new form. On February 10, 1946, Lt. Governor-General H. J. van Mook presented proposals for a federal state of Indonesia, with the promise of a commonwealth relationship to the Kingdom of the Netherlands. These proposals served as the basis for negotiations with the Republic, held under the auspices of the British, which eventuated in the Linggajati Agreement. The principal provisions of this agreement were that the Dutch government recognized the Republic as the de facto authority in Java and Sumatra and that both sides undertook to work toward establishment of "a sovereign, democratic, federal state," the United States of Indonesia, consisting of the Republic of Indonesia (Java and Sumatra), Borneo (Kalimantan), and the Great East (Sulawesi, the Lesser Sundas, the Moluccas, and West New Guinea). This federal state would then join with the Netherlands in a Netherlands–Indonesian Union. Within the Republic there was considerable opposition to these terms, which at least temporarily conceded to the Dutch their control over regions of Indonesia outside Java and Sumatra. Although initialled in November 1946, the agreement did not receive endorsement from the Republic's Central National Committee (KNIP) until early March 1947 at a meeting at Malang, at which Sukarno and Hatta made the issue one of confidence in their leadership. Endorsement of the agreement had a dampening effect on resistance in those parts of the archipelago where the Republican leadership had acknowledged Dutch authority.

Only four months later, on July 21, 1947, charging violations of the Linggajati Agreement, the Dutch launched their first major attack on the Republic (an attack they euphemistically termed a "police action"). Through military operations they extended their control over about two-thirds of Java and over a smaller area of Sumatra—one incorporating most of the island's large plantations and oil fields. But the attack hurt the Netherlands' image in the international community. In direct reaction India and Australia brought the Dutch-Indonesia dispute before the United Nations at the end of July, and the Security Council set up a Good Offices Committee, charged with settling the dispute by peaceful means. The committee was made up of three representatives: Belgium, chosen by the Netherlands; Australia, chosen by Indonesia; and the United States, as a third "neutral" member acceptable to both sides.

Under the auspices of the Good Offices Committee, the Republic and the Netherlands met for talks in December 1947 on neutral territory—the U.S. ship *Renville* anchored off the Java coast. At these meetings, the Indonesian delegation headed by Prime Minister Amir Sjarifuddin ultimately signed the Renville Agreement of January 19, 1948. This agreement proclaimed a ceasefire but acknowledged temporary Dutch control over areas their military forces had overrun, pending a plebiscite to be held in all Dutch-controlled territories to determine whether the local people wished to be governed by the Republic or to become part of the Dutch-sponsored federal system.

In the regions they occupied, the Dutch had already begun in 1946 to set up states and autonomous territories which were to form part of the projected Federal State of Indonesia, and they continued to do this in the territories they had invaded in July 1947. In total, the Dutch created fifteen such federal units, six of which were termed states and the remainder having the status of autonomous territories. The strongest states were Pasundan (West Java), Sumatera Timur (East Sumatra), and, particularly, Negara Indonesia Timur (NIT, State of East Indonesia).

Defying the ceasefire sponsored by the UN under Renville, the Dutch again attacked the Republic on December 19, 1948, occupying its capital, Yogyakarta, and arresting and exiling most of its top leaders, including Sukarno and Hatta. As a contingency move, Hatta had earlier sent Minister of Economic Affairs Sjafruddin Prawiranegara to Sumatra to establish a government presence there should the Dutch succeed in overrunning Java. On hearing of the fall of Yogyakarta, Sjafruddin on December 22 proclaimed an Emergency Government (PDRI, Pemerintah Darurat Republik Indonesia) headquartered in the interior of West Sumatra, with himself at its head. And while Sukarno and most of the Republic's top civilian leaders remained in Dutch detention—nearly all on the island of Bangka off Sumatra's southeast coast—the Emergency Government on Sumatra, together with the Republican army under General Sudirman on Java, continued the struggle against the Dutch. Despite the apparent success of the initial Dutch attack, the vigor of Republican guerrilla resistance and pressure from the international community ultimately forced the Netherlands toward accommodation. Formal talks were begun on April 14, 1949, between a Dutch delegation, headed by J. H. van Royen, and a Republican delegation, led by Mohamad Roem. A compromise American-sponsored formula, known as the Roem–van Royen agreement, was accepted by both sides on May 7. Although this did not call for Dutch withdrawal, except from the Republican capital of Yogyakarta, it did provide for the release of the Republican leaders, and also for the convening of a Round Table Conference in The Hague to discuss the transfer of authority to a United States of Indonesia. Sukarno and Hatta returned to Yogyakarta on July 6.

Both the armed forces and the PDRI at first denounced Republican concessions in the Roem–van Royen talks, but Sjafruddin finally decided that it was futile to oppose the Sukarno/Hatta leadership and he returned his mandate as head of the Emergency Government to Sukarno in Yogyakarta on July 13. During the remainder of July, Republican representatives held discussions with representatives both of the Netherlands and of the Dutch-sponsored Federal Consultative Assembly (BFO, Bijeenkomst voor Federaal Overleg) representing the Dutch-created federal states. To the surprise of the Dutch, in the UN-sponsored Round Table Conference that opened on August 23 in The Hague, the representatives of the BFO acted as allies of the Republic. On November 2 the conference reached an agreement providing for the Netherlands to transfer sovereignty over all the Dutch East Indies except West Irian (West New Guinea) to a Republic of the United States of Indonesia by December 30, 1949.

The federal system did not survive. Although the Round Table Conference agreement provided for a federation of fifteen states plus the Republic, most of these states were weak and enjoyed negligible popular support. A mixture of persuasion and coercion on the part of the Republic, together with actions initiated by local nationalists, were enough to bring them into the Republic and a new unitary Indonesian political order. Of the stronger states, Pasundan and West Kalimantan were irrevocably compromised by the alleged involvement of their leaders in abortive anti-Republic coups, mounted in Bandung and Jakarta in January 1950 by the notorious Dutch counterinsurgency expert, R. P. P. "Turk" Westerling. The two strongest, East Sumatra and East Indonesia, were the last to go, succumbing in May 1950 to internal and external pressures.

Rumors of the imminent dissolution of the NIT sparked separatist movements within eastern Indonesia among pro-Dutch elements and former KNIL soldiers. In April 1950, KNIL (Royal Netherlands Indies Army) units awaiting demobilization in Makassar, led by Captain Andi Azis, rebelled in support of the East Indonesian State, and later that month pro-Dutch elements and former KNIL soldiers in Ambon proclaimed an independent Republic of the South Moluccas (RMS, Republik Maluku Selatan), which endured until crushed by the Indonesian army in the closing month of the year.

A unitary nation state, the Republic of Indonesia, superseded the Dutch-tainted federal order on August 17, 1950. But with the end of the nationalist struggle, the thrust of regional political pressures aroused in the revolution did not entirely subside, and the new state's central leadership had to confront regional concepts of what the revolution meant and should lead to, which often differed in important respects from their own.

Internal Dissension in the Republic

The proclamation of independence of 1945 had called forth much greater enthusiasm than the Dutch expected. Nevertheless, basic philosophical and strategic divisions weakened the Republic in confronting the Dutch. Several interrelated disputes, affecting revolutionaries in both the regions and the center, dominated the struggle from its inception and influenced its course until the transfer of sovereignty more than four years later. One of the most important of these concerned the relationship between the national independence struggle and internal social revolution.

In much of Indonesia the economic misery and widespread suffering of the closing years of the Japanese occupation had pushed large sections of the population, particularly in the rural areas of Java, to the point where, with nothing to lose, they were willing to support a revolution not only against the return of the Dutch but against the whole Indonesian social order through which the Dutch had governed. Demands arose in town and countryside for all those who had acted as agents for the Dutch and/or Japanese to be removed. Not only were the Indonesian officials or traditional rulers who had cooperated with the colonial authorities targeted, but so were Chinese and Eurasians who had often benefited economically from colonial rule. The widespread hatred against all who had served or profited from the colonial system was reinforced by a suspicion that they retained their loyalty to the Dutch and would work to facilitate their return. In the early months of independence, not only Socialist or Communist parties but also traditional and religious groups headed uprisings both against the return of the Dutch and against the existing political, social, and economic order—its Indonesian as well as Dutch and Chinese components. Many of these revolutionaries also attempted to replace the former hierarchy by an egalitarian society with democratically elected leaders.

But most Republican leaders at the center, whatever their political affiliation, adopted what they thought was the pragmatic view that achievement of independence should precede any such restructuring of Indonesian society. In discouraging or attempting to suppress the local revolutions that broke out in many parts of Java and Sumatra as the Japanese withdrew, the Republic's leaders—whether or not they had collaborated with the Japanese—were not only fearful of the chaos that might result from such uprisings; they were also preoccupied with demonstrating to the Allied powers (particularly Britain and the United States) that the Indonesian Republic was capable of governing the archipelago. Netherlands officials already scoffed at such a contention, and Dutch assertions that the Indonesian people were unable to govern themselves would thus seem more credible if violence and disorder became widespread. The Western-educated nationalist leaders feared that uncontrolled violence, besides antagonizing potentially sympathetic international opinion, could undermine a social system many elements of which they wished to retain. In their view, if the independent Indonesian state was to function effectively, it needed the services of experienced administrative and technical officials. The most qualified of these had been trained by the Dutch, and most had retained their posts under the Japanese. Republican leaders, then, saw premature removal of such officials as likely to undermine the national cohesion and economic strength needed to face Dutch power most effectively.

Nevertheless, despite their support—often grudging—of the old administrative order, most of the Republic's predominantly Western-educated leaders did want to create a more egalitarian and democratic society. They believed this could be realized more successfully at this time, not through violently overturning the social order, but through instituting a democratic political system by which far-reaching social and economic measures would be introduced in an orderly manner on the basis of careful planning. They also felt the need to refute Dutch accusations that the Republic was a Japanese creation—a fascist puppet regime that the Allies should dismantle. Both the Republic's vice-president, Mohammad Hatta, who had worked with the Japanese authorities, and its first prime minister, Sutan Sjahrir, who had remained aloof from them, were leading advocates of a pluralistic polity. They saw this as best attained through establishing a multiparty system, and on November 3, 1945, Hatta issued a decree authorizing its formation. Well before that date, many political parties had in fact already sprung up independently. By the end of the year, most of the prewar parties were again in existence and numerous new political organizations had been born.

The Republic was also riven by internal disagreements on the best way to attain the goal of independence: whether the primary emphasis should be on armed struggle *(perjuangan)* or on diplomacy. The top leadership never considered the two concepts to be mutually exclusive, perceiving them in fact as in varying degrees complementary, with the military struggle providing the leverage for the diplomatic efforts. While often opposing some of the specific concessions made to the Dutch, few of those in power believed that, given the fact of Allied military strength in the Pacific region, independence could be gained for all Indonesia without some degree of compromise. From the beginning it was difficult to isolate the Dutch from their allies, for when British forces began landing in September 1945 to carry out their assigned task of repatriating the Japanese and freeing Allied prisoners of war, they brought with them officials from the Netherlands Indies Civil Administration (NICA). The Republic then faced the immediate problem of how far resistance against the returning Dutch officials and soldiers would necessarily involve war against their British ally.

In the "struggle" versus "diplomacy" debate, those on the "struggle" side argued that the Dutch were exhausted from the war and, with no more than toe-holds on the islands of Java and Sumatra, were incapable of occupying these islands by force against stubborn local resistance. The diplomatic counterargument was that the Republic's strength on Java and Sumatra was matched by Dutch strength in the eastern archipelago; and there was no way by which the Republic could regain these extensive areas militarily, given American and British support of the Dutch. The only means by which the Republic could ever extend its authority outside Sumatra and Java would be through negotiated agreements with the Netherlands, guaranteed by other nations.

These various issues became part of a single debate by the end of 1945. Tan Malaka, the radical activist of the 1920s who had slipped back to Indonesia during the Japanese occupation, became the major exponent of uncompromising resistance to the Dutch, and he tied this stance to a demand for what he termed "100-percent independence." He argued that the realization of complete independence demanded a true social revolution, whereby not only would the old officials be removed, but so would all foreign control over Indonesia's economy—in other words, the Republic should confiscate the Dutch-controlled rubber, coffee, and sugar plantations and the oil fields and industrial installations. He further contended that, by establishing political parties, the Republic's leaders were weakening the ability of the Indonesian people to focus all their energies on the anticolonial struggle. He believed that domestic political allegiances would destroy national unity and argued instead for a single national front to confront the Dutch.

In January 1946 Tan Malaka directly challenged the Republican leadership's policies by establishing his Persatuan Perjuangan (PP, Union of Struggle), known on Sumatra by the Dutch name, Volksfront (People's Front). This front incorporated political parties and military organizations and had a program that emphasized national solidarity and a refusal to negotiate with the Dutch until after their departure from Indonesia. It appealed to the desire for revolutionary change in much of Indonesia and soon attracted a large following, establishing branches throughout Java and on Sumatra. Sukarno, Hatta, Sjahrir, and other Republican leaders saw the burgeoning movement as a direct challenge to their authority, and in mid-March 1946 Tan Malaka was arrested, together with some of his closest and most influential followers, and held in prison until September 1948.

Internal dissension did not end with his imprisonment and again began to intensify in the early months of 1948. By then many Republicans in both the regions and the center had become increasingly disillusioned by the number of concessions the Republic had made, particularly those agreed to in the Renville Agreement of January 1948. Several political parties in the cabinet, including the PNI and Masyumi (Council of Indonesian Moslems), withdrew their support from Amir Sjarifuddin, who had signed the agreement, compelling him to resign his post as prime minister. Sukarno then appointed Vice-President Hatta to head a non-party presidential cabinet, believing him to be a person above party conflicts who was strong enough to implement the unpopular policies demanded by Renville. In reaction to these moves and in opposition to the presidential character of the new cabinet, a coalition of left-wing parties and workers' and peasants' alliances reorganized themselves in February 1948 into a broad People's Democratic Front (FDR, Front Demokrasi Rakyat), which Amir himself soon joined. In March, the FDR repudiated the Renville Agreement and adopted an increasingly radical line in opposition to the Sukarno-Hatta leadership.

At the same time dissension was also increasing within the Republican army. Three years earlier, demobilized Peta or Giyūgun soldiers had been the initial core of the Badan Keamanan Rakyat (BKR, People's Security Organization), established on August 22, 1945, as a provisional Republican peacekeeping force. These official armed forces had been supplemented by numerous independent bands of young people *(pemuda),* some of whom had received basic martial training in Japanese-sponsored youth groups, while others had been members of prewar boy scout or youth organizations allied with political, religious, or educational associations. Many of the militia bands (known in the early weeks as *badan perjuangan* [struggle groups] and later as *lasykar)* sprang up spontaneously around a particular prewar opposition political or religious leader, and some had as their basis bandit and other outlaw groups that had long existed on the periphery of the colonial society in rural areas. Some of the lasykar units eventually joined with the BKR, while others jealously guarded their autonomy or allied themselves with the emerging political parties.

As the character of the Republican army changed between 1945 and 1948, so did its name. On October 5, 1945, the first steps were taken toward creating a military structure embracing both Java and Sumatra when Sukarno proclaimed formation of the TKR (Tentara Keamanan Rakyat, Army for People's Security) to replace the original BKR and appointed Urip Sumohardjo, a former major in the Royal Netherlands Indies Army (KNIL) to head its general staff. Tensions were high within the TKR between the Dutch- and Japanese-trained officers, and only six weeks later, on November 12, top military commanders elected General Sudirman, a Japanese-trained officer, and not Urip, as the TKR's commander-in-chief *(panglima besar).* On January 25, 1946, as the center tried to strengthen its control of the command structure and organization, the army's name was changed to TRI (Tentara Republik Indonesia, Army of the Republic of Indonesia). Finally, on May 5, 1947, at the same time that the order went out for all independent militias and lasykars affiliated with the political parties to be incorporated within the official military structure, the armed forces were given the name they continued to hold after the transfer of sovereignty, Tentara Nasional Indonesia (TNI, Indonesian National Army).

During the three and a half years of independence up to the launching of the Netherlands' second major attack on the Republic in December 1948, Hatta and elements of the Republican army's high command continually struggled to assert control over, and impose a structure upon, the motley bands that had taken up arms to realize the revolution and prevent the return of the colonial order. The center's efforts culminated in 1948 in a "rationalization" program for the armed forces that had the ultimate goal of reducing their numbers from a total of nearly half a million regular and irregular soldiers to a force of 57,000 mobile, well-trained, and well-armed troops. The officer who planned and tried to implement this process was not Panglima Sudirman, but his Chief of Staff, Col. A. H. Nasution, initially trained in the KNIL and former commander of the Republic's West Java-based Siliwangi Division. In his efforts to consolidate and streamline the armed forces, Nasution worked closely with Vice-President Hatta, who from January 1948 held the posts of both minister of defense and prime minister. The drastic measures that they pressed through provoked widespread resentment among the Republic's armed forces, both regular and irregular.

These pressures helped precipitate the Madiun rebellion of September 1948, the greatest internal challenge mounted during this period against the central Republican government. Initiated by second-echelon Communists and disaffected military units who seized power in Madiun, the uprising soon embroiled all top leaders of the FDR and of the Communist party. A long-exiled prewar PKI leader, Musso, who had returned to Indonesia from Moscow only the previous month and now headed the Communist party, assumed leadership of the uprising, together with senior party colleagues and former prime minister Amir Sjarifuddin.

The Madiun revolt did not, however, develop broad support. Any possibility of it doing so was destroyed when Musso openly accused Sukarno and Hatta of betraying the revolution and put himself forward as an alternative leader. The TNI counterattack crushed the rebellion and destroyed the parties that had supported it, killing Musso, along with many of his fellow rebels. Amir and several of his colleagues escaped, but they were captured at the end of November and executed by the TNI at the time of the second Dutch attack the following month. Poorly coordinated and limited in scope, the Madiun rebellion attracted little support in other regions of the Republic; many local Communist party branches, even on Java, openly repudiated it.

The final major rift within Republican ranks occurred some six months after the second Dutch attack and was precipitated by the participation of the imprisoned Republican leaders in further negotiations with the Dutch. Neither the Emergency Government headed by Sjafruddin Prawiranegara nor the top Indonesian military commanders on Java and Sumatra were willing to accept the validity of these negotiations, believing that those still fighting should now represent the Republic and that they alone could appreciate the relative strength of Republican and Dutch forces in Indonesia. By this time too, the guerrilla leaders deeply mistrusted the negotiating process, viewing it with a suspicion grounded in the history of previous agreements. Many believed the Roem–van Royen talks and the negotiations subsequently held in The Hague to be merely another step in the series represented by Linggajati and Renville, wherein, in their opinion, the Dutch negotiated only when hard-pressed militarily, breaking the agreements as soon as they had rebuilt their strength. It was, then, only with extreme reluctance that many of those who had continued the guerrilla war against the Dutch ultimately agreed to accept the negotiations, which—though involving some unpalatable concessions —did in fact lead to the transfer of sovereignty to the Republic of the United States of Indonesia at the end of 1949.

This sketch of the course of the revolution and some of the major disputes within the Republic can serve as a backdrop to the following accounts of how eight of Indonesia's regions responded to the challenges posed first by the growth of the nationalist movement and later by the years of physical struggle with the Netherlands military forces. Echoes of clashes at the center reverberated locally, but in no consistent pattern, and the distant sounds were often drowned out by the tumult of the more immediate struggles.

Many skirmishes and some real battles were fought in Medan, Makassar, Banda Aceh, Padang, and Jakarta between the more cautious Republican office holders and the young, impatient revolutionaries whose hopes had been raised by their military training under the Japanese and the proclamation of independence. And in the countryside of Banten, the Tiga Daerah, and many parts of Sumatra, the rural population often took matters into their own hands, forcing local officials out of office and seizing rice and other food supplies from the Japanese stores. Prewar political parties were reestablished, but in many of the regions, particularly on Sumatra, Tan Malaka's Struggle Union was welcomed and became for a time the spearhead of the revolution. The Linggajati Agreement exerted particular influence in South Sulawesi, where the revolutionaries felt betrayed by the Republican leaders' acquiescence to Dutch control outside Java and Sumatra, and where the ill-equipped militias became easy prey for Dutch military suppression. And in many parts of Java and Sumatra the local armed forces combatted efforts by the central command to "rationalize" their units by mass demobilizations and subsequently, as guerrilla fighters, in 1949 opposed the final compromises made to the Dutch.

The basic initial determinant of the course of events in these regions, however, was probably the extent to which the Dutch were able to build up a sufficiently powerful military presence during the British interregnum to reassert their control thereafter. It is this factor that has dictated the organizational format of the subsequent chapters: the first section includes three regions (the Tiga Daerah, Banten, and Aceh), which during their major revolutionary upheavals were largely free of external authority; the second, two regions (East Sumatra and West Sumatra), where, after the withdrawal of British forces, the Dutch and the Republicans competed to establish state authority; and the third, three regions (Jakarta, South Sulawesi, and Ambon), where Allied forces ensured that the reconstituted Dutch colonial state was soon dominant. Such a progression also coincides generally with a chronological framework: all the regions in the first grouping experienced violent upheavals during the early months of independence, and the three authors are primarily concerned with the causes, course, and outcome of this early period of violence. Attention in the remaining five sections is spread more evenly over the revolutionary years, but the last one emphasizes the final months, when the situation in Ambon assumed the character of revolutionary action against the Republic's authority as it became increasingly clear that it was triumphing over the Dutch in the independence struggle.

The contributors were given only very general guidelines for writing their histories, and they themselves selected the developments that, in their view, stamped the particular character of the revolution in their region. For this reason there is no close congruity of treatment among them from which easy comparisons can be drawn. A number of common themes do emerge, however, and these will be considered in the concluding section.

PART I

REGIONS FREE OF EXTERNAL AUTHORITY

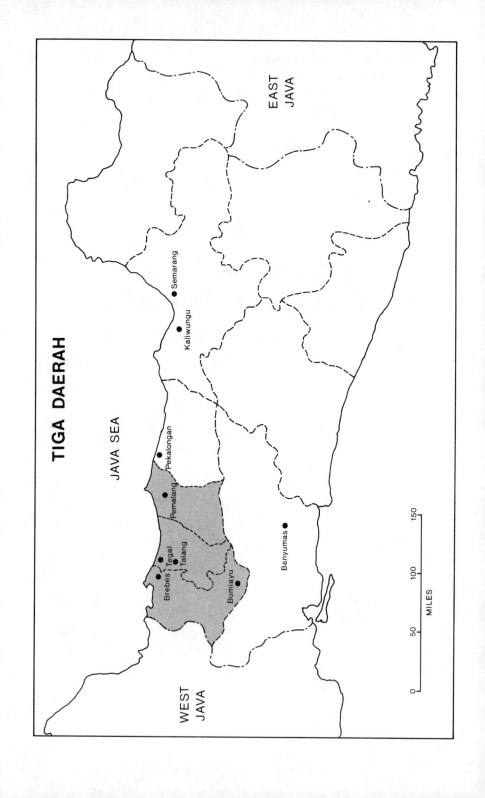

THE TIGA DAERAH AFFAIR: SOCIAL REVOLUTION OR REBELLION?

Anton Lucas

The Tiga Daerah (Three Regions) Affair, which took place in north central Java in the latter part of 1945, was one of several local[1] social upheavals that occurred in Indonesia during the months following the proclamation of independence on August 17, 1945. Many of the surviving participants still refer to the turbulent events of those months as the social revolution. In the residency of Pekalongan, this revolution removed the entire bureaucratic elite of the three regencies of Brebes, Pemalang, and Tegal, the so-called Tiga Daerah.[2]

During this period, the national leadership supported, indeed encouraged, the peaceful takeover or transfer of power in all regions of Indonesia from the Japanese- and Dutch-trained bureaucratic elite. But no one at the national level seems to have shared the local perception that this transfer provided an opportunity for real social and political change. Although Prime Minister Sjahrir in his pamphlet *Our Struggle* described the *pangreh praja* (administrative corps, Java) as nothing more than the "henchmen of the colonialists" and "an instrument fashioned by Dutch colonialism from the feudal heritage of our society,"[3] his government's reformism (which consisted of replacing officials who had cooperated with the Japanese) stopped well short of supporting social revolution. Furthermore, the need for change was always tempered in the minds of Sjahrir, Vice-President Hatta, and others in the Socialist party cabinet by the need to attract the sympathy of the Western powers for Indonesia's struggle. They feared that the violence of the social revolution in the Tiga Daerah that shattered the old order locally could also shake the international foundations of the new Republic and the policy of diplomacy through which the leaders were trying to build an image of a stable and viable independent Indonesia.

Social revolutions in other areas of the new Republic—Aceh, Banten, and East Sumatra—generally conformed to regional (provincial) or ethnic boundaries. The Tiga Daerah, on the other hand, although fairly homogeneous linguistically, ethnically, and geographically, were only a part of the residency of Pekalongan. And Pekalongan residency, though separated by a range of mountains from Banyumas in the south, nonetheless has a basic cultural similarity with the rest of the province of Central Java.[4]

Except for the group of Communists, whose leadership was crucial in establishing a new order during the social revolution in the Tiga Daerah, local participants had no sense of carrying their revolution beyond the boundaries of the residency. On the other hand, symbolic elements in language and ritual that characterized the period in the Tiga Daerah were probably shared with other areas. Whether the local groups were Islamic, Communist, or nationalist, whether they were urban or rural, whether veterans of the 1920s or *pemuda* (youth), a shared set of perceptions, a revolutionary consciousness initially bound them to each other and to the wider Indonesian revolution.

Background

The socioeconomic origins of the social revolution of October–December 1945 in the Tiga Daerah go back to the intrusion of Western capitalism into the region with the introduction of the forced cultivation system in the nineteenth century. The most successful cash crop was sugar, and by the time of the depression of the 1930s all but four of the residency's seventeen sugar mills were in the Tiga Daerah. These mills took over most of the available wet-rice land along the rich alluvial coastal plain. Thirteen of the mills closed during the depression, ending seasonal part-time employment. While twelve had reopened by 1939, wages paid to day laborers by the local mills during the 1930s (especially in Tegal) were lower than elsewhere in Java.[5]

Of crucial importance to the sugar industry was the assistance given by the local bureaucratic elite in helping the mills obtain an adequate supply of wet-rice land on which to plant sugar and ensuring first priority for the cane fields in the distribution of irrigation water. The mills had invested large sums in local irrigation systems to secure their water supply, but at the village level the competition between sugar and rice for water caused much social tension.[6] In order to maximize sugar content, the cane was cut as late as possible; thus when land was returned after leases had expired, it was often too late in the year for the peasants to take advantage of the seasonal rainfall to plant their paddy fields.

In the early years, cane-field arson was the only means of protest available to the peasantry, but by 1918 the local Sarekat Islam had begun openly to take up the peasants' cause in disputes with the mills. Unions had also begun to campaign actively for better wages and working conditions for their members, the consequent unrest culminating in the railway workers' general strike of 1923.[7] By this time the Indonesian Communist Party (PKI) exercised considerable influence in this area of Java, and local branches of its People's Unions actively supported peasant opposition to burdensome taxes. Pekalongan residency became a center of radical political activity, and PKI adherents in Tegal and Pekalongan were leading proponents of a violent uprising against the Dutch in 1926. In March a premature revolt broke out in Karangcegak south of Tegal, and there were three further attempts at rebellion in August and September of that year. The Dutch were then able to trace PKI leaders in Tegal and Pekalongan and arrest virtually all of them, so that these places, which had been among the strongest proponents of the rebellion, were silent on November 12, 1926, the date fixed for the nationwide uprisings.[8] Most of the local nationalist leaders were either imprisoned elsewhere in Java or Madura or exiled to Boven Digul in West New Guinea.[9] During the premature revolts in Pekalongan residency, many Moslem supporters of the People's Unions were arrested along with the other rebels. Although subsequently the Dutch sugar mills tried to conciliate the local religious elite by building prayer houses in the villages around the mills, most religious leaders in the Tiga Daerah remained hostile to the colonial authority and to its Javanese representatives, the pangreh praja.

During the Japanese occupation, Pekalongan residency was hard hit by wartime economic policies. The Japanese requisitioned up to half the rice crop in some areas of the Tiga Daerah to feed their 16th Army, stationed in Java, as well as the Japanese civilian population and various semi-military groups, and to provide rations for the corvée working on projects within and outside the residency.[10] Under the Japanese army's policy of economic self-sufficiency, regions had to feed their populations on the rice that was left over. The ban on trade between regions, together with inflation and skyrocketing black-market prices, offered widespread opportunities for corruption and illegal traffic in rice. In implementing their rice-requisitioning and rationing schemes, as well as in the recruitment of corvée, the Japanese relied on the cooperation of the bureaucratic elite, who, willingly or not, became economic supervisors for the local Japanese administration. Officials at the subdistrict level, whose wives controlled the distribution of cloth, often exploited opportunities for corruption. By the end of the occupation most peasants did not have enough cerecloth (needed for wrapping the dead), but they knew that corrupt officials were hoarding precious supplies of cloth. The Japanese forced village headmen into the role of landlords, extracting rice from the peasantry to fulfill delivery quotas set at the regency level, and they also had to help their subdistricts meet their corvée quotas. Precipitated in part by a long dry season and late arrival of the monsoon rains, famine conditions existed in the Tiga Daerah by late 1944; people were reported to be eating snails, banana roots, and forest plants, and even to be dying in the streets.

The standard of living among the bureaucratic elite and the Japanese-created Indonesian militia, Peta, contrasted sharply with that of the rest of the population in Pekalongan residency. Both groups received rations and were well paid; further, under their economic self-sufficiency policy, the Japanese allocated Peta companies such assets as ducks, goats, fishponds, and wet-rice fields to manage. After Peta was disbanded in August 1945, these assets were supposed to be handed over to the local Republican government, but in Pemalang they were seized by the people.[11]

During the last decade of their rule, the Dutch had kept Islam at arm's length and harassed the nationalists. The Japanese, in contrast, made use of both religious leaders and nationalists, as well as the bureaucratic elite. Religious and nationalist leaders held key positions in such Japanese-organized bodies as Putera (Center of People's Power), the Barisan Pelopor (Pioneer Corps), and the Pekalongan Residency Advisory Council. The pangreh praja, however, still monopolized the bureaucracy and the two lower ranks of Peta. By August 1945, the occupation had badly eroded, if not destroyed, the traditional patron-client ties between the bureaucracy and the peasantry, and the socioeconomic cleavage between the two groups had widened further. The overriding sentiment among the lower classes in 1945 was that they were being exploited by the bureaucratic elite; with that sentiment went a conviction that "they would take their revenge in the future."[12]

The Course of the Tiga Daerah Affair

The initial response in Pekalongan residency to the proclamation of independence on August 17, 1945, was elation among the nationalists and confusion in the ranks of the bureaucratic elite and the Japanese. The older radicals of the prewar nationalist movement, together with a handful of younger pemuda figures, picked up news of the Japanese surrender via various clandestine radios throughout the residency; the bureaucratic elite, however, knew nothing of the event, and their confusion was the greater because their only source of information was local Japanese officials, who refused to confirm or deny the surrender rumors.

The proclamation of independence created a dilemma for local officials over the attitude to be taken toward the Japanese civilian and military officials still in power in the residency. Some officials waited for the Japanese either to affirm or to deny the declaration; others felt that the Allies would soon return to restore Dutch power. For the regional head *(bupati)* of Brebes, for example, the proclamation had no meaning until the Japanese in Pekalongan residency formally transferred power to the local Republican administration.[13] Only on September 27, when this occurred, was the problem "of having to submit to two different governments" removed for the bureaucratic elite.[14] In the intervening period, the attitudes of local officials varied from unofficial acceptance of pemuda demands to fly the new Indonesian flag, through expressions of private misgivings about the situation, to outright public denials that the proclamation had any validity. They urged caution until the Allied forces should arrive.

The first action of local nationalist leaders was to send couriers to various contacts in Jakarta to discover what was happening in the capital. These couriers soon returned, with messengers sent independently from Jakarta, carrying printed texts of the proclamation and revolutionary slogans, mainly in English. Reprinted and distributed locally, the slogans soon began to appear on the walls of government buildings. For many people in the rural areas the first news of the proclamation came in messages scrawled in Javanese on passing goods-train wagons.

Loosely knit groups of local revolutionaries, known as struggle organizations, played a crucial role in this urban-based campaign. These groups usually sprang up around an older radical of the prewar nationalist movement. The degree of formal organization and leadership style of these struggle groups varied considerably among districts, but in the first few weeks of the revolution their priorities were the same: to spread the news of the proclamation as quickly as possible; to keep the Indonesian flag flying in the face of Japanese opposition to the lowering of their own flag; and to obtain arms from the Japanese. In areas where there was no nationalist veteran of the prewar movement to lead the local revolutionary struggle, the popularly chosen Indonesian national committees (KNI) became the basis of local revolution at the district or subdistrict level.[15]

In other parts of Java, on September 5, the Jakarta government appointed as Republican residents officials who had served as vice-residents under the Japanese; but no resident for Pekalongan was appointed until September 21, and then only after the Pekalongan national committee had petitioned the Republican secretary of state.[16] The central government's hesitation probably reflected the fact that the vice-resident, Mr. Besar, was from neither the nationalist movement nor the bureaucratic elite, as were other vice-residents. In any event, the delay in his appointment diminished his authority, for it was generally believed to mean that he had doubted the proclamation or was pro-Dutch, or both.[17] Mr. Besar's position was further undermined by a breakdown in negotiations for the transfer of arms from the Japanese military police, the Kenpeitai, to local Republican forces. In Tegal, national committee leaders successfully negotiated the transfer of arms with only one casualty, but in the residency capital bloody fighting broke out on October 3 during negotiations between Resident

Besar and the Kenpeitai. In the battle that ensued thirty-seven Indonesians and about seventeen Japanese were killed.[18] After a three-day siege by Republican forces the Kenpeitai eventually surrendered, partly as a result of the diplomacy of the resident of neighboring Banyumas (Mr. Iskak Tjokroadisoerjo), whose arrival in Pekalongan with two Japanese advisers ended the deadlock. The remaining Japanese civilians and soldiers were subsequently evacuated south to Banyumas. On October 7, 1945, Pekalongan residency became the first region in Indonesia to be free of Japanese power.

On the following day the first incident of the social revolution occurred when a village headman was humiliated and removed from office in a subdistrict in southern Tegal. Within a week the revolution had swept through the rural areas of the Tiga Daerah. A district head and two subdistrict heads were killed; so too were an unknown number of village headmen, officials, and police. The revolutionary wave engulfed the regency towns of Pemalang and Tegal on October 19 and November 4, and Brebes at some time in between. In Pemalang, on the night of October 19, local revolutionary leaders removed the bupati, along with the remainder of the town's bureaucratic elite, to the safety of the jail as a crowd ransacked their houses looking for corrupt officials.[19] On November 4 a more coordinated mass demonstration in Slawi, center of the local sugar industry twelve miles south of Tegal, began at the headquarters of a group of radicals calling themselves AMRI (Angkatan Muda Republik Indonesia, Younger Generation of the Republic of Indonesia) and gathered strength as the crowd marched toward the town. According to an eyewitness:

> The group in front was wearing slings of *janur kuning* [the young yellow leaf of the coconut palm], those at the back headbands of the same, and another group was wearing it as a belt. All were chanting fiercely in Arabic la ilaha illa llah ("there is no god but Allah"), over and over again. Some were waving drawn swords. . . . It was frightening . . . and it raised the hairs on the back of my neck, like seeing . . . a hungry tiger about to fall upon its victim.[20]

The "victims" included at least three officials, but, as in Pemalang, other office holders, including the mayor, took refuge in the jail on the advice of local national committee leaders. The crowd also occupied the regency office for a time, turning its contents upside down, but the bupati himself escaped.[21] The local Republican army (TKR) battalion came under attack, and they defended themselves, with arms obtained earlier from the Japanese, by firing over the heads of the revolutionaries. Later, on orders from military headquarters in Yogyakarta, army units in Tiga Daerah withdrew to Pekalongan to prevent further clashes with the people.[22]

In Brebes, where the army withdrawal was more orderly, revolutionary violence began in the regency town itself and was directed against the Chinese and Eurasians. Eurasians were again its victims in the vicinity of the regency's sugar mills. The three most important members of the bureaucratic elite in Brebes—the bupati, his deputy, and the Brebes district head—were kidnapped by national committee leaders from Tegal, where they were taken and held captive for the following two months.

Thus, while the bureaucratic elite were the particular targets, revolutionary violence was directed too against the Chinese and Eurasians. The visible signs of Chinese wealth, their shops and rice mills, were either ransacked or taken over. Eurasians also were viewed as aliens occupying a privileged economic position, as most of them had been employed in the local sugar industry. Interned by the Japanese at the beginning of the occupation, many had emerged bitter and resentful on their release in September 1945, expecting the Dutch to return to restore their prewar status. Ironically, it was the arrival of the Dutch as part of the Allied (British) reoccupation of Java in late September 1945 that sealed the fate of the Eurasian population in Pekalongan residency. Rumors of Dutch terrorism against the Jakarta population fanned a fierce anti-NICA (Netherlands Indies Civil Administration) movement in the Tiga Daerah.[23] At the height of the revolutionary violence in mid-October, more than one hundred Eurasians, Ambonese, and Menadonese were killed in Tegal and Brebes for being "pro-NICA" or "betraying the national revolution."[24]

By early November 1945, the social revolution had swept away the older order in both the regency towns and the rural areas. Discredited in the eyes of the people by their role as representatives of Dutch and Japanese authority in Pekalongan residency, the bureaucratic elite's passive wait-and-see attitude toward the proclamation of independence had alienated the local revolutionaries even more. Resident Besar's subsequent use of the army in his efforts to protect the lives and property of Eurasians and officials and maintain law and order further undermined his authority. A large number of the bureaucratic elite, as well as the army, took refuge in Pekalongan. This widened the gulf between the residency capital and the revolutionaries, for the fate of the other officials who stayed in the Tiga Daerah was unknown in Pekalongan, although in fact many of them were safe, having moved voluntarily or been taken to local jails. In the wake of news of bloody massacres of Eurasians during the anti-NICA movement, however, government officials in Pekalongan feared the worst.

Leadership Struggles

In the weeks following the overthrow of the bureaucratic elite, local revolutionary groups from the regency to the village level throughout the Tiga Daerah sought candidates to replace the administrators who had been removed or killed. The method of appointing new officials was as varied as the candidates chosen. In Pemalang, Soepangat, a skilled medical orderly who had been a central figure in the prewar nationalist movement, was acclaimed bupati at a mass meeting in the town square; in Tegal, after prolonged negotiation, the radical Islamic nationalist K. H. Abu Sudja'i, whose resistance to the Dutch and Japanese was widely known, emerged as a candidate acceptable to both orthodox Moslems and Dutch-educated nationalists; in Brebes, where there was less violence during the social revolution, Kyai Syatori, a local mosque official and a vice-chairman of the Brebes Masyumi, had most support and became the new bupati.

The outcome of the struggle for political power and social ascendancy varied among regions and was different at village and subdistrict levels. The degree of violence in village-level upheavals depended on the impact of wartime depredations, the extent of corruption in the old administration, the intermediary role of the radical prewar leadership, and the rivalry between the local religious establishment and semi-bandits known as *lenggaong*. In colonial times these local leaders had gained a livelihood from providing security to various groups within the village, as well as from banditry outside it.

The most famous local figure to adopt the lenggaong style was Kutil from Talang, a subdistrict south of Tegal. A barber by trade, Kutil was

regarded by many as a *guru* or semi-religious figure[25] and an intermediary between the religious establishment, the lenggaong, and Dutch-
educated nationalists. Kutil and his followers during the social revolution tried to achieve a redistribution of wealth in the region. They
ransacked the houses of local Dutch and Eurasian sugar-mill employees and distributed the contents, seized the local village headman's
lands, and dispensed cloth to villagers. Kutil himself ended up as Tegal
regency police chief.[26] Indeed, such was his notoriety during this
period that the Tiga Daerah Affair is often referred to in Indonesia as
"Kutil's Movement."[27]

Outside the regency towns, with no instructions coming from the
residency, or from the provincial, or the central government, local
revolutionaries usually made leadership changes by organizing elections to find local candidates acceptable to all groups. This task was
easier at the district or subdistrict than at the village level, where economic and cultural cleavages were more evident. Nevertheless, the
leaders in most of the villages were replaced, with a sizable number of
the new headmen coming from groups within the village that had
not previously supplied office holders, such as lenggaong, struggle
groups, or peasants.[28] Elections were informal affairs but served their
purpose. The following account of the procedure in a village is typical:

> There were three candidates; each candidate had his own round bamboo
> cylinder, with his symbol (all leaves) above it. My symbol was *turi* leaves;
> Satum [who had been headman for seventeen months under the Dutch
> before being dismissed for corruption] used janur kuning; and the other
> candidate used *kluwih* leaf. People used short sticks [as ballot papers],
> which they placed in the cylinder. Everyone in the village could vote.[29]

In many districts and subdistricts, similar methods were used to
choose officials and members of local national committees. Ninety-
seven percent of district and subdistrict officials were changed, the
majority of the new incumbents coming from previously excluded
groups, namely the orthodox Islamic teachers and local nationalists,
including school teachers and KNI leaders.[30] Thus, at the subdistrict
and district levels, the revolutionary struggle took on the nature of a
popular movement against the pangreh praja.

In the residency and regency, once the bureaucratic elite was removed, three groups contended for power: the Communist-led popular front, the Islamic establishment, and the army. These groups' varying perceptions about the nature of the struggle they wanted to lead reflected their different backgrounds, compositions, and objectives.[31]

First were the local Communists, who on November 16 established a popular front, the so-called GBP3D (Gabungan Badan Perjuangan Tiga Daerah, Federation of Resistance Organizations of the Three Regions). With its headquarters in the Tegal branch of Amir Sjarifuddin's Socialist party,[32] the popular front's main priority was to seize political power at the residency level. Organizationally, it consisted of three separate committees under a secretariat, with each of the three regions (Tegal, Brebes, and Pemalang) having a representative on each committee. Of its ten members, six, including one Chinese, were local Communists (three members of the early PKI, two ex-Digulists), while three others were members of the PNI Baru (Hatta and Sjahrir's prewar party) or of the early PNI (Indonesian Nationalist Party). There were no Moslem representatives (possibly because the new bupatis of Tegal and Pemalang were from the Islamic group) and no army men.[33] Regency-level working committees, set up in Tegal and Brebes in early November to replace the nonfunctioning national committees, were also dominated by radicals. Although in theory advising the Moslem bupati, these working committees (whose membership in both cases overlapped with the GBP3D) in practice took over most of the functions of local government in Brebes and Tegal between early November and December 14.

K. Midjaja, the central figure in the Tiga Daerah movement, was responsible for establishing both the popular front and the working committees.[34] A railway unionist, journalist, and pemuda leader, he had joined the Illegal PKI in 1939 and been forced to flee Solo in the face of Kenpeitai arrests in April 1942. He then joined with the remnants of the Surabaya-based Illegal PKI to continue a local underground PKI under the leadership of Widarta, also a member of the Illegal PKI.[35] Their main aim was to continue the united front against fascism, in accordance with the line set forth by Musso in his brief visit to Surabaya in late 1935 when the Illegal PKI was established. Making Java's north coast the center of his activities, K. Midjaja began in

1943 to renew contacts with labor unionists and helped to arrange codes and cover for fugitives from Kenpeitai raids in other parts of Java who were given sanctuary in the teak forests south of Pemalang. After the proclamation of independence, Widarta's PKI group, being numerically small and weak, decided that they should continue operating underground, working with local progressive forces—the national committees and struggle organizations—against feudalism and capitalism.[36] Widarta himself, who was in Jakarta at the time of the proclamation, came to Pekalongan as a top Pesindo (Indonesian Socialist Youth) leader and as representative of the Minister of Information, Mr. Amir Sjarifuddin.

The objectives of the Communists are reflected in the popular front's program, enunciated in late November.[37] According to this program, the local economy was to be run by cooperatives under centralized control, with the central cooperative renting businesses and determining prices. Export of foodstuffs from the region was to be strictly controlled and the output of house gardens increased by encouraging planting of cash crops, such as cotton. Pemuda were to lead a campaign to popularize the revolution among the people. The region was to have its own military units, including a two-hundred-man Executioner's Brigade, which would be given ideological as well as military training.[38]

While the broad strategy of the popular front was the same as that of the national leadership—to defend the Republic against outside attack—its political demands were not.[39] Set out in a printed leaflet and a letter sent to the acting resident in early December 1945, these demands stated that Pekalongan residency needed "an orderly government based on socialism . . . sharing the same ideology." This could not be achieved while the Tiga Daerah and Pekalongan continued to be administered separately. Consequently, the residency government "must be handed over to the people immediately," with those members of the bureaucratic elite in the residency capital who could not follow the revolutionary way resigning, and all those "acting like NICA or who are procolonialist" to be purged.[40]

The second group contending for power, the Moslems, had two streams, the Islamic nationalists and the modernist Muhammadiyah. Those of the first stream, who were the majority in the Tiga Daerah, saw themselves as part of the strong local anticolonial tradition begun by the Sarekat Islam (the first nationalist political organization) and continued by its successor, the PSII (Indonesian Islamic Unity Party), and attracted both urban and rural support, the latter from the ortho-dox religious teachers *(ulama),* including K. H. Abu Sudja'i, the future revolutionary bupati of Tegal.

At the district and subdistrict levels, 22 percent of the new officials appointed in the social revolution came from the Moslem group: four district and twelve subdistrict heads.[41] Two of the bupati in the Tiga Daerah were also from this group. Of the nine Moslem leaders whose biographies are known, all were popularly elected during the social revolution, and their prewar experience and strong anti-pangreh praja sentiment identified them with the aspirations of the social revolution in the Tiga Daerah in contrast to the Pekalongan-based Muhammadi-yah. Although all nine were born locally (unlike Communist leaders K. Midjaja and Widarta), all had spent time during the colonial period as pupils in Islamic schools outside Pekalongan residency, five of them at the well-known Tebu-ireng school at Jombang, in East Java, under the strongly nationalist and most famous traditionalist Islamic teacher in Java, K. Hasjim Asj'ari.[42] Two who had gone on the *haj* had stayed on in Mecca to study. Returning to their home areas when political activity in the residency was curtailed by the Dutch after 1926, all had either founded their own Moslem schools or taught in well-known local institutions. Several had become involved in pre-war Moslem youth groups. During the Japanese occupation, most of the nine worked in some way with the Japanese, either in local offices of the Department of Religious Affairs, on the Residency Advisory Council, or in leadership positions in Masyumi, Hizbullah (the militia attached to the Masyumi party), or the Barisan Pelopor. The Islamic nationalists dominated the Barisan Pelopor in Tegal, where seventeen of twenty-four of its local district and subdistrict leaders were mem-bers of the orthodox religious elite.[43]

Islamic nationalists such as K. H. Abu Sudja'i (himself imprisoned under both the Dutch and Japanese regimes) considered the second Moslem stream, the Muhammadiyah, "very moderate and pro the colonial government," while people in Pemalang town contrasted the unpopular wealthy *priyayi* (governing elite) class—mostly Muham-madiyah members—with *santri rakyat* or poor santri. The stronghold of the Muhammadiyah was in the batik and textile community of

Pekajangan, south of the residency capital of Pekalongan.[44] A branch of the Muhammadiyah had been founded by this self-contained trade-oriented community in 1922, and the profits of the Pekajangan Batik Cooperative founded in 1937 went toward establishing a private Dutch-language primary school, run by the Muhammadiyah. This acceptance of Dutch education reflected a difference in attitude between the two Moslem groups, for Islamic nationalists in Tegal would never let their children "sit at the desk of a Dutch school."[45] Pekajangan lifestyles were also very different from those of the poorer Moslem communities in the Tiga Daerah.[46]

While K. H. Abu Sudja'i symbolized the Moslem-radical national-ist alliance in the Tiga Daerah, K. H. Iskandar Idris symbolized the Moslem-TKR alliance in the residency capital of Pekalongan. Appointed by the Japanese to lead the Peta battalion in Pekalongan, Idris was chosen as commander of the newly formed TKR in October 1945, more out of loyalty on the part of his former Peta subordinates than his suitability for the job. This brings us to the third group vying for leadership—the military.

To understand the unpopularity of the Republican army in the Tiga Daerah, and why it was forced to lauch a counterrevolution in alliance with Pekajangan Moslems against the popular front, it is necessary to look at the social origins of its leadership and the economic conditions of Peta members during the Japanese occupation. All the officers of the Republican TKR regiment in Pekalongan had belonged to the two Peta battalions established by the Japanese. Most Peta company commanders had been recruited from bureaucratic elite families, at least two of them having served as subdistrict heads before the occupation.[47] Together with Peta platoon commanders, these men made up the officer corps of the TKR regiment's four battalions.

Their immediate priority during the closing months of 1945 was to fight the British forces that had landed in Semarang on October 20. From late October, several TKR battalions (including one from Pekalongan) were stationed at Kaliwungu, to the west of Semarang, to block any British advance along the north coast. There was a bloody, five-day battle with the Japanese in Semarang in October, and subsequent fighting against the British. These confrontations made TKR leaders view defense of the Republic as of much greater urgency than the social revolution in the Tiga Daerah.

Counterrevolution

Following the clash in Pekalongan between local revolutionaries and the Kenpeitai in early October, the governor of Central Java had sent Sayuti Melik, Sukarno's personal secretary, to Pekalongan as his envoy. After an initial visit to the residency capital, Sayuti Melik returned again in early November, with the task of ratifying the local leaders' choice of new revolutionary officials. His formal authority as the governor's representative and his political influence as the president's personal secretary meant that his opinions carried considerable weight in and outside the residency. Melik believed that Resident Besar's position had become untenable because the resident's actions to protect the lives and property of the local Eurasians had strengthened allegations that he was pro-NICA. At Sayuti Melik's request, Yogya military headquarters on November 5 ordered the TKR to arrest Besar, but local army leaders felt unable to carry out these instructions.[48] On being informed of the order, however, Besar left the residency of his own accord. On November 6, R. M. Soeprapto, a high official in the governor's office in Semarang and a member of the old bureaucratic elite, arrived in Pekalongan as the new acting resident.[49] Apparently, the provincial government either saw the appointment as a temporary one or it hoped that Soeprapto would be acceptable to the Tiga Daerah leaders. But he was not, and the local revolutionaries set about finding a suitable candidate to replace him.

A further incident at this time raised tensions between the popular front leaders and other contending groups in the Tiga Daerah. A regional Muhammadiyah conference held near Tegal on November 3 was attended by Pekalongan military commander Iskandar Idris. While there, Idris decided that he would go to Talang to try to meet Kutil, and Sayuti Melik accompanied him. Believing the two men to be officials attempting to escape, radical pemuda captured them south of Tegal and eventually took them to Slawi. Melik was recognized by pemuda leader Soewignjo—a former friend from Boven Digul—and was escorted safely back to Tegal;[50] but Idris remained in Slawi (willingly, according to his later account) for the next six weeks. Neither the military in Pekalongan nor Muhammadiyah leaders in Pekajangan were aware of the facts, and both groups believed Idris was the prisoner of pemuda radicals.[51]

The capture of their commander, Idris, was only a minor element in the army's strained relations with the popular front. The fact that after his return to Pekalongan Idris never regained his command position suggests that he had indeed been appointed originally primarily because of the loyalty of his former Peta subordinates. A more important aspect of army-GBP3D relations were such popular front actions as sealing the army's warehouses containing supplies (including rice) and insisting that army vehicles leaving the residency capital needed to obtain permission from the popular front. In addition, pemuda guards would stop and search the vehicles for runaway officials.

The popular front's first priority at this time was to find a suitable resident to replace acting resident Soeprapto. After considering several possible candidates, they finally approached Sardjio from Purworejo.[52] At a crucial meeting in Pemalang on December 9, they secured the agreement of the acting resident and of Pekalongan revolutionary leaders to this appointment. The new resident arrived in Pekalongan at noon on the following day with a sixty-man pemuda escort and a takeover staff. They set up their headquarters in a local hotel, and from there they directed the revolutionary government for the next four days. After the acting resident had formally handed over his position to Sardjio, the new government's first act was to freeze all government department funds in order to undertake a review of residency finances. They invited the uneasy bureaucratic elite of Pekalongan to a special goodwill meeting, where it was explained that the popular front's first aim was to make local government structures more democratic. To this end, working committees were to be created at the district, subdistrict, and village levels to bring Pekalongan into line with the Tiga Daerah. In the few instances where local officials had left their posts, local working committees were to carry on the administration.

During a mass meeting held in Pekalongan on December 12 to introduce Resident Sardjio to the people, the political atmosphere underwent a dramatic change. In his speech to this meeting, popular front chairman K. Midjaja observed that Pekalongan Moslem pemuda were less revolutionary than those in other areas and that religion should be "put aside" in the interests of revolution. Local Islamic groups felt threatened by these remarks,[53] so that the alliance between the Pekajangan Moslems and the TKR was broadened to include

Moslem groups from the capital itself. Iskandar Idris' brother, a Peka-jangan Muhammadiyah teacher, asked the police in Pekalongan for permission to organize a Moslem demonstration against the popular front on the following day, and he and other Pekajangan Moslems led the countermovement. On the morning of Friday, December 14, Resident Sardjio, K. Midjaja, and a small staff group were ambushed at Pekajangan while on their way to visit the southern subdistricts, and Midjaja was slightly wounded.

Later that day the TKR arrested Sardjio, his takeover staff, and the escort company (170 people in all); three days after that, the army launched a full-scale counterrevolution against the Tiga Daerah. In the military operation, TKR units and Moslem groups from Peka-jangan and Pekalongan swept through the Tiga Daerah, arresting about 1,600 people and releasing former members of the bureaucratic elite (including the bupatis of Brebes and Pemalang) who had been living in local jails since the start of the social revolution.

Although most of those arrested were released fairly quickly, legal and political battles over the fate of about thirty prisoners went on for more than a year. Six, including Midjaja, were brought to trial in Pekalongan in April 1947, charged with "attempting to change the structure of government by force" or "inciting revolt."[54] The government based its position on the fine distinction between righteous revolution and criminality. Up to November 1945, popular actions against officials were to be seen as pure and pardonable, but those taking place after November would be considered criminal offenses. The trial was adjourned several times, until on July 21, 1947, just before the first major Dutch attack on the Republic, it was reported that President Sukarno had announced an amnesty for the remaining prisoners.[55]

Perceptions of Revolution in 1945

The Tiga Daerah movement was aimed at removing the bureaucratic elite that had governed on behalf of the Dutch in the decades of colonial rule and replacing it by an Indonesian authority with radically different values and attitudes. Hence the perception of revolution in this area in 1945 was cast in particular cultural terms.

During the social revolution, popular front leaders attempted to overthrow forever the dominant value system and ethos of the Javanese bureaucratic elite and to replace it with a more egalitarian, less hierarchical system. As part of the rejection of the old social hierarchy, the use of different speech levels was rejected—a radical move in the Javanese context. Thus, when Sardjio became resident he abolished aristocratic forms and titles in Pekalongan. In order that local government administration should be based on "democracy and family spirit," all communications between officials and the people were to employ the term *bapak* (father) as the form of address for officials, from the resident down; otherwise, *bung* or *saudara* (brother) were to be used; such feudal terms of address as *paduka* (your honor) and *ndoro* (your servant) were banned, and, to make the Javanese system of titles more democratic, all males and married and unmarried women were to be addressed in the same way.[56] In his campaign to popularize the new speech movement, K. Midjaja addressed the workers at the sugar mills:

> Beginning now, there is no longer any *Raden Mas, Kanjeng Gusti* or *Raden Tumenggung* [priyayi titles]. Everyone is the same now. If you mention the president, you don't need to use Your Excellency; it is enough to say Bung Karno. Likewise, other important people should be called Bung. You should not be afraid of others; all are the same. *Kromo* [high Javanese] is no longer necessary. You should all use just *ngoko* [low Javanese] and Indonesian.[57]

The old language hierarchy was prized by the bureaucratic elite. It could be manipulated not only to maintain their power but also to restore order and stability in insecure situations at the village level. The bureaucratic elite believed kromo to have such power that, if they used it to speak to angry peasants, it would defuse social unrest. Some officials believed too that, by making the peasants use kromo, they could constrain them: "in ngoko they could express demands strongly, with anger, but in kromo they could not."[58]

The dominant elite value system was overturned not only in the realm of language but also in other aspects of urban and rural life. Through ritual actions, known as *dombreng,* in the rural areas, hated corrupt or oppressive officials were exposed in symbolic public unmaskings and shamed by being paraded around.[59] In one such action occurring at the beginning of the social revolution, the headman was dressed in sacking, while his wife was made to wear a necklace of paddy, symbolizing the role of the village headmen as economic supervisors for the Japanese. Both were publicly paraded, to the accompaniment of the headman's own gamelan orchestra, and were further humiliated by being treated "like fowl"—that is, being made to drink unboiled water from a coconut shell and to eat the rice bran usually fed only to chickens.[60] The plays presented by urban-based groups, too, often portrayed the revolution as a struggle to overthrow the old master, be he bureaucratic elite or former colonial ruler. Also in the distribution of cloth a new ideal of fairness or democracy was evident. According to this ideal, everyone should get the same amount of cloth, regardless of need, though in one village this led to each person getting only four inches. Notions of equality and fraternity expressed the values of the social revolution. Those taking part in the struggle shared an inner spirit, or being, or soul.

This emphasis on cultural matters in the perception of the revolution at the local level played a part in the conflict between the Tiga Daerah and the central government. The great gulf between local realities and national priorities was felt by those on both sides.

At the national level, in order to present the Republic as a *fait accompli* to the Allies and the rest of the world, the first Republican cabinet's top priority was to demonstrate its authority over an orderly population. To this end, Sukarno and Hatta tried from the start to avoid having a dual—Japanese and Republican—system of administration. As Hatta put it, "Orders were issued to every government official to acknowledge himself as an official of the Republic of Indonesia and be ready to accept only orders given him by superiors of Indonesian nationality."[61] At a conference of officials from throughout Java and Madura that began in Jakarta on August 30, Sukarno reassured the assembled officials that they would get "the proper place they deserved" in the new Republic. This undertaking referred to the deal worked out with the bureaucratic elite whereby they would stand behind the Republic if their positions and status were guaranteed. Only on September 25, however, were all Japanese-appointed officials formally declared civil servants of the new Republic.

The agreement between the national leaders and the bureaucratic elite had been possible only because of the position taken by the older moderate nationalists who formed a majority in the first Republican cabinet. Such a deal was unthinkable, given the political realities, in the Tiga Daerah, where the older nationalists were the radicals and did not hold power. Even if the Japanese in Pekalongan had transferred power earlier and Resident Besar had been able to declare himself for the Republic on September 5, as the nationalist resident of Banyumas to the south had done, rather than on September 27, the polarization between the revolutionary movement and the bureaucratic elite could not have been prevented.

This polarization must be seen in the context of the growing isolation felt by all groups in the Tiga Daerah. Feeling abandoned and lacking instructions from above, super-cautious and bureaucratic as a result of their Dutch training, local officials waited for orders that never came.[62] The feeling of isolation from the national government was equally frustrating for local revolutionaries. Following the kidnapping of the bupati of Brebes and other offcials in mid-October, two local leaders decided to seek advice in Jakarta on how to stop the unrest. However, officials there explained that the problem of local unrest could be solved only by the Brebes national committee, because "the center had not had the chance to work out a solution." The home affairs ministry then sent the two revolutionaries to Semarang with a letter for the governor of Central Java. There they were told "to wait for instruction from above," which would be issued as soon as possible. After the Magelang affair had been dealt with, Brebes would get its turn.[63]

No strong regional or ethnic ties linked local with national leaders. Connections with national-government figures were personal rather than organizational. The foremost national-level figure from the Tiga Daerah in 1945 was Supeno, a prominent member of Prime Minister Sjahrir's Socialist party and of the fifteen-man working committee of the KNIP. Later chairman of both these bodies, Supeno was the key defense lawyer in the trial of the Tiga Daerah leaders in early 1947.[64] Born in Tegal, Supeno had kept in contact with several local national committee leaders with whom he had been at school in the early 1930s. The same local group of Sjahrir-type Marxists had links with another prominent nationalist from Tegal, Soebagio Mangunrahardjo, the last PNI Baru chairman and also a close friend of Sjahrir.

Local Communists had links with Amir Sjarifuddin through underground work during the occupation.

The political isolation of the Tiga Daerah was reflected in, indeed may have been a result of, a great sense of physical isolation, which members of the revolutionary movement recall today as a central feature of this period. Although for a time following the proclamation there was contact with Jakarta via couriers, after mid-October when the social revolution had swept away the old order in Pemalang, communications between the Tiga Daerah and the residency capital were cut. Post offices remained open, but there was apparently no mail from outside the region, and few people dared travel the roads because of the rural unrest. The residency's two local newpapers, *Pelita Rakjat* in Tegal and *Pantjaran Nasional* in Pekalongan, must have been the only source of outside news for those without radios.

One response by Jakarta to the social revolutions occurring in various regions was a political announcement signed by Sukarno and Hatta on October 27. Warning people that acting by themselves would only result in anarchy, it specified that demands for the replacement of local officials should be *"made via the government or with the mediation of the national committees* as the temporary representatives of the people."[65] By this time, however, the entire government apparatus at the district and subdistrict levels in the Tiga Daerah was in disarray and, as we have seen, the local national committees, as well as the police, had ceased to function. All the Tegal KNI could do for officials, who early in November felt their lives to be threatened, was to suggest that they move to the only safe place remaining, the local jail.

Another response by the government was to send a delegation of four Socialist party leaders, including two ministers, to Pekalongan to try to mediate between the Tiga Daerah and the residency capital, instructing them to explain to the bureaucratic elite that the new revolutionary government had the center's support and to Tiga Daerah leaders in Pemalang "that Sjahrir wasn't supporting feudalism but could not tolerate the lawlessness of the social revolution."[66]

Finally, on December 22, Sjahrir, Sukarno, Hatta, and their entourage arrived in Pekalongan. There they found a situation where the Communist resident, his staff, and the entire leadership of both the popular front and the revolutionary movements throughout the Tiga Daerah had been imprisoned by the TKR. But they largely ignored this military counterrevolution, saying little about the situation in public and only calling privately on the TKR commander to explain the army's action.

Sjahrir soon made his own attitude clear. He complained in a speech that he had more difficulty in dealing with Pekalongan than with the outside world and went on to express his disapproval of the local struggle, using an analogy with building materials. There were two kinds, said Sjahrir, those that passed the quality test and those that did not. "It was as if Pekalongan had not passed the test," recalls an official who was present.[67] In Sjahrir's view, the transfer of power that passed the quality test was one that was peaceful and orderly. Peacefully replacing a Japanese-appointed official was one thing, violent social upheaval quite another.

Sukarno appears to have made only one reference to the situation. This was during a brief stopover in Tegal, when he mentioned the "Talang State," suggesting that the social revolution was a separatist movement.[68] Hatta reportedly complained in December 1945 that there was "too much popular sovereignty" in Pekalongan residency. The people could not get rid of the pangreh praja just like that, said Hatta; only the government had that right.

Aftermath

The social revolution of October–December 1945 saw the complete overthrow of the bureaucratic elite, the ruling class in the Tiga Daerah. The old order was gone for good. The TKR counterrevolution in mid-December did not reestablish the bureaucratic elite in their former position; it merely removed certain radicals—but not the Moslem bupatis of Tegal and Brebes—from the local administration and disbanded the regency working committees in Tegal and Brebes.[69] The impossibility of reestablishing the old order was clear when the next resident, Soemitro Kolopaking, a former bupati from an old Banyumas bureaucratic elite family, tried to replace Moslems chosen during the social revolution with former officials.[70] Local opposition to such a return to the status quo ante forced the center to find a fourth resident in as many months. This time, Wali al-Fatah, a radical Moslem leader prominent in the national left-wing coalition, Persatuan Perjuangan (Struggle Union) and a Masyumi vice-chairman, was chosen.[71] With the replacement of Soepangat (arrested by the army) as bupati of Pemalang by a local religious teacher, the ascendancy of Islam in Pekalongan residency continued until, in late 1948, two of the santri bupatis (of Brebes and Pemalang) died as heroes at the hands of the Dutch during the guerrilla war.

The bureaucratic elite thrown out during the social revolution were in most cases reappointed to jobs either in the civilian police or in autonomous towns elsewhere in Central Java. When the Dutch occupied areas of the north coast after their first attack of 1947, some officials worked, willingly or otherwise, for their former Dutch superiors. Others (such as the bupati of Brebes), whose experiences during the social revolution had made them staunch Republicans, refused to cooperate and set up local Republican governments-in-exile in the mountains near Wonosobo to the south.

At the district and subdistrict levels, the orthodox Moslem teachers chosen during the social revolution stayed in office until after the transfer of sovereignty, when many moved to local departments of religious affairs in the regency towns. Most local nonreligious nationalists chosen by the people in 1945 also made careers in the civil service after 1950, as did some struggle movement leaders. One important result of the social revolution was thus an opening-up of the civil service at the local level. Most of the new village headmen retained their posts until well after the transfer of sovereignty in 1950, some until after the upheaval of 1965, when nearly all who had been in office since the Tiga Daerah Affair were removed.

The power struggle between the revolutionaries and the bureaucratic elite in the Tiga Daerah was more than just a struggle for administrative positions. It was not just a case of new wine in old wineskins, or old structures manned by new people—although in the colonial context of monopolization of these jobs by the bureaucratic elite, this change in itself would have been no small achievement. Local revolutionaries clearly saw that the structures themselves had to change. To make the administrative structure of local government more democratic, it was necessary to increase the people's participation through the creation of representative councils at all levels. Many local leaders saw first the local national committees, then the working committees, and finally the popular front that replaced them in the Tiga Daerah as sharing for the first time the bureaucratic power previously monopolized by the Dutch-trained elite. The change was not something they would give up lightly.

Notes

1. That is, at the residency level or below (regency, district, subdistrict, and village).

2. The Pekalongan residency in 1945 consisted of four regencies: the Tiga Daerah and the huge Pekalongan regency, which made up almost a third of the residency. The local Javanese bureaucratic elite consisted of the Dutch-trained *pangreh praja* (lit., rulers of the realm), a salaried class of officials, and below them the village headmen. For the formation of the elite as a class in Java, see Heather Sutherland, *The Making of a Bureaucratic Elite, the Colonial Transformation of the Javanese Priyayi,* ASAA Southeast Asia Publication Series, no. 2 (Singapore: Heinemann, 1979).

3. Soetan Sjahrir, *Our Struggle,* trans. Benedict Anderson (Ithaca: Cornell Modern Indonesia Project, 1968), p. 26.

4. This is not to say, of course, that Tegal and Pekalongan do not have their own linguistic and cultural peculiarities: low Javanese, for example, is pronounced in a distinctive way in the Tegal region, which also has its individual music and *wayang* (traditional Javanese drama, particularly by shadow puppets) tradition.

5. *Indisch Verslag* (The Hague/Batavia: Landsdrukkerij, 1931, 1935, 1938).

6. Sugar needs almost three times as much water as wet rice.

7. For a discussion of this strike, see John Ingleson, " 'Bound Hand and Foot': Railway Workers and the 1923 Strike in Java," *Indonesia* 31 (Apr. 1981): 53–87. Unions representing pawnshop employees, dockworkers, and sugar-mill workers also organized strikes in Pekalongan residency during this period.

8. See Ruth T. McVey, *The Rise of Indonesian Communism* (Ithaca: Cornell University Press, 1965), pp. 331–333, 340.

9. At least one religious leader was among those exiled to Boven Digul, and later to Australia. This was Haji Moeklas, the father of M. H. Lukman, the PKI politbureau leader in the post-1951 PKI headed by D. N. Aidit. Although

he was still overseas in 1945, other veterans of this early period returned to the region before the Japanese occupation and played key leadership roles in the Tiga Daerah Affair.

10. Rice was also requisitioned for stockpiles needed lest there be an attack on Java from the south and, in the last year of the war, for the Seventh Division headquarters in Singapore. For details on the amount of rice requisitioned in various parts of the Tiga Daerah, see Anton Lucas, "The Bamboo Spear Pierces the Payung: The Revolution against the Bureaucratic Elite in North Central Java in 1945" (Ph.D. dissertation, Australian National University, 1980), p. 52, table 2.

11. Transcript of taped interview with Djuweni Wimbohandoko, Tegal Peta battalion commander, Yogyakarta, Apr. 17, 1975.

12. This phrase comes from a conversation between Dr. Moerjawan, Pemalang regency's medical officer, and a patient, the driver of a horse cart, late in the Japanese occupation, recorded in Moerjawan, "Ichtisar" (typescript, [1946]), inventory 201, "Omwentelingzaak te Pekalongan." This is a collection of Republican documents relating to the Tiga Daerah Affair seized by the Dutch from Yogyakarta in 1949, now part of the Archief Procureur-Generaal bij het Hoogerrechtshof van Nederlandsch-Indië, Algemeen Rijksarchief, The Hague [hereafter *Proc. Gen.*].

13. Sarimin Reksodihardjo (bupati of Brebes), "Kenang Kenangan dari Masa yang Silam" (typescript, 1965). He recalled in these memoirs that "Japanese officials in the region kept completely silent" about the surrender.

14. Sarimin Reksodihardjo, Question 15, "Keterangan," Jan. 31, 1946, *Proc. Gen.*

15. Not all these national committees were chosen by local revolutionary groups; some were appointed by local officials. The former were more effective, usually taking the initiative in relieving economic distress by distributing surplus cloth and rice.

16. The petition, "Mosi Komite Nasional Daerah Pekalongan" [Motion of the Pekalongan Region National Committee], Sept. 12, 1945, was replied to by a letter from Secretary of State A. G. Pringgodigdo to Dr. Soembadji, Pekalongan KNI chairman, Sept. 21, 1945. I am grateful to the late Besar Martokoesoemo S. H. for allowing me to use these documents from his personal collection.

17. For an appreciation of Besar's contribution to the legal profession in Indonesia, see Daniel S. Lev, "In Memoriam: Besar Martokoesoemo S. H. (1894–1980)," *Indonesia* 30 (Oct. 1980): 121–123.

18. *Warta Berita,* Oct. 8, 1945; *Buku Kenangan Pembangunan Monumen Pahlawan Pekalongan* (Pekalongan: n.p., 1964).

19. For a more detailed account of these events, see Anton Lucas, "Social Revolution in Pemalang, Central Java, 1945," *Indonesia* 24 (Oct. 1977): 108–120.

20. Marsum Hardjoprajitno, "Ceritaku: Percikan Peristiwa Bersejarah Hari Proklamasi Kemerdekaan Indonesia di Daerah Tegal dan Sekitarnya" (typescript, 1974).

21. He was later able to leave Tegal in the cabin of a locomotive, dressed as a driver.

22. Several people were wounded in the clashes with the TKR. Transcript of taped interview with Djuweni Wimbohandoko, Yogyakarta, Apr. 17, 1975.

23. The Netherlands Indies Civil Administration (NICA) arrived in Jakarta with a company of the Royal Netherlands Indies Army (KNIL), together with the British forces, on September 29, 1945.

24. Interviews in Tegal in February and April 1973, and in Brebes and Tegal, Balapulang, and Jatibarang in November 1975; Soesmono (Tegal regency KNI vice-chairman), typescript, 1972; Kartohargo (Brebes KNI chairman) (proces-verbaal), Pekalongan, Oct. 23, 1946, *Proc. Gen.*

25. Sartono Kartodirdjo describes a guru as one of the charismatic powerful natural leaders in the village forming an unofficial religious elite with contacts and authority over a wide area. See his "Agrarian Radicalism in Java," in Claire Holt et al., eds., *Culture and Politics in Indonesia* (Ithaca: Cornell University Press, 1972), p. 78.

26. From interviews with Tauchid (village headman of Kajen village), Kajen, Feb. 9, 1973, and Nov. 29, 1975; Kutil's son in Pemalang, Nov. 1974; Abdul Latip (Talang KNI chairman), Tegal, Feb. 6, 1973; and Kho I Sin (Kutil's Chinese chauffeur), Tegal, Feb. 21, 1973.

27. Kutil, held responsible for the murder of a number of officials, was sentenced to death by a Pekalongan court on October 21, 1946, according to Pekalongan Court Declaration no. 1, 1950 (Diponegoro Division, [Kodam VII], military history section, Semarang). Because Kutil escaped in July 1947 as the Dutch were occupying Pekalongan, the sentence was not carried out until May 5, 1951, when he was executed by firing squad after President Sukarno had rejected an appeal for clemency. "Keputusan Presiden Republik Indonesia no. 336/G, 21 April 1951" (Diponegoro Division, military history section); Maj. Gen. Soedharmo (Pekalongan TKR leader), interview, Jakarta, Oct. 23, 1971.

28. Interviews in Brebes and Bumiayu subdistricts of Brebes, Watureja and Balapulang in Tegal, and Ulujami, Comal, and Moga in Pemalang, February and November 1975.

29. Interview with village KNI chairman, Krasak village, Dec. 5, 1975.

Turi is a marsh legume (*Sesbania* sp.) used for food in time of want; *kluwih* is a species of *Artocarpus,* a relative of the breadfruit, used as a vegetable.

30. Sixty-one out of sixty-three subdistrict and district heads were replaced. Among the new officials were seventeen members of the former elite, fourteen Moslem leaders, and fourteen school teachers. For further details, see Lucas, "Bamboo Spear," Appendix E, pp. 421–424.

31. Although in this discussion Moslems and Communists are treated separately, in the Tiga Daerah Affair (as in the planned uprising in 1926) a clear line cannot always be drawn between them. In the regency town of Pemalang and at the district/subdistrict level in the radical centers of Ketanggungan West, Slawi, Adiwerna, Jatinegara, and Randudongkal, Moslem teachers and nonreligious radicals worked actively together in local revolutionary movements.

32. The Barisan Pelopor (Pioneer Corps), the town's largest revolutionary group, run by veterans of the prewar nationalist movement, was replaced by Parsi (Partai Sosialis). In December 1945, however, Parsi became part of the Indonesian Socialist Party established in Yogya on November 1.

33. For the composition of the GBP3D, see Lucas, "Bamboo Spear," Appendix G, p. 428.

34. Kamidjaja or K. Midjaja (as he wrote his pseudonym), the son of a small peasant farmer, was born on August 7, 1909, near Kartasura, in Central Java. After village primary school he worked on the railways (except for two years in prison after the attempted Communist rebellion of 1926) until 1933, when he was dismissed for passive resistance against the railway company's order banning employees from joining the Railway Workers' Union. From 1935 to 1941 he was an editor of *Mimbar Boeroeh* in Solo and a leader of the prewar labor movement.

35. The PKI had been clandestinely reconstituted in 1935 by Musso and became known as the "Illegal PKI." Its main base of strength was in East Java. Subandi Widarta, born about 1913 in Kediri, was educated at a Dutch-language primary school in Surabaya, but dropped out of intermediate school (MULO). He was active in various youth groups, and after joining the Illegal PKI in 1936 he went to South Sumatra to work in the labor movement at the oil refineries in Palembang and Sambu Island. Forced to leave by the Dutch after strikes in the refineries, he returned to Java, joined Gerindo (Indonesian People's Movement), and worked as a journalist in Semarang. For the activities of Widarta's underground PKI, see Lucas, "Bamboo Spear," pp. 92–105, and Anton Lucas, "Reminiscences of Underground Work in Java during the Japanese Occupation" (Clayton, Victoria: Monash Univesity Centre of Southeast Asian Studies, forthcoming).

36. Interview with a former underground member, Jakarta, July 5, 1978.

37. This program is clearly spelled out in the minutes of the GBP3D's second meeting, Nov. 25, 1945, *Proc. Gen.* For a translation, see Lucas, "Bamboo Spear," p. 429.

38. Negotiations were under way with military headquarters in Yogya to reestablish a TKR presence in Tegal, but members of the popular front disagreed about whether to invite the TKR back or establish their own militia. Eventually the latter alternative was chosen.

39. Minutes of popular front meeting, Tegal, Nov. 25, 1945 *(Proc. Gen.),* translated in Lucas, "Bamboo Spear," p. 434.

40. The leaflet "Toentoetan Rakjat 3 Daerah Brebes, Tegal, Pemalang Terhadap Pemberesan Daerah Pekalongan" [The demand of the people of the Three Regions of Brebes, Tegal, and Pemalang for the settlement of the conflict in Pekalongan Region] and letter *(Proc. Gen.)* are translated in Lucas, "Bamboo Spear," pp. 439–440.

41. If those *santri* (devout Moslems) who were also KNI leaders or teachers were counted as part of the Moslem group, the total would be 28 percent. Of the four district heads, two served successively as *wedana* (district head) of Slawi for only a matter of days. The first, a Muhammadiyah teacher (the only modernist Islamic representative to obtain bureaucratic power in the Tiga Daerah), was removed after four days in office; his successor, a former vice-consul in Jeddah, was killed.

42. During the Japanese occupation K. Hashim Asj'ari held two important posts: chairman of Masyumi and (from mid-1944) head of the Office of Religious Affairs. After Masyumi was reorganized as a political party in November 1945, Asj'ari was elected chairman of its first party council. K. H. Fachruri, when interviewed in Slawi on December 15, 1972, could still recite in Arabic an Indonesian song he learned from K. Asj'ari while studying in Tebu-ireng, a free English rendition of which would go:

> We the people of Indonesia,
> Let us unite in our own groups,
> We shall organize for our faith.
> We must be true!
> We must hold fast to our weapons.
> To strengthen the ranks of Islam,
> For the glory of Islam.
> To educate our youth for the struggle.

43. Interview with K. H. Fachruri, Slawi, Dec. 15, 1972. The Tegal regency-level leader of the Barisan Pelopor, K. H. Fachruri later became wedana of Adiwerna during the social revolution.

44. For an account of the Pekajangan community, see Suzannah Price,

"Religion, Social Organisation, and Textile Production in a Javanese Village" (M.A. thesis, Australian National University, 1978).

45. Abu Sudja'i, interview in Tegal, Nov. 20, 1975.

46. In 1953 the Muhammadiyah batik entrepreneurs, who had opposed the social revolution in 1945 so vigorously, were living "on a scale comparable to that of the upper middle class of the west; large well furnished houses, radios, a protein-rich diet, college education for their children and perhaps an automobile." Boyd Compton, "Letter to the Institute of Current World Affairs in New York," Jakarta, Jan. 11, 1953.

47. One of the two Peta battalions stationed in the residency of Pekalongan was in Tegal and the other in Pekalongan itself. Of the eight company commanders whose backgrounds are known, six were from pangreh praja families and two were prominent religious teachers. For Peta/TKR social backgrounds, see Lucas, "Bamboo Spear," pp. 350–352 and 442–448.

48. Major General Soedharmo (Pekalongan TKR leader), in an interview in Jakarta, on March 26, 1973, stated this was because of the TKR's strong ties to the bureaucratic elite.

49. According to his account in a printed interview, Sayuti Melik played no part in Soeprapto's appointment. See "Latar Belakang 'Peristiwa Madiun,'" *Berita Buana,* Jan. 13, 1977. In an interview in Jakarta on October 30, 1971, Sayuti Melik recalled that, during his first visit to Pekalongan, he canvassed the possibility of himself becoming resident to replace the beleaguered Besar, but this was greeted without enthusiasm in Pekalongan "because I was not a member of the Pangreh Praja." Ideological differences with Communist popular front leaders Widarta and K. Midjaja also made him unacceptable in the Tiga Daerah. Soesmono (Tegal KNI vice-chairman), typescript, 1972.

50. For two accounts of this incident, see the interview with Sayuti Melik in *Berita Buana,* Jan. 13, 1977, and Soewignjo's version in "Sebuah renungan kecil: Penyelamat jiwa Sayuti Melik," *Berita Buana,* Apr. 28, 1977.

51. According to an account written later by Idris, he lived in a house outside the Slawi pemuda headquarters with some of his family. Iskandar Idris, "Sedikit catatan sekedar yang saya alami dan ketahui" (typed notes of Armed Forces Museum, Jakarta, interview team, July 26, 1972). Soewignjo claimed that, although Idris was not a prisoner, he had been told his safety could not be guaranteed if he returned to Pekalongan. Interview, Jakarta, Dec. 12, 1971.

52. Sardjio was a former member of the PNI Baru; during the Japanese occupation he was elected a member of the Kedu Residency Advisory Council and later appointed to the All-Java Advisory Council. Arrested by the Japanese in 1944 on suspicion of being a member of the underground PKI, he was serving a thirteen-year jail sentence when released in late September 1945.

53. "The Crisis in the Region of Pekalongan Residency," unsigned letter from the Tegal branch of the Indonesian Workers' Party, Dec. 20, 1945, *Proc. Gen.*

54. They were charged under section 107 of the criminal code, for which the maximum penalty was fifteen years in jail. See Yap Sin Fong, *Kitab Undang-Undang Hukum Pidana Indonesia* (Jakarta: Saksama, 1954), p. 50.

55. Iwa Kusumasumantri, *Sedjarah Revolusi Indonesia,* vol. 2 (Jakarta: Grafica, n.d. [1965]), p. 68; "Daftar Nama-Nama Perintis Kemerdekaan dalam Periode 1908–1945 dengan Sejarah Perjuangan Singkatnya" [A list of Pioneers of Independence from 1908–1945 with brief biographical notes] (membership book kept by the Tegal branch of Pioneers of Independence). Sukarno's amnesty is recorded under the entry for Amir, the Communist popular front leader from Pemalang.

56. "Announcement of the Republican Government of Pekalongan Residency, no. 1/B, 11 December 1945," *Proc. Gen.,* translated in Lucas, "Bamboo Spear," p. 441. See also Benedict Anderson, "Sembah-Sumpah: The Politics of Language and Javanese Culture" (Paper delivered at the Conference on Multilingualism in Modern Indonesia, Puncak, Aug. 1981).

57. This example of a speech by K. Midjaja was provided by a Brebes sugar-mill employee in an interview in Tegal, Nov. 19, 1975.

58. Wadyono (Pekalongan TKR commander), interview, Semarang, Aug. 27, 1971.

59. The word *dombreng* comes from *tong* and *breng,* two onomatopoeic Javanese words for the sounds of banging on wood or metal. To be "dombreng-ed" during the social revolution meant to be paraded around to the accompaniment of clanging tin pots and wooden clappers.

60. Interview with a son of the former village headman, Jatinegara, Feb. 13, 1975.

61. Benedict R. O'G. Anderson, "The Pemuda Revolution: Indonesian Politics, 1945–1946" (Ph.D. dissertation, Cornell University, 1966), p. 116.

62. Not one of my pangreh praja informants remembered the national conference of their spokesmen and the national leaders or recalled anyone attending from Pekalongan residency.

63. Kartohargo (Brebes KNI chairman), Question 5 (proces-verbaal), Jan. 15, 1947, *Proc. Gen.* The Magelang affair mentioned here refers to the fighting between British and Republican forces in that Central Java town on November 1, 1945.

64. Minister of defense in Amir Sjarifuddin's first cabinet, Supeno was shot by the Dutch during the second "police action."

65. Koesnodiprodjo, *Himpunan undang2, peraturan2 penetapan2 pemerintah Republik Indonesia, 1945,* rev. ed. (Jakarta: Seno, 1951), p. 68.

66. Interview with Soebadio Sastrosatomo, Jakarta, Aug. 7, 1972.

67. Transcript of taped interview with Soedjono (Pekalongan assistant-resident), Puncak, July 30, 1973.

68. As mentioned earlier, Talang, a subdistrict south of Tegal, was renowned because of the activities of Kutil.

69. On his release in July 1947, Kamidjaja returned to union activities. Before 1965 he was for a number of years a secretary of the PKI's Verification Committee (the party's watchdog responsible to congresses for its financial affairs). He died on March 6, 1966. Widarta was executed in the year following his release from prison in mid-1947 as the result of an internal PKI dispute.

70. Soemitro Kolopaking arrived in Pekalongan on January 23, 1946, to replace acting resident Suprapto (who had been called back by Pekalongan's Pesindo on December 17 after the arrest of Sardjio by the army). See *Antara,* Jan. 25, 1946.

71. Wali al-Fatah took up the position on April 16, 1946. *Antara,* April 18, 1946. For a biographical note on him, see Benedict R. O'G. Anderson, *Java in a Time of Revolution: Occupation and Resistance, 1944–1946* (Ithaca: Cornell University Press, 1972), p. 455.

BANTEN: "RICE DEBTS WILL BE REPAID WITH RICE, BLOOD DEBTS WITH BLOOD"

Michael C. Williams

Prologue

Three strands run through Banten's history in the Indonesian revolution. These three strands can briefly be identified as regionalism, anticolonialism, and social revolution. The revolution in Banten was characterized by a strong regional perspective, manifested in a distrust of the central Republican government and in a desire for as much autonomy as possible. It was also characterized at all stages by constant and unremitting anticolonialism. Like Yogyakarta, Banten was not reconquered by the Dutch until 1948, and it was one of the few regions of Indonesia not to be drawn into Dutch federalist projects. In addition, the period between 1945 and 1950 was marked by a strong social revolutionary impulse, demonstrated most spectacularly by the overthrow of the old administrative structure and the establishment of the Dewan Rakyat (People's Council), which ruled Banten between October 1945 and January 1946. These three strands intertwined to create the particular pattern of the revolutionary process in Banten: often one element assumed more importance than another, but at no time was any strand absent from the politics of the region.

During the revolution, Banten's distinctive history, leadership, and political direction caused constant friction between the regional leaders and the authorities in Yogyakarta. On occasion the central government forcibly suppressed local initiatives that did not accord with national policies and directions, and in 1949 it crushed a revolt against its authority in the region. Further tension sprang from Banten's traditionally strong radical tendencies. In the nineteenth century, this revolutionary tradition found expression in a series of revolts that culminated in the Cilegon uprising of 1888. Later, in 1926, Banten was the scene of a serious uprising by the PKI (Indonesian Communist Party). That revolt, with its strongly anti-*priyayi* (indigenous governing elite) and anticolonial emphases, had a profound influence on the revolution of 1945, most dramatically through a common leadership of both revolts.[1]

Economically and politically isolated in the nineteenth century,[2] Banten was a region renowned for its rebelliousness and religious fervor. The last vestiges of its independence disappeared only in 1832 when the Dutch abolished the sultanate. Ironically, this allowed the sultanate to remain, until modern times, a powerful symbol of Banten's past and a beacon for revolutionaries in the region. No revolt in later times was complete without ritual affirmation of its contact with the past. The leaders of these rebellions were preponderantly the *ulama* (Islamic scholars), but they also included descendants of the sultans and the old displaced aristocracy.[3]

The *pangreh praja* (administrative corps) were in most cases recruited from outside the region, principally from the Sundanese heartland of the Priangan. They were regarded with scant respect by the majority of the local population, whose first loyalties were still to the ulama. Banten remained a profoundly conservative region, stubbornly resisting most manifestations of Islamic modernism. Even in the 1920s, the Indonesian Communist Party achieved its remarkable revolutionary mobilization only through a close alliance with, and ultimate subservience to, sections of the ulama. The leadership of the 1926 revolt was in fact unique in that it linked three elements, the ulama, local Communists, and the *jawara*—the regional men of violence who traditionally exploited the power gap between the peasantry and the pangreh praja.

The coalescence of these three groups in the 1920s was based primarily on their common hatred of Dutch colonial rule. But more than this was needed to bind the three into a successful revolutionary alliance. A key element was the acceptance by the local PKI of the undisputed political hegemony of the ulama in Banten. The cooperation of the local jawara was sought because the PKI lacked an armed wing and had pitifully few weapons. The failure to maintain a similar coalition in 1945–1946 was seriously to weaken the social revolutionary strand of the struggle against the Dutch.

The failure of the PKI revolt of 1926 marked a turning point in Banten's political development. In its aftermath four men were hanged, ninety-nine sent into exile in Boven Digul in West New Guinea, and hundreds of others imprisoned for long periods. Deep scars were left in Bantenese society; the result was an abiding hatred of the pangreh praja, the revolt's main targets, as well as of the Dutch. Subsequent colonial repression left Banten politically isolated and neutralized in the period to 1942. The ulama and jawara saw modern urban-based parties of the 1930s as a threat, unlike the PKI in the 1920s, which had basically not sought to challenge their traditional roles. Distrusted by the orthodox ulama and lacking a significant intelligentsia in the region to which it could appeal, the nationalist movement found no meaningful political constituency in Banten. The only challenge to the colonial law and order came from the jawara, who retained clandestine links with some recently released Communists and with underground groups.[4] By the late 1930s, the jawara had developed an organization of their own that had political overtones, but this was broken by the Dutch between February and May 1940 when seven bands totalling 175 men were arrested.[5]

During the Japanese occupation, small underground opposition groups managed to survive. The oldest of them consisted of former PKI members, including many ex-Digulists and others who had fled to Malaya following the collapse of the 1926 revolt. Some of the latter had established contacts in exile with Pari (Partai Republik Indonesia), the party established by Tan Malaka following his break with the PKI.[6] Partly because of this, the PKI/Pari split was not to become a bitter dispute in Banten until well after the declaration of independence. By the late 1930s, after their return from exile, this group had contacts with local jawara and also with Batavia-based labor unions such as Persi (Persatuan Sopir Indonesia, Drivers' Union). More ex-Digulists returned home in 1939–1940, among them Kyai Achmad Chatib, the most important ulama to have adhered to the Communist cause in 1926, and became loosely associated with this group and its leader, Tje Mamat, who was to play an important part in the social revolution of 1945.

Tje Mamat had been secretary of the PKI branch in Anyer in 1926 and was one of those who fled to Malaya following the failure of the PKI uprising and were recruited into Pari.[7] He returned to Indonesia in 1930 and set up a political study club in Palembang with Mohammed Arif Siregar. In 1932, following the arrest of Tan Malaka's aide, Djamaluddin Tamin, the Palembang cell was broken up; Tje Mamat was detained for several weeks but released for lack of evidence. He then returned to Banten, where he earned a living as an unlicensed attorney, frequently appearing on behalf of jawara brought before the local courts.

During the war years, Tje Mamat and his colleagues maintained contact with groups outside Banten, including the underground movement of Mr. Jusuf, a radical lawyer who had headed the Persi union before the war and who was to revive the PKI in October 1945.[8] On the whole, Tje Mamat and his associates abjured any contact with markedly pro-Japanese groups or individuals, though they did maintain links with Kyai Chatib, who was appointed battalion-commander in the Peta (Japanese-sponsored volunteer army), and with some pemuda (young people) who had been drawn into Japanese-sponsored youth groups.[9] Tje Mamat and many of his associates were arrested in 1944 by the Kenpeitai (Japanese military police). Tje Mamat himself was imprisoned and tortured; two other leaders of the group, Haji Sinting, an ex-Digulist, and Hidayat, died in detention.[10] The experiences of this group during the war left them with a hatred not only of the Japanese but also of the Indonesian officials and police whom they saw as willing collaborators.

Other Bantenese, however, were willing to work with the Japanese. Tomegoro Yoshizumi, who before the war had been a correspondent in Batavia for the To Hindo Nippō, was head of the Kaigun Bukanfu Daisangka (Japanese Naval Counter-Intelligence) in Banten. He appears to have visited Banten frequently before 1942, and during the occupation he recruited several Bantenese to his office.[11] Of a younger generation than the veterans of 1926, most of these Bantenese had been working in Batavia in 1942. After 1945 all of them became closely associated with Tan Malaka's Persatuan Perjuangan (Struggle Union). Some contact seems to have been maintained between Bantenese of the Kaigun group and the PKI group, and on at least two occasions the former intervened with the Kenpeitai to secure the release of ex-Digulists from prison.

Toward the end of 1944, the Kaigun Bukanfu Daisangka began to take an increasing interest in Banten although, formally, Kaigun (the Japanese Navy) had no authority in Java. Rudimentary guerrilla training was given in Jakarta under the auspices of Yoshizumi's office to jawara leaders from West Java, including Jaro Karis and Jaro Kamid from Banten. In May 1945 Yoshizumi followed this up by visiting the region with Entol Chaeruddin, a Bantenese aide who later became bodyguard to Tan Malaka. The two men met with prominent ulama and jawara and, as a result of their visit, the Bukanfu Daisangka trained 400 young men in Serang during the month of June.[12] Most of those who received training appear to have been nominated by jawara leaders; they were later to associate with the Dewan Rakyat.

During the occupation, the positions of the two dominant social groups in Banten, the ulama and the pangreh praja, changed markedly. The war years brought to Islam an official importance that had been systematically denied it during the Dutch colonial period. Almost certainly, expectations of receiving greater political power were raised among the ulama when for the first time the government accorded them limited political recognition. The most dramatic expression of their changed position came with the appointment of Kyai Chatib and Kyai Sja'maun as commanders of two of the four battalions of Peta in the region.[13] Other ulama were named to official positions, largely in nominal bodies dealing with religious or social affairs. Control of the administration, however, remained firmly in the hands of the Japanese and the pangreh praja. Even in the Peta, with the exception of a few ulama, officers were almost exclusively from priyayi rather than *santri* (devout Moslem) backgrounds. The appointment of a few ulama seems to have been designed to appease local sentiment, but the all-important recruitment to the Peta was organized through local government. The officers were overwhelmingly young men with at least Dutch elementary education, and care seems to have been taken even with recruitment to the lower ranks. There was thus no question of ulama entering en masse with their santri followers.

The position of the pangreh praja in Banten was substantially eroded during the occupation years. Strictly speaking, their control of local administration and their political status remained intact, but it was precisely because of the former that they came increasingly into conflict with other local interests. The police, most of whose senior officers in Banten were from outside the region, were given the task of hunting down suspected Allied or leftist sympathizers and of curbing the restless jawara.

First Moves in the Revolution

The situation in Banten began to deteriorate markedly in 1945. Shortages of food and clothing became particularly acute. By the end of 1944, rice deficiencies in the Menes region had begun to cause considerable unrest, with peasants refusing to make deliveries of rice to the authorities and even denying them permission to visit villages.[14] Then allegations of widespread official corruption in the collection of the rice harvest and the distribution of cloth increased the resentment and bitterness of the peasantry toward the priyayi. By mid-1945 unrest had spread even to the ranks of the Peta, with desertions reported from the Labuan and Cilegon battalions.

The first sign that the simmering social tensions were likely to give way to widespread disorders occurred in August 1945 when rioting broke out in the Anyer district of Serang regency. A PKI stronghold in the 1920s, Anyer's local economy had been sharply hit during the war years by the complete standstill of the copra industry. The immediate cause of the rioting appears to have been food shortages caused by the rice delivery system and the failure of the assistant-*wedana* (district head) of Cinangka to distribute cloth in exchange for rice. New regulations for rice deliveries introduced in 1945 required peasants to surrender between 66 percent and 75 percent of their crop.[15]

On August 16, peasants in Cinangka approached the assistant-wedana, Tb. Mohammed Arsad, demanding that cloth in his possession be turned over to them. When he refused, his residence was promptly ransacked, whereupon he fled to Anyer to seek help. The wedana of Anyer, Raden Soekrawardi, returned to Cinangka with the assistant-wedana and two policemen, but when they entered the village, they were attacked by peasants armed with machetes. In the melee, Raden Soekrawardi was killed; other officials managed to escape.[16] The rioting was not suppressed until the 18th, when thirty policemen together with Japanese soldiers entered the village. In the fighting that followed, one policeman and seven peasants were killed.

The Cinangka incident was in many ways the opening shot in the struggle that was soon to develop between the pangreh praja and the social revolutionaries. Although the disturbances were over in a few days, the repercussions were widespread. Nervousness and unease increased among the Japanese and Indonesian officials in August and September. The Kenpeitai tried to keep matters under control by making arrests and showing their presence in the region, but further indications of unrest were not long in coming. In late August, an Indonesian police patrol was attacked and fired on near the village of Taktakan, just outside Serang, a senior officer, Tjokrosuwiryo losing an eye in the engagement.

In the weeks after the Cinangka incident, it was the ulama and jawara, together with the small underground Communist groups, that seized the initiative, not the pemuda who were so active in the cities. The absence of large towns and of a significant intelligentsia or middle class in Banten explains why pemuda did not become the critical revolutionary group there, as they did in many other areas. Peta had been disbanded prior to the proclamation of independence and former Peta officers in the region were reluctant to lead a struggle that they might not be able to control. Many therefore left the region for Jakarta and Bandung. In some quarters the Peta were already being denounced as collaborators; a whispering campaign attacked their "treachery" during the occupation. There was strong resentment of the privileged access the Peta had had to food and clothing, as well as of their close personal relations with Japanese.[17] Their priyayi backgrounds also made most of the Peta officers fear the outcome of any reenactment of the 1926 revolt.

September 1945 was marked by growing tension throughout Banten. The violence of events in Cinangka had an unsettling influence on pangreh praja and local police officials. Jawara bands began to emerge into the open, and authority was more and more flouted. Revolutionary groups increasingly began to steel themselves for combat. The ulama, local Communists, and jawara became convinced that, in the absence of any pro-Republican leadership at the top in the residency or any initiative from the former Peta, they would have to act. The conviction was also spreading that a complete overhaul of the existing system of government in the region would be necessary as the Japanese were removed.

The revolutionaries were probably fortified in this conviction by the presence and advice of Tan Malaka. Using the pseudonym Ilyas Husen, the veteran Indonesian Communist had lived for more than two years, since 1943, in south Banten, working in the offices of the Mitsubishi coal mine in Bayah.[18] During the occupation years he had made contact with a number of young Indonesians active in Japanese youth organizations in the region, including the son-in-law of Kyai Achmad Chatib. Whether he had any direct contact with the local underground Communists is more difficult to determine. What is certain is that on August 9, 1945, he was asked by a small group in Rangkasbitung to represent Banten at a forthcoming pemuda meeting in Jakarta.

In late September, Tan Malaka returned to Banten, spending several days in the region before leaving for Central Java. Contacting the son-in-law of Kyai Chatib, he asked to be introduced to the future resident of Banten.[19] There followed a series of meetings in Serang of core revolutionary leaders, many of them ex-PKI and former Digulists, addressed by Tan Malaka. One of the men present at these meetings recalled the atmosphere:

> In late September I attended a secret meeting in Serang at which Tan Malaka and Tje Mamat were the main speakers. There were about forty people present, including many from Tanggerang such as Kyai Achmad. There were many ex-Digulists. Tan Malaka made a passionate speech advocating the early transfer of power from the Japanese and the creation of genuine people's organs. Some of those present advocated the execution of all pangreh praja and the feudal class in order to complete the aims of 1926.[20]

How much direct influence Tan Malaka had on the events that followed, however, is not so clear. He left Banten on October 5, 1945.

The hesitation and extremely cautious approach adopted by the local administration to the declaration of independence in Jakarta increased the militancy of revolutionary groups. While the Jakarta government promoted Indonesian vice-residents to full resident in most areas on September 5, 1945, the vice-resident in Banten, Raden

T. R. Tirtasujatna, was appointed resident of Banten only on September 29.[21] As in Pekalongan, where a similar delay had taken place, the suspicions of local revolutionaries were aroused; it was widely assumed that Tirtasujatna, who was not Bantenese, was guilty of serious shortcomings, even that he was pro-Dutch. Rightly or wrongly, it was held that it was because Tirtasujatna doubted the wisdom of the proclamation of independence that his appointment was delayed.

Thus the polarization increased between the loose coalition of local Communists, ulama, and jawara on the one hand, and the local administration on the other. The revolutionaries were further emboldened by the increasingly obvious reluctance of the Japanese to support the Indonesian administration. On October 6 a mass public meeting of several thousand people in Serang elected Kyai Chatib resident. At the same time the regent in Pandeglang, Raden Djumhana Wiriaatmadja, refused to fly the Indonesian flag and, after an argument with local revolutionaries, left Banten.[22]

In an attempt to avoid direct clashes, the Japanese, who had remained in formal control until late September, withdrew their remaining forces to Serang. In the process, however, a clash occurred at Warunggunung, near Rangkasbitung, when four Japanese soldiers were attacked and killed by several hundred peasants. The remaining two hundred Japanese soldiers in Serang rejected any further negotiations about the surrender of arms, and on October 9 a battle ensued that pitted the jawara, peasants, and a handful of Peta soldiers against the Japanese garrison. The jawara were led by Soleiman Gunungsari, Haji Mu'min, Jaro Kamid, Kyai Abdulhadi (a former Digulist), and Salim Nonong (a former Peta officer active before the war in Persi).[23] The fighting ended the following day when the Japanese broke out of the town.

The withdrawal of the Japanese from Banten, the immediate object of the social revolutionaries, was a symbolic victory of great significance. For the first time in the history of social and political unrest in Banten, the rebels, at least in their own eyes, had achieved not a temporary defeat of the colonial power but a complete and lasting victory that was to leave the Bantenese in charge of their own house. How to manage that house became the principal issue on the revolutionaries' agenda.

The traditional hatred of the pangreh praja and the police, and the preponderance of jawara among the revolutionaries, determined the choice of the former as the next target of the radicals. First an attack was mounted on the main prison in Serang, which was largely undefended. Many jawara imprisoned there, including Achmad Sadeli, Mad Duding, and Wadut, were released. On the night of October 13 the rebels killed six Europeans detained in the jail; among them was a former captain in the Dutch army, Faber, who had arrived in Banten only a few days earlier from Sumatra. At the same time, the rebels seized the almost deserted regency office and imprisoned the regent, Hilman Djajadiningrat, in the jail, where he was held for several months. Several other priyayi, including the wedana of Ciomas, Raden Sastradikaria, were arrested and imprisoned.

The Dewan Rakyat (People's Council)

In the next few days there followed an almost total disintegration of local government and police activity in the region.[24] Throughout the residency, all pangreh praja, from assistant-wedana to regent, were replaced by ulama. In some instances the change took place seemingly spontaneously; elsewhere, revolutionary bands appeared, claiming that they acted on the orders of the resident, Kyai Chatib. In a number of places the changeover was accompanied by violence. Policemen were killed in Pandeglang, Mancak, and in Menes. In Pabuaran, near Ciomas, the assistant-wedana, Tb. Entik Surawijaja, was killed when a large band under Haji Saldi, a veteran of 1926 and a former Digulist, attacked the assistant-wedana's residence. Invoking the memories and aims of the 1926 revolt, Haji Saldi intended to proceed to the neighboring villages of Baros, Petir, and Ciruas to remove other officials. The timely intervention of an emissary personally dispatched by Kyai Chatib prevented the violence from spreading.

The pattern of revolt followed in many respects the precedents of the uprisings of 1888 and especially 1926. The targets of revolutionary violence, as on those occasions, were Dutch and Indonesian officials and policemen, and, as before, there appears to be no record of attacks on Chinese. The rebels were mostly peasants; the revolutionary leadership, as in 1926, consisted of a loose alliance of ulama, Communists, and jawara. The main feature distinguishing 1945 from

1926 and 1888, however, was the virtual absence of resistance or reaction from the authorities, at least for several months. The very success of the rebels was, ironically, to lead to an unraveling of the revolutionary coalition.

For the most part, the revolutionary upheaval took place without violence, if only because most officials and senior police officers had wisely taken the precaution of leaving Banten in early October for the comparative safety of Jakarta or Bandung. Public meetings were held at which new officials were elected, most of them ulama.[25] The atmosphere in which officials were replaced was graphically recalled by a former senior police officer in Cilegon at the time:

> The confusion increased greatly in October particularly around the 15th. Leaflets and posters began to appear everywhere with the hammer and sickle. After Natadiredja, the head of the police in Banten, had fled, the prisoners in the Cilegon jail were freed and the police station was looted of its arms. . . .
>
> Because we did not feel safe in our own house, from the 20th I took refuge in the house of a friend. Many people were pouring into Cilegon from the surrounding villages—Kramatwatu, Merak, and Anyer. Meetings of thousands were held in the town square. It was decided to share all looted goods [from the houses of officials and Chinese]. The question also arose of what to do with me and the wedana. Most of those who had come into Cilegon were in favor of execution, while the townspeople wanted us detained. A decision on the matter was finally taken at a secret meeting on October 20. Some of my own police agents were present at the meeting. The majority view propounded by Kyai Suhaimi prevailed. We were to be spared and expelled from Banten. I eventually left Cilegon on October 27 for Bandung.[26]

Local Communists did not oppose the choice of ulama to fill official posts. To have done so would have prompted the early breakup of the alliance. Instead, they concentrated their efforts on the establishment of the Dewan Rakyat, which was set up by the revolutionaries, under the self-appointed chairmanship of Tje Mamat, alongside the ulama-dominated civil administration. In ceding control of the local administration, at least nominally, to the ulama, the PKI/Pari group in the Dewan tacitly acknowledged the dominant social position of the ulama in Banten. The revolutionaries grouped around Tje Mamat clearly hoped, however, that real political control would be vested in the Dewan. In this division of responsibility lay the seeds of future conflict.

In the aftermath of the Japanese withdrawal from Banten and in the absence of any countervailing structures, the Dewan rapidly assumed the function of the main executive body. It had only tenuous links with the Republican government in Jakarta, which, at least until December 1945, seems to have despaired of the situation in Banten.[27] The Dewan, for its part, was strongly under the influence of such former PKI/Pari cadres as Tje Mamat, Alirachman, Tb. Hilman, and Haji Joes, and prominent jawara, among them Soleiman Gunungsari and Jaro Kamid, who were at best skeptical of the Republican leadership and sometimes openly hostile. A striking illustration of their attitude was the Dewan's refusal to countenance the existence in Banten of the officially sanctioned KNI (Indonesian National Committee) because it was not sufficiently revolutionary.

The dominant figure within the Dewan was Tje Mamat, often referred to at the time as "Bapak Rakyat" (Father of the People). He appears to have worked closely with Kyai Chatib, the resident. Chatib's authority and influence were based above all on his leadership of the 1926 revolt and his position as son-in-law of Kyai Asnawi, the most famous Bantenese Digulist and member of the wartime underground.[28] The Dewan's chief political and social constituency was the peasantry and jawara of the region. It successfully marshaled its most fervent supporters into various *lasykar* (militia) and even into a reconstituted police force. With their traditional antipathy to the pangreh praja, the jawara were natural allies of the Dewan. But their indiscipline and easy resort to violence were later to prove a disadvantage.

Amongst the peasantry, the Dewan made an immediate impression. Its revolutionary and populist slogans—"the people will become judge," "one for all and all for one," "rice debts will be repaid with rice, blood debts with blood"—seemed aptly to express the essence of the revolutionary struggle. The proliferation of revolutionary emblems and insignia—the red flag, the hammer and sickle, and the Dewan's own red triangle on a white background—further contributed to the heady and insurrectionary atmosphere of October 1945. The Dewan soon formed its own police force, known at first as the People's Security Police, and later as the Special Police, under a well-known jawara, recently released from Serang prison, Achmad Sadeli. Most important, the Dewan successfully managed the task of food distribution through a People's Economic Council. The Dewan took over Japanese stocks of rice, salt, sugar, and tapioca and distributed them through a primitive rationing system until December 1945, when supplies ran out. (Significantly it was at about this time that public opinion began to shift against the Dewan and Tje Mamat.) It also organized raids on the homes of priyayi and saw to the distribution of food and clothing found there.

The period of the Dewan's ascendancy in Banten was, however, comparatively short, almost exactly three months. Having seized power, the revolutionaries had great difficulty in consolidating their hold on the region. The absence of any favorable revolutionary developments at the national level, and particularly the slowness with which Tan Malaka and the PKI regrouped into coherent political factions, were frustrating to a social revolutionary movement such as the Dewan in Banten. As in 1926, the local revolutionaries were undercut by lack of support at the national level. After the initial revolutionary euphoria, internal local factors also began to work against the Dewan. By November, under instructions from the central army leadership, former Peta officers and men who had not left the region had begun to regroup themselves as a unit of the TKR (Republican armed forces). They chose as their leader the former Peta commander and new regent of Serang, Kyai Sja'maun.[29] Similar developments occurred in Rangkasbitung and Pandeglang, as former Peta units tried to reconstitute themselves and sought contact with the more conservative ulama.

These moves came at a time when the Dewan's difficulties were increasing. The council had few trained officials at its disposal. Indeed, many of its prominent members rejected the need for tax collection or education as contrary to the revolutionary ideals. The ulama themselves were singularly inexperienced in administration. Some lower-level office personnel had been retained by the Dewan, but they seem to have adopted an obstructive attitude to the new administration and been unwilling to cooperate with it.[30]

Most damaging for the Dewan were the strains that had been allowed to develop in its relations with the ulama. In this respect, Tje Mamat and his associates had been far less circumspect and subtle than had Puradisastra, the PKI leader in 1926. Kyai Chatib and a handful of other ulama who were veterans of 1926 may have had a wider vision, but for most of the religious leaders, their long-cherished goal had been achieved once local government was transferred from the pangreh praja to the ulama. Few wanted to venture further. Rumors of land distribution and of black lists of persons to be tried before the Dewan, as well as charges that the ulama were indulging in shows of luxury, alienated the religious leaders. The lead given by Kyai Sja'maun in siding with the TKR was soon followed by other Moslem leaders. A wave of kidnappings and killings in December 1945 finally ruptured the links between the ulama and the Dewan. The time for Islam and communism to go their own ways had arrived.

The Dewan experienced growing difficulties not only with the ulama and the TKR; divisions were also beginning to arise in the revolutionary left. While councils similar to the Dewan, and operating under its tutelage, had been formed in Labuan and Rangkasbitung, in Pandeglang events had taken another course. There, Mohammed Ali (Mamak), a former Digulist, had formed a Komite Revolusioner Indonesia (KRI, Indonesian Revolutionary Committee), which, although it cooperated with the Dewan, increasingly found itself at odds with the Dewan's policies. This was also the experience of veteran Communist and ex-Digulist, Achmad Bassaif, who returned to Serang from Australia in November 1945.[31] Together with other ex-Digulists, such as Tb. Hilman and Agus Soleiman, this group increasingly saw a policy of outright opposition to the Republic as futile. They saw as more realistic an attempt to consolidate a Communist hold within the Republican administration.

This withdrawal of support for the Dewan by the moderate PKI groups left the pro-Tan Malaka faction of Tje Mamat and Alirachman dangerously exposed. They were still supported by important jawara leaders, such as Soleiman Gunungsari, Jaro Kamid, and Jaro Angling, but in terms of political leadership the Dewan was, by December 1945, fatally weakened. Many of the jawara bands proved difficult to control, and killings and robberies continued unabated. Most critical for the Dewan was the wavering attitude of the resident, Kyai Chatib, who by January 1946 was not prepared to accompany the Dewan on another bout of fratricidal killings.

The Dewan's difficulties in Banten coincided with mounting opposition to local social revolutions from the Republican government in Jakarta. The Jakarta leadership was concerned, particularly after the formation of the Sjahrir government in November 1945, that revolutionary unrest in Banten and Tanggerang might spill over into the Batavian hinterland. If this were to occur, the British and Dutch would almost certainly react unfavorably and use the opportunity to demonstrate the Republic's inability to keep its own house in order. It was in the Republic's interest for developments in such regions as Banten to be brought into line.

The Republic's concern about events in Banten was enhanced by rumors, sometimes bordering on the fantastic, brought by travelers from the region that Banten intended to declare itself independent, that the Dewan intended to challenge the legitimacy of the rule of President Sukarno, and even that the Bantenese sultanate was to be restored. By late October 1945, these rumors had begun to appear in the Jakarta press.[32] The body of stories about social revolution and impending anarchy was fed by the steady stream of former officials, policemen, and even Peta officers fleeing Banten. Most members of the large and influential Djajadiningrat family, for example, had left the region following the death of Raden Soekrawardi in August and the imprisonment of Hilman Djajadiningrat in October.[33]

If the tactical advantage had been overwhelmingly with the revolutionaries in October, within weeks the tide was flowing in the other direction. The absence of any social-revolutionary element in the Indonesian independence struggle on the national plane was a decisive factor. The leaders of the Dewan did not accept the legitimacy of the Sukarno-Hatta leadership of the Republic and, indeed, openly derided it; yet until the formation of the Persatuan Perjuangan, in late January 1946, there was no countervailing revolutionary force at the national level. The Republican government was, of course, militarily weak and had only limited ability to impose its will, yet it had political clout; *faute de mieux,* it was leading the struggle for independence. In the absence of any contending national force, this fact was gradually accepted, even in Banten; and acceptance was accelerated by the growing disillusionment with the Dewan.

The visit of Sukarno and Hatta to the region in December 1945 played an important part in changing the situation for the Dewan. By this time, the TKR was increasingly confident that support from the

Republic would enable it to turn the tables in Banten. In Jakarta, the Republican leadership was making more and more concessions to the Allies. On November 19 the Sjahrir cabinet had declared the capital a diplomatic city and formally withdrawn all Republican army units. These moves aroused great suspicion in Banten, where the Dewan saw the Republic as opposed not only to social revolution but also to a fight with the Dutch.

By December, the Republican government, and especially senior army officers, some of whom had family connections in Banten, had become extremely disturbed by the unwillingness of the Dewan to accept the Republic's authority. The presidential visit provided an opportunity to gauge the extent of local support for the Dewan and led to talks with the region's army leaders on the need to curb the Dewan's activities. More important, it reminded the local people of the presence of the central government.

Sukarno and Hatta, accompanied by Kasman Singodimedjo, the attorney-general, spent December 9–12 in Banten.[34] In speeches in Serang and Rangkasbitung, the Republican leaders warned their audiences that the notion of people's sovereignty was not to be interpreted literally; on the contrary, the people must remember their responsibilities to the state. They also emphasized the need for national unity in the struggle against the Dutch. Hatta went out of his way to describe the Dewan as meaningless and to call for its dissolution.

In public, Tje Mamat replied that the Dewan represented the only true people's democracy, while the KNIP (Central Indonesian National Committee) was simply a hand-me-down from the Japanese. Elements within the Dewan sought to use the occasion of the presidential visit to demonstrate their revolutionary militancy. While Sukarno and Hatta were staying in Rangkasbitung, Dewan supporters kidnapped and killed R. T. Hardiwinangun, who had been regent of Lebak until 1945.[35] This incident made a showdown with the army inevitable.

Before the presidential visit and Hardiwinangun's death, the TKR had been afraid to take action against the Dewan for fear of reaction by local ulama and peasants. The murder of Hardiwinangun, however, lost the Dewan considerable support; the ulama, particularly, were increasingly perturbed by the course of events. The urgency of the situation for the army was dramatically underlined on December 31, when Dewan lasykars in Serang arrested Entol Ternaja,[36] a senior

TKR officer, and Iskandar Kusumuningrat, the former police chief of the residency. The two men were taken to Ciomas, a Dewan stronghold, to be tried for crimes committed under the Dutch. The same day, a clash took place in Pandeglang when Dewan supporters tried to seize arms from the local TKR unit. On January 2, 1946, the Dewan in Rangkasbitung demanded the replacement of the regent, Kyai Abuya Hassan, and the appointment of a directorium to supervise all branches of the government and all revolutionary armed forces.

The TKR in Rangkasbitung replied with an ultimatum of their own, demanding the dissolution of the Dewan; when this attempt failed, fighting took place in the town, in which the Dewan forces, poorly armed and ill trained, were quickly routed. Sensing that events had turned in their favor, TKR forces in Banten's three main towns moved against the Dewan forces in Ciomas on January 8. The fighting lasted for more than twenty-four hours, leaving at least fifteen dead on the Dewan side, and was stopped only by the personal intervention of the resident, Kyai Chatib.[37]

The ceasefire that followed led to the dismemberment of the Dewan. Several revolutionary leaders, including Tje Mamat, Alirachman, and Achmad Bassaif, were arrested; Hilman Djajadiningrat and other priyayi still imprisoned were freed and taken to Sukabumi. The position of the resident, Kyai Chatib, remained unchallenged, however, and ulama continued to occupy all the administrative posts of importance.

The Aftermath of the Dewan: Banten 1946–1949

With the suppression of the Dewan in January 1946, radicalism in the region suffered a severe setback. Politically and organizationally, the Dewan had been unable to develop structures and programs capable of sustaining it in the face of local and national opposition. The Dewan's elimination meant that the social revolutionary strand in Banten's history in the revolution was eclipsed but not extinguished. Regionalism and anticolonialism became the more important elements, both in the revolutionary struggle and in the continuing tensions between Banten and the Republican government in Yogyakarta. The regionalist strand demonstrated itself in the desire of Banten's leaders for a meaningful degree of autonomy for the region, the anti-colonialist strand in their constant distrust of the diplomatic maneu-verings of the government.

The Dewan may have been removed, but there was to be no coun-terrevolution—no immediate restoration, for example, of the old pangreh praja to their former posts. For the moment, the ulama con-tinued to occupy all administrative positions, although later, between 1947 and 1950, they were to be gradually eased out. Kyai Chatib, despite his earlier sympathies with the Dewan, remained resident, thanks largely to the enormous influence he exercised throughout the region. More orthodox Communists who had distanced themselves from the Dewan remained in influential advisory positions. In Pan-deglang, Mohammed Ali (Mamak) dissolved his Revolutionary Com-mittee soon after the fall of the Dewan and formed instead a Komite Nasional Indonesia in conformity with the structure of Republican administration elsewhere. In Serang, three key PKI figures, all ex-Digulists, Agus Soleiman, Mohammed Noer, and Tb. Hilman, set up a People's Information Bureau to develop and consolidate PKI influ-ence and support in the region. Agus Soleiman and Mohammed Ali also became members of the five-man executive of the Banten KNI.[38] Many former PKI leaders also continued to occupy important posi-tions in the administration; Haji Afif became wedana of Cilegon; Tb. Emed, Achmad Chatib's brother-in-law, was appointed wedana of Labuan; and Achmad Rifai held the position of political secretary to Kyai Abdulhalim, the regent of Pandeglang.[39]

Nevertheless, conservative tendencies and forces had been strength-ened by the Dewan's fall, and disillusionment with the anarchy and looting of the latter period of its rule reinforced these tendencies. Most notably, the former Peta and Heihō (auxiliary forces under the Japa-nese) soldiers, now regrouped in the TKR as the "1,000 Division," had achieved absolute military superiority in the region. At the same time, the second year of the revolution saw a renewal of regionalism and a return to the banditry that had disturbed law and order in the late 1930s. Large jawara bands such as those of Soleiman Gunungsari, Jaro Kamid, and Haji Armana, took to the hills once again and renewed their contacts with the Jakarta underworld.[40]

The Republican government in Yogyakarta remained concerned by the situation in Banten, especially when regionalist desires seemed to be re-emerging. The main cause of the government's alarm was a program launched in September 1946 by Kyai Chatib to restore the old town of Banten, together with its harbor, destroyed by the Dutch in 1832. Rumors spread rapidly that this effort was but the preliminary to a full restoration of the old sultanate, with Chatib himself, a descendant of the last sultans, first in line to inherit the title. Such was the alarm felt in Yogyakarta that Hatta returned to Banten in October to meet with the resident.[41]

Hatta was sufficiently disturbed by what he learned about the situation in Banten to call for decisive action on both the political and the military fronts. Earlier, in May, following the formation of the Siliwangi Division in West Java, Colonel A. H. Nasution, its first commander, had visited Banten to try to bring the 1,000 Division into line with other Siliwangi units. Thus the TRI units in the region became Brigade I of the Siliwangi, with Kyai Sja'maun as commander and Lieutenant Colonel Sutalaksana as chief of staff.[42] The brigade remained far weaker than other Siliwangi units, however, being poorly armed and critically short of officers as a result of the exodus of many former Peta officers from the region in October 1945. After Hatta's visit to Banten, Nasution consolidated the brigade further, sending Lieutenant Colonel Sukanda Bratamenggala, accompanied by several hundred troops from the East Priangan, to Banten in December 1946 to take command. At the same time several key appointments were made on the political level. While the government recognized, albeit reluctantly, that the position of Kyai Chatib as resident was unassailable, it tried to limit his room for maneuver by appointing Joesoep Adiwinata as governor of West Java, based in Serang, and Semaun Bakri, Sukarno's wartime secretary, as deputy resident.[43]

Beginning in 1947, the Republican government made a determined attempt to put the clock back to 1945 and curtail the powers of both the ulama and the irregular lasykar. In February, the regent of Pandeglang, Kyai Abdulhalim, was replaced by Mas Sudibja, the former subregent of Serang.[44] Increasingly, the government brought in officials from the Priangan to serve in Banten, a practice that had always aroused intense resentment in the colonial period. In March 1947, the Council of Ulama in Banten reacted by urging the government to review its policy of appointments in the region.[45]

These political changes were coupled with an increasing militarization of the local administration. In order to supplement and neutralize the ulama, who continued to occupy most posts, the central government appointed civil and military wedana. Military courts were also established, and a special unit of Priangan troops, the Garuda Company, was formed to deal with the problem of irregular lasykar and banditry. The complaint was frequently heard, and not without justification, that more effort was expended on controlling unruly elements in Banten than on fighting the Dutch. The Siliwangi was referred to derisively as Tentara Wilhelmina ([Queen] Wilhelmina's army), and the cry was often heard, "Banten dijajah lagi oleh Priangan" (Banten is colonized again by Priangan), because of the preponderance once more in Banten of officials and police from the Priangan. Resentment at the changes imposed by the Republican government in the name of order led at times to open conflict with the Siliwangi troops. Armed clashes occurred in October 1947 and again in February and March 1948,[46] the latter prompted in part by the humiliating Renville Agreement of January 1948, which left Banten the only unoccupied area of West Java. The army's ability to contain the threat posed by this renewed unrest in Banten was due in no small measure to the failure of the lasykar and jawara to unite under one political flag, as they had done temporarily under the Dewan in 1945.

The one serious attempt at cooperation in 1947–1948 was made under the auspices of the BPRI (Badan Pemberontak Republik Indonesia, Insurgent Corps of the Indonesian Republic). BPRI, whose origins lay in the 1945 fighting in Surabaya, had been founded by Bung Tomo and was distinctly pro-Tan Malaka in its political leanings. It stood, above all, for uncompromising militancy and resistance to the Dutch.[47] The commanders of BPRI in Banten were Mohammed Chusnun and Entol Mohammed Mansjur, both of whom had worked in Jakarta during the war for Kaigun Bukanfu Daisangka.[48] Not surprisingly, given the wide interpretation applied by the Siliwangi to controlling unrest in Banten, support for BPRI was widespread. The large bands of Jaro Kamid and Soleiman Gunungsari joined after another leading jawara, Haji Armana, was shot dead in an army ambush. But the BPRI was no match for the better armed TNI, and in March 1948 it was successfully dispersed and several of its leaders arrested.

The most serious revolutionary challenge to the Republic in Banten occurred in the wake of the Dutch military occupation of the region in December 1948.[49] Throughout 1948, resentment and distrust of the Republican government had been increasing in Banten. The agreements of Linggajati and Renville, followed by the re-imposition of Dutch colonial rule after a seven-year break, were regarded at best as compromises, but finally as betrayals. This sense of betrayal ran deep in Banten, especially when many of the civil servants appointed by the Republic in 1947–1948, and even some Siliwangi units, went over to serving the Dutch after December 1948. Elsewhere in West Java this alienation from the Republic took the form of support for the Darul Islam movement which was striving to establish an Islamic State of Indonesia.[50] In Banten, however, radical traditions were upheld, and unrest once again assumed a leftist guise. The social revolutionary stand of the struggle for independence had emerged again.

After the Dutch military action of December 1948, most TNI units in Banten, together with part of the civilian administration, withdrew to the isolated southwest of the region. Only irregular lasykar and jawara bands were left operating in the north and west. Pro-Tan Malaka elements tried to regroup these bands in a new guerrilla force.[51] Mohammed Chusnun, the former BPRI chief, had by this time returned to Banten and linked up with the jawara leader, Soleiman Gunungsari. He made contact as well with other jawara and lasykar leaders and with Kyai Chatib, who remained resident. During the early part of 1949, the guerrilla movement developed strength in Banten and established links with dissident pro-Murba groups elsewhere in West Java, notably in the Krawang and Sukabumi regions. However, the capture of Chusnun by the Dutch and the shooting of Soleiman Gunungsari by an Indonesian military police unit in July dealt the group a serious blow.

Despite these setbacks, Murba leaders in West Java decided to continue with their plans to establish a base in Banten for resistance to both Dutch and Republican forces. An "Indonesian People's Republic" was to be formed under the leadership of Chaerul Saleh (a key pemuda leader in 1945 and close follower of Tan Malaka)[52] and Achmad Chatib. The armed forces of the new government were to be officially termed Bambu Runcing (lit., sharpened bamboo, i.e., spears). Although the initial plan was to dispatch 400 armed men from Krawang to Banten in August 1949, this was delayed by the announcement of a ceasefire between Dutch and Republican forces. Instead, the move took place later and via southern Banten in order to avoid Dutch and Republican forces who were regrouping in the north of the residency, where most forces that might have been sympathetic to the new rebel movement were scattered. In the first week of October, Chaerul Saleh's People's Army moved into southern Banten. They seized Malingping and Cibaliung, killing Jusuf Martadilaga, the Republican police chief of Banten, and Fathoni, the deputy resident, as well as ten TNI soldiers. These killings alienated supporters of the movement in Banten, and in late October Siliwangi units led by Major Sudarsono successfully suppressed the rebels. Both Chaerul Saleh and Kyai Chatib were later arrested and detained by the Indonesian authorities.[53] With this episode the revolution in Banten drew to a close as it had begun—violently and again demonstrating the link between Islam and radicalism in the region.

The Bambu Runcing affair of October 1949 is a fitting end to the history of Banten during the struggle for independence. Briefly it brought together again the three strands of the revolution in Banten— anticolonialism, regionalism, and social revolution. The movement sought to tap those energies and forces that the PKI had mobilized adeptly in November 1926 and the Dewan temporarily in October 1945, a combination of radicalism, militant anti-imperialism, and a profound distrust of outside forces that refused to accept the realities of Banten. In all three strands of Banten's revolutionary experience, one man was involved above all others, Kyai Achmad Chatib. In his character, Chatib combined the three aspects of the revolution there.

The Bambu Runcing episode was but a pale reflection of the movements of October 1945 and November 1926. Four years of struggle against the Dutch, coming after three and a half years of occupation by the Japanese, had sorely tested the people of Banten and greatly depleted their appetite for radicalism. Serious tactical errors by the movement's leaders in seeking to establish a base in isolated south Banten rather than among the restless jawara of the north further reduced the movement's chances of success.

And, even more than in October 1945, it proved impossible to create an alliance of the left, the ulama, and the jawara. The left, always a small but vocal and influential group in Banten, had by 1949 become permanently fractured into PKI and Tan Malaka wings, and further cooperation between them had become impossible. Among the ulama, although there were reservations about the Republican government, the expulsion of the Dutch and the experience of the years since 1945 had largely removed any temptation to cooperate with political radicalism. Only the jawara bands were left to carry on a desultory campaign of harassment against the authorities into the mid 1950s. The revolution had played its course. The inability of the three component forces of the successful 1926 alliance to cooperate doomed any further attempt at a social revolution.

Notes

1. For further background on the 1926 revolt, see Michael C. Williams, *Sickle and Crescent: The 1926 Revolt in Banten* (Ithaca: Cornell Modern Indonesia Project, 1982).

2. There was no industrial development in the region and very few plantations. In 1930, Serang, the largest town, had a population of only 10,000 in a region of approximately one million inhabitants.

3. In many cases the two groups overlapped. Many religious leaders were also male descendants of the sultans. During the nineteenth century some elements of the old aristocracy were incorporated into the Dutch colonial order but for the most part they found no place in the new regime. See Sartono Kartodirjo, *The Peasants' Revolt of Banten in 1888* (The Hague: Martinus Nijhoff, 1966), especially pp. 74–90.

4. On jawara and social banditry in Banten, see T. H. M. Loze, "Iets over eenige typische Bantamsche instituten," *Koloniaal Tijdschrift* 23, no. 2 (Mar. 1934): 171–173; P. M. van Wulften Palthe, *Psychological Aspects of the Indonesian Problems* (Leiden: E. J. Brill, 1949); D. H. Meyer, "Over het bendewezen op Java," *Indonesie* 3, no. 2 (Sept. 1949): 178–189. See also Meyer's *Japan wint den Oorlog: Documenten over Java* (Maastricht: NV Leiter-Nypels, 1946), pp. 15–22 and 24; and *Het Dagblad* (Jakarta) Feb. 21, 1946, where possible links with the Japanese are mentioned. See also the series of articles by R. M. Slamet Sudbyo, "Perampokan," *Asia Raya,* June 11, 12, 13, 18, 19, and 22, 2602 [1942].

5. Meyer, *Japan wint den Oorlog,* p. 30. The author was assistant-resident of Serang, 1938–1942.

6. Interviews with Tje Mamat, Serang, Apr. 14, June 14, 1976; and Tb.

Alipan, Pandeglang, Jan. 7, 1976. See also Harry A. Poeze, *Tan Malaka: Levensloop van 1897 tot 1945* (The Hague: Martinus Nijhoff, 1976), pp. 411 (where Tje Mamat is referred to as Tjeq Man) and 418–419. It seems they were initially recruited into Pari by Sarosan.

7. See Williams, *Sickle and Crescent,* p. 64; and Djamaluddin Tamin, "Sedjarah PKI" ([Jakarta?], 1957, mimeographed), p. 52.

8. Sidik Kertapati, *Sekitar Proklamasi 17 Augustus 1945,* 3rd. ed. (Jakarta: Jajasan Pembaruan, 1964), pp. 27–29.

9. On Haji Sinting and Hidayat, see "Zaman Menteng 31," *Galanggang Repolusi Kenangan 10 Tahun Proklamasi* (Jakarta: Badan Penerbit Nasional [U.P.M.I.], n.d.), pp. 107–116; and Soepardo et al., *Manusia dan masjarakat baru Indonesia* (Jakarta: Dinas Penerbitan Balai Pustaka, 1962), pp. 24–25.

10. Interviews cited in note 6.

11. Interviews with Mohammed Chusnun, Bogor, Apr. 19, 1976, and Entol Mohammed Mansjur, Menes, Mar. 19, 1976. Both worked for the Kaigun Bukanfu Daisangka. On this office, see Entol Chaerudin, "Proklamasi 17 Augustus 1945 dan Pemindahan Kekuasaan" (n.p., n.d.). See also the article on Kaigun Bukanfu Daisangka in *Het Dagblad,* Mar. 14, 1946.

12. Chaerudin, "Proklamasi," p. 15. See also Warsa Djajakusumah, "Api '45 Dari Masa ke Masa. Kisah Pengalaman Perjoangan Kemerdekaan R.I. 1945–50" (n.d., mimeographed), pp. 3–7.

13. The other two battalion commanders in Banten, Entol Ternaja and R. Sutalaksana, were recruited from the pangreh praja.

14. Interview with Amanan Satiahardja (who was assistant-*wedana* [district head] in Menes), Bogor, Mar. 14. 1976.

15. See Benedict Anderson, "The Problem of Rice," *Indonesia* 2 (Oct. 1966): 88–89.

16. For biographical details on Raden Soekrawardi, see *Orang Indonesia jang terkemoeka di Djawa* (Jakarta: Gunseikanbu, 2604 [1944]), p. 80. Soekrawardi was the son of Raden Mohammed Isa, chief *penghulu* (head of religious officials at regency level) of Serang, 1920–1938, and first president of the Court for Islamic Affairs. Interviews with Oma Natadredja (Serang police chief in 1945), Bandung, Oct. 23, 1975.

17. Interviews with several ex-Peta officers in Banten. One former Moslem leader in the region described the Peta officer group as *"anak ambtenaren, senang pakaian, ideologis kosong"* (children of officials, comfortably clothed, empty in ideology).

18. See Poeze, *Tan Malaka,* pp. 516–533, and Tan Malaka, *Dari Penjara ke Penjara,* vol. 2 (Yogyakarta: Pustaka Murba, n.d.), pp. 146–183. In April of the previous year Tan Malaka had left Palembang via Banten for Jakarta. In

Dari Penjara ke Penjara, 2:128–132, he refers to meetings with "mang Mamat," an alias of Tje Mamat, in both Lampung and Serang at that time.

19. See H. Ayip Dzukri, "Proklamasi dimulai dari Banten," *Warta Harian,* Aug. 16, 18, and 19, 1969, and Tan Malaka, *Dari Penjara ke Penjara,* vol. 3 (Jakarta: Widjaja, n.d.), p. 62. Tan Malaka apparently identified himself.

20. Interviews with Haji Mohammed Tahir, Serang, Dec. 9, 1975, and Maruto Nitimihardjo, Jakarta, June 10, 1976.

21. For biographical details, see *Orang Indonesia jang terkemoeka,* p. 104.

22. See *Kami Perkenalkan* (Jakarta: Kementerian Penerangan, 1954), p. 63.

23. For a report on the fighting, see *Berita Indonesia,* Oct. 16, 1945.

24. Most of this account of the Dewan is based on interviews. There are few written sources, but see "Verslag, Ontwikkeling Situatie in Bantam tot 11 Maart 1946," Archief Algemene Secretarie Batavia, 1ᵉ zending, Kist 1, Bundel 36, Algemeen Rijksarchief, The Hague [hereafter ARA], and "De Ongeregeldheden binnen de Republiek Indonesia," Archief Procureur-Generaal [hereafter *Proc. Gen.*], no. 35, inv. no. 157, ARA, "Laporan Politik, Ekonomi, Social, Keamanan d.s.b. dari Daerah Banten" [Official Republican document] (1949, Mimeographed), pp. 1–2. See also *Republik Indonesia Propinsi Djawa Barat* (Jakarta: Kementerian Penerangan, 1953), pp. 54–55 and 150–151, and *Ra'jat,* Dec. 29, 1945.

25. In Serang, Kyai Sja'maun, the grandson of Kyai Wasid, one of the principal leaders of the 1888 revolt, was elected regent. Kyai Sja'maun was the former commander of the Cilegon battalion of Peta. He had spent many years in Mecca and had attended the Al-Azhar University in Cairo, a most unusual place for a Bantenese ulama to study. Kyai Sja'maun was also one of the few appointees who was not of the 1926 generation. In Pandeglang the new regent was Kyai Abdulhalim, a former Digulist. In Lebak (Rangkasbitung), Kyai Abuya Hassan was appointed regent.

26. Interview with former police chief in Cilegon.

27. Interview with Kasman Singgodimedjo (attorney-general in 1945), Jakarta, June 6, 1976.

28. Kyai Asnawi died in 1938. For further details on his life, see Williams, *Sickle and Crescent,* pp. 28, 30, 40, and 48.

29. The TKR was actually formed on September 10, but little had become of it before October.

30. See "Laporan Politik" (in *Proc. Gen.*), pp. 1–2.

31. On the role of Achmad Bassaif in 1926, see Williams, *Sickle and Crescent,* pp. 12–13, 35–37, 42, and 58.

32. See *Sin Po,* Oct. 29 and 30, 1945; *Berita Indonesia,* Nov. 1, 1945; and *Het Dagblad,* Dec. 9 and 11, 1945.

33. Soekrawardi was a nephew of Hilman Djajadiningrat.

34. For press reports, see *Ra'jat,* Dec. 13, 1945, and *Boeroeh,* Dec. 14, 1945.

35. R. T. Hardiwinangun was born in Pandeglang in 1897. In 1926 he was appointed wedana of Menes, replacing the murdered wedana Raden Partadinata. From 1934 to 1939, when Ch. van der Plas was resident of Ceribon, Hardiwinangun was *patih* (chief minister of regent) of Indramayu. See *Orang Indonesia jang terkemoeka,* p. 40. In November 1945 Hardiwinangun went to the Hotel des Indes in Jakarta for a meeting with van der Plas. Probably the visit became known to the Dewan.

36. Entol Ternaja had been assistant-wedana of Menes in 1926.

37. The TKR forces were far better armed than the Dewan, having received directly from the Japanese most of the former Peta arms. It also seems that the TKR received arms from Indonesian army units elsewhere in West Java after the presidential visit in December.

38. The other members were Kyai Sjadeli Hassan and Fathoni of Masyumi and Gogo Sanjadirdja of the PSII.

39. All three were ex-Digulists.

40. Some of the bands went so far as to announce that in future they would rob only the rich, who were denounced for not having fulfilled their responsibilities in regard to *fitrah* (obligatory gift of rice at the end of the fasting month) and *zakat* (religious tax). See *Ra'jat,* Feb. 23, 1946.

41. *Berita Indonesia,* Oct. 30 and Dec. 30, 1946. Haji Chatib defended his actions in a long report (twenty-one handwritten pages) in February 1947, "Laporan tentang Pembangunan Banten," in which he estimated that up to 320,000 people had been involved in the restoration work. He denied that this was part of a plan for a new Bantenese sultanate. The numbers involved in the work certainly ran into the tens of thousands, all voluntary labor, with wood and stone being brought from south Banten. The work was regarded as *waqaf* (religious obligation). In some quarters it was even felt that participation in the project was comparable with the pilgrimage to Mecca.

42. Nefis [Netherlands Forces Intelligence Service] "Weekelijksche Militair Overzicht," July 8, 1946, FYS/33507/G, Bundel 1074, and Nefis, "Verkort Politiek Situatie-Overzicht van Nederlandsch Indie," January 1947, no. 1103/xAG, Kist 42, Bundel 16 (Ministerie van Defensie [hereafter MvD], The Hague). See also, *Siliwangi dari Masa ke Masa: Sedjarah Militer Kodam VI Siliwangi* (Jakarta: Fakhta Mahjuma, 1969), p. 81.

43. Sukanda Bratamenggala had led the youth section of Paguyuban Pasundan, a strongly regionalist Sundanese organization with little support in Banten, before the war. During the war he was head of the Bandung Seinendan. For further details, see Benedict R. O' G. Anderson, *Java in a Time of Revo-*

lution (Ithaca: Cornell University Press, 1972), pp. 25, 337, 430, and 445–446. On Adiwinata, see *Orang Indonesia jang terkemoeka*, p. 7.

44. *Antara*, Feb. 11, 1947. On Sudibja, see *Orang Indonesia jang terkemoeka*, p. 81.

45. *Antara*, Mar. 10, 1947.

46. Overzicht en Ontwikkeling van het Toestand, Mar. 26, 1948, no. 50, Terr. Tpn. Commandant West Java, Archive of the Headquarters of the General Staff, Kist 20, Bundel 25, and Toestand Bantam, Apr. 1948, Nefis, GG 39, Bundel 9907 (MvD). See also *Sin Po*, Sept. 15, 1948.

47. See Anthony J. S. Reid, *Indonesian National Revolution* (Hawthorn, Victoria: Longman, 1974), p. 57, and George McT. Kahin, *Nationalism and Revolution in Indonesia* (Ithaca: Cornell University Press, 1952), pp. 163–164. On the BPRI in West Java, see Warsa Djajakusumah, "Api '45," pp. 41–42.

48. Both men had been in Banten in 1945 but accompanied Tan Malaka when he left.

49. For details of the occupation, see *Siliwangi*, pp. 199 and 354ff; *Herrineringsalbum 1ᵉ InfanterieBrigade Groep Divisie 7 December*, vol. 4 (Leiden: Sijthoff, n.d.), pp. 21–92, and Alfred van Sprang, *Wij werden Geroepen: De Geschiedenis van de 7 December Divisie* (The Hague: Van Hoeve, 1949), pp. 187–206.

50. See C. van Dijk, *Rebellion under the Banner of Islam* (The Hague: Martinus Nijhoff, 1981), pp. 81–100.

51. See *Propinsi Djawa Barat*, pp. 242–245; *Sin Po*, Aug. 25, Nov. 17, and Dec. 24, 1949; and *Siliwangi*, pp. 354–358 and 370–373. "Wekelijkse territoriale inlichtingenrapporten van Commando West Java," HKGS 1949, Bundel 314A, weekly, nos. 32–37, Oct. 13–Nov. 18, 1949 (MvD). "Rapport betreffende de Politieke Ontwikkeling en de Algemene Veiligheidstoestand T. B. A. Gebied Bantam sedert de Wapenstilstandsovereenkomst," *Proc. Gen.*, no. 186, ARA. Between December 23, 1948, and June 30, 1949, some forty-six officials, mainly village headmen, were killed by the dissident pro-Murba groups.

52. On Chaerul Saleh, see Anderson, *Java in a Time of Revolution*, pp. 58–59, 327–328, 415.

53. See *Merdeka*, Oct. 17, 1949. Chatib was taken to Yogya and held in the Hotel Garuda. He was released in 1950 but rearrested the following year and imprisoned for four months in Bandung. In 1955 he became a member of parliament representing the PSII and in 1958 was appointed a member of the DPA (Dewan Pertimbangan Agung, High Advisory Council) by President Sukarno. Chaerul Saleh was released from prison in 1950 and went into exile in West Germany for several years.

ACEH: SOCIAL REVOLUTION
AND THE ISLAMIC VISION

Eric Morris

During the four years of anti-Dutch resistance, Aceh remained stead-fastly loyal to the fledgling Republic. Why is it, then, that only three and a half years later the Acehnese rose in rebellion against the central government? Was there an inherent contradiction between the goals of the Acehnese leadership in the independence struggle and those of the Indonesian national leadership? In attempting to answer these questions, scholars tend to focus on the ethnic distinctiveness and Islamic fervor of the Acehnese.[1] One should go beyond these attributed characteristics, however, to examine what the revolutionary experience meant to those Acehnese who led the struggle for independence. The argument to be presented below is that Acehnese leaders thought and acted in Acehnese, Islamic, and Indonesian terms, with little awareness at the time of the possibility—and certainly no sense of any inevitability—of conflicts among the three.

Background: The Colonial Period

The Dutch attacked the capital of the sultan of Aceh in April 1873, the first action in what became known as the Aceh War, which lasted, according to the Acehnese, seventy years.[2] The consequences of the Aceh War were different for the sultan, the *uleebalang*[3] (territorial chiefs), and the *ulama* (Islamic scholars).

During the first thirty years of the Aceh War, the sultanate remained what it had been since the decline of Acehnese power in the seventeenth century—an object of great reverence but with little actual power over the uleebalang who were nominally subordinate. By the time Sultan Muhammad Daud surrendered to the Dutch in 1903, the colonial authorities were in a sufficiently strong position that no serious thought was given to establishing the sultan as a "native ruler." Aceh would henceforth be without a sultan.[4]

With a few notable exceptions, there were clear limits to the extent to which an uleebalang would commit himself to the resistance movement. As Snouck Hurgronje put it, "The great defect in most of the hereditary chiefs consisted and still consists in this, that their religious and political convictions never impel them to action on behalf of *Acheh;* they wait as long as possible to see whether their own territory will be threatened."[5] By 1904 most uleebalang were no longer involved in the resistance movement and were being made administrators of the Dutch East Indies government.

Since the chiefs were for the most part incapable of working together, and since the sultan was not in a position to coordinate the resistance, the ulama emerged from their *dayah* (Islamic boarding schools) to lead the *perang sabil* (holy war) against the infidel invaders. Snouck Hurgronje noted: "What the Dutch have had opposed to them in Acheh is not a Keumala party (such has never existed) nor disconnected bands of marauders, but a national party, as far as that is possible in Acheh, held together and organized by the ulama."[6] The most powerful weapon in the ulama arsenal was an epic poem—the "Hikayat Perang Sabil" (The epic of the holy war)—which recounted the fantastic rewards awaiting the faithful in paradise should they fall in the holy war against the infidels.

The uleebalang became the cornerstone of Dutch colonial policy in Aceh. Governor Goedhart's analysis of the situation in 1928 illustrates the importance the Dutch attached to them:

I have not lost hope that eventually good feelings will exist between us and the Acehnese. Their exclusivity and keen sense of self-esteem will in time, I anticipate, lead them to prefer close relations with us rather than with other 'Indies' peoples. The Acehnese are too intelligent not to understand that eventually, in view of the numbers, they will be dominated by other 'Indies' ethnic groups. Discussions with intelligent Acehnese youths have confirmed my opinion. In order to attain good feelings it is first of all necessary that we remember that our power in Aceh, aside from the force of arms, depends in the main on the *uleebalang*s. Through them and with them we can win over the people. Without them in the long run we will accomplish nothing in Aceh.[7]

There was a contradiction in the Dutch perception of uleebalang; this perception entailed a contradiction in colonial policy as well. On the one hand, uleebalang were seen as *adat* (customary) rulers. As such, they represented the continuity of real Acehnese tradition, in opposition to the aspirations of the ulama. As Piekaar saw it, with Dutch colonialism "the traditional superiority of the uleebalang was restored."[8] On the other hand, the Dutch clearly felt that colonial governance demanded incorporation of the chiefs into a rationalized native administration.

Dutch rule served to buttress uleebalang authority by providing them with unprecedented security of tenure. With the boundaries of their territories clearly demarcated, the chiefs were no longer compelled to fight among themselves over territorial rights. At the same time, colonial policies transformed their economic position, depriving them of their accustomed grip on the flow of goods in and out of their territories. They had to forego their pivotal role in trade and the collection of tolls on goods in favor of administrative security, but they were compensated with government salaries. Under the Dutch, levies on pepper, areca nut, and other products, as well as revenues derived from judicial fines, went into regional treasuries instead of to the uleebalang.[9] No longer able to acquire wealth by controlling the movement and marketing of cash crops, the chiefs were compelled to look within their territories for new sources of income to supplement their salaries. The most important such source was ownership and control of ricelands. Consequently, landholdings were increasingly concentrated in uleebalang hands, particularly in the ricebowl of Pidie, and this development exacerbated relations between the chiefs, who were no longer dependent on local support, and the peasantry.[10]

In precolonial times, administration of the law had provided an ideological justification for the uleebalang's position in Acehnese society. That not all chiefs took this task seriously did not deter the Dutch from attempting to use them as the means to establish a uniform system of justice throughout the region.[11] As administrators of the colonial system of justice, the uleebalang increasingly became the target of popular resentment. Much more significant in defining attitudes toward them, however, was the fact that the uniform system of justice rested upon a forced congruence between what the Dutch took to be a separate symbolic entity of adat (what was customary) and the institutionalization of uleebalang as "*adat* potentates." Such a forced congruence brought into bold relief a conflict that the Acehnese would previously have said had no meaning, namely a conflict between adat and Islamic law.

Central to the transformation of the uleebalang class was Dutch language schooling in the European stream of the colonial education system. Colonial education policy further isolated the uleebalang at the top of a new, foreign-imposed stratification system frozen according to ascriptive criteria. The long-term consequence was the creation of a cultural divide between the chiefs and the society around them.

The nature of the postcolonial reaction against the uleebalang was the result not only of their position as tools of the colonial power, but also, and more important, of the contradictory character of their authority. On the one hand, the uleebalang, in their "traditional superiority" as the Dutch would have it, represented the particularism of their many territories. This particularism constituted an obstacle to the transformation of Aceh along the lines envisioned by reformist ulama, for whom, as will be shown, unity was a rallying theme. On the other hand, certain segments of the uleebalang class, those with a Dutch education, were becoming acculturated. Both aspects of uleebalang came to be seen as contrary to the ulama vision of a revived and unified Islamic community.

Acehnese Islam changed during the colonial period. Those ulama who emerged as the leaders of change can be identified as the local proponents of the reformist movement that spread throughout the Islamic world in the early twentieth century. Reformist Islam in Aceh found organizational form in PUSA (Persatuan Ulama2 Seluruh Aceh, All-Aceh Ulama Association), founded in 1939, which represented the culmination of a decade of effort to reinvigorate religious education. In the late 1920s, new schools, called *madrasah,* which fused traditional religious education with the modern methods used in government primary schools, began to replace the traditional religious dayah schools. In time the madrasah curriculum was extended beyond religious subjects to include more secular subjects.[12] The most prominent leader of the madrasah movement was Teungku M. Daud Beureu'eh who established the Madrasah Sa'adah Abidiyah in Pidie.[13] By 1936 there were more than one hundred madrasah throughout Aceh.[14] Staffing them as teachers were Acehnese who had attended middle-level religious schools and teacher-training schools in West Sumatra, an experience that strengthened their reformist and anticolonial sentiments.[15]

The reformist ulama of the 1930s did not limit their efforts to education. Attempting to mobilize support for their vision of an Islamic society, they held large public meetings throughout Aceh. Their appeal linked Islamic reformist goals with the historical renovation of the Acehnese community. They spoke of a golden age identified with the Acehnese sultanate at the height of its power, but their purpose was not to restore an idealized version of this golden age. More concretely they spoke in terms of a future in which all Moslems would be united through religious law and attributed the shameful present decline to failure to adhere to the law. The proposed remedies for the decline were unity and consciousness. And it was in terms of unity and consciousness that the reformists attacked the traditional religious practices of mysticism and saint-veneration (and the practitioners, conservative ulama) which they saw as being in conflict with a purified Islam.[16]

Linking reformist goals with community revival allowed the Acehnese to perceive themselves in a new light. The result was a heightened consciousness of their identity as Acehnese Moslems that transcended kinship, village, and territorial identities. But the idea of Acehnese revivalism did not preclude notions of an overarching Indonesian unity, as is made clear by A. Hasjmy in an article on the medium of instruction in the madrasah. Contending that the use of Acehnese in government-run village primary schools had been a Dutch attempt to isolate the Acehnese, he goes on to say: "When our children had forgotten their national language [Indonesian] which had become the language of unity . . . when our children had been isolated from the language of unity, the madrasahs appeared to restore the Indonesian language, requiring our children to use it again."[17]

The young activists produced by the madrasah system naturally saw Dutch colonialism as the major obstacle to achievement of their revivalist goals. Organized in the Pemuda PUSA (PUSA Youth) under the leadership of Teungku Amir Husin al Mujahid, the young people were to become the driving force of the struggle waged during the Japanese occupation and the revolution. Abdullah Arif illustrated the importance of Pemuda PUSA in these terms: "If PUSA can be seen as the locomotive of the struggle and movement in Aceh, then Pemuda PUSA can be seen as the wheels of the struggle."[18]

The Japanese Occupation

Dutch rule came to a sudden end with the Japanese invasion of March 1942. Despite its brevity (three and a half years), the Japanese occupation set internal forces in motion in a way that resulted in a violent transition to independence. Acehnese leaders perceived the Japanese interregnum as a time of shifting gains and losses for both uleebalang and ulama, as Japanese military authorities attempted to balance the two groups.

The Japanese made it clear that they intended to continue the Dutch colonial policy by leaving native administration in uleebalang hands. Most of the uleebalang, save those seen as irremediably pro-Dutch, were confirmed in their positions. The bonus was that the administrative positions at the district level that had been held by Dutchmen were given to Acehnese, and seventeen of the nineteen Acehnese appointed were uleebalang; at the end of the occupation, all such district-level positions were held by uleebalang.[19]

Yet time proved the continuity of uleebalang authority to be illusory. As the war turned against the Japanese, and as the military authorities came to exact more from the Acehnese in preparation for an Allied counteroffensive, the Japanese made concessions to those persons who were seen to be popular leaders—the ulama. By far the most important change entailing an abridgment of uleebalang authority was the revamping of the judicial administration that was carried out in early 1944.

One aspect of this judicial reorganization was the establishment of a separate court system for the implementation of Islamic law in cases involving marriage, divorce, inheritance, religious taxes, religious trusts, and the status of orphans.[20] The new religious judicial system was a major triumph for the implementation of Islamic law. Piekaar, rephrasing Snouck Hurgronje, saw the result in these terms: "The adat was no longer the mistress and the hukum [Islamic law] her obedient slave girl."[21]

Displeased as uleebalang were with the religious court system, they were even more opposed to the Japanese proposal for a new secular court system, for this change meant the total loss of their judicial authority. The position of uleebalang as adat potentates was drawn into question once they were deprived of the institutional base for carrying out adat functions. Replacing the uleebalang as administrators of the law was a five-man court in each territory.[22] This change was certainly of great significance in Pidie, where uleebalang had used their judicial powers to settle land control and ownership disputes in their own favor. This loss of authority was exacerbated for the uleebalang by the fact that the Japanese relied heavily on the advice of PUSA leaders in appointing members of the new courts.[23]

What remained for the uleebalang? In a word, administration. But under the Japanese, administration involved separating the farmer from his rice crop to supply the occupation army and recruiting manpower for forced labor to construct defense installations.[24] Without question, the trade-off was a bad one; the uleebalang had been confirmed in their positions as rulers, but the prerogatives of rule were stripped away, leaving them to perform only those tasks that aroused popular resentment. PUSA leaders participated, on the whole energetically, in various organizations established to encourage mass support for Japanese war goals, but when the rice crop was collected and manpower for forced labor needed, the responsibility consistently fell on the uleebalang. It is therefore questionable that the two groups "paid the same price" for cooperating with the Japanese.[25] The uleebalang were to pay a much higher price.

From the beginning of the occupation, the Japanese had established indigenous paramilitary bodies, but the most important was formed only in late 1943—the Giyūgun, a separate military unit with its own lower-grade Indonesian officers. Most of the Giyūgun officers were from uleebalang families, but the overwhelming majority of the soldiers were PUSA youths. This delicate military balance may have served Japanese defense purposes, but it stood little chance of survival once the occupying power had been removed.

The Early Days of the Republic in Aceh

In late August 1945 the Japanese military authorities announced publicly that the war was over. A number of weeks passed, however, before knowledge of the August 17 declaration of independence in Jakarta became widespread in Aceh. The newly appointed Republican governor of Sumatra named Teuku Nya' Arif, who had been the highest-ranking local official during the Japanese occupation, as resident for Aceh.[26] Both the Dutch and the Japanese had been wary of Teuku Nya' Arif's strong streak of independence, but his long-standing nationalist credentials were soon called into question by pemuda activists who were convinced that he had been concealing the news of independence. Teuku Nya' Arif's appointment of lower-level territorial administrators followed Dutch and Japanese practice: all assistant-residents and district administrators were uleebalang. To PUSA activists, then, the meaning of independence was obscure, inasmuch as the new official Republican leadership was virtually to a man the uleebalang establishment.

Many of the nominal leaders of the Republic in Aceh fully expected the return of Dutch authority as part of the Allied occupation of Indonesia, and therefore, they were reluctant to take any initiatives. Consequently, the revolutionary impulse came from a coalition of PUSA ulama and pemuda educated in the madrasah. The contrast between this group and the official Republican leaders was apparent in the words they used to justify their actions; official leaders took action "in the name of the Indonesian government," PUSA and pemuda leaders, "in the name of the people."

The fate of the Republican leaders, and of the uleebalang class of which they represented the apex, was determined in large measure by the pemuda movement. All of the prominent youth leaders had been involved in the prewar Pemuda PUSA and, from their earlier commitment, believed they possessed a special responsibility in developing those attributes of unity, consciousness, and awakening that would lead to the new era. In giving expression to their cause, Acehnese pemuda shared an Indonesian-language vocabulary with youth activists throughout Indonesia. The rallying words were *merdeka* (freedom), *revolusi* (revolution), *perjuangan* (struggle), and *bersiap* (vigilant). The urge to identify with an Indonesia-wide pemuda consciousness was also apparent in the choice of a name for the youth organization in Aceh. On October 6 the BPI (Badan Pemuda Indonesia, Indonesian Youth League),[27] was established under the leadership of Ali Hasjmy,[28] but within a matter of days the name was changed to PRI (Pemuda Republik Indonesia, Youth of the Republic of Indonesia) in response to instructions from pemuda leaders on Java. In December the name of Ali Hasjmy's group was changed once again to Pesindo (Pemuda Sosialis Indonesia, Indonesian Socialist Youth). This name remained of crucial importance to Acehnese pemuda leaders, for what was involved was the naming not simply of an organization but of a cause, a consciousness, and a predilection for direct, spontaneous action. What was being named was a commitment to a common struggle, one in which Indonesia-wide identities were formed that were at once transcendent and transitory.

Support for the Republic from older religious leaders came on October 15 with the "Declaration of Ulama Throughout Aceh," signed by four eminent ulama: Teungku M. Daud Beureu'eh and Teungku Ahmad Hasballah Indrapuri, both PUSA leaders; Teungku Ja'far Sidik, an elderly dayah-based ulama; and Teungku Hasan Kreueng Kale, the foremost conservative ulama. The declaration urged the people to unite behind "our great leader Sukarno" in resisting a Dutch return to "our fatherland Indonesia." Since the Dutch would once again "try to destroy our pure religion as well as repress and hamper the glory and prosperity of the Indonesian people," the four ulama stated that the struggle for independence was a sacred cause properly known as a perang sabil.[29]

United as pemuda leaders and PUSA ulama were to be throughout the struggle for independence, the two groups did have somewhat different perceptions of the revolution. There was little difference between them regarding the Indonesia that was to emerge from the independence struggle. Both held firmly to the idea that independence should lead to the establishment of an Islamic state. Rather, the difference lay in the ulama conviction that a moral reformation must accompany the political struggle. Teungku M. Daud Beureu'eh, in a message to a Pesindo congress in January 1946, argued, for example, that physical freedom from colonialism was incomplete without spiritual freedom. To lack spiritual freedom was to be enslaved to passion, a condition that led individuals to give precedence to base and narrow self-interest over the well-being of the community of the faithful. And passion would

> destroy physical freedom, for whatever the outward appearances it is not truly freedom since it benefits only a few individuals or those of a certain lineage. . . . For this reason I urge the people, the glorious people, to liberate their souls from Satan's domination; but first they must destroy that traitor, *hawa nafsu* [passion], along with all his foul accomplices. Only then can we carry out deeds in accord with our words, only then can one see that we are a people capable of working in accord with what we proclaim. Only then will we be strong, only then will we be firmly united, [and] solidarity will replace conflicts.[30]

Thus, PUSA ulama who hoped for the moral perfection of society were confronted by pemuda leaders who believed that priority should be given to the political and social revolution. Earlier reformist ulama opposition to uleebalang rule had not involved a desire to usurp institutional power. During the revolution, pemuda leaders believed that only by taking over the offices of government could true independence be realized.

In the face of the spontaneous mobilization of pemuda and PUSA forces and the establishment of Pesindo and Mujahidin militias,[31] the uleebalang who represented Republican officialdom found themselves without an effective counterweight. Efforts to remedy this situation centered on the establishment of the Indonesian army in Aceh.

Teuku Nya' Arif envisaged an army based on the expertise and experience of those who had received officer training from the Japanese. This meant, in effect, that leadership of the army was given to a small group of trained men, most of them uleebalang,[32] for few pemuda identified with PUSA had received officer training from the Japanese. Had Teuku Nya' Arif and the Japanese-trained officers possessed sufficient resources, they might have succeeded in founding an army responsive to the official Republican leadership. As it was, they succeeded only in alienating the pemuda leaders who were allowed no role in it.

The Social Revolution

The wave of internal violence in late 1945 and early 1946 that led to the overthrow of the uleebalang came to be known as the social revolution, though the label was applied only after the event, to identify it with popular uprisings occurring elsewhere on Sumatra and Java. That the social revolution began and reached its most bitter intensity in Pidie was not coincidental. The proximate cause of the conflict was the vacuum of authority, the absence of anyone claiming to represent Republican authority who was acceptable to both chiefs and PUSA activists. Under the Dutch, Pidie had been the stronghold of uleebalang power. After the collapse of the Japanese, the initial challenge for the territorial chieftains of Pidie, and to varying degrees for those of other regions, was to restore the felicitous trinity of outside backing, judicial authority, and economic power that had served them so well during the colonial period. Allied landings in other regions of Indonesia and the Dutch presence on Sabang Island (off Aceh Besar) convinced them that it was only a matter of time before the prewar status quo was restored. The uleebalang leader was Teuku Muhamad Daud Cumbo, "territorial ruler of Cumbo" under the Dutch, district administrator of Lammeulo under the Japanese, and newly appointed by the Republic as *wedana* (district head) of Lammeulo. Uleebalang held most of the military power in Pidie, for several Japanese-trained officers who were ostensibly local TKR (Republican armed forces) representatives joined a militia established by the chiefs. The ease with which this militia obtained arms led pemuda leaders to suspect that local Republican officials were diverting weapons to it.

Young PUSA activists, meanwhile, were organizing themselves into PRI (later Pesindo) chapters and raising the Indonesian flag, activities that led to confrontations with the uleebalang. Any possibility that widespread bloodshed in Pidie could be avoided disappeared in the first week of December when uleebalang forces moved into Sigli, capital of Pidie, in an attempt to seize Japanese armaments. Thousands of pro-PUSA villagers surrounded Sigli. After several days of skirmishing between uleebalang forces and PUSA sympathizers the TKR chief-of-staff managed to arrange a ceasefire whereby both sides returned to their strongholds outside Sigli. The leaders of the anti-uleebalang movement saw the official vacillation and compromising in the face of

increasing chaos in Pidie as little more than conspiracy with uleebalang forces. Confronted with a spontaneous movement over which he
had no control, Teuku Nya' Arif voluntarily took leave from his duties
as resident, although he still continued as supervisor of the TKR in
Aceh with the rank of major general.[33]

Sporadic fighting continued in Pidie for the rest of December.
Uleebalang forces established four strongholds in various parts of
Pidie and had the greater firepower, which allowed them to launch frequent raids. Their opponents organized themselves into a People's
General Headquarters. Residency officials took no heed of the activists' demands that the entire Republican establishment in Pidie be
replaced and reconstituted on the basis of "people's sovereignty."

The outcome of the battle of Pidie was determined in part by political maneuvering in Kutaraja and in part by the move of PUSA forces
from North Aceh into Pidie. In the face of official hesitancy, PUSA and
pemuda leaders argued their case for action against uleebalang in the
residency KNI (Indonesian National Committee). At the same time,
Teungku M. Daud Beureu'eh instructed PUSA leaders in North Aceh
to mobilize Pesindo and Mujahidin members for an attack into eastern
Pidie. Chosen as commander of this force—known as the People's
Corps—was Teungku Abdul Wahab Seulimeum, the leading reformist
ulama from Aceh Besar. The People's Corps attracted village pemuda
as it moved into Pidie in the last week of December.

As thousands of pemuda and villagers converged on the uleebalang
headquarters at Lammeulo, the denouement was at hand. But its
nature was determined in Kutaraja, where PUSA ulama and pemuda
leaders had finally prevailed in their efforts to compel the hesitant
Republican leaders to turn against the Pidie uleebalang. On January 8,
1946, the residency government and the General Headquarters for the
People's Struggle and Defense[34] issued two joint announcements. The
first labeled the forces centered at Lammeulo "traitors and enemies of
the Republic of Indonesia." The second demanded that they surrender
their arms. These two announcements did not change the outcome of
the conflict in Pidie, but they did provide an aura of legality that the
social revolutionaries later felt compelled to invoke to justify their
actions. In S. M. Amin's words, "PUSA's actions, which initially had
to be considered illegal, had been made legal. The regional government legitimized PUSA's actions and 'took over' PUSA's attempts to

destroy the uleebalang who were declared to be 'traitors to the State,' which meant that the government accepted full responsibility for the consequences of the Cumbo affair."[35]

The Pidie uleebalang ignored the ultimatum. In a matter of days, Lammeulo fell, and subsequently all of the chiefs' leaders were captured. The residency government requested that the uleebalang be brought to Kutaraja to stand trial. But there were to be no trials. "At the time," a Pesindo leader wrote, "the people's hearts reverberated with the slogan: 'The People have become the Judge.' "[36] With the people as the judge, the Pidie uleebalang were virtually eliminated. Pesindo and Mujahidin forces executed all but two of those who had served as territorial chieftains under the Dutch and the Japanese. Also killed were those notables who had been appointed to Republican military and civilian positions in Pidie. Then villagers turned on surviving family members, in some cases killing all related males and in others sparing only the youngest boys. The survivors were quickly dispossessed as villagers took over uleebalang property. The greatest windfall was that most prized possession in Pidie, rice land. Tenants took over land they had been cultivating for chieftain owners. And those who believed that uleebalang had wrongly deprived them, or their ancestors, of their land quickly laid claim to rice fields, coconut groves, and areca-nut gardens.[37]

After the uleebalang had been vanquished, the leaders of the People's General Headquarters convened public meetings to establish a government based on "people's sovereignty." Teungku Abdul Wahab Seulimeum, the commander of the People's Corps from North Aceh, was chosen as the new assistant-resident for Pidie, and Hasan Ali, the Pesindo leader, was chosen as his deputy. PUSA loyalists took over almost all lower-level government positions "in the name of the people."

The repercussions of Pidie were soon felt in other parts of Aceh. In mid-February 1946, twenty-three uleebalang in Aceh Besar declared that, in response to "people's sovereignty," they were stepping aside in favor of popularly chosen territorial heads.[38] Chiefs still retained their positions in the residency government and in the regions outside Pidie, but this situation would soon change.

In February, disturbances broke out in East Aceh that heralded the second phase of the social revolution. Teungku Amir Husin al Mujahid, the founding chairman of Pemuda PUSA, declared himself commander of the TPR (Tentara Perjuangan Rakyat, People's Struggle Army), a force established to depose those uleebalang who, in Teungku Amir Husin al Mujahid's view, were pro-Dutch. The TPR was, in fact, never much of an army, its recruits possessing little or no military training. But Teungku Amir Husin al Mujahid's ardent call to the revolutionary cause, his colorful personality and inimitable allegorical oratory soon attracted hundreds of village pemuda to his force. After deposing the uleebalang officials of East Aceh and appointing their successors, Teungku Amir Husin al Mujahid installed a PUSA ulama as the new assistant-resident for North Aceh. The TPR then continued its march along the north coast toward the residency capital.

At the beginning of March, the TPR, now numbering in the thousands, moved into Kutaraja. Teungku Amir Husin al Mujahid demanded the dismissal of Major General Teuku Nya' Arif, Colonel Syammaun Gaharu, and several other officers from the army command. Army leaders found themselves isolated and were thus compelled to comply.[39] Teungku Amir Husin al Mujahid assumed Teuku Nya' Arif's title as army supervisor with the rank of major general, and Husin Yusuf, the highest ranking army officer with PUSA connections, replaced Syammaun Gaharu as division commander. On the civilian side, acting-resident Teuku Chi' Muhamad Daud Syah was elevated to resident, a position he held for the remainder of the revolution, and Teuku M. Amin, secretary of PUSA, was appointed assistant-resident.

In a matter of days, a number of uleebalang and former army officers, including Teuku Nya' Arif and Syammaun Gaharu, were placed under arrest. The TPR detained the Aceh Besar uleebalang, even those who had voluntarily stepped aside a month earlier. Then a pemuda force moved down the west coast in a roundup of most of the uleebalang of West Aceh and South Aceh. Some sixty were interned in the mountains of Central Aceh, among them Teuku Nya' Arif, who died two months later.[40]

By the end of March 1946 the social revolution was completed. Yet the Acehnese experience was not accepted as a legitimate part of the struggle for independence by an Indonesian national elite intent on maintaining a distinction between national revolution—the struggle against Dutch colonialism—and social revolution, the fight against indigenous power structures. For the Acehnese, the two revolutions were inseparable; only by overcoming those who awaited the return of the Dutch, those who prevented the mobilization of the people, and those who, even if nationalist in the past, lacked the requisite spirit, could true independence be attained.

That the social revolution in Aceh was so complete and successful is attributable to the presence of a cohesive group that, under the guidance of PUSA ulama, possessed its own shared experiences and symbols from the reformist and revivalist movement of the 1930s. For a people who had suffered the shock of defeat at Dutch hands, PUSA ulama attempted to provide new categories of meaning. In the process, the position of the ulama in Acehnese society was transformed. In contrast with the conservative ulama, who remained in their dayah, reformist ulama emerged to mobilize mass participation in their revivalist movement. In contrast with conservative ulama, who maintained that the esoteric meanings of Islam were open to only a small group of initiates, reformist ulama proclaimed the message that the meaning of the scriptures was available to all believers. Against this background, the significance of the revolution becomes clear. The point is not simply that a contending group replaced an established elite. Rather, the social revolution confirmed and consolidated the position of reformist ulama as popular leaders. Central to this changed role was the idea of "people's sovereignty."

But what shared idiom bound the people to social revolutionary leaders who claimed to be working on behalf of popular sovereignty? Two ideas were central to the social revolution: the idea of equality in Islam and the idea of transcending particularistic self-interest through joint struggle. A fundamental tenet of Islam is the equality of all believers before God and before the law revealed to His Prophet— what Clive Kessler calls "a profound moral egalitarianism."[41] Such a belief has relevance for social life if only because of the glaring incongruity between moral egalitarianism and social realities. Prophetic voices have promised social egalitarianism as well, if only Moslems could transcend their base self-interest and act on behalf of the community of the faithful. Since passion is an inherent part of human nature, believers must content themselves with an abstract moral egalitarianism; yet the hope of realizing the other remains. Ritual tempo-

rarily bridges the gap; religious occasions, such as celebration of the
pilgrimage and observance of the fast, allow believers to join together
in equality before God, leaving behind the particularisms that divide
them in everyday life.[42]

Aside from ritual occasions, there are times of upheaval when the
expectations of normal life are suspended and the prospect of realizing
the implicit promise of social equality assumes an aura of immedi-
acy.[43] The social revolution in Aceh was one such time. But the prospect of realizing equality on this earth, however transitory, is not
dependent just on upheaval. Rather, it depends on what believers do in
a time of crisis, whether they perceive themselves to be acting in a dis-
interested way, transcending their individual interests. Here the idea of
struggle is important. The participants in the social revolution perceived themselves as acting on the basis of principle in behalf of the
community of the faithful. In that struggle the ritualized community of
equal believers came closest to realization. In these terms, Teungku M.
Daud Beureu'eh's remark, that "the people were free of the grip of passion" makes sense. He was not blind to individual interests and ambitions, but for the moment they paled to insignificance in the face of the
overarching commitment to the struggle in which the faithful were
unified and the particularist identities that divided men during cor-
rupted times did not exist.

Consolidation of the Republic

During the revolution, the Dutch did not re-establish a presence in
Aceh, save for the island of Sabang off Aceh Besar. The beleaguered
central Republican leadership, far away on the island of Java, could
offer neither rewards nor sanctions to affect the situation in Aceh. Precisely because Republican authority rested solely on moral suasion,
the central leadership enjoyed a high degree of popularity and compliance in Aceh. Following the first Dutch military offensive against the
Republic in July 1947, the central government appointed Teungku M.
Daud Beureu'eh as military governor for Aceh. Daud Beureu'eh's commitment to the Republic remained steadfast, as is demonstrated by his
response to a proposal in early 1949 that Aceh could be self-governing
in a Dutch-backed federal system:

There are no regional feelings in Aceh; thus we have no intention of establishing a Great Aceh state as we are Republican spirited. . . . The loyalty of the people to the Republic of Indonesia is neither pretended nor fabricated but rather is honest and sincere loyalty which comes from pure heart-felt commitment as well as from firm calculations and considerations. The Acehnese people are convinced that separate independence, region by region, state by state, can never lead to enduring independence.[44]

Since the Dutch did not attempt a move into Aceh, Acehnese merchants were able to carry on a lucrative barter trade across the Straits of Malacca with Penang and Singapore. Initially, trade was unhampered, as the Dutch had not yet gained control over the straits. By 1947, the Dutch had established a naval blockade that made passage dangerous, but this did little to deter the Acehnese traders. The most important export commodities were rubber and palm oil, first from stockpiles left behind by the Japanese and then from the plantations of East Aceh. Copra and areca nut from small holdings also commanded high prices in Malaya. The trade was as firmly under PUSA control as were the administrative apparatus and military forces. PUSA members were appointed to direct the various residency government-financed trading companies. But not all the export earnings were used in Aceh; consequently the Acehnese described their area as *"daerah modal"* ("region of capital"). Acehnese merchants donated a portion of their profits to support the Republic's foreign emissaries and, in 1948, provided foreign exchange for the purchase of two airplanes.[45]

The post–social revolution government in Aceh operated with almost complete autonomy. PUSA leaders thus had the opportunity to take some initial steps in accord with what they perceived to be the imperatives of Islam, steps that would become contentious issues between Aceh and the central government once the revolution was over. More problematical than any given policy initiatives was the underlying attitude of Acehnese ulama; they were presuming to make a contribution to the national ideological debate, to indicate what they believed should be the foundation for a postrevolutionary Indonesian state. During the revolution, Teungku Nur el Ibrahimy, a leading PUSA ulama, put forward the rationale for "a state based on Islamic ideology." Arguing against the claim that Islam is a personal matter, outside the political realm, he asserted:

Within the glorious Koran we find abundant evidence that Islam does not only provide guidance to mankind in matters of divinity and religious duties but also provides guidance in social problems so that mankind can truly achieve prosperity and happiness in this life as well as in the hereafter. . . .

Do not think that all of these laws are suitable for the age of the camel only, for they are also suitable for the modern age, the age of the airplane, of the radio, of the atom; moreover, they will be suitable for a future that mankind has yet to imagine.[46]

The transcendent appeal of a state based on Islam must be seen in the light of the urgent desire to redeem the indignities of colonization. For the Acehnese ulama who, in the 1930s, explicitly linked Islamic reformist goals with the historical renovation of the community, the struggle necessarily entailed the concept of an Islamic state; such an entity would be manifest evidence that the circle was complete, the indignities redressed.

Even though the appeal of the idea is evident, the concept of the Islamic state remains elusive. To gain a better understanding of the concept, a simple question should be posed: had the Acehnese ulama succeeded in gaining an Indonesian state called Islamic, what would they have proposed to do with it? For the reformist ulama were not employing religious symbols in pursuit of political goals, but rather were using political means to achieve what they conceived as religious ideals. The one ideal having transcendent appeal is the possibility of the faithful overcoming the particularisms of self-interest, kinship, and locality to act in unity and harmony as true Moslems and equals before God and His law. The ideal is not so much one of the perfectability of man as it is of realizing that the establishment of the community of the righteous can come only through complete submission to God. Nonetheless, the ideal is optimistic. There is also, however, a profound pessimism that a unified and harmonious community of the faithful can be maintained over the long run, for passion is an innate part of human nature. The apparent contradiction between an optimistic vision of community and a pessimistic view of human nature is not recognized by a Moslem as contradiction but is seen rather as a tension central to the Islamic faith.

This tension is crucial to an understanding of what Acehnese ulama had in mind when they spoke of a state based on Islam. They believed that the state should be centrally concerned with this tension and define and promote those tenets of the Faith that motivate believers to act on the basis of a higher principle than self-interest. Further, an Islamic state should foster and protect a society with a shared awareness that justice and righteousness come only through complete submission to God and His law. The institutional form such a state would take remained unclear, and to some extent irrelevant. The compelling question for the proponents of an Islamic state was not one of institutions but of how public authority could be used to create and maintain a unified and harmonious community of the faithful. When proponents spoke of an Islamic state, they had little to say about the state as such; their real interest was the quality of society, and the state entered into their thinking only insofar as it served the ends of achieving the ideal society.

Although PUSA ulama did not during the revolution openly press their claims for an Islamic state on the beleaguered Republican central leadership—this would come once the Republic was victorious—they were nonetheless intent on giving the revolution in Aceh a distinctive Islamic flavor.

The ulama saw a close connection between moral rectitude and piety, on the one hand, and a sense of community and purpose, on the other. In an effort to enforce public morality, the military governor proclaimed that those deemed guilty of gambling, adultery, or theft, whether formally charged or not, whether acquitted of charges or not —indeed even those only suspected of these transgressions—could be interned in the interests of public security.[47] Such apparent disregard for evidentiary requirements naturally outraged Dutch-trained lawyers. This negative reaction raised disturbing questions; in the words of a PUSA leader, "Why couldn't we implement Islamic law? We wanted to do away with gambling and the like, but we were told that we did not have the legal authority to do so. It appeared that we could not carry out our goals because the center insisted on following Dutch law."[48]

Attempts to enforce moral rectitude were extended to religious ritual as well. In 1948 the residency Office of Religious Affairs, along with "ulama throughout Aceh" issued a joint decree forbidding various traditional religious practices that were deemed to be local accretions and anathema to a purified Islam. The prohibition included the whole complex of rituals associated with death—the elaborate feasts that were held at fixed intervals following the burial of a relative, the incessant chanting of prayers and other efforts at intercession on behalf of the soul of the departed. In addition, the reformists forbade such Acehnese variants of saint veneration as feasts and the recitation of the Koran and worship at the tombs of famed ulama whose grace and mercy were invoked to grant a wish or cure an illness.[49]

While PUSA ulama did not think primarily in terms of institutions when they spoke of implementing Islamic law, they nonetheless wanted to consolidate the judicial reforms of the Japanese occupation. In August 1946 the residency government officially established, without central government authorization, Islamic courts at several administrative levels and an appellate court in Kutaraja. In January 1947, the governor of Sumatra instructed residents throughout Sumatra to establish religious courts, in part to meet the demand for Islamic courts in other parts of Sumatra, where, in contrast to Aceh, the Japanese had not separated religious judicial matters from the customary courts, and in part to control, in Daniel Lev's words, "what appeared to be a wild situation in Atjeh."[50] Since Islamic courts already existed in Aceh, local leaders chose to interpret the governor's instruction as allowing for an even broader competence of the courts. From the beginning, Islamic courts had jurisdiction over family matters, which were seen as the traditional concern of religious courts. More problematical in terms of judicial competence were issues of inheritance and religious trusts. The legislative assembly in Aceh decided that inheritance was strictly within the competence of Islamic courts and denied civil courts the right to hear inheritance cases.[51]

These judicial initiatives later became an issue of contention between the center and Aceh, reflecting the broader problem of whether postrevolutionary central governments acknowledged the existence of legitimate Republican authority in Aceh during the revolution. Only ten years later did the central government decree that the governor's order of January 1947 establishing Islamic courts on Sumatra was a legitimate act of the Republic. The delay in confirming the governor's instruction called into question the entire Islamic legal apparatus on Sumatra and, to PUSA leaders, was a disturbing portent.[52]

Another important item on PUSA's agenda was the future of the madrasah. For PUSA leaders the madrasah were the cornerstone of the struggle for independence. In 1946 the residency government decreed that the madrasah were state schools receiving government subsidies and madrasah teachers state employees receiving government salaries.[53] This step, predictably, encouraged the establishment of even more religious schools; by the end of the revolution, the residency government was funding more than two hundred madrasah. Natural as the reformist ulama found support for the madrasah, they were, nonetheless, aware of the potential for problems. When central government officials visited Aceh, the question of what to do with the state-supported madrasah invariably came up; nowhere else had a local government completely taken over responsibility for Islamic elementary schools. But no central government decree was forthcoming to regularize what ministry of education officials considered to be a highly unusual state of affairs.[54] An intense commitment to a religion-based elementary education, combined with an awareness that there were forces working against acceptance of the madrasah as a part of state education, led PUSA leaders to propose the integration of madrasah and village schools. In the event, the merger did not come about. Nor did subsequent attempts to integrate religious and secular elementary schools succeed, for the central government was unwilling to allow such an exceptional local initiative. Yet the idea that Acehnese children should receive an education based on the madrasah model remained. During the revolution, PUSA leaders successfully institutionalized the madrasah to such an extent that it could not easily be dismantled by unsympathetic education officials at the center.

Following the second Dutch offensive against the Republic in late December 1948, the autonomy of the Acehnese leadership increased as Dutch forces captured the central Republican leaders and as Republican strongholds on Sumatra were cut off from Java. By July 1949, Dutch-Indonesian negotiations had led to the release of the central Republican leaders. Given the uncertain prospects for the continuing negotiations with the Dutch, President Sukarno appointed Sjafruddin Prawiranegara as deputy prime minister, giving him the power to decree government regulations for Sumatra, subject to central government review.[55] At the urging of Acehnese leaders, Sjafruddin used his extraordinary powers to issue a government decree establishing Aceh as a separate province.[56] This decree, in December 1949, preceded by

only a few days the formal transfer of sovereignty from the Netherlands to the Republic of the United States of Indonesia. Preparations
were then made in Aceh to establish a provincial government. In a
matter of days, however, a cable from the ministry of home affairs
stated that Sjafruddin's decree was in violation of an earlier decision
dividing Sumatra into three provinces. A subsequent cable said that
preparations for the province could continue pending a definite decision. On this ambiguous and problematical note the revolution in
Aceh came to an end.

Acehnese revolutionaries took pride in their loyalty to the Republic
during the struggle for independence. As Ali Hasjmy, in his tribute to
those who had fought during the revolution, said, "Many of our
youths fell as martyrs. But they did not die in vain. . . . Their struggle
and their sacrifice were successful, for the Dutch army was unable to
occupy Aceh. Thus there remained a single region of the Republic of
Indonesia which was still one hundred per cent in Indonesian hands.
That was Aceh!"[57]

Given the intensity of Acehnese commitment to the Republic, why
was there such an early challenge to the center following the revolution? The challenge came because the Acehnese revolutionary experience entailed a great deal more than supplanting Dutch colonialism.
Acehnese revolutionaries had gone beyond the boundaries of national
revolution—they were social revolutionaries also. Postrevolution central governments were never willing to acknowledge the social revolution in Aceh as a legitimate and valued part of the national revolutionary heritage. One result of the social revolution was the removal of an
elite possessing the one characteristic seemingly necessary for successful relations with the center—a mastery of the colonial language that
provided a shared modality of thought with the national elite. Lacking
as they did the colonial language, and lacking the shared experiences
and implicit meanings that its mastery provided, the Acehnese social
revolutionaries were unable to operate comfortably or effectively in
postrevolutionary Jakarta, where the Dutch language was centrally
important.

Furthermore, the Acehnese revolutionaries began to think about
how to make the postrevolution state one that would be based on

what they thought were the dictates of Islam. Indonesia, however, was not to be an Islamic state. Despairing of achieving their goals, in 1953 the Acehnese revolutionaries retreated to the mountains in rebellion against what they saw as a secular central government. All the while, the Acehnese were careful to identify their rebellion as part of an Indonesian Islamic struggle, to claim for themselves the national revolutionary legacy.

Notes

1. As Benda put it: "Under the banner of a distinctly Islamic local and ethnic patriotism, Aceh thus entered independent Indonesia as a virtually autonomous *imperium in imperio.*" Harry J. Benda, "South-East Asian Islam in the Twentieth Century," in P. M. Holt, Ann K. S. Lambton, and Bernard Lewis, eds., *The Cambridge History of Islam,* vol. 2 (Cambridge and New York: Cambridge University Press, 1970), p. 204. Also representative of the standard view is Anthony Reid's statement, "The leadership of the dominant popular force, PUSA, indisputably thought in Atjehnese and Islamic rather than in Indonesian terms," in his "The Birth of the Republic in Sumatra," *Indonesia* 12 (Oct. 1971): 42, n. 76.

2. That the Aceh War never ended, in the sense that the Acehnese were not completely subjugated by the Dutch, is also the thesis of Paul van't Veer, *De Atjeh-oorlog* (Amsterdam: Uitgeverij De Arbeiderspers, 1969).

3. I include in this group both the territorial rulers, of whom there were slightly over one hundred, and the broader social formation that can be roughly described as the nobility or gentry.

4. On the role of the sultan during the Aceh War, see J. Jongejans, *Land en Volk van Atjeh Vroeger en Nu* (The Hague: Hollandia Drukkerij N. V. Baarn, 1939), pp. 303–306.

5. C. Snouck Hurgronje, *The Acehnese,* vol. 1, trans. A. W. S. O'Sullivan (Leiden: E. J. Brill, 1906), p. 174.

6. Ibid., p. 188. The Keumala party refers to the sultan, whose court during the war was at Keumala, Pidie.

7. "Politiek Verslag Atjeh," in Mailrapport 221x/28, Archive of the former Ministry of the Colonies, The Hague.

8. A. J. Piekaar, "Atjeh," in *The Encyclopaedia of Islam,* new ed. (Leiden: E. J. Brill, 1960), p. 745.

9. For a discussion of Dutch regulations on the chiefs' income, see J. Kreemer, *Atjeh,* vol. 2 (Leiden: E. J. Brill, 1922), pp. 248–257.

10. A. J. Piekaar, *Atjeh en de Oorlog met Japan* (The Hague: van Hoeve, 1949), p. 8.

11. For a description of the system of justice in Aceh during the colonial period, see A. D. A. de Kat Angelino, *Colonial Policy,* trans. G. J. Renier (The Hague: Martinus Nijhoff, 1931), pp. 178–180.

12. Mahmud Junus, *Sedjarah Pendidikan Islam di Indonesia* (Jakarta: Pustaka Mahmudiah, 1960), p. 157. In time, PUSA leaders established a standard curriculum for five years of instruction; roughly 30 percent of the curriculum was devoted to secular subjects. "Rantjangan Leerplan boeat sekolah2 agama rendah diseluruh Atjeh," *Penjoeloeh* 2, 10 (Aug. 1941): 139–141.

13. Teungku M. Daud Beureu'eh, born in 1899 in a village near Beureuneun, Pidie, studied at three different dayah in Pidie. Before establishing his madrasah, with the assistance of Teungku Abdullah Ujong Rimba, he had taught at several dayah in Pidie and North Aceh.

14. One source lists more than ninety madrasah in 1936, but the region of Lho'seumawe was not included. "Verslag Tablegh Akbar di Loeboek, III Mks. Keurekon dan Pertemoean Oelama-Oelama di Koetaradja, 1–2 October 1936," (typescript), pp. 10–12.

15. In 1940 there were approximately 150 Acehnese studying in West Sumatra. *Seruan Kita* 2, 37 (Apr. 5, 1940): 766.

16. For a PUSA critique of Acehnese saint-veneration, see M. Joesoef Ibrahim, "Pemoeda tanah Rentjong . . . insjaflah!" *Penjoeloeh* 2, 12 (Oct. 1941). Also see Ismail Yakub's comments on the mystical practices of the followers of Habib Seunagan in West Aceh in the Medan newspaper, *Pewarta Deli,* Nov. 21, 1939.

17. A. Hasjmy, "Bahasa Indonesia disekolah-sekolah agama," *Penjoeloeh* 2, 3 (Jan. 1941): 3.

18. Abdullah Arif, *Tindjauan Sedjarah Pegerakan Atjeh* (Kutaraja?: Panitia Raja Kongres Besar Pusa/P. Pusa, Seksi Penerangan, 1950), p. 23.

19. For a list of appointments, see Piekaar, *Atjeh in de Oorlog met Japan,* pp. 339–343.

20. "Atjeh Syu Rei (oendang-oendang Atjeh): Tentang soesoenan Syukyo Hoin (Mahkamah Agama) didalam Atjeh Syu" and "Atjeh Syu Kokusi (Makloemat Pemerintah): Perihal peratoeran jang berkenaan dengan Oendang2 tentang soesoenan Syukyo Hoin didalam Atjeh Syu," *Beberapa Pemandangan Tentang: Kehakiman di Daerah Atjeh,* Boeah dan Pati dari permoesjawaratan Hakim2 (Sinapankan dan Sinpankanho) seluruh Atjeh, 305 Boelan X, 2604 (Kutaraja: n.p., 1944), pp. 55–60.

21. Piekaar, "Atjeh," p. 746.

22. "Oendang-oendang tentang soesoenan Hakim dan Mahkamah didae-

rah Atjeh" and "Penerangan-penerangan jang berkenaan dengan oendang-oendang tentang soesoenan Hakim dan Mahkamah didaerah Atjeh," *Beberapa Pemandangan Tentang: Kehakiman di Daerah Atjeh,* pp. 48–55.

23. In late December 1943, those Japanese officials responsible for judicial reform asked PUSA leaders to select candidates for the new courts on the basis of three criteria: the trust of the people, knowledge of adat law, and courage to withstand uleebalang interference. Summary translation by Mitsuo Nakamura of Eigoro Aoki, "Achie no Mingoku-undo" [National movement in Atjeh] (June 1, 1955, Mimeographed). Film 905, no. 1, John M. Echols Collection, Cornell University Library, p. 3.

24. For a personal account of the hardships of Japanese rule in Aceh, see Abdullah Hussain, *Terjebak* (Kuala Lumpur: Pustaka Antara, 1965).

25. Cf. Anthony Reid, "The Japanese and Rival Indonesian Elites: Sumatra in 1942," *Journal of Asian Studies* 35, 1 (1975): 49–61.

26. Teuku Nya' Arif (1899–1946) was *panglima* (commander) of sagi XXVI mukim, a subdivision of Aceh Besar. He received his education at a training school for indigenous officials in Serang, West Java. Based on his service as Aceh's representative in the Volksraad (a quasi-representative body for the Netherlands East Indies), he emerged as the most influential uleebalang. Piekaar, in his *Atjeh en de Oorlog met Japan,* p. 11, calls Teuku Nya' Arif a "strong nationalist."

27. On the BPI, see Tuanku Hasjim, "Detik-Detik Proklamasi 1945," *Warta Pendidikan dan Kebudajaan* 7 (Aug. 1971): 16–17.

28. Ali Hasjmy was born in Aceh Besar in 1917. He studied at several dayah in Aceh before attending an Islamic secondary school in West Sumatra, where he was chairman of an association of Acehnese students. After returning to Aceh in 1939, he taught at Teungku Abdul Wahab's madrasah in Seulimeum. He was an active leader in Pemuda PUSA's scouting organization and a prolific contributor to the PUSA journal, *Penjoeloeh.* Involved in the Seulimeum uprising before the Japanese invasion, he served as editor of the newspaper *Atjeh Shinbun* during the occupation.

29. For the "Makloemat Oelama Seloeroeh Atjeh" (Declaration of U!ama Throughout Aceh), see Seksi Penerangan/Dokumentasi Komite Musjawarah Angkatan 45 Daerah Istimewa Atjeh, *Atjeh: Modal Revolusi 45* (Kutaraja: n.p., 1960), p. 61.

30. Teungku M. Daud Beureu'eh, "Merdekakanlah bathinmoe! Katakanlah jang benar walau pahit sekalipoen," in *Sang Saka: Kenangan Berlangsoengnja Konperensi Daerah Jg Kedoea* (Kutaraja: Badan Penerangan Markas Daerah "Pesindo" Atjeh, 1946), pp. 24–25. The choice of words to depict Satan and passion creates a nice parallel with the external situation: Satan's

domination is *penjajahan,* literally, colonial domination; passion is the traitor *(pengkhianat)* who must be destroyed before the threat of colonialism can be removed.

31. A. Hasjmy established the Pesindo militia, made up of pemuda who had received some military training from the Japanese. PUSA leaders founded the Barisan Mujahidin as a separate militia to mobilize youth in rural areas.

32. The commander was Syammaun Gaharu, a young man of twenty-nine, who, though born in Pidie, had never been part of the madrasah movement; he attended teacher-training college in Pematang Siantar, returned to Aceh to teach at the nationalist Taman Siswa school in Kutaraja, and then continued his education at an agricultural teacher-training school in Bogor. On the early days of the army in Aceh, see *Dua Windhu Kodam-I/Iskandar Muda* (Kutaraja?: Sedjarah Militer Kodam-I/Iskandar Muda, 1972), pp. 81–83.

33. Teuku Nya' Arif was suffering from diabetes, but his decision to take leave was also determined by the increasingly untenable position in which he had been placed.

34. This body had been established in December 1945 to coordinate the activities of government agencies, independent militias, and political parties. Col. Syammaun Gaharu, as TKR commander, was its first chairman.

35. S. M. Amin, *Disekitar Peristiwa Berdarah di Atjeh* (Jakarta: Soeroenga, 1956?), p. 14.

36. Excerpts from a personal account of events written shortly after the social revolution (typescript).

37. Several months later, the residency government established a special court to resolve the many property disputes that grew out of the Pidie social revolution. See "Peraturan Daerah No. 1–24 Djuni 1946—Peraturan Tentang Menguasai Atau Memiliki Harta Benda Peninggalan Pengchianat-Pengchianat N.R.I. Daerah Atjeh," in Teuku Ali Basjah Talsya, *Sedjarah dan Dokumen-Dokumen Pemberontakan di Atjeh* (Jakarta: Kesuma, 1955?), pp. 21–25.

38. T.M.A. Panglima Polem, *Memoir (Tjatatan)* (Banda Aceh: Alhambra, 1972), pp. 28–29.

39. Syammaun Gaharu recounted that as the TPR approached Kutaraja he instructed his officers to deploy those "soldiers who could still be controlled." Syammaun Gaharu, "Beberapa Catatan Tentang Perjuangan Menegakkan Kemerdekaan" (Revised version of a paper presented at the Seminar on the Acehnese Struggle from 1873 to Indonesian Independence, Medan, Mar. 1976), p. 52.

40. See "Besluit Residen Atjeh dari Negara Republik Indonesia no. 591/ N.R.I., 13 Augustus 1946." Most of the internees were from Aceh Besar, West Aceh, and South Aceh; in these three regions, in contrast to Pidie, East Aceh, and North Aceh, there were few uleebalang fatalities. Beginning in mid-1947,

a number of the less important internees were allowed to leave Central Aceh with the stipulation that they not return to their home regions. On the releases, see "Notulen Rapat Gaboengan dari Dewan Pertahanan Daerah, Badan Pekerdja Dewan Perwakilan Atjeh, Wakil2 Partai serta Wakil Tentera, Polisi, Kedjaksaan dan Kehakiman, 21 April 1947"; "Notulen Rapat Gaboengan Dewan Pertahanan Daerah, Badan Pekerdja D.P.A. serta oendangan, 19 Djoeni 1947"; and "Petikan dari Kepoetoesan Badan Pekerdja Dewan Perwakilan Atjeh, 4 Desember 1947, no. 36." (Typescripts in the author's possession.)

41. See Clive S. Kessler, *Islam and Politics in a Malay State: Kelantan, 1838–1969* (Ithaca: Cornell University Press, 1978), p. 212.

42. Here I am following Kessler, whose analysis of Islam I believe to be applicable to Aceh (ibid., p. 216). For his analysis, Kessler in turn depends on Siegel's description of the Acehnese celebration of the pilgrimage; see James T. Siegel, *The Rope of God* (Berkeley and Los Angeles: University of California Press, 1969), pp. 260–275.

43. Kessler says: "In time of political crisis or religious climax, all are faced equally by the same overriding issue. This transcendental if momentary equality gives intimations of the ideal Islamic community, harmonious, solidary and egalitarian. Even though it remains uninstitutionalized in this life, the ideal is kept alive: instead of being projected into the life to come, it is made to impinge upon and insinuate itself into the life of this world by which it is yet disappointed." Kessler, *Islam and Politics in a Malay State,* p. 246.

44. *Semangat Merdeka,* Mar. 23, 1949, quoted in *Dua Windhu Kodam-I/ Iskandar Muda,* p. 154.

45. For trade with Malaya and Aceh's contribution to the Republic, see T.M.A. Panglima Polem, *Memoir,* pp. 32–42; Talsya, *Sedjarah dan Dokumen-Dokumen Pemberontakan,* pp. 27–28; and Ong Poh Kee, "Trade of Penang with Atjeh, 1945–1955" (Honors thesis, University of Malaya, Singapore, 1956).

46. Mohd. Noer el Ibrahimy, "Islam dan Politik," *Kebangoenan Islam* 1, 3 (Mar. 1948): 51–52.

47. "Soerat Penetapan No. Gm/25, 29 November 1948" and "Makloemat GM 12 M, 18 September 1948," in Amin, *Disekitar Peristiwa Berdarah,* pp. 289–291.

48. Interview, Banda Aceh, Oct. 13, 1976.

49. The list of forbidden practices is found in "Kepoetoesan Sidang Badan Pekerdja Dewan Perwakilan Atjeh, 27-7-1948" (typescript).

50. Daniel Lev, *Islamic Courts in Indonesia* (Berkeley: University of California Press, 1972), p. 82.

51. Amin, *Disekitar Peristiwa Berdarah,* pp. 43–47.

52. For a discussion of this problem, see Soufjan Hamzah, "Kedudukan Pengadilan Agama di Sumatera," *Mimbar Indonesia* 39 (Sept. 24, 1955): 10–12.

53. PUSA's teacher-training school was converted into a state school at the same time.

54. Interviews, with a PUSA leader, Banda Aceh, Oct. 27, 1976, and Feb. 8, 1977.

55. "Undang-Undang No. 2 1949 Tentang Kedudukan dan Kekuasaan Wakil Perdana Menteri Jang Berkedudukan di Sumatera," in Amin, *Disekitar Peristiwa Berdarah,* pp. 279–281.

56. "Peraturan Wakil Perdana Menteri pengganti Peraturan Pemerintah No. 8/Des/WKPM tahun 1949 tentang pembentukan Provinsi Atjeh," in ibid., pp. 276–277.

57. A. Hasjmy, "Apa Sebab Belanda Sewaktu Agressi Pertama dan Kedua Tidak Dapat Memasuki Atjeh?" *Atjeh: Modal Revolusi 45,* p. 63.

PART 2

BATTLEGROUNDS FOR COMPETING STATES

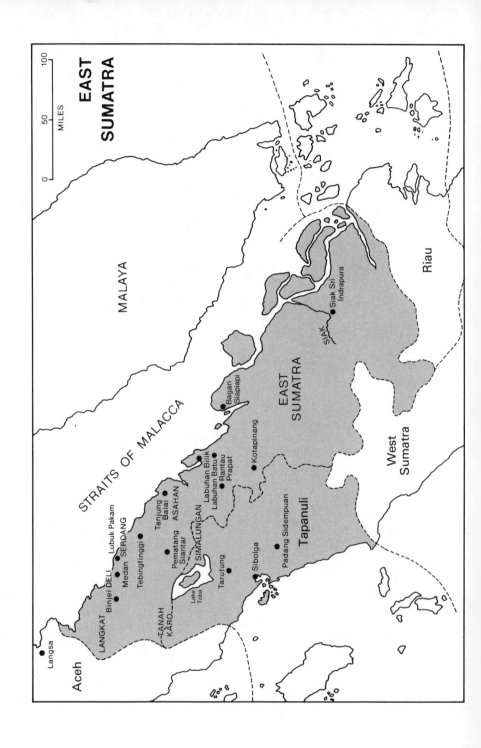

EAST SUMATRA: ACCOMMODATING AN INDONESIAN NATION WITHIN A SUMATRAN RESIDENCY

Michael van Langenberg

> Between 1945 and 1950 we entered a new world. We were
> liberated from an enforced childhood and entered an adult
> world of opportunities, freedom, uncertainty, and fear. We
> had to find our own identity and survive while trying to
> build a new civilized order. We all knew we had experi-
> enced a revolution. We now had to accommodate an Indo-
> nesian nation within our souls.
>
> *From personal recollections*
> *of two leading participants in the*
> *revolution in northern Sumatra*

The Indonesian national revolution that occurred in the residency of
East Sumatra between 1945 and 1950 was certainly part of a much
larger struggle for national independence, encompassing both Java
and the rest of Sumatra, and was seen as such by those within and outside the residency. Important initiatives, vitally affecting the course of
developments in the region, were taken by outsiders—by the Japanese,
the British, the Dutch, and the nationalist leadership on Java. But
overall, the events of 1945–1950 took place with a high degree
of regional isolation. At all times the leadership of the revolution
remained in local hands.

At the heart of the revolution in East Sumatra was the confrontation between local institutions, loyalties, and consciousness on the one
hand and national (Indonesian) ones on the other. A rapidly expanding national consciousness, interpreted through different and often
contradictory subnational values, came into play. Conflicts resulting
from competing local loyalties and traditions became more intense.
Thus the relative degree of autonomy and stability that had characterized most social structures at the local level in colonial East Sumatra

immediately prior to the Japanese occupation in 1942 were undermined. In this sense the revolution was much more than a crisis in relations between the indigenous peoples and the Dutch. It was also the
first stage in the working out of the reality and meaning of Indonesia
and of being Indonesian.

Background: The Colonial Experience

In the approximately seventy years from about 1870 to 1942, Dutch
colonial rule incorporated a mosaic of kingdoms, petty principalities,
and village communities into a relatively centralized political economy. Thirty-four native states in the residency of Sumatra's east coast
(Oostkust van Sumatra) were granted varying degrees of self-governing status within the Indies colonial system.[1] In effect, however, by
1942, administration was in the hands of Dutch colonial officials governing subresidency regions and responsible, via the residency administration, to the Netherlands East Indies government in Batavia. While
day-to-day administration involved a continual process of accommodation between local indigenous elites and Dutch colonial officials,
there was no question that ultimate authority lay with the latter.

Colonial rule brought some great changes to the society. Class
structures, cultural and demographic patterns, and economic systems
were altered. A highly diverse social structure had emerged by 1942.

A vast plantation economy dominated the region. The plantations
occupied nearly one million hectares, producing rubber, tobacco,
palm oil, and sisal that accounted for 64 percent of the value of all
exports from the residency in 1938.[2] Hundreds of thousands of
laborers, first from southern China and later from Central and East
Java, were brought in to work the estates. By 1930, there were
192,000 Chinese and 590,000 Javanese in the residency. Other Indonesians had also begun to migrate into the region, attracted by the
prosperous plantation economy. As a result, by 1930 the three ethnic
groups that considered themselves indigenous to Sumatra—the Malay,
the Karo, and the Simalungun—had been reduced to a minority of 39
percent of the total Indonesian population of East Sumatra. The
Javanese had become the largest single ethnic community in the residency and the Chinese, the third largest.[3]

A few big urban centers had developed to service the plantation economy, notably Medan, Pematang Siantar, and Tebingtinggi.[4] Thousands of Chinese and other nonindigenous migrants had moved into the towns. By 1942, most of the small- and middle-scale commerce was in Chinese hands, the remainder being carried out by Indians, Minangkabau, or Tapanuli Bataks. The Javanese, Toba, Angkola, Mandailing, Minangkabau, Acehnese, and other nonindigenous Indonesians had found jobs as, for example, domestic servants, factory workers, school teachers, clerks, or junior civil servants. From the port towns along the coast, notably Tanjung Balai and Labuhan Bilik in the south and Langsa in the north, a substantial commerce controlled by Chinese merchants linked East Sumatra with Penang and Singapore.

The class structure of colonial East Sumatra was extremly complex and regionally varied. At the top was a ruling elite constituting an identifiable colonial establishment. This elite in itself was made up of several layers. First were the Europeans—colonial officials, planters, and businessmen. Next came the ruling families of the six main Malay sultanates—Langkat, Serdang, Deli, Asahan, Kotapinang, and Siak. Third were the ruling families of the smaller Malay principalities, the Simalungun and Karo rajas, the Western-educated Indonesian professionals (doctors, lawyers, senior civil servants), and the wealthier Chinese, Indonesian, and Indian merchants. The majority of the Indonesian professionals and merchants were nonindigenous, originating mostly from Java, Tapanuli, West Sumatra, Aceh, and East Indonesia.

The class differences between elite and masses varied considerably from region to region. In the towns and plantation region of East Sumatra, a vast gap separated the colonial establishment from the mass of plantation workers, urban labor, and peasantry. The Malay sultans in particular had become immensely rich from their relationship with the colonial system and pursued extravagant and notably indolent lifestyles. The Simalungun and Karo rajas had gained nothing like the same wealth from the colonial relationship but, nonetheless, lived much more prosperously than had their predecessors of even thirty years before. They enjoyed considerable benefits from their membership in the colonial establishment.

Cultural diversity was significant and manifold. The Malay, Karo, and Simalungun were intensely aware of being the indigenous peoples. This awareness was heightened by the presence of the large nonindigenous majority. But other factors served to divide the indigenes. The Karo and most Simalungun were either animist or Christian and hence consciously apart from the Islamic Malays. Also, contractual arrangements between the Malay sultans and the Indies government had given the Malay peasantry special rights of access to plantation land, rights not enjoyed by most non-Malays. This served to make most Karo and Simalungun resent Malay privilege, from which they were excluded. The large Javanese community also remained quite distinct. Most Javanese were either plantation laborers or urban proletariat and conspicuously nominal Moslem *(abangan)*. The stigma of being coolies, only recently freed from the notorious penal contract system under which they had been brought to East Sumatra, made most Javanese acutely aware of being especially discriminated against within the colonial system.

The region was pervaded by intense racism and ethnocentrism. The colonial system as a whole was dominated by the foreign-controlled plantation economy and the special relationship between the Malay aristocracy and the colonial authorities. Malay culture had a political primacy, and the vast majority of non-Malays among the Indonesian population thus had both political and cultural reasons for feeling discriminated against in what they saw as a system of European-Malay hegemony.

Along with interethnic tensions, Dutch colonial rule had also produced a milieu in the burgeoning urban centers, notably Medan and Pematang Siantar, where a new Indonesian superculture was evident by 1942. In this new Indonesian environment, organized opposition to colonial rule and a conscious search for a new national identity developed. A branch of the Java-based cultural nationalist organization, the Budi Utomo (High Endeavor), had been formed in Medan as early as the end of 1908, only a few months after its parent body on Java. By 1919 the nucleus of a nationalist movement had come into being in the plantation region with the establishment of branches of Sarekat Islam (Islamic League) and of the Eurasian-oriented radical party, Insulinde.

During the 1920s a radical sector of this movement emerged to articulate an overtly confrontative stance against Dutch colonial rule. Three organizations gave the radical movement form and coherence: the PKI (Indonesian Communist Party) led by Abdul Xarim MS; a radical modernist Islamic movement, the Sumatra Thawalib, based in the Minangkabau and Mandailing regions; and a vocal anticolonial minority within the Batak Christian church, led by the Batak Christian Association. Common to all the groups making up the radical sector was an uncompromising opposition to Dutch colonial rule, to the Dutch-supported aristocracies, and to the foreign-owned plantation economy.[5]

By the early 1930s, radical activity had declined. The Communist party had been banned in 1927, and most of its leaders were in prison. The Sumatra Thawalib and the Batak Christian Association had gradually disintegrated under combined pressure from the colonial authorities and local indigenous elites. Branches of the newer, militant, Java-based nationalist parties—the PNI (Indonesia Nationalist Party) and its successor Partindo (prewar Indonesian Party)—enjoyed only a brief legal existence in East Sumatra. Through the early and mid-thirties the legal, organized nationalist movement functioned almost wholly through more moderate organizations such as the modernist Moslem Muhammadiyah, Taman Siswa (lit., Garden of Pupils), the cultural-nationalist education system, and Parindra (Greater Indonesian Party) led by nationalist sympathizers from the colonial establishment. Support for these nationalist organizations came overwhelmingly from the non-Malay ethnic groups, particularly the Javanese, Karo, Toba, and Minangkabau.

The establishment of a new organization, Gerindo (Indonesian People's Movement), in the later 1930s stimulated renewed radical activity. With many of its leaders having been associated with one or more of the main radical organizations of earlier years—the PKI, PNI, Partindo, and Sumatra Thawalib—Gerindo represented a broad alliance of radical nationalists in the region. It maintained a strongly anticolonial, anti-European, and anticapitalist line, urging complete national independence, destruction of feudal aristocratic systems, nationalization of all capital enterprises, and restoration of indigenous land rights. Land rights and opposition to the East Sumatra aristocracy became a central issue in the party's program. Campaigns for the redistribution of plantation land to peasant farmers brought wide support from the Javanese, Karo, and Toba communities.

Cadre-training courses begun by Gerindo in 1938 produced a nucleus of nationalist-minded youth, strongly imbued with a radical ethic. Although no more than a couple of hundred in all by 1942, they added considerable momentum to the organized movement. Among the Karo and Simalungun, a network of young leaders had begun to challenge the traditional rights and authority of the aristocracy, attacking the sultans and rajas as colonial lackeys. In the urban centers, thousands of young men, many from nonelite backgrounds and many unemployed, responded enthusiastically to this movement.

As the orbit of the Pacific war expanded toward the Netherlands Indies, a significant sector of the population of East Sumatra was conscious of being deprived by the existing social order and eager for opportunities to improve their lot. Opposition to colonial rule and aristocratic privilege lay at the heart of this movement. Encompassing proletariat, plantation workers, peasant farmers, Islamic reformers, Christian modernizers, social revolutionaries, and a broad spectrum of nationalist-minded young men and women, the movement numbered in the hundreds of thousands by 1942.

The Japanese Occupation

The Japanese occupation from 1942 to 1945 coincided with a widespread awareness of a new age, particularly among the youth.[6] This awareness, a new consciousness, was produced by the socioeconomic changes of the previous three decades brought about by the combined impact of the colonial economy and the spread of Indonesian nationalist ideals. The three-year Japanese occupation was thus integral to the larger national revolution, constituting for the people of East Sumatra the first stage in that revolutionary era. It served to accelerate the spread of nationalist consciousness. It brought radical change to the social structures of the region. It brought into being new values, new motivations, new ambitions, new institutions, and new patterns of behavior and social relationships. Out of the occupation emerged a key revolutionary force, the *pemuda* (youth). Military government gained in legitimacy. Social mobility increased markedly. Destruction of the basis of the colonial economy, the plantation system, began. Political unity and factionalism among Indonesian nationalists were intensified simultaneously. Politics became dominated by values of activism, heroism, authority, and discipline.

The Japanese brought a large number of nationalists, both radicals and moderates, into their administrative system and gave them access to the instruments of political propaganda and mass mobilization. Several thousand young men, many from nonelite backgrounds, were given military training. This training emphasized the basic Japanese military ethics of discipline, stoicism, and other virtues of the violent warrior spirit and also appealed to a nationalistic, anti-Western consciousness. Recruits had impressed upon them their role in the defense of the fatherland. Radical nationalist leaders were frequent participants in indoctrination classes given at the training center.

By early 1945 the idea of an independent Indonesian nation had become an important social reality within the collective consciousness of most local communities, particularly the non-Malay. Youth, the mass component of this nationalist movement, had been defined as a special category and invested with special status in the social order. Out of the military organizations had emerged a new, ambitious, highly motivated, nationalist elite committed to the idea of an independent Indonesia and convinced of their rights to political leadership.

From the beginning of the occupation, the Japanese severed administrative and political links between Sumatra and Java. Until May 1943 Sumatra and Malaya were a single administrative region. Thereafter, a separate military administration for Sumatra operated from Bukittinggi in West Sumatra. As a result, politics during the occupation became increasingly internalized within each of the main administrative regions, the former residencies. Japanese and Indonesians sought to utilize one another in a continuous strategic play of factional politics, with each side exploiting factional divisions within the other.

By the end of the occupation, the old norms of political behavior and social status had been seriously challenged. The destabilizing and socially dislocating effects of this challenge produced an essentially anarcho-revolutionary condition that was all too obvious to those living in the region in August 1945.

Leadership of the Revolution

Leaders of the revolution in East Sumatra can be grouped into four main categories, based on a combination of class, ideological orientation, nationalist seniority, and social mobility.

First were a number of prominent members of the prewar colonial establishment who either had been active in nationalist organizations or had developed strong sympathies for the idea of national independence. Prominent among them were Mr. Teuku Mohammad Hasan, who became governor from 1945 to 1948; Dr. Mohammad Amir, deputy governor until his defection in April 1946; and Mr. Abdul Abas, at various times deputy governor and military governor until 1948.[7] Leaders in this category had in common a Dutch tertiary education, in many cases in Holland, professional careers as either doctors, lawyers, or senior civil servants, distinctly Western lifestyles, moderate political orientations, and membership of traditional aristocratic families.

In the second category were those persons who had been prominent activists in the prewar nationalist movement and who, after 1945, drew on this background in asserting their leadership of the revolution. Ideologically, they encompassed a wide spectrum. They included radicals such as the prewar PKI leaders Abdul Xarim MS and Natar Zainuddin, leaders of the PNI–Partindo–Gerindo network such as Mohammad Saleh Umar and Marzuki Lubis, Islamic nationalists (both moderate and conservative) like Hamka and Haji Abdul Rahman Sjihab, and more moderate nationalists from Parindra and Taman Siswa backgrounds. Many of these people had been imprisoned by the Dutch in the 1920s and 1930s. A few, such as Xarim and Natar, had the added nationalist status of having been interned in the notorious West New Guinea penal settlement of Boven Digul. Several came from lesser elite or nonelite backgrounds. Almost all of them were administrators and/or political propagandists during the Japanese occupation.[8]

Third, were the younger nationalists who reached senior positions via the Japanese-established military organizations. A few, such as Mohammad Jakub Siregar and Selamat Ginting, had been active in the nationalist movement in the late 1930s (notably in Gerindo). Others, like Ahmad Tahir and Hopman Sitompul, reached officer rank in the

Giyūgun (the Japanese-sponsored volunteer army on Sumatra), where they became committed nationalists. Many, including Jakub Siregar, took a leading part in forming and training auxiliary units such as the BHL (Barisan Harimau Liar, Wild Tigers) and Naga Terbang (Flying Dragon) toward the end of the occupation. All men in this category were unquestionably radical in their political commitments by the time the occupation ended.[9]

Fourth, were those who rose to prominence during the revolution itself. In almost all cases they established themselves as leaders of armed *lasykar* (militias) early in the revolution. Many had been active in military units or youth organizations during the occupation. In this context they had revolutionary careers in common with many of those in the third catetory and with some in the second. In class background they were extremely varied, encompassing aristocratic, urban middle class, proletariat, and peasant backgrounds. A few had connections with the prewar nationalist movement, usually as members of leading nationalist families. As with those in the third category, all were identifiable by an assertive radicalism throughout their careers during the revolution. Typical of this fourth category were such young lasykar commanders as Bedjo, Timur Pane, Pajung Bangun, Saragiras, Nip Xarim, Sarwono S. Soetardjo, and Liberty Malao. They represented the archetypical young freedom fighter of the revolution.[10]

Overlapping these four categories was a division between old and new elites—between those whose claims to leadership rested principally on their prewar nationalist or establishment credentials and those (mostly pemuda) who rose to leadership as activists in the post-1945 struggle. This distinction encompassed both a generation gap and a division between radicals and moderates. A few among the old elite, such as Xarim MS and Natar Zainuddin, bridged the generational divide. Others from the new elite shifted position as the revolution progressed and, while continuing to maintain their new generational identity, allied themselves with moderate sectors of the old elite in opposition to pemuda radicalism.

An important feature of the leadership of the revolution in the region was the emergence of a few persons whose authority was based as much on the psychological intangibles of charisma as on any of the other factors mentioned above. Persons like Xarim MS, Moh. Saleh Umar, Timur Pane, and Bedjo exercised considerable authority through their ability to present themselves as symbols and representatives of the heroism and fighting spirit of the revolution. A search for charisma and an emphasis on style was especially prevalent among the new elite that emerged out of the pemuda movement after 1945.

Ethnicity was a key factor in the exercise of leadership throughout the revolution. Many Republican leaders drew heavily on support from their own ethnic communities. Ethnic loyalties were frequently called upon in intraelite conflicts and, just as frequently, set the conditions for such conflicts.

In the months between the proclamation of the Republic in Medan in October 1945 and the social revolution of March 1946, almost all senior positions in the provincial administration were held by men from the first category—establishment moderates such as Governor Hasan and his deputy Dr. Amir. These leaders showed a marked reluctance to confront the Japanese and British occupation forces in proclaiming and establishing the Republic and a willingness to try to reach accommodation with the pro-Dutch aristocracy.[11] Growing radical frustration with such a cautious approach rapidly widened the differences between radicals and moderates. In part, the intense violence of the social revolution was to reflect these frustrations.[12]

The Pemuda

Impetus and style came to the revolution from the armed pemuda. Young men socially dislocated, ambitious, highly politicized, and imbued with a militaristic ethic and heroic values, they provided the spirit, the visible evidence that the struggle for independence was under way. They were the clearest sign of the Republic's existence and of its ability to survive and control the future. These young men affected a range of heroic styles, which quickly became dominant in the style of the revolution itself.

Widely prevalent were the cowboy and the samurai—pistol or Japanese sword hanging low from their waists, adorned with an array of other accoutrements, and affecting a conscious swagger. So too was the more indigenous *jago,* or fighting cock—long hair, unkempt appearance, boastful and pugnacious manner, the heroic social deviant.[13] There were also other styles drawn from particular cultural heroes. Among the Toba, there was the model of the last Singamangaraja, the lone guerrilla warrior pursuing a final confrontation with the Dutch until death. Javanese pemuda used the model of Diponegoro. Among Acehnese, Minangkabau, and Mandailing youth, there was the Islamic style and the models of Imam Bondjol and Teuku Umar—requiring a dagger or sword tied to the waist, talisman worn around the neck or upper arm, and white cloth tied around the forehead to signify the purity of the Holy War.[14]

At the same time, the armed pemuda was more than a mere reflection of heroic styles. Style was itself a reflection of social and psychological needs in the conditions of social dislocation. The pemuda

> needed to be able to stand alone and take care of himself like the individual cowboy, or to entrust himself to a self-sufficient fraternity like that jago band. In a time of danger he needed the assurance of invulnerability. . . . He needed self-confidence, romance, a style for heroes.[15]

These needs, and the style they generated, determined the importance of the charismatic leader, the leader who displayed special bravery, panache, and organizing ability. He would gather followers often because of an acquired reputation for heroism or even cruelty.[16] He was the magnet that held the armed pemuda group together.

Revolutionary Violence

The combination of class tension and ethnic hostility brought to the revolution in East Sumatra a consistently high level of violence throughout the 1945–1950 period. So, too, did the ethic and style of violence inherent in the pemuda personality that had developed since the Japanese occupation. Added to this was the approved value of aggression in most Batak cultures.[17] Finally, the emphasis on struggle and radical activism of the prewar nationalist movement attracted many of the nonelite pemuda who rose to lead armed units after 1945.

The first major outbreak of revolutionary violence was the social revolution of March 1946. Class and ethnic tensions, building up since the early 1920s, exploded as Republican supporters among the main non-Malay ethnic groups wreaked vengeance upon the aristocratic sector of the colonial establishment. The prime targets were the sultans and rajas and their families. Also, non-Malays turned upon Malays in reprisal against what the former saw as the special privileges enjoyed by the latter under the colonial system.

Throughout most of March 1946, armed pemuda—mostly belonging to lasykar units from Pesindo (Indonesian Socialist Youth), Napindo (Indonesian Nationalist Youth), the BHL, Barisan Merah (Red Front of the PKI), and Hizbullah (Army of Allah)—supported by Javanese plantation workers and Karo and Toba farmers, ran riot through East Sumatra, killing, arresting officials, and seizing property. Outside Medan (which was garrisoned by an Allied military force), most of the palaces and houses of the aristocrats were attacked and ransacked. Members of aristocratic families and alleged colonialist collaborators were attacked. All the main sultans and rajas (an exception was the sultan of Deli, guarded by British troops in Medan) were either killed or arrested. Altogether, nearly ninety prominent aristocrats lost their lives and hundreds were arrested.[18] Large numbers of officials of the native states were also killed or arrested. A great quantity of property (including money, gold, and jewelry) was seized by raiding lasykars.[19] Plantations across the residency were occupied by lasykar units, and plantation land was distributed to former plantation workers and non-Malay farmers. Many Malay farmers were evicted from plantation land they had been cultivating under the special access rights of the prewar plantation contracts.[20]

In a sense, the social revolution took place on two levels. On the politically articulated level, all nationalist leaders sought to promote or restrain the violence in accord with their perceived interests and aims. On a more spontaneous level, social frustrations and communal hatreds were vented in the name of the national revolution. In the latter case, many of the attacks and killings reflected a complex mixture of class and ethnic conflicts. Javanese and Batak pemuda would attack Malays on the grounds that, ipso facto, they were supporters of the aristocracy or Dutch spies. Alternatively, many of the attacks on the Karo and Simalungun aristocrats were carried out by Karo and Simalungun pemuda against their own traditional chiefs. In this case, an important motivation was the desire to destroy what was seen as an exploitive ruling class. But there was also a much more subtle ethnic aspect, one which helped to sharpen the class consciousness itself. Several of the Karo and Simalungun aristocratic families, because of intermarriage and close social relationships with the Malay aristocracy, were regarded by the pemuda as having become Malayized, of being traitors to their own cultural identity, their *suku* (ethnic group) and *adat* (custom). It was an alienation produced by mutually reinforcing class and primordial consciousness. Beyond the ethnic aspect, many people were killed or arrested simply because they displayed an obvious Westernized lifestyle and a reluctance to join the anticolonial cause. Many of the attacks were motivated by a desire to expropriate property. In some cases it was to meet specific group (e.g., lasykar) needs. In others it was a matter of indiscriminate looting.

The social revolution was far more than a localized outbreak of violence manipulated by a few radical leaders exploiting conditions of administrative breakdown. It was, in a very real sense, an expression of class, ideological, and ethnic tensions that had been building up for over forty years and from which the prewar nationalist movement had gathered much of its momentum. The tensions underlying the violence of the social revolution were basic to the dynamics of the larger national revolution itself. In this sense, the social revolution reflected the deep hostilities that many thousands of non-Malays felt against a colonial system they considered especially discriminatory.

In this context, the social revolution set the scene for much of the later violence and internal conflict that was to be characteristic of the 1945–1950 period as a whole. It heightened the sense of heroics and aggressive group identity of the lasykar units. It gave the armed pemuda a greater sense of power and consciousness of their role as leaders of the revolution. It also gave them access to political authority and economic resources, upon which later warlord fiefdoms would be built. The social revolution also sharpened the divisions between moderates and radicals, another conflict that was to be played out for the remainder of the 1945–1950 period and later. It consolidated the alienation of the great majority of the East Sumatran aristocracy and the mass of the Malay population from the Republic and ensured these groups' support for the Dutch military occupation of the residency in 1947. Finally, the social revolution shook the confidence of the more conservative Republican leaders in the ability of the Republic to offer a greater degree of freedom than the colonial alternative.

To the extent that internecine violence is characteristic of any revolutionary situation, the events in northern Sumatra were typical revolutionary phenomena. The pressures of intensely competing interests in a condition of accelerated social change had brought old vested interests and new motivations into violent collision. The conclusion of the national revolution in 1950 did not resolve the conflicts that revolutionary conditions had set in motion. Many of those conflicts have still to find peaceful resolution.[21]

The Warlords

A crucially important feature of the revolution in East Sumatra and in the adjoining residency of Tapanuli was the power exercised by leaders of large armed units in control of territory and significant economic resources. By late 1946, a warlord structure had been established and these emerging warlords were providing the greatest momentum to the physical armed struggle. In command of armed units affiliated with either the official Republican army or with one of the major lasykar (Napindo Halilintar, Naga Terbang, BHL, and so on), they built up territorial fiefdoms based on control of local civil administrations and local trade and commerce. By the end of 1946, local government in most of the region was in the hands of such warlords.[22]

Control of the plantations in East Sumatra provided the military units with the mainstay of their political autonomy. Via Chinese traders, military commanders began exporting large quantities of plantation products (especially rubber, palm oil, and sisal) to Penang and Singapore. There they were sold or bartered for weapons and other military supplies.[23] By August 1946 the armed units engaged in this trade were acquiring quantities of rifles, machine guns, motor vehicles, uniforms, and other equipment from Malaya and Singapore. Within a few months a powerful group of military entrepreneurs had established themselves. Timur Pane's force, the Naga Terbang, was perhaps the largest and best armed. Other powerful units were the Napindo Halilintar in Tanah Karo and the Pesindo in Langkat. By mid-1947, Pane had entered into alliances with neighboring lasykar units and expanded his own force, renaming it, more grandiosely, Tentera Marsose (Territorial Army).[24]

Following the Dutch military occupation of most of East Sumatra in July 1947, Republican armed units retreated into those parts of the countryside beyond effective Dutch control. Bedjo, with his mostly Javanese lasykar (designated as Brigade B of the TNI, the Indonesian National Army) soon emerged as a rival warlord to Pane. In the south Asahan/Labuhan Batu region, Bedjo, Pane, and the commanders of some smaller units stepped up production from the big rubber and oil palm plantations in their territories. They also gathered in large quantities of smallholder rubber from nearby villages, partly by purchase and partly as tax. Through the ports of Labuhan Bilik and Bagan Siapiapi, farther south, these goods became part of an expanding trade with Penang and Singapore.[25]

By mid-1948, huge quantities of goods were being shifted along the trade networks in and out of Langsa, Labuhan Bilik, Penang, and Singapore. Hundreds of boats—small diesel freighters, motorized junks, speedboats, and sailing vessels—were working the trade, making a mockery of Dutch attempts to impose a naval blockade on the Malacca Straits.[26] In southern East Sumatra, a largely barter trade from Labuhan Bilik linked Singapore with Bukittinggi via Padang Sidempuan in south Tapanuli. Hundreds of tons of goods—rice from Tapanuli, rubber and palm oil from East Sumatra—flowed out from Labuhan Bilik. From Langsa, agricultural products from Dairi and western Tanah Karo went to Penang.[27]

Soon some Republican military commanders and civil servants moved into full-time trading activities, acting as agents for both the warlords and Chinese traders. Some set themselves up in business in Penang or Singapore.[28] There were big profits to be made. Though most of these profits continued to flow to Chinese traders in Sumatra, Penang, and Singapore, many of the new Indonesian entrepreneurs became rich men during 1948.

At the end of that year the second Dutch military offensive brought the remaining urban centers of East Sumatra under Dutch control. Republican military units were forced to disperse into the countryside, from where they conducted a remarkably effective guerrilla campaign against the occupying Dutch forces.[29] The changed circumstances of course brought about a contraction of the previous commercial activities of Republican military commanders. In several regions, however, military guerrilla administrations still controlled political and economic structures, enabling the Republic to remain relatively self-sufficient despite Dutch occupation of the towns. In parts of Langkat and

Labuhan Batu, former warlords still controlled large areas of rubber and oil palm estates and access to trading networks out of the coastal ports. At the same time, many military commanders began to trade in less bulky and more profitable items, especially opium.[30]

Many of the more independent-minded warlords failed to survive the combined effects of the Dutch military occupation of 1949 and the earlier internecine conflicts of 1947 and 1948.[31] By August 1950, when East Sumatra was incorporated into the unitary Indonesian state, together with Tapanuli, as the province of North Sumatra, control of the political economy of the region was in the hands of the TNI. The warlord era had provided the basic structural conditions for the distinctly garrison-managerial polity that emerged in postindependence North Sumatra.[32]

Leadership Factionalism and Internecine Conflicts

The pattern of conscious ethnocentrism promoted during Dutch colonial rule bedeviled Republican unity throughout the revolution. With the end of the Japanese occupation and the proclamation of the Republic all ethnic groups had felt the need to protect their particular community interests. Republican leaders sought to build their power bases on these communal loyalties. Ethnicity, ideology, and group material interests were compounded to produce intense factional conflict.[33]

In most cases, each of the armed pemuda groups that were formed to defend the Republic during 1945 and 1946 was composed of young people from one particular ethnic group. Given the highly personalized relationships between pemuda leaders and followers, the basic needs of communication in times of chaos made this pattern inevitable. Later, as pemuda networks such as Napindo and Pesindo developed, they encompassed strongly ethnocentric factions. Each of the bigger lasykar forces was made up of units composed largely of pemuda from a single ethnic group.[34] Particularly charismatic leaders like Timur Pane managed to forge interethnic alliances, but they were always unstable and, as in Pane's own case, temporary.

As warlord control of the Republican areas grew during the latter part of 1947, ethnic differences and competition for control of territory and resources acted to increase hostilities. The first open clash occurred in November 1947 between Pane's lasykar army (called by then the Legiun Penggempur, Stormtroop Legion) and an alliance of TNI units that included Bedjo's Brigade B. Thus began a struggle to control the Republican areas of southern East Sumatra and the trading networks between East Sumatra and Padang Sidempuan. After a month of armed conflict, peace negotiations initiated by the Sumatran provincial government in Bukittinggi brought Pane's retirement and the breakup of the Legiun Penggempur.[35]

Bedjo and Liberty Malao, Pane's former deputy, were then left as the premier warlords, controlling between them most of southern East Sumatra and Tapanuli. Attempts by the military governor, Dr. Gindo Siregar, and his successor, Mr. Abdul Abas, to implement central government plans to rationalize all Republican armed forces under a more centralized command brought the combination of ethnic hostilities and warlord interests to open civil war. On September 10, 1948, Bedjo, determined to forestall rationalization, attacked the largely Toba TNI unit in Padang Sidempuan, killing its commander. The TNI unit was disarmed and the military governor, Mr. Abas, arrested. With the non-Toba forces in control of south Tapanuli, TNI units in the north joined Malao in an opposing alliance. Only when Vice-President Hatta arrived in Padang Sidempuan on November 22 and pleaded for a restoration of Republican unity was a ceasefire arranged. The rival forces agreed to recognize a new regional military command. But the crux of the agreement was the allocation of specific regions to each of the major military units.[36] The warlord structure was given de facto government recognition.

By 1947, firm alliances had been established between radical politicians and like-minded warlords.[37] Both were determined to resist what they regarded as moderate willingness to betray the true ideals of the revolution.

On several occasions, the course that radicalism was taking forced senior moderates away from the Republic and into the arms of the Dutch. The first, and most notable, occasion was the decision by the deputy governor, Dr. Mohammad Amir, to defect following the social revolution.[38] Later, in 1947 and 1948, others, including such prominent Batak nationalists in East Sumatra as Dr. F. J. Nainggolan, chose to cooperate with the Dutch-sponsored East Sumatran state movement.[39] Such efforts failed ultimately to offer a suitable alternative outside the Republic. In the end, it was the new military elite of the TNI, increasingly conscious of law and order, that, in 1950, took control of the Republic in the region and began a purge of the remaining radical leadership.

Popular Support for the Revolution

Given the highly factionalized and culturally diverse context of East Sumatra, assessing popular support for the Republic becomes an impressionistic exercise. But despite the divisions resulting from ethnic differences and other primordial factors, the Republic clearly had widespread popular support. For the overwhelming majority of Javanese, Karo, Toba, Angkola, Mandailing, Minangkabau, and Acehnese, the Republic best represented their communal interests. To this extent, primordialism and support for the national revolution were deeply intertwined.

The large numbers of pemuda from both urban and rural areas who joined the various armed units provided the most visible evidence of popular support for the Republic. A few of them may have been motivated primarily by desire for adventure, even plunder, in a time of acute social dislocation. A larger number moved in and out of armed units, often as a result of the factional conflicts that saw some units disbanded and/or amalgamated with others. But there seems little doubt that the vast majority of armed pemuda were deeply committed to the nationalist ideals of the revolution. As to how many young men joined the various armed units during the revolution, it is impossible to arrive at any accurate assessment, given the fluidity of membership. By 1948, however, the five main warlord forces—Legiun Penggempur, Brigade A, Brigade B, Napindo Halilintar, and the TNI—seem to have had a total strength of only between 4,000 and 5,000 men.[40]

At the time of the proclamation of independence and the establishment of a Republican administration in East Sumatra, rallies in support of the Republic were attended by thousands of enthusiastic supporters. Republican flags, anti-Dutch slogans, and people wearing red and white armbands were well in evidence.[41] Later, during the social revolution in East Sumatra, mass gatherings of Republican supporters shouted their approval for the destruction of the sultanates and the native-state administrations.[42]

Perhaps the best evidence of Republican support was the continued viability of the Republic during 1949, following the Dutch military occupation of most of the region, and the extent of opposition to the Dutch-sponsored East Sumatra State (Negara Sumatera Timur, NST).

After 1947, the emphatic Malay ethnocentrism of the East Sumatra State increased non-Malay support for the Republic, especially among the Javanese, Karo, and Toba. With these three ethnic groups alone making up more than half the total Indonesian population of the residency, the Republic had a substantial mass base. In the rural areas of Asahan, Labuhan Batu, parts of Simalungun, the Karo highlands, and in western Langkat, Republican guerrilla administrations operated with the support of large sectors of the population.[43] A network of Republican organizations, supported by an active Republican press, made for an energetic and articulate movement—holding meetings, circulating propaganda, and recruiting members.[44] A National Front, established in Medan with branches in Deli, Serdang, and Simalungun, provided a loose coordination of this movement.[45] The National Front, despite divisions between radicals and moderates among its leaders, was, by late 1948, instrumental in giving organized coherence to a radical movement across East Sumatra.[46] In early 1950 this movement, drawing on the support of thousands of urban workers, squatters on plantation lands, and peasant farmers among the non-Malay population, took to the streets demanding an end to the East Sumatran State and the incorporation of East Sumatra into a unitary Republican state.[47]

In general, the period of guerrilla rule in much of the region seems to have consolidated popular acceptance of the Republic. Despite the fact that the great majority of the population had taken little or no part in the armed guerrilla actions and despite many having had occasion to resent the economic demands of the guerrillas, all indications are that by August 1949 there were far more committed supporters of the Republic in East Sumatra than at the start of the revolution four years earlier. The adversity of the guerrilla struggle had greatly strengthened the commitment of large sections of the population to the Republic. Among its more active supporters, the guerrillas helped to provide a greater sense of solidarity than had previously existed.

Factionalism had certainly not disappeared, nor were its causes removed, but the sense of common antagonism against the Dutch military occupation and the common struggle for survival seem to have brought a deepened sense of national identity to a great many people in the region. It brought the nation much closer to the village.

Opposition to the Republic

Nevertheless, there was also deeply felt and well-organized opposition to the Republic in East Sumatra. In 1945 Republican supporters among the East Sumatra colonial establishment were in the minority. With a few exceptions, the aristocracy had little sympathy for the Republic, given the intensely antiaristocratic views of the radical movement. For the ethnic Malays, the Republic threatened an end to the protection and privileges they had enjoyed under colonial rule. By the end of 1945, the Malay peasants were particularly aware of the large non-Malay majority's eagerness to dispossess them of their special land rights.[48]

From April 1946, following the social revolution, aristocratic leaders beset the returning Dutch colonial administration with accounts of the sufferings of the indigenes at the hands of Republican extremists. They demanded that the Netherlands government intervene in East Sumatra to restore law and order and the customary rights of the Malay and other indigenous communities.[49] At the same time, some of the more conservative indigenous members of the colonial establishment, particularly some Toba leaders, shifted appreciably further into the anti-Republican camp, fearful of what they saw as extremist domination of the Republican government.[50]

The large Chinese community in East Sumatra, too, supported the restoration of Dutch colonial normalcy. In the early months of the revolution, the Chinese, highly visible and relatively prosperous, were frequent victims of pemuda violence. Pemuda gangs regularly raided Chinese shops and warehouses, seizing allegedly hoarded goods.[51] In response, vigilante units were formed in the Chinese districts of the bigger towns. Clashes with Republican pemuda became frequent. Despite affirmations by the powerful Overseas Chinese Association of willingness to cooperate with the Republic,[52] Chinese community leaders turned increasingly to the British occupation forces, and later to the Dutch, for protection. In early 1946, an armed Chinese security force, the Poh An-tui, equipped by the British military command, had small units patrolling the Chinese sectors of Medan, Binjei, and Pematang Siantar.[53]

Despite extensive Chinese participation in the warlord economy of the Republic after mid-1946, the political sympathies of the great majority of the Chinese leaders were against the Republic. In July 1947, Poh An-tui units joined Dutch forces in their occupation of East Sumatra.[54] By the end of that year, prominent Chinese were involved in preparations for setting up the East Sumatran State sponsored by the Dutch and local aristocrats.

The East Sumatra State movement represented the broadest alliance of opposition to the Republic, drawing together the Malay aristocracy, most of the Simalungun rajas, some of the Karo chieftains, and most Chinese community leaders. The state was officially proclaimed in January 1948 and lasted until August 1950, when it was disbanded as a result of the combined pressure of mass internal opposition and the success of the antifederalist movement in Java.[55] The state enjoyed the support of perhaps one-third of the population of the residency. But, beset by severe internal divisions (ethnic and intraelite), it proved unable to survive once Dutch military support had been withdrawn.

Changing the Social Order

By the end of 1950, most of the institutions basic to the stability of the social structures of colonial East Sumatra had either been destroyed or diminished severely in functional importance. The indigenous hereditary elites, the base upon which the colonial political economy had been built, were no longer of major political significance. Lineage and genealogy were far less important prerequisites for positions of political authority than they had once been. Social mobility had been increased greatly. New motivations and ambitions challenged the old social norms that were no longer able to provide the psychological and material security they once had. At the same time, these newly broadened horizons, and the new motivational forces within each of the cultural traditions, brought different primordial identities and loyalties into closer, more frequent, contact—and conflict. As the national revolution and a growing national consciousness imposed themselves upon local social structures, the primordial conflicts became more intense.

In this sense, primordial identity, especially ethnic, gave great impetus to the revolution in East Sumatra. It provided a frame of reference against which national identity was interpreted and given meaning. For those involved in the civil wars of 1947 and 1948, the very strength of their national consciousness contributed significantly to the conditions making for internecine conflict. Thus, primordial identity and national consciousness together operated as mutually reinforcing factors. As Donald Emmerson has pointed out, "Statemaking raised choices between alternatives in which different groups had stakes; creating unity meant confronting disunity." And the resulting dislocation "required some reaffirmation of cultural identity to render the chaos interpretable."[56]

The stimulus provided to primordial conflicts by the events of the revolution became a dominating feature of the postindependence North Sumatra. On the other hand, by mid-1950 the nation, the unitary Republic, had become a reality firmly rooted in the collective consciousness of all communities.

The revolution brought important changes to village life in the region. The evolutionary process of change that village societies had undergone since the 1870s were dramatically speeded up. The former native states vanished as administrative entities, absorbed within a national bureaucratic system. Local adat councils and law courts were in some cases disbanded. Most were subsumed within new institutions asserting superior legitimacy based upon an Indonesian nationalist identity.[57] Tradition and kinship, while not ceasing to be important in the exercise of political authority, functioned also as structures of meaning in the interpretation of a new national identity.

The old social order in East Sumatra was altered markedly between 1945 and 1950. The superiority of the aristocrats and the Malays within the colonial polity had ended. Once the social revolution had taken place, aristocratic authority rapidly declined. Not even during the NST, despite the efforts of the sultans, was its prewar eminence restored. Malay land rights and customary law were no longer given any special recognition. Tens of thousands of non-Malays (mostly

Javanese, Toba, and Karo) were farming huge areas of the former tobacco plantations. The giant prewar plantation economy was greatly attenuated. The revolution had destroyed the structural links connecting Malay ethnic and aristocratic class interests to the plantation economy built up under Dutch colonial rule since 1870. At the same time, the revolution freed the large Javanese community from the stigma of being coolies and made Javanese ethnicity a positive rather than a negative factor in the social order. After 1950, the relationship between the Republican military and the Chinese trading network linking East Sumatra with Malaya and Singapore, upon which the revolutionary warlord structure had been based, was further consolidated. Chinese control of the regional economy became considerably greater than it had been in 1942. Finally, the ethnic map of East Sumatra changed. Between 1950 and 1956, more than 250,000 people, eager for access to land and other economic rewards of the revolution, moved from northern Tapanuli into the former plantation region.[58] The Toba population of East Sumatra increased at least fourfold, making it probably the second largest ethnic community in the residency. Ethnic hostilities between Toba and non-Toba became a major feature of postrevolution politics.

By 1950, the military was established as the main political and governing institution in the region. The TNI officer corps was the new ruling elite. Being a member of the TNI meant access to status, power, and economic resources. Military control encompassed virtually the entire range of political activity and economic enterprise: the supervision of government and public administration, the maintenance of law and order, and extensive involvement in the regional economy. Political parties, the civil bureaucracy, trade unions, mass organizations, plantations, trade and commerce, finance, social welfare, public works, and transportation were all subject to military control. The military functioned as soldiers, politicians, policemen, administrators, managers, and entrepreneurs. Civilian politicians came to accept this pattern as a fact of life. Since 1950, no political organization in East Sumatra has been able to maintain influence without the patronage and protection of alliances established within the regional military command.

The pemuda had been a major revolutionary force. Most of the postrevolution military elite came out of the pemuda movement after

1945. The armed pemuda most directly challenged and helped destroy the colonial system. The large numbers of pemuda from nonelite backgrounds helped shake the rigidity of the colonial class structure. Even though many who moved into elite positions during the late 1940s and early 1950s aspired, at least in part, to the lifestyles and values of their colonial predecessors, their different experiences ensured a fundamental break with the past.

The revolution also brought important changes in relations between elites and the masses. Before 1945, the tightly controlled system of regional and local government, and the ensuing limitations on social mobility, had meant that leadership interests tended to be contained within specific levels in the social pyramid. Those in leadership positions at the middle and lower levels knew their place. After 1945, however, as upward mobility increased, leadership interests at these levels became more transitory and exploitative. With much greater opportunities for control of power and resources, community interests often became expendable in the scramble up the elite ladder. There was a greater temptation for political leaders to exploit ethnic and other communal interests as a means to personal achievement. Hence internecine violence, profiteering, and corruption became a feature of the East Sumatran revolution.[59]

The disorder and factional conflicts of the revolution were accompanied by a significant growth in the importance of corporate ties and patron-client structures within political institutions. Beyond the links provided by ethnicity and religion, group identity and the more personal patron-client relationships became important in providing social and economic security. Within the lasykars, the TNI, and political parties, strong corporate ties, based on loyalty to the organization, developed. Frequently, primordial identity, patron-client relationships, and corporate loyalties reinforced one another, as in many of the lasykars. At other times, primordial and corporate loyalties challenged each other, resulting in factional conflict. The patronage networks became basic to the Republican polity, providing important brokerage functions and institutional coherence. They acted as links in the accommodation process between the new national identities and the local/primordial ones.

The social order in 1950 in East Sumatra was vastly different from that of eight years previously. There is little question that the region had experienced a revolution. It was a revolution that had been distinctly regionally based, to the extent that much of what occurred involved the playing out of local and communal issues. But it had also been a strongly national-focused revolution. The search for the nation-state had focused attentions beyond the region. The accommodation with the nation-state had been a specifically local and regional problem.

Notes

I am indebted to the Koninklijk Instituut voor Taal-, Land- en Volkenkunde in Leiden (particularly to Frits Jaquet and Pram Soetikno) and to the School of Humanities of the Universiti Sains Malaysia for providing facilities which contributed greatly to the completion of this study.

1. During most of the revolution some Republican government leaders, notably Vice-President Hatta, tried to create three provinces—North, Central, and South Sumatra—out of the single province of Sumatra. The proposed North Sumatra province was to incorporate not only the residencies of East Sumatra and Tapanuli but also that of Aceh. Although a law creating three Sumatran provinces was passed in 1948, it was never really implemented until after the transfer of sovereignty from the Dutch, when the province of North Sumatra included only East Sumatra and Tapanuli. On the traditional and colonial structures of East Sumatra, see H. Mohammad Said, *Suatu Zaman Gelap di Deli: Koeli Kontrak Tempo Doeloe Dengan Derita dan Kemarahannya* (Medan: Waspada, 1977); Mahadi, *Sedikit "Sejarah Perkembangan Hak Suku Melayu atas Tanah di Sumatera Timur" Tahun 1800–1975* (Jakarta: Badan Pembinaan Hukum Nasional, 1978); Anthony Reid, *The Blood of the People: Revolution and the End of Traditional Rule in Northern Sumatra* (Kuala Lumpur: Oxford University Press, 1979); Karl J. Pelzer, *Planter and Peasant: Colonial Policy and the Agrarian Struggle in East Sumatra 1863–1947* (The Hague: Martinus Nijhoff/Verhandelingen van het Koninklijk Instituut voor Taal-, Land- en Volkenkunde, 1978); and Michael van Langenberg, "North Sumatra under Dutch Colonial Rule: Aspects of Structural Change" (Part One) in *Review of Indonesian and Malayan Affairs* 11, 1 (1977): 74–110, and (Part Two) in ibid., 11, 2 (1977): 45–86.

2. On the plantation economy, see The Kian Wie, *Plantation Agriculture and Export Growth: An Economic History of East Sumatra 1863–1942* (Jakarta: National Institute of Economic and Social Research, 1977).

3. See *Volkstelling* 1930 (Batavia: Departement van Economische Zaken, 1935), vol. 4.

4. Between 1920 and 1930 the population of Medan increased by 69 percent and that of Pematang Siantar by 62 percent. See figures for major towns cited in van Langenberg, "North Sumatra under Dutch Colonial Rule" (Part One), p. 110.

5. For details of the history of the prewar nationalist movement in northern Sumatra, see Said, *Suatu Zaman Gelap;* Hamka, *Kenang-Kenangan Hidup* (Kuala Lumpur: Pustaka Antara, 1966); Reid, *Blood;* William J. O'Malley, "Indonesia in the Great Depression: A Study of East Sumatra and Jogjakarta in the 1930s" (Ph.D. dissertation, Cornell University, 1977); Julia Niblett, "The Development of Nationalist Activity, 1926–1931: An East Sumatra Case Study" (B.A. thesis, University of Sydney, 1978); Karen Entwistle, "The 'Pergerakan' Movement in East Sumatra, 1938–1942" (B.A. thesis, University of Sydney, 1979); Michael van Langenberg, "National Revolution in North Sumatra: Sumatera Timur and Tapanuli, 1942–1950" (Ph.D. dissertation, University of Sydney, 1976), pp. 118–165; and Lance Castles, "The Political Life of a Sumatran Residency: Tapanuli 1915–1940" (Ph.D. dissertation, Yale University, 1972).

6. For details of the developments during the Japanese occupation, see Reid, *Blood,* ch. 5; Anthony Reid, "The Japanese and Rival Indonesian Elites: Sumatra in 1942," *Journal of Asian Studies* 35, 1 (1975): 49–61; Anthony Reid and Saya Shiraishi, "Rural Unrest in Sumatra, 1942: A Japanese Report," *Indonesia* 21 (Apr. 1976): 115–133; Tengku Lukman Sinar, "The East Coast of Sumatra Under the Japanese Heel," *Berita Kajian Sumatera/Sumatra Research Bulletin* 1, 2 (1972): 29–43; van Langenberg, "National Revolution," pp. 166–295; and Michael van Langenberg, "North Sumatra, 1942–1945: The Onset of a National Revolution," in Alfred W. McCoy, ed., *Southeast Asia Under Japanese Occupation* (New Haven: Yale Southeast Asia Monographs no. 22, 1980), pp. 33–64.

7. For biographical information on Hasan, Amir, and Abas, see Reid, *Blood,* pp. 144–145, and van Langenberg, "National Revolution," pp. 241–242 and 247–248.

8. See Reid, *Blood,* pp. 79–81, and van Langenberg, "National Revolution," pp. 189–215.

9. See Reid, *Blood,* pp. 81 (n. 5) and 178 (n. 18), and van Langenberg, "National Revolution," pp. 170 (n. 5) and 521 (n. 61).

10. See Reid, *Blood,* ch. 6, and van Langenberg, "National Revolution," chs. 2–4.

11. See Reid, *Blood,* pp. 155–172.

12. The events of the social revolution outlined in this chapter are given in much greater detail in Reid, *Blood,* pp. 185ff; H. Mohammad Said, "What Was the 'Social Revolution of 1946' in East Sumatra?" *Indonesia* 15 (Apr.

1973): 145–186; PRIMA (Pejuang Republik Indonesia Medan Area), Biro Sejarah, *Medan Area Mengisi Proklamasi, Perjuangan Kemerdekaan dalam Wilayah Sumatera Utara* (Medan: Badan Musyawarah PRIMA, 1976), passim; and van Langenberg, "National Revolution," pp. 426–487.

13. On these styles, see John R. W. Smail, "On the Style of the Indonesian Revolutionaries" (Paper no. 89 delivered at the International Conference on Asian History, Hong Kong, 1964).

14. An article in the nationalist journal *Radikal* 1, 3–4 (Feb. 1946), published in Kabanjahe (Tanah Karo), appealed to the pemuda to "shape your spirits to become those of a young Diponegoro, a young Teuku Umar, a young Tuanku Imam Bondjol, a young Singamangaradja."

15. Smail, "On the Style," p. 6. Generally on the need for style in this context, see Jacques Barzun, "Cultural History: A Synthesis," in Fritz Stern, ed., *The Varieties of History from Voltaire to the Present* (London: Macmillan, 1970), pp. 399–400.

16. See the description of Timur Pane in Mohammad Radjab, *Tjatatan di Sumatera* (Jakarta: Balai Pustaka, 1949), p. 69.

17. The Toba, Karo, and Simalungun lasykars, like Naga Terbang, the BHL, and Napindo Halilintar, gained a particular reputation for violence and ruthlessness.

18. Among those killed were the sultans of Kotapinang and Kualuh, the sultan of Bilah, and the Simalungun rajas of Raya, Pane, Silimakuta, Tiga Dolok, and Pematang Raya. The arrested included the sultans of Langkat, Serdang, and Asahan, the Simalungun rajas of Panai and Purba, the Karo sibayak of Lingga and Barusjahe, about thirty leading aristocrats from Asahan, more than a dozen from Langkat, and about twenty from Deli.

19. See Reid, *Blood,* chs. 8 and 9.

20. On these special land rights, see Mahadi, *Sedikit Sejarah,* and Pelzer, *Planter and Peasant.*

21. Interethnic conflicts dominated regional politics in East Sumatra and Tapanuli throughout the 1950s; see John R. W. Smail, "The Military Politics of North Sumatra December 1956–October 1957," *Indonesia* 6 (Oct. 1968): 128–187, and William R. Liddle, *Ethnicity, Party and National Integration: An Indonesian Case Study* (New Haven: Yale University Press, 1970), pp. 189–196. A major issue in these conflicts was that of ethnic land rights. See Karl J. Pelzer, "The Agrarian Conflict in East Sumatra," *Pacific Affairs* 30, 2 (1957): 157–159; and Ahmad Fauzi Ridwan, "Sekitar Perkembangan Hukum Tanah Dalam Tindjauan Masa Lampau dan Datang" (Skripsi, Universitas Sumatera Utara, 1960). That issue and the resulting interethnic tensions continue to be central to internal politics in northern Sumatra.

22. The first to emerge as a major warlord was the former Medan pick-

pocket and gang leader, Timur Pane. By mid-1946 he commanded a large armed force, built up from a pemuda street gang in Medan, controlling a fiefdom centered upon Perbaungan in Serdang. From there he controlled several plantations (mostly rubber) and a profitable trading network with Malaya via the port of Pantai Labu near Lubuk Pakam.

23. The main ports from which this trade was conducted were Langsa in southern Aceh, Bangkalan Susu in Langkat, Tanjung Balai in Asahan, and Labuhan Bilik in Labuhan Batu.

24. The most detailed account of the development of the Republican armed units is given in PRIMA, *Medan Area*.

25. See Nefis [Netherlands Forces Intelligence Service], Batavia, "Chinese Press (N.E.I.), no. 81, 1948" (Algemeen Rijksarchief, The Hague [hereafter ARA]).

26. A. H. Soomers, "Relaas over de Situatie in Zuid-Sumatra's Oostkust ('t-Asahanse) en in Tapanoeli," Medan, Sept. 21, 1948, p. 6; Hidayat, "Report on the Situation in South Sumatra's East Coast Area," Medan, Sept. 13, 1948, pp. 2–3 (ARA).

27. Soomers, "Relaas," p. 6; Hidayat, "Report," pp. 2–3; Regeringsadviseur voor Politieke Zaken op Sumatra, Medan, "Politiek Verslag van Sumatra over Augustus 1948," p. 5; Centrale Militaire Inlichtingendienst, Batavia, "Signalement no. 21, Sept. 30, 1948," pp. 2–3; Consulaat Generaal der Nederlanden, Singapore, "Rapporten, 1947" (ARA). A detailed account of trading operations between Labuhan Bilik and Singapore in 1947–1948 is given in Consulaat Generaal der Nederlanden, Singapore, "Rapport," Nov. 16, 1948, pp. 6–9. A summary of this report is given in van Langenberg, "National Revolution," pp. 952–958.

28. Mahroezzar (a younger brother of the Republic's prime minister, Sutan Sjahrir), who had become the army chief of supply and then military resident for East Sumatra in 1946, had extensive trading contacts in Penang that employed a number of former TRI officers. In 1948 a former Pesindo commander, Abu Bakar Lumbantobing, set up the Star Trading Company in Singapore. For details of these trading operations, see van Langenberg, "National Revolution," pp. 363–365, 462, 527–531, 557–560, 673–677, 732–734, and 749–752.

29. For Dutch reports attesting to the effectiveness of the guerrilla operations, see Algemene Secretarie, Wali Negara van Soematera Timoer, "Verslag v.d. Politieke en Economische Toestand in de Negara Soematera Timoer," Jan.–Apr. 1949, and Letter from Assistant Resident, Balige to Regeringsadviseur voor Politieke Zaken op Sumatra, Apr. 8, 1949 (ARA).

30. See Consulaat Generaal der Nederlanden, Singapore, "Rapporten, 1949"; "Letter from Kepala Djabatan Pabean Republik Indonesia, Sumatera

Utara, Kotaradja to Atjeh Trading Company, Penang, Aug. 10. 1949"; "Letter from Kepala Djabatan Keuangan Republik Indonesia, Sumatera Utara, Kotaradja to Indonesia Office, Penang, Jun. 28, 1949"; and "Letters from Perdagangan Masjarakat Indonesia, Penang to Indonesia Office, Penang, Sept. 13, Oct. 5 and 29, and Nov. 1, 1949"; and "Letters from Perdagangan Masjarakat Indonesia, Penang to Atjeh Trading Company, Penang, Sept. 29 and Oct. 29, 1949" (ARA). See also reports in *Free Press* (Singapore), Apr. 29, 1949, and *Straits Times,* July 6, 1949.

31. In the first three months of 1949, a major purge of radical lasykar leaders was carried out on the orders of the TNI commander, Colonel Kawilarang; see *Waspada,* Jan.–Mar. 1949.

32. On the concept of the garrison state, see Harold Lasswell, "The Garrison State Hypothesis Today," in Samuel P. Huntington, ed., *Changing Patterns of Military Politics* (New York: Free Press, 1962), pp. 51–70. For a picture of a garrison-managerial polity in North Sumatra in the 1950s, see R. Boyd Compton, "Army Smuggling, North Sumatra," *Newsletter of the Institute of Current World Affairs* (New York), July 13, 1956, and Smail, "Military Politics."

33. In May 1946, the information office of the Republican governor's office in Pematang Siantar was referring to three different Republican authorities in East Sumatra: the government and the TRI, the radical People's Front (Volksfront), and "wild and obscure groups"; see "Resident der Oostkust van Sumatra (C.O.AMACAB), Half-maandelijksch Verslag, May 1–15, 1946," p. 3 (ARA), and *Soeloeh Merdeka,* May 3, 1946.

34. For example, the Karo units led by Pajung Bangun and Selamat Ginting, the Simalungun lasykar commanded by Saragiras, Bedjo's mostly Javanese force, and the Toba unit led by Liberty Malao.

35. Pane retired to take up trading activities in Sibolga. For details of the armed clashes and the eventual peace negotiations, see Indonesia, Kementerian Penerangan, *Republik Indonesia: Propinsi Sumatera Utara* (Jakarta: n.p., n.d. [1954?]) (hereafter *Propinsi*), pp. 146–148 and 170–171; Lance Castles, "Internecine Conflict in Tapanuli," *Review of Indonesian and Malayan Affairs* 8, 1 (1974): 73–80; Kadiran, "Tjukilan sebahagian tentang data2 pengalaman dalam kisah sedjarah perdjuangan Korps Brigade Mobiel Kepolisian Republik Indonesia dalam menegakkan kemerdekaan Republik Indonesia" (typescript, Medan, 1971), pp. 32–34; and van Langenberg, "National Revolution," pp. 679–684.

36. For details of the events of the civil war and the issues involved, see Kadiran "Tjukilan," pp. 35–40; Castles, "Internecine Conflict"; *Propinsi*, pp. 174–176; van Langenberg, "National Revolution," pp. 693–724; and *Waspada,* Oct.–Nov. 1948.

37. Politicans such as Abdul Xarim, Jakub Siregar, and Saleh Umar were working closely with Timur Pane, Bedjo, Saragiras, and Pajung Bangun.

38. On Amir's defection, see Reid, *Blood*, p. 244; Said, "What Was the Social Revolution"; and van Langenberg, "National Revolution," pp. 502–503.

39. See van Langenberg, "National Revolution," pp. 593–594.

40. This assessment is based on information provided by several informants during 1969–1971.

41. See S. Woodburn Kirby, *The War Against Japan*, vol. 5 (London: H. M. Stationery Office, 1969), pp. 356–357, and *Aneka Minggu* (Medan), June 2, 1970.

42. See Reid, *Blood*, ch. 8; *Soeloeh Merdeka*, Mar. 8–12, 1946; *Kesoema Negara*, Mar. 20, 1946; Indian Division, Medan, Weekly Intelligence Summary, no. 21 (1946), p. 6; and Ministerie van Overzeese Gebiedsdelen (Minog), The Hague, "Nota inzake de politieke ontwikkeling der gebeurtenissen op Sumatra tot ultimo Mei 1946," p. 1 (ARA).

43. See Algemene Secretarie, "Wali Negara van Soematera Timoer, Verslag, Jan.–Apr. 1949"; "Letter from Assistant Resident, Balige to Rapolsum, Medan, Apr. 8, 1949"; reports from F.C.A. Delegation, Local Joint Committee, Medan, concerning "violations of ceasefire," dated Sept. 6 to Nov. 10, 1949 (appended to "letter from Nederlandse Civiele Vertegenwoordiger v.d. Plaatselijke Gemengde Commissie, Medan, to Departement van Binnenlandse Zaken, Batavia, Nov. 12, 1949"); and "Ged. Hoge Vertegenwoordiger v.d. Kroon, Soematera Timoer, Maandrapport, Sept.–Oct. 1949" (ARA).

44. The Republican organizations included the Muhammadiyah, the Taman Siswa, and such peasants' organizations as the Gaperta (Gabungan Persatuan Tani, Federated Union of Farmers). The two largest-circulation newspapers were the Medan dailies *Mimbar Umum* and *Waspada*. Other pro-Republic journals and newspapers were *Waktu* (weekly), *Pedoman* (an Islamic monthly), *Setaraf* (weekly), *Angkatan Muda* (monthly), *Pemuda Merdeka* (monthly), *Mimbar* (weekly), and *Mimbar Islam* (bimonthly). On the activities of the movement, see Regeringscommissaris voor Bestuursaangelegenheden, Medan, "Verslag betreffende de politieke en economische toestand in de Negara Soematera Timoer, Mar.–Jun. 1948" (ARA).

45. See *Waspada*, July 9, 1948.

46. See van Langenberg, "National Revolution," pp. 649–651.

47. See *Waspada*, Feb. 1950; *Waktu*, Mar. 4, 1950; "Aksi Tuntutan Rakjat Kabupaten Tanah Karo" (typescript), "Tiga Nderkat," Feb. 28, 1950; "Letter from R.R.M. Harahap, Kabanjahe, to Menteri Dalam Negeri R.I.S., Jakarta, Feb. 20, 1950"; Makmun Sumadipradja, "Perkembangan Politik di Negara Sumatera Timur," report by Ketua Panitia Negara R.I.S., Mar. 1950; and

"Tuntutan Rakjat Republikein didaerah-daerah Kab. Karo dan Serdang Hulu jang dilakukan dengan demonstrasi" (typescript, n.p., Feb. 1950).

48. By October 1945, a militant Malay youth organization, the Persatuan Anak Deli Islam (Association of the Islamic Indigenous People of Deli), originally formed by rural Malay Islamic students in 1938, had established a number of armed units in Deli to defend Malays against Republican lasykar. See Reid, *Blood,* pp. 97 and 165, and van Langenberg, "National Revolution," p. 318.

49. See "Letter from Regeringsadviseur voor Politieke Zaken op Sumatra to Lt. Gouverneur-Generaal, Batavia, Dec. 1, 1947" (ARA).

50. See Michael van Langenberg, "Class and Ethnic Conflict in Indonesia's Decolonialization Process: A Study of East Sumatra," *Indonesia* 33 (Apr. 1982): 11.

51. See *Kerakjatan,* Dec. 2, 1945; H. Mohammad Said, *Empat Belas Boelan Pendoedoekan Inggeris di Indonesia* (Medan: Berita Antara, 1946), pp. 121–122; "26th Indian Division, Medan, Weekly Intelligence Summary," no. 12 (1945), p. 2, and no. 15 (1945), p. 2; and Resident der Oostkust van Sumatra (C.O. AMACAB), "Half-maandelijksch Verslag, Jan. 1–15, 1946," p. 6 (ARA).

52. See *Kerakjatan,* Dec. 18 and 21, 1945.

53. By September 1947, this security force had a strength of about 1,000, made up of fifteen operational units. Letter from Territoriaal tevens Troepcommandant "Z" Brigade, Medan, to Commandant het Leger, Batavia, Sept. 16, 1947 (Archives of the Ministerie van Defensie, The Hague).

54. *New China Times,* July 23–24, 1947.

55. On the history of the NST and its internal structure, see van Langenberg, "Class and Ethnic Conflict."

56. Donald K. Emmerson, "Thoughts on 'Remembered History' as a Subject of Study, with Reference to Indonesia's Revolution," *Review of Indonesian and Malayan Affairs* 8, 1 (1974): 5 and 6.

57. See Daniel Lev, "Judicial Unification in Post-Colonial Indonesia," *Indonesia* 16 (1973): 16–18.

58. See Clark E. Cunningham, *Postwar Migrations of the Toba Bataks to East Sumatra* (New Haven: Yale Southeast Asia Studies, Cultural Report Series no. 5, 1958).

59. See, for example, some of the contemporary descriptions recorded by the journalist Mohammad Radjab in his *Tjatatan di Sumatera.*

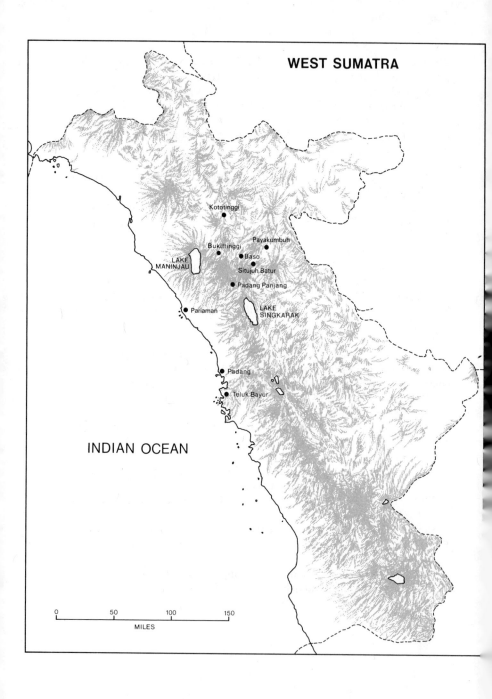

WEST SUMATRA

Kototinggi

Payakumbuh

Bukittinggi

Baso

Situjuh Batur

LAKE
MANINJAU

Padang Panjang

LAKE
SINGKARAK

Pariaman

Padang

Teluk Bayur

INDIAN OCEAN

0   50   100   150

MILES

WEST SUMATRA:
OUTPOST OF THE REPUBLIC

Audrey R. Kahin

The home of nearly three million Minangkabau—the largest ethnic group outside Java—West Sumatra had an importance to the Indonesian revolution that was primarily symbolic. No major military battles were fought in the region, but it was always a political center staunch in opposition to compromise with the Dutch. Following the first "police action" of July 1947, its capital, Bukittinggi, became capital of all Sumatra, and until January 1948, Vice-President Mohammad Hatta headed the Republic on Sumatra there while President Sukarno led it on Java. After the second "police action" of December 1948, when Dutch forces occupied Yogyakarta and arrested the central Republican leaders, it was in West Sumatra that the Emergency Government of the Republic of Indonesia was proclaimed. Advantaged by their region's minimal economic importance to the Dutch and its mountainous terrain that hampered foreign occupation, local revolutionaries created a state with many unique Minangkabau characteristics but also an unshakeable loyalty to the central leadership of the Republic.

The Nationalist Movement in West Sumatra

In combatting Dutch efforts to reimpose their rule, the people of West Sumatra were strengthened by certain underlying characteristics of their society. Of fundamental importance was the autonomy traditionally enjoyed by the region's more than five hundred *nagari* (extended villages) and the ethnic homogeneity of its people. A social structure with fewer socioeconomic inequalities than most other parts of the archipelago also aided its cohesion in facing the Dutch. Less directly, the Minangkabau were also helped by their long experience in resolving such sharp contradictions within their community as that between the strong Islamic beliefs of most of the people and the matrilineal *adat* (customary law) that ordered the inheritance and social stratification of the society.[1] The ideal in which these elements could come together harmoniously was expressed in a popular local saying: "Adat is led by the *penghulu* [adat heads of the extended family], religion by the *ulama* [Islamic scholars], the government by the intellectuals, and all three entwine together to form one."[2]

The underlying tensions of this complex society were mitigated by the large-scale migration *(merantau)* of young men from their home villages to seek knowledge and wealth outside their communities.[3] By the early years of this century, this migration had resulted in sizeable concentrations of Minangkabau in the centers of learning, religion, and trade throughout the archipelago and had brought to their home area a more direct consciousness of regions of Indonesia outside West Sumatra.

The Dutch viewed the religious and matrilineal components of Minangkabau society as fundamentally incompatible. From the early 1830s, when they extended their control to the upland areas by defeating the Islamic fundamentalist movement, the Padri,[4] they were suspicious of the religious elements in West Sumatra. Accordingly, in governing the region they strengthened and built on the base of the adat authorities, isolating the ulama outside the colonial administration. Dutch hostility to Islamic forces was increased by the strong support that local uprisings against colonial rule always attracted on the basis of religious appeals.[5]

In contrast to most of the rest of Indonesia, from early in this century West Sumatra enjoyed a broad second track of high quality, locally financed education alongside the modest government facilities. Established by modernist ulama, these private religious schools were inextricably linked to the development of the nationalist movement in the region. Financed largely by Minangkabau merchants, the modernist schools, known after 1918 as the Sumatra Thawalib, differed from the traditional *surau* (Moslem houses of prayer and education) in their innovative teaching methods, their introduction of secular subjects into the curriculum, and in the nature of their religious instruction, which emphasized the individual mind and judgment rather than mere acceptance of traditional Islamic teachings. Although the first generation of modernists restricted observance of these principles to religious matters, their students saw no reason to do so and sought to reconcile Islamic beliefs with anticolonial nationalism and socialist thought. Many were attracted to communism. The disputes between the first generation of modernists and their pupils over politicization of the schools split the Sumatra Thawalib in the early 1920s,[6] with many of the students eventually participating in the Communist-led uprisings that broke out in West Sumatra in January 1927.[7] When these were suppressed by the Dutch, there was, however, a resurgence of religious-led nationalist activity in the region.

The major vehicle for this new movement was Permi (Persatuan Muslimin Indonesia, Moslem Union of Indonesia),[8] a locally rooted political party founded in 1930 by Thawalib graduates and soon joined and led by ulama recently returned from their studies in Cairo. Permi leaders embraced Islam and nationalism as equally important elements in the anti-Dutch struggle, contending that religion could not be separated from the political movement.[9] Their stance was opposed not only by the older modernist ulama but also by the major nationalist parties based in Jakarta. It was also challenged by one of the most prominent Minangkabau on the national scene, Mohammad Hatta, who, although himself a devout Moslem, strongly believed that religion should be separated from politics. When he visited his home region in 1933 on returning from studies in the Netherlands, he founded there a branch of his party PNI Baru (New PNI), and appointed Chatib Suleiman, a young teacher with close ties to both the trading community and religious schools, to head it.[10]

When the colonial government cracked down on nationalist activity throughout Indonesia in 1933, they arrested many Permi members including its top leaders together with the foremost leaders of the other radical religious party in West Sumatra, the PSII (Indonesian Islamic Union Party), but not those of the more secular PNI Baru.[11] Dutch repression eventually forced Permi to dissolve, but throughout the 1930s teachers in the Thawalib schools, the Islamic colleges, and youth organizations still instructed their pupils in the same combination of Islamic and nationalist ideals that had characterized Permi. As a former student recalls the anticolonial activity in the schools during these years:

> There were demonstrations two or three times a year, against the Wild Schools ordinance and whenever the teachers were arrested. . . . The teachers went to jail, perhaps for a week or two, then they came back. Someone else would take their place teaching school. Then they would be arrested. If the schools were shut down another school would open. . . . When they banned the schools we responded with demonstrations.[12]

In the late 1930s, Jakarta-based nationalist parties that were willing to cooperate with the Dutch gained no great following in West Sumatra; but as Dutch rule drew to a close, former Permi members and competing religious and secular political and adat organizations joined together on a number of occasions, usually in response to Dutch moves threatening either the religious or the adat traditions of the region.[13] Such rapprochements were possible in part because party ideologies had generally been superimposed on a shared acceptance of basic Islamic and adat principles, with members often belonging to more than one party and differences between them frequently a question more of priority and personality than of basic political ideology.

Japanese Occupation

During the Japanese occupation, the 25th Army governed Sumatra first from Singapore and then, beginning in April 1943, from new headquarters in Bukittinggi. In establishing their government apparatus in West Sumatra, as in other parts of the island, they retained in their previous administrative positions the Indonesian officials who had been trained and appointed by the Dutch. No strong anti-Japanese movements ever developed in West Sumatra, and widespread resentment against their rule became evident only during the last year of their occupation, when Sumatra was virtually cut off from outside supplies and Japanese economic and manpower demands became nearly intolerable.[14] On the eve of the Japanese invasion, the colonial authorities transferred Sukarno from his exile in Bengkulu to Padang, and when the area first came under Japanese control, he acted as intermediary between Minangkabau groups and the Japanese military commanders until his return to Java. His example of cooperation probably influenced the attitude of the local nationalists toward their new rulers.

In West Sumatra, as in other regions of Indonesia, until they had consolidated their control the Japanese tolerated nationalist activities. And even after the first few weeks of leniency had passed, the local people were largely shielded from many of the harsher Japanese policies by Yano Kenzo,[15] who arrived in August 1942 to take up his appointment as governor of Padang. Something of a maverick among the Japanese governors, Yano was fascinated by Minangkabau culture and from his earliest days in office encouraged the establishment of adat study groups, which he was soon using as advisory councils. He expanded membership of these bodies to include religious and intellectual as well as adat representatives.[16] Two of Yano's closest Indonesian advisers were Mohammad Sjafei, a respected nonpolitical educator,[17] and Chatib Suleiman, the former PNI Baru leader, who had been arrested by the Dutch in March 1942 for organizing antigovernment demonstrations and later freed by the invading Japanese forces.[18] With Chatib Suleiman as his deputy, Mohammad Sjafei became head first of the governor's informal advisory body and then of the provincial advisory council (Shū sangikai) established in November 1943, and its successor Hōkōkai, which had local offices throughout the region.[19] In May 1945 the Japanese appointed Sjafei chairman of the new All-Sumatra Advisory Council.

Governor Yano and his advisers were influential in determining the local character and organization of the Sumatran Giyūgun, the paramilitary forces established by the Japanese in late September 1943. Yano himself publicly proclaimed that this army was to become an instrument for achieving Indonesian independence.[20] Chatib Suleiman was appointed to head the Giyūgun's sponsoring committee, which later became its support organization.[21] He and his colleagues were responsible for selecting recruits for officer training and traveled to villages throughout the region to encourage local leaders, ulama and penghulu, to enroll their followers in their volunteer army.[22] The Giyūgun support organization was later expanded to include a women's branch, and it had offices in villages and towns throughout West Sumatra, which raised food and supplies for the military units, helping their families and acting as liaison between military and civilian leaders.[23]

The Giyūgun forces were trained by Japanese instructors, but most of the soldiers had local Indonesians as their immediate superiors. The first officer trainees were drawn from the ranks of prewar nationalists, particularly from the Moslem community. Most important were Dahlan Djambek, son of the modernist ulama, Syekh Djamil Djambek;[24] Sjarief Usman, who was also the son of an ulama and had a record of anti-Dutch activities through most of the 1930s;[25] Dahlan Ibrahim, likewise from a strongly Islamic family, and himself a religious teacher;[26] and Ismael Lengah, Western educated and without close ties with the Moslem leaders, who had taught in the technical school in Padang.[27] These four officers became the core leadership of the Republican postindependence army in West Sumatra.[28] In contrast to the situation in most other areas, the Giyūgun was the only paramilitary force the Japanese promoted in the region. With its reliance on a network of village support groups to which adat, religious, and secular leaders belonged, it provided territorial links and bases of understanding that were to be important in the subsequent struggle.

The Character of the Revolution in West Sumatra

The declaration of independence in 1945 elicited an immediate response in West Sumatra. The telegraph and telephone offices in Padang and Bukittinggi apparently received news of the proclamation on August 17 from Indonesian friends employed in the Japanese news agency on Java;[29] copies were duplicated and distributed to most of the province's main towns within two or three days. Almost immediately afterwards, Ismael Lengah set up the first of the Republican associations in Padang, the BPPI (Balai Penerangan Pemuda Indonesia, Indonesian Youth Information Office). In Bukittinggi before the end of August, Minangkabau youths returning from Java established a P[R]I (Pemuda [Republik] Indonesia, [Republic of] Indonesian Youth), patterned on the Java-based youth association. Dahlan Djambek in

Bukittinggi and Ismael Lengah in Padang organized Giyūgun officers and soldiers into the BKR (Badan Keamanan Rakyat, People's Security Organization),[30] that was to form the nucleus of the Republican army. On August 27, the Japanese-sponsored Hōkōkai met and changed its name to the West Sumatra KNI (Indonesian National Committee). On August 29, the closing day of the KNI's first session, its head, Mohammad Sjafei, officially welcomed the independence proclamation on behalf of the Indonesian people on Sumatra. On September 1, after consulting with the Japanese authorities, the KNI elected Sjafei as the first Republican resident of West Sumatra.

The hiatus between the Japanese surrender of mid-August and the first British landings nearly two months later gave the Republicans an opportunity to establish their authority and the viability of their administration in a way that the Dutch were never able to counter effectively. British forces, accompanied by Dutch officials, did not land in Padang until October 10; a small contingent was also stationed in Bukittinggi until early December, when all British forces were consolidated in Padang to avoid the danger that the Republicans might sever their communications lines. Until their departure in December 1946, the British controlled no more than parts of the coastal town, with convoys keeping open the road to Tabing airport three miles to the north and the seaport of Emmahaven (Teluk Bayur) some five miles to the south.

The character of the revolution in West Sumatra was always influenced by the limited territorial control exerted by outside powers. There being no important local military, economic, or strategic objectives, the Dutch were unwilling, when they took over from the British in late 1946, to devote the amount of manpower and resources that would have been necessary if they were to regain effective control of the region. The first "police action" of July 1947 expanded Dutch territorial governance only to the boundaries of the narrow coastal plain, and it was not until the second attack, in December 1948, that an attempt was made to occupy the vast highland areas and establish footholds in all the major towns from which to conduct patrols and try to reimpose their authority over the countryside.

As in many of the other regions, particularly during the early days of the revolution, the young people *(pemuda)* were the spur and spearhead of the struggle, both urging their more cautious elders on to decisive, irrevocable action and being their instrument in carrying out such action. In contrast with most parts of Indonesia, however, in West Sumatra the political consciousness of the pemuda had been aroused earlier, well before the closing years of the Japanese occupation, because of the character of prewar education there. Most of these pemuda had received at least part of their education in the 1930s and early 1940s in the private religious schools. Even those who had only attended government schools up to the highest available level in West Sumatra—the MULO (junior high school)—had usually belonged to a nationalist youth organization, such as the Hizbul Wathan of the Muhammadiyah (a modernist Islamic association). They had been aware from their earliest years of the religious and nationalist aspirations of their teachers and fellow students, for it was the issue of the schools and the nature of the education offered there that was so frequently the trigger for protests and demonstrations against the Dutch. The young people may have received their first military training from the Japanese, but the political side of their army training was generally conducted by Indonesians, so that Japanese ideals and concepts were interpreted in terms of Indonesian nationalist and religious aims.

On the eve of their capitulation, the Japanese disbanded the Giyū-gun, sending the soldiers home. But in the early days of independence, top Giyūgun officers and political leaders instructed their subordinates to organize the young people in their villages into paramilitary groups and *lasykar* (militias) to defend the Republic. Throughout the revolution, military and political leaders consciously tried to prevent the establishment of independent youth bands. Young men with arms or military training were encouraged to remain either under the jurisdiction of the official army or political party structure or in their home villages, where they were subject to the restraints imposed by family, neighbors, and traditional and religious leaders. The early avowedly pemuda organizations, the BPPI and the PRI were, therefore, ephemeral, being replaced by the TRI (Army of the Indonesian Republic), the lasykars of the political parties, and later the security organizations in the villages. Never developing into autonomous supralocal groups bound by generational unity, the pemuda in West Sumatra remained rooted in their own localities. Rather than forming independent forces, they became internal pressure groups for more radical action within the army, the political lasykars, and the villages themselves.

Throughout the first year of the revolution, when West Sumatra, like other regions of Indonesia, was rocked by violence and rapid change, the KNI, in which all major contending groups and individuals had a place, was a major stabilizing force. Drawn largely from the Hōkōkai, most KNI members were initially territorial or functional group representatives.[31] With the establishment from November 1945 of political parties,[32] however, party allegiances began to play a more important role in KNI deliberations. In every important crisis, particularly during the first two years of independence, the KNI provided a forum for airing, and sometimes resolving, disagreements. Similar bodies existed in all Republican-controlled residencies of Indonesia, but in West Sumatra the institution was particularly strong, probably because of the traditional emphasis in Minangkabau government on consensus democracy.[33] Until June 1946, when a Regional Defense Council was established,[34] the KNI's executive council governed, together with the resident, as the executive body of the regional government.

Although the consultative character of Minangkabau governance worked well in maintaining societal equilibrium and preventing disturbances from tearing the social order apart, such a system was not designed for rapid and decisive action. For this, a strong leader with an understanding of local political dynamics was needed to guide and shape KNI actions. In the closing months of 1945, no one among the residency leadership was able or willing to perform this role. During the final period of the occupation, when Japanese economic and physical demands had weighed most heavily on the local people, Chatib Suleiman's prominence aroused popular resentment against him;[35] this reaction probably made him reluctant to attempt to exert any decisive leadership in the immediate postindependence period. The first strong resident, Mr. St. Mohammad Rasjid, did not assume the post until July 1946, nearly a year after the independence declaration. Once he was firmly in place, the autonomous influence of the KNI soon declined.

Another stabilizing factor, which helped initially to prevent local policy disagreement from erupting into large-scale internal dissension and later to avoid schisms that could be exploited by the Dutch, was the disproportionate Minangkabau representation in the highest levels of the Republic's central leadership on Java. In addition to Vice-President Hatta, national leaders who came from the Minangkabau included: the charismatic nationalist-Communist Tan Malaka, who established on Java the Persatuan Perjuangan (Struggle Union), the first major group to offer radical opposition to the policy of negotiation with the Dutch, and who had a large following among both civilian and military leaders in West Sumatra; Mohammad Yamin, allied to Tan Malaka in the Persatuan Perjuangan but also close to Sukarno; the cosmopolitan Westernized socialist, Sutan Sjahrir, head of the Socialist party and twice prime minister; Mr. Asaat, chairman of the working committee of the central KNI; and two of the principal Western-educated Islamic leaders, Haji Agus Salim, minister of foreign affairs, and Mohammad Natsir, minister of information and a leader of the powerful Masyumi (Council of Indonesian Moslems) party.[36] The presence of so many Minangkabau among the Republic's national leaders gave the local people a greater sense of identification with the center, for despite the wide spectrum of political ideas and ideologies these leaders embraced, all were Republican nationalists. As the Dutch resident in West Sumatra recognized, shortly before the transfer of sovereignty: "People don't forget that the really big figures in Djokja [Yogyakarta] such as Hatta, Soetan Sjahrir, and Hadji Agoes Salim are Minangs, and that the Djokja government can with almost as much justice be called a Minangkabau government."[37]

The long-term migration of Western-educated Minangkabau to the administrative capital on Java was one of the factors ensuring that most of the top Republican leaders in West Sumatra itself were not Western-educated. Another was the fact that those Minangkabau who had had advanced Western education but had not migrated to Java had usually been part of the colonial administration; they therefore found it hard even to retain the positions they held at the beginning of the revolution.

The group that dominated the leadership in West Sumatra from the middle of 1946 onward consisted mostly of men who had been educated locally, often in religious schools, at least at the secondary and tertiary levels. Many of them had been active in the prewar trading, financial, and private educational network that had competed with the Dutch in West Sumatra. The group was characterized by pragmatism, moderation, absolute loyalty to the Republican national leadership, and opposition to the Dutch. Few of its members were closely tied to any specific political party, either religious or secular, though they had often belonged for a while to either the PNI Baru or Permi, or both. Most of these leaders had worked together in the 1930s and during the Japanese occupation. They managed and controlled the course of the revolution in the region and stamped its character. But this moderate pragmatic leadership emerged only after a period of apparent chaos.

The Initial Year of Confusion

The first year of independence was marked in several parts of West Sumatra by small-scale local uprisings protesting economic hardship and directed against unpopular officials who had retained the posts they had held in the Dutch and Japanese periods. In addition, among local leaders disputes raged over the political and economic policies of the fledgling Republican government and the military posture it should adopt vis-à-vis the Dutch.

In the closing months of 1945, in West Sumatra as in other regions, the Republic's leaders attempted to retain the old colonial administrative apparatus, confirming officials in their previous positions under the Dutch and Japanese. By early 1946, however, the government had begun to realize the depth of bitterness toward these men[38] and that, if the Republic was to retain the support necessary for governing the region, it would be necessary to introduce popular leaders into positions of responsibility. At the same time, however, the residency leadership still felt it necessary to retain many experienced administrators in their posts, in order both to avoid alienating the whole group of Dutch-trained officials and to maintain efficiency in the day-to-day running of the administration. As Sumatra Governor Hasan said, in addressing a KNI meeting in Bukittinggi: "[if removed from their posts] the old experienced government officials will be compelled to go over to the NICA [Netherlands Indies Civil Administration]. It may be true that our young leaders have a better political training, but the facts are that the old district heads have more experience and influence. . . . If they are not respected by the youth movement, they will become disappointed and an easy prey for our enemies."[39] In broadening its popular base, the residency government observed guidelines whereby the appointment of a popular but inexperienced leader was balanced by that of a trained administrator, one being made deputy to the other. Dutch-trained officials who kept their positions at the district level and above were usually transferred to regions where they had not served as members of the Dutch or Japanese administrations.[40]

The turmoil that characterized these early months was in part the result of the general atmosphere of uncertainty throughout Indonesia about the country's future, but it also reflected the lack of effective leadership within West Sumatra itself. During the first twelve months of the revolution, four residents followed one another in rapid succession. The first, Mohammad Sjafei, was neither a politician nor an administrator. Unwilling to confront the problems raised by the Allied landings, and lacking the expertise to create an effective administrative apparatus, he handed over power at the beginning of November 1945 to Roesad Dt. Perpatih Baringek, who had been one of the highest Indonesian officials in the prewar colonial administration of West Sumatra.[41] Mounting antagonism against all officials who had served the Dutch and the Japanese led to Roesad's forced resignation in mid-March 1946. In his place the KNI elected Mohammad Djamil, a medical doctor with no political experience, whose oratory had made him popular. Social, political, and personal conflicts reached their height under Djamil, who was ultimately forced out of office at the end of June, being replaced in mid-July 1946 by the astute and well-educated lawyer, Mr. St. Mohammad Rasjid.[42]

In the meeting of March 13–15, 1946, when Djamil was elected to replace Resident Roesad, the KNI also established the Volksfront (People's Front) patterned on the Persatuan Perjuangan on Java. The local branch of the front was headed by Chatib Suleiman and Bachtaruddin, the commander of the Communist military force, Temi (Tentara Merah Indonesia, Indonesian Red Army) in West Sumatra; other leaders were drawn from the more radical political parties and from trading groups.[43] The KNI delegated many of its powers, particularly control over the West Sumatran economy, to the Volksfront, which in the following weeks clashed repeatedly with Resident Djamil over the economic measures it tried to introduce.[44]

As the Japanese units were withdrawn, and concurrent with the growth of the Volksfront, a number of local armed challenges were being posed to the authority of the government in several parts of the residency. The most powerful of these was the Baso movement, led by two ulama brothers, Raham Tuanku Nan Putih and Burhanuddin Tuanku Nan Hitam, who were long-time followers of Tan Malaka, and had reportedly reestablished a branch of his Pari (Republic of Indonesia Party) in the Baso region.[45] The community they headed controlled a large area only seven miles from Bukittinggi, with a well-armed militia, whose weapons probably came from the Japanese forces who had been regrouped in the Baso area before their evacuation from West Sumatra. Officials of the Republic accused the Baso group of establishing a counter-government, of kidnapping and murdering local officials and of conducting a campaign of terror in the area they controlled.[46]

On April 13, 1946, four days before a central government delegation headed by Minister of Defense Amir Sjarifuddin was due to arrive in Bukittinggi, Panglima (Commander) Dahlan Djambek ordered local TRI (Army of the Indonesian Republic) units to launch an attack on the strongholds of the Baso movement. In "the largest police action undertaken by the army during the physical revolution in Central Sumatra,"[47] these units crushed the movement, killing its leaders and more than a hundred of their followers. The operation, which was completed the day before the Sjarifuddin delegation reached Bukittinggi, was clearly aimed, at least in part, at demonstrating to the national leadership the ability of the local authorities to crush internal dissidence.

It may also, however, have been a warning to the leaders of the local Volksfront.[48] A month earlier, the central government in Yogyakarta had arrested the national leaders of the Persatuan Perjuangan, including Tan Malaka and Mohammad Yamin, and Amir Sjarifuddin's visit to Sumatra was in part an effort to exert central government control over Volksfront branches there, which were viewed as responsible for the most violent acts of the social revolution in East Sumatra. In West Sumatra, Sjarifuddin appears to have encouraged Resident Djamil to move more decisively against Tan Malaka's followers, for within two days of the government delegation's departure the resident arrested the Volksfront's six top local leaders.

The character of the front in West Sumatra, however, differed markedly from the Persatuan Perjuangan on Java. Of its two principal leaders, Chatib Suleiman's closest ties had always been with Sjahrir and Hatta rather than Tan Malaka, while Bachtaruddin's ties were with the PKI (Indonesian Communist Party). In contrast with its experience in other Republican-controlled territories, the front's West Sumatra branch continued to enjoy the support of the KNI, and its district and village branches formed part of the official administrative structure. Although at loggerheads with the resident, the front was generally regarded favorably in West Sumatra as a radical defender of complete independence. The arrest of its leaders, instead of solving the resident's problems, further complicated them. Local army units responded by detaining Djamil himself, and he was persuaded to release the Volksfront leaders a month after they had first been arrested. Although Djamil briefly resumed his position as resident, within a few weeks he was gently eased from the post.[49] His successor, St. Mohammad Rasjid, had close rapport with the Volksfront leaders, and although the front's importance as an organization declined over the following months, its leaders retained their positions and influence around the new resident.

During the early months of 1946, the Republican government's hold on power was precarious, leading it to realize the urgent need to strengthen further its ties with the village population by going beyond the modest administrative reforms introduced in January under Resident Roesad. There was widespread dissatisfaction in the villages over the extent to which nagari heads and councils from the Dutch time still held authority. Republican leaders believed that the loyalty of religious groups and pemuda in the villages would be strengthened if they could participate in the selection of their own nagari officials. Consequently, at its meeting of March 16–18, 1946, the residency KNI decided that elections should be held for the nagari heads' positions and for membership of representative councils to govern the nagari. The elections for these councils were held on June 25 and for nagari heads on July 10, 1946. Most candidates came from the political parties, and the major beneficiary of the elections was the Masyumi party, whose members, usually former teachers in the religious schools, largely replaced the traditional lineage heads as village leaders.[50] These elections thus marked a major shift in power at the lowest level of government.

The March 3 Affair

The election of Rasjid as resident and his informal alliance with several of the Volksfront leaders laid the basis for an effective exercise of power in the residency government; the elections for village heads and councils had a similar effect there. A discrepancy, however, was evident in the power of the Islamic parties at the two levels. The paradox of the elections was that they aligned much of the village population with the Republic while at the same time alerting the Moslem parties to the contrast between their grassroots strength and their limited influence in the upper reaches of the residency government. Although Islamic teachers and ulama had largely replaced the lower Indonesian officials of the Dutch administration, several Western-educated officials still played important roles at the residency level; and many men allied with the nonreligious parties exerted great influence in the civilian and, to a lesser extent, the military leadership.

Within the army, the Moslem parties saw their direct influence declining as the military structure was shaped to accord with national priorities. Initially, the Republican army was little more than a group of partially armed bands, usually led by men who had been trained by the Japanese but who, in the egalitarian days of the early revolution, were assigned no military ranks. In January 1946, in accordance with directions from Java, many military units came together to form Division III (Banteng), one of six Republican army divisions on Sumatra, with responsibility for West Sumatra and Riau. The Sumatra command appointed Dahlan Djambek as divisional commander. Long after that, however, there were many armed bands that remained essentially autonomous, their commanders deciding independently whether to remain that way or to ally the band with either the regular army or the newly formed political parties.

A large proportion of these armed bands were concentrated in small groups around Padang, the front line of the struggle against the Dutch throughout the first two years of the revolution. The Masyumi party's lasykar, the Hizbullah (Army of Allah), was by far the strongest and best organized of these irregular forces, and it held independent responsibility for several portions of the front line around Padang.[51] During 1946, when several of the smaller armed bands were incorporated into a battalion of the Banteng Division, no effort was made to bring either the Hizbullah or the Sabilillah (Path of Allah, a militia also affiliated with the Masyumi party) under the command of the regular forces.

Nevertheless, for at least the first year of the struggle for independence, most leaders of Islamic lasykars acknowledged the overall authority of the Banteng commanders at the front and were willing to cooperate with them. The accommodation was based chiefly on their earlier relationship with the regular officers in the Giyūgun, where both groups had received their initial military training. In the early postindependence period, Moslem Giyūgun officers headed both the local Banteng division and the Islamic lasykars.

This situation began to change in the summer of 1946, when Ismael Lengah replaced Dahlan Djambek as division commander, and many of the other top first-generation officers moved up to positions in the all-Sumatra command and ceased to have regular direct contact with the soldiers in the field. The major grievance of the lasykars was that the government channeled most supplies for the front-line forces directly to the TRI, leaving the political parties to support their own militias.[52] At the same time, however, the government was gradually arrogating to itself sole authority for collecting public contributions of food and money for the armed forces, forbidding party leaders to solicit aid from nonparty members.

Probably these complaints would not have reached crisis proportions had it not been for the leadership of Saalah J. St. Mangkuto, who had been one of the most fiery and outspokenly nationalistic of the Muhammadiyah leaders in the 1920s and 1930s.[53] St. Mangkuto felt that Masyumi support in the villages should be translated into power in the residency government. Although he himself had been appointed to a relatively high position, *bupati* (equivalent of regency head) of Solok, he was very conscious of the discrepancy between the status of the Masyumi party in West Sumatra compared with that in Aceh, an area where Islam was equally strong and where Islamic leaders and parties dominated civilian and military offices. He became spokesman and head of an antigovernment movement most of whose leaders were from the Masyumi party and lasykars. Its appeals linked the grievances of these religious groups with the general popular discontent that was felt over the compromises the Republic was making with the Dutch in the Linggajati Agreement. At a meeting of ulama from all of Sumatra, held in Padang Panjang from February 28 to March 3, 1947, disgruntled Islamic spokesmen voiced their suspicion that such Western-educated leaders as Resident Rasjid and Divisional Commander Ismael Lengah had Dutch sympathies and ways of thinking and were thus less patriotic than the Moslem leaders.

On the night of March 3, 1947, St. Mangkuto and his associates launched a coup attempt against the residency administration. Hizbullah units and several other lasykar groups and regular army units staged uprisings in several of the upland towns, and in Bukittinggi aimed to seize Rasjid and Lengah and other top officials. Although the rebels were successful in kidnapping a large number of lower officials, mostly former members of the colonial Dutch and Japanese administrations, Rasjid, Lengah, and other top leaders had been expecting trouble[54] and their guards were able to protect them. By withdrawing some of their troops from the front line around Padang, Banteng Division commanders were able to prevent the dissident Hizbullah units from even reaching the center of Bukittinggi. By the morning of March 4, it was clear that the coup attempt had failed, and intermediaries, particularly Islamic TRI officers, were trying to get the two sides to compromise.

Despite Lengah's demand that their leaders should be shot,[55] the rebels were not punished severely. The military participants were disarmed and sent home; only one of the political leaders was sent to jail for a year, the others, including St. Mangkuto, receiving at the most suspended sentences. Masyumi's national leadership launched an investigation into the causes of the revolt, which led to a direct confrontation between Lengah and both national and local Masyumi leaders. Lengah's refusal to return the confiscated weapons to the rebel Hizbullah forces, even when he was asked to do so by such national figures as Hatta and Mohammad Natsir, confirmed Moslem hostility toward him and earned him the disapproval of the vice-president. And, despite the lenient treatment they had received, some of the rebel leaders continued to harbor resentment toward the residency government. Although the bitterness engendered by the affair did not soon dissipate, it was the last serious internal challenge mounted against the local Republican government in West Sumatra.

Attempts at Consolidating the Regional Defense

As early as the end of 1946, the Banteng command had already made some efforts to bring irregular forces under its authority, but these attempts had been restricted to the weaker secular lasykars. As a consequence of the events of March 3, 1947, the residency government and the army command felt it imperative that Moslem lasykars also be brought under direct army control. Former Giyūgun officer Sjarief Usman, who had been in charge of mobilizing and coordinating the people's lasykars on Sumatra since mid-1946, was put in command of a Legiun Syahid (Legion of Martyrs) that was to be made up of armed Hizbullah, Sabilillah, and Lasymi (Lasykar Muslimat) units, and some smaller groups from the Hulubalang, Temi, and others.[56] However, as all members of the legion had to possess their own weapons, only a relatively small proportion of the total lasykar forces were able to join.[57] The legion was in existence by the end of 1947, and throughout 1948 efforts were made to amalgamate it with the Banteng Division. Battalion-size units were eventually incorporated under their own officers, but several lasykar commanders in the legion continued to refuse to subordinate themselves to the authority of the TNI.[58] Nevertheless, in West Sumatra in general, efforts to incorporate the irregular forces into the Banteng Division were more successful, and faced fewer problems, than comparable efforts in other parts of Indonesia; with the assent of party leaders, the armed lasykars were at least officially integrated into the regular army structure before the end of 1948.

Unarmed militia members were demobilized during 1947 and 1948; in addition, many regular TNI soldiers were discharged as part of the government's 1948 rationalization program. Under this program, each of the four Sumatran TNI divisions was to be reduced to a mobile brigade, which, in West Sumatra, meant that about two-thirds of the regular army was to be partially demobilized into local security forces and one-third was to stay on.[59] Vice-President Hatta worked

with the deputy-commander of the TNI, A. H. Nasution, to implement the plan on Sumatra in the face of widespread local opposition
headed by the commander-in-chief of the TNI on Sumatra, Suhardjo
Hardjowardojo, and by Ismael Lengah, who believed the program to
be suited to Java but not Sumatra. Because of their intransigence,
these two officers were removed, and an officer from West Java's Siliwangi Division, Colonel Hidayat, was appointed to head the Sumatra
command, while authority over the TNI in West Sumatra was divided
between Col. Dahlan Ibrahim and Col. Abdul Halim.[60] Although the
Sumatra TNI offered no armed opposition to the government's moves,
the local armed forces were left resentful and disorganized and in a
poor position to put up an effective defense when the Dutch launched
their second attack in December 1948. The burden of defense then fell
on other organizations in West Sumatra.

During 1947 and 1948, a network of local security, tax, and administrative organizations was established that not only did much to com-
pensate for the initial chaos within the regular army but also added a
new and important dimension to the anti-Dutch effort in West Sumatra. This was the concept of Chatib Suleiman and was based on the
support organizations for Giyūgun, which he had headed during the
Japanese period. In January 1948, People's Defense organizations
were set up in West Sumatra at residency, district, and nagari levels.
Tied at the residency level to the Regional Defense Council, they were
headed at all levels by civilians, with the highest ranking military or
police officer as deputy head. These organizations were responsible
for coordinating all defense efforts in the region. At the village level
the People's Defense organizations were given authority over the local
militia, established a year earlier.[61] All pemuda between the ages of
seventeen and thirty-five who were not members of the armed forces
were required to join this village militia, called the BPNK (Badan
Pengawal Nagari dan Kota, Body for Guarding the Villages and
Towns). Although they were not armed, members of these bodies
received basic military training from local army units. In the wake of
the incorporation of the armed lasykars into the TNI and the moves to
rationalize the TNI itself, the BPNK provided a place where demobilized regular and irregular forces could still play an active role in the
defense of their home regions. Soon these village-based militias became the most potent security force in the region. Their leaders, offi-

cially subject to civilian local authorities,[62] were in no position, however, to build up the type of warlord fiefdoms that emerged in other regions of Sumatra.

The Second Dutch Attack

The Dutch launched their second major attack against Republican forces in West Sumatra in the early hours of December 19, 1948, at the same time as their assault on Yogyakarta. Present in Bukittinggi at the time was Sjafruddin Prawiranegara, the Republic's minister of economic affairs, who had been asked by Hatta to begin planning an emergency government on Sumatra in case the Dutch should succeed in occupying the Republican capital on Java. The difficulty of the terrain prevented the Dutch forces from occupying Bukittinggi until December 22, and during this two-day period of grace, all the Republican leaders had the opportunity to retreat from the town, along with much of its population. On December 22, in a village outside Payakumbuh, about thirty miles from Bukittinggi, Sjafruddin proclaimed the establishment of the Emergency Government of the Republic of Indonesia with himself at its head.

By early January 1949, Dutch forces had occupied most of the major towns in the heartland of West Sumatra. The attack shattered the remaining structure of the regular army there, and many of its units, being taken by surprise and lacking firm leadership, scattered in disarray. In most regions, the TNI was not able to begin operating effectively again until about March 1949. With the Republic's front-line defenses crumbling in the face of the Dutch assault, there was a period of panic at all levels of government, described vividly in an instruction from Military Governor Rasjid[63] on January 11, 1949:

> Most of our administrative officials did not know where to go; the lower levels of the administration, unable yet to stand on their own feet, were like chickens that had lost their mother; some of the people's leaders were frantic; and the army itself, if we are willing to face up to it frankly, was in a state of chaos. The psychological effect of the Dutch attack was temporarily tremendous. Most of all, those villages that had not previously been subject to air attack were in a state of panic.[64]

The instruction concluded, however, that "now gradually we are beginning to rebuild our government and army."

The first major step in this direction, a meeting at the village of Situjuh Batur to discuss reorganization of the administration and security forces in West Sumatra, resulted in disaster. Alerted by a spy, Dutch forces encircled and attacked the group, killing sixty-nine of them, including Chatib Suleiman, the architect of the security network the Republicans were trying to reestablish.[65] Despite this setback, Republican leaders continued their attempt to erect a defense barrier for the region, utilizing the People's Defense organizations, particularly in the villages, and the BPNK militias.[66] Their aim was to block Dutch penetration of the villages and thus prevent any substantial number of villagers from shifting their allegiance from the Republic. The defense measures taken were not only military. An economic program was introduced covering a universal 10 percent tax in cash or kind, increased food production and, to exclude the Dutch-occupied towns from the regional economy, the establishment of secure markets away from Dutch-controlled areas.[67]

By March 1949 these efforts were yielding results. The Dutch resident described the situation in West Sumatra as "strongly reminiscent of the Netherlands under German occupation," and, according to him, the village militias were "present everywhere," and "the struggle stretching from the front to the kampung" was "a true reflection of the ideas Tan Malaka developed in his brochure 'Sang Guerilla dan Gerpolek' where he sought to emphasize the Murba—the common people." As a result, "the Netherlands is only strong enough to hold the occupied towns; outside of these, the TNI, BPNK and guerrillas rule."[68]

Even within the occupied towns, Dutch efforts to detach groups and individuals from the Republic failed. Prior to December 1948, Dutch-sponsored organizations which advocated formation of a Minangkabau state had to restrict their activities to the area controlled by the Dutch around Padang.[69] Most leaders of these organizations were former minor Indonesian officials in the prewar colonial administration.[70] The second "police action" dramatically enlarged the scope for the Dutch to promote such organizations, and they mounted a major drive to win support for a Minangkabau state that could become a component of the Dutch-sponsored Federal Consultative Assembly.

Competition between the Netherlands and the Republic in the towns differed from the struggle in the countryside in that it took place in areas actually administered by the Dutch and was conducted by both sides more through persuasion than through physical violence.[71] The basic Dutch assumption was that the people would accept only leaders whose authority rested on traditional adat qualifications and that the Minangkabau people resented the potential Javanese dominance of the Republic. From the Dutch point of view, therefore, the most welcome, as well as the most viable, solution for West Sumatra would be a Sumatran federation in which a Minangkabau autonomous territory could play a large role and the tie with Java would be more symbolic than real.[72] This argument disregarded the loyalty of the Minangkabau population to the Republic's national leadership, Minangkabau representation at the center, and the extent to which local adat authoritites had been discredited by their close links to the colonial administration.

An underground Republican shadow government within the town combatted the move for a Minangkabau state. At the same time, an openly pro-Republican urban political movement presented counterarguments that were apparently more persuasive than those of Dutch supporters.[73] At both levels Dutch efforts at consolidation of control were impeded, even within the larger towns where most of their forces were concentrated.

Communications routes between the towns remained tenuous, and within as well as outside the urban areas Dutch forces continued to encounter persistent small-scale guerrilla opposition. Despite the ease of their advance and their few casualties they were unable to consolidate control of the occupied areas. The traditional importance of the autonomous village in Minangkabau governance meant that the shock and disarray of the early weeks of the attack did not for long cripple the functioning of the Republic's resistance. So long as the military government in Kototinggi was able to issue general guidelines, the method of their implementation could be decided at the local level. Through the BPNK and the People's Defense organizations, opposition to the enemy was so effectively decentralized that there were no critical targets against which the Dutch could focus efforts to regain military and political control.

The course and consequences of the Roem–van Royen discussions of April 1949 between representatives of the Republic and the Netherlands initially aroused dismay in West Sumatra, particularly among the armed forces and the leaders of the Emergency Government. The Republic's leaders were again thought to be ignoring the strong position of the guerrilla forces throughout Sumatra and going too far in their compromises with the Dutch.[74] During the latter half of 1949, however, the psychological atmosphere in the region changed dramatically. Although small-scale military skirmishes continued after the ceasefire order of mid-August, the principal focus of attention shifted to the emerging domestic postrevolutionary situation in Indonesia. The dissatisfaction among elements of the armed forces and some of the political parties with the Republic's choice of the path of diplomacy and accommodation was for the time overshadowed by the general feeling of relief within the region that after a decade of hardship peace was finally at hand.

Conclusion and Epilogue

The need to accommodate peacefully conflicting adat and religious components in Minangkabau society had led in the closing decade of colonial rule to the emergence of an important element identified with neither the adat nor religious groups but with ties to and an understanding of both. Many of the traders and teachers who became leaders at the residency and village level during the revolution were such people—not belonging exclusively to one group but recognizing the dangers of alienating either. The effort at accommodation was made easier in that the segments of the society were not mutually exclusive; a penghulu was often also an ulama, and with sufficient education to be regarded as an intellectual.

The type of struggle conducted in West Sumatra was well suited to the strengths of Minangkabau society. As there was little open warfare, the principal need was to maintain solidarity in the face of hardships and attempts at subversion directed from outside. Competition between component groups in the society could be subordinated to the task of confronting the external threat posed by the Netherlands forces, while at the same time this impingement of Dutch power could be blamed for the hardships and injustices the people were experiencing. Within that framework, cleavages and tensions could be largely contained.

Nevertheless, the seeds for future conflict both within the society and against the center were sown during these years, and occasionally sprang up in such upheavals as that at Baso and the March 3 affair. They were also perceptible in the tension and dissatisfaction within the armed forces engendered by the policies being imposed by the army's central command. At the local level there was also resentment among the more conservative adat groups because so many of the positions of leadership in the villages had passed from their hands into those of teachers, traders, and ulama.

Having fought a local struggle within a national context, where they saw ultimate success as being achieved more in spite of the actions of the central government than because of them, the Minangkabau people emerged with unrealistic expectations for the future of their region within an independent Indonesia. Being only part of the struggle and seeing so many government positions at the center in the hands of leaders from West Sumatra, they expected that in postrevolutionary Indonesia their region would retain considerable self-direction and administrative autonomy. But this perception underestimated the prejudices against decentralization among the national leaders, whatever their own region of origin, that resulted largely from Dutch attempts throughout the 1945–1949 period to win adherents through exploiting interethnic antagonisms. Moreover, many of the factors that seemed to augur well for West Sumatra's retention of a favored place in this new Indonesian nation now in fact worked against it. Over the previous years, it had demonstrated its loyalty to the national government, and this, together with its disproportionate participation in the center's leadership, made the Jakarta government even less circumspect in its political and military demands on the region. With national independence finally accomplished, local dissatisfaction at the center's policies emerged almost immediately. Led by disgruntled military leaders, efforts to achieve greater autonomy for West Sumatra gained a growing following until eventually a region that had been steadfastly loyal throughout the anticolonial struggle went into open rebellion against the central leadership seven years later.

Notes

I am particularly grateful to Fulbright-Hays, which supported my original research; the Rockefeller Foundation's Villa Serbelloni at Bellagio, where I was able to do some of the writing; the Social Science Research Council for their support in 1981; and the Institute of Southeast Asian Studies in Singapore, where I completed the final work. In Indonesia my special thanks go to Dr. Taufik Abdullah and to Drs. Azmi, Drs. Buchari Nurdin, Dr. Imran Manan, and Fatimah Enar of the I.K.I.P., Padang, as well as to the many informants who gave so generously of their time and memories.

1. The best short analysis of these contradictions appears in Taufik Abdullah, "Adat and Islam: An Examination of Conflict in Minangkabau," *Indonesia* 2 (Oct. 1966): 1–24.

2. This saying is known as the "Tali Tigo Sapilin." Interview with H. A. K. Dt. Gunung Hijau, Padang, July 9, 1976.

3. On the tradition of *merantau,* see Taufik Abdullah, "Modernization in the Minangkabau World," in Claire Holt et al., eds., *Culture and Politics in Indonesia* (Ithaca: Cornell University Press, 1972), pp. 179–245, and Tsuyoshi Kato, *Matriliny and Migration* (Ithaca: Cornell University Press, 1982).

4. On the Padri, see in particular Christine Dobbin, *Islamic Revivalism in a Changing Peasant Economy: Central Sumatra, 1784–1847* (London and Malmö: Curzon Press, 1983). See also Muhammad Radjab, *Perang Paderi di Sumatera Barat 1803–1838* (Jakarta: Kementerian P.P. & K., 1954).

5. This was true in 1897, in 1908, and in 1927, although the uprisings did not necessarily have religious aims. On 1897 and 1908, see Akira Oki, "Social Change in the West Sumatran Village: 1908–1945" (Ph.D. dissertation, Australian National University, 1977), pp. 71–73 and 75–82; on the 1927 uprisings, see in particular Harry J. Benda and Ruth T. McVey, *The Communist Uprisings of 1926–1927 in Indonesia: Key Documents* (Ithaca: Cornell Modern Indonesia Project, 1960).

6. Hamka (Haji A. Malik Karim Amrullah) presents the view of the older generation on this split in his biography of his father, *Ajahku* (Jakarta: Djajamurni, 1967).

7. See Benda and McVey, *Communist Uprisings.*

8. On the growth and decline of Permi, see Taufik Abdullah, *Schools and Politics: The Kaum Muda Movement in West Sumatra 1927–1933* (Ithaca: Cornell Modern Indonesia Project, 1971), pp. 157–163, 172–177, 202–206, and 224–225.

9. Statement by Muchtar Luthfi, recorded in Memories van Overgave [hereafter MvO] B. H. F. van Heuven, Dec. 31, 1934, Mailrapport [hereafter

Mr.] 254/35, dos AA 236, Algemeen Rijksarchief, The Hague [hereafter ARA].

10. The son of a trader, Chatib Suleiman was born in the village of Sumpur in 1906. When his father went bankrupt at the end of World War I, another local trader helped him attend government junior high school for two years. In the 1920s Chatib worked as a violinist in the Padang movie theater, then headed one of the youth organizations of the Diniyyah schools in Padang Panjang. In the 1930s he headed the Merapi Institute, a private religious educational institution, taught also in the Muhammadiyah school, published and wrote in various ephemeral magazines, was active in the local traders' associations, and was a founder, with Anwar St. Saidi, of the National Bank in Bukittinggi.

11. PNI Baru leaders in Jakarta, however, including its founders, Sutan Sjahrir and Mohammad Hatta, were imprisoned in February 1934. The colonial authorities arrested PSII leaders only in West Sumatra and Tapanuli, not elsewhere in Indonesia. For Resident Spits' descriptions of Permi and PSII in West Sumatra, see MvO A. I. Spits, Mr. 504/37, pp. 44–48, dos AA 236, ARA.

12. Interview with Kamaluddin Muhamed, Kuala Lumpur, Dec. 21, 1981. Born in Malaya, he had attended the Sumatra Thawalib schools from 1932 to 1935 and, after 1937, first the Islamic College in Padang and then the Islamic Training College in Payakumbuh.

13. Examples of this were the Majelis Pertahanan Islam (Islamic Defense Council) and the Badan Permusyawaratan Islam Minangkabau (Minangkabau Islamic Discussion Body), both of which were formed to protest the possible repeal of restrictions on Christian schools in Moslem areas. People belonging to the organizations included members of the PNI Baru, Permi, PKI, PSII, and also the Muhammadiyah (Mr. 1230, geh/39 and Mr. 1406 geh/39, ARA).

14. On the situation in West Sumatra during this period, see Audrey Kahin, "Struggle for Independence: West Sumatra in the Indonesian National Revolution" (Ph.D. dissertation, Cornell University, 1979), pp. 86–88.

15. Yano was the only governor on Sumatra who had held a similar position previously in Japan. He had been governor of Toyama prefecture until he was removed from his post because he objected to government policies which, in his view, violated indigenous characteristics of Toyama. Interviews with Mrs. Aminah Madjid Usman, Tokyo, Dec. 13, 1976, and Yuichi Sakamoto, Ithaca, N.Y., May 14, 1977; see also Yano Kenzo, "Saigo no kaigi" [The last conference], Sekido hyo, no. 82 (Apr. 10, 1967).

16. Kita Sumatora Sinbun, Aug. 4, 1943; interviews with Mrs. Usman.

17. The adopted son of a Minangkabau official, Mohammad Sjafei (1897–

1969) attended the Sekolah Radja in Bukittinggi from 1908 to 1914 and was a member of the Budi Utomo, and later of the Indische Partij. He founded the Indonesische Nederlandsche School (INS) in Kayu Tanam in 1926, changing its name to Indonesia Nippon School under the Japanese and to the Indonesian National School after 1945.

18. In the early days of March 1942, Chatib Suleiman tried to organize demonstrations demanding that the Dutch transfer authority to the Indonesians so that they could negotiate surrender terms with the Japanese. He and his colleagues were imprisoned in north Sumatra until the Japanese took over the jail. See Leon Salim, "Tawanan Kutatjane" (Bukittinggi, typescript, 1953), and Ribai Abu and Abudullah Suhadi, *Chatib Suleman* (Jakarta: Departemen P. dan K., 1976).

19. On the Shū sangikai, see *Kita Sumatora Sinbun*, Nov. 25, Dec. 10, 1943, and on the Hōkōkai, ibid., Dec. 16, 1944.

20. Yano claimed that he had been encouraging recruitment of a volunteer army since February 1943: "Because only the dream of independence, not money was enough to motivate the native people to fight . . . in this voluntary army recruitment campaign I freely encouraged their dream of independence." See *Sekido hyo,* no. 79 (Jan. 10, 1967), "Fostering the Indonesian Dream," and ibid., no. 17 (Jan. 10, 1966), "The First Meeting with Sukarno: Prelude to Independence."

21. Headed by Chatib Suleiman and Mohammad Sjafei, the committee included among its members Syekh Djamil Djambek, one of the original modernist ulama, and adat leader Dt. Simarajo. Interviews with Dt. Simarajo, Simabur, Batu Sangkar, Aug. 22, 1976, and Ismael Lengah, Jakarta, Apr. 17, 1976.

22. See *Kita Sumatora Sinbun,* Oct. 13, 21, and 28, and Nov. 2 and 17, 1943.

23. Ibid., Dec. 16, 1944.

24. Born in 1917, Dahlan Djambek had his initial schooling in West Sumatra but was then sent by his father to a Christian high school in Jakarta for three years. He returned to West Sumatra shortly before the Japanese invasion. He had excellent relations with the Japanese and was responsible for training the Seinendan youth forces.

25. Sjarief Usman, who was born in 1917 near Solok, graduated from a Permi religious school in Bukittinggi in 1934 and was leader of an Islamic youth group. He attended the Islamic College in Padang, was arrested twice by the Dutch, attended high school and law school in Jakarta, and returned to Padang at the outbreak of the war.

26. Dahlan Ibrahim, whose father had fought in both the 1908 and 1927 uprisings, attended the Thawalib school in Padang Panjang and then became a

religious teacher in his home village before entering the Islamic Training College in Payakumbuh.

27. Born in Padang in September 1914, Ismael Lengah was the son of a merchant. After attending elementary school in Padang, he attended technical school, first in Jakarta and then in the Netherlands, before returning to Padang in 1935. He states that he joined the Giyūgun at the personal request of Chatib Suleiman. Interview, Jakarta, Apr. 17, 1976. See also BPSIM (Badan Pemurnian Sejarah Indonesia—Minangkabau), *Sejarah Perjuangan Kemerdekaan Republik Indonesia di Minangkabau 1945-1950,* vol. 1 (Jakarta: BPSIM, 1978), p. 85.

28. Dahlan Djambek became the first commander of Division III (Banteng) of the Republican armed forces; the others commanded the division's three West Sumatra regiments. Ismael Lengah succeeded Djambek as divisional commander in August 1946, when Djambek was promoted to the Sumatra command.

29. See account of Nasrun A.S., in *Haluan* (Padang), Aug. 10, 1976.

30. In Padang, there was no clear division between the BPPI and the BKR in these early days. According to Ismael Lengah, his BPPI was to form an acceptable facade behind which military actions could be organized, and the young people joining the BPPI soon became leaders of the BKR security forces. In Bukittinggi, however, there were few ties between the youth organization of the P[R]I and Dahlan Djambek's BKR, which was established toward the end of August.

31. They included representatives of the army, police, officials, workers, cooperatives, political, adat, religious, and economic groups, women, farmers, teachers, fishermen, and youth. Detailed information, including lists of members, appears in Kementerian Penerangan, *Propinsi Sumatera Tengah* (n.p., n.d.), pp. 380–391.

32. The Communist party (PKI) was established on November 12, 1945; the PSII on November 18; the traditional religious Perti (Persatuan Tarbiah Islamiah, Islamic Education Association) on November 26; the adat MTKAAM (Majelis Tinggi Kerapatan Adat Alam Minangkabau, High Consultative Council of Adat of the Minangkabau World) on December 20; and the MIT (Majelis Islam Tinggi, High Council of Islam) on December 25. The Partai Sosialis (PS, Socialist party) was formed on January 12, 1946. See Fatimah Enar dkk, *Sumatera Barat 1945-1949* (Padang: Pemerintah Daerah Sumatera Barat, 1978), p. 72.

33. Discussion leading to consensus is a decision-making process recognized by many other societies, particularly in Indonesia, but it is institutionalized and probably implemented to a far greater extent in the Minangkabau region than in most other areas.

34. This council was headed by the resident, with the West Sumatra TRI division commander as vice chairman. Two of its members came from the KNI's executive council and two from the political parties.

35. Sjahrir sent messages urging him to distance himself from the Japanese, and some Socialist party members plotted at one stage to assassinate him. Interviews, Tamimi Usman, Kota Baru, Padang Luar, Bukittinggi, June 22, 1976; and Almunir, Padang, July 20, 1976.

36. On Java the Masyumi was set up by the Japanese on November 7, 1943, as a successor to the MIAI (Majlisul Islamil a'laa Indonesia, Islamic Council of Indonesia) of the late colonial period. The Republican Masyumi held its first congress in Yogyakarta on November 7, 1945. In West Sumatra, the MIT and Muhammadiyah fused to form the Masyumi only in early 1946.

37. "Overzicht Situatie," Padang, Sept. 12, 1949, Mr. 781/49, ARA.

38. At the beginning of October 1945, Resident Sjafei, in accordance with orders from Jakarta, had confirmed current offficials in the positions they had held under the Dutch and Japanese. They were called to Padang in mid-October to take an oath of loyalty to the new government. Several, however, had already fled their posts because they feared reprisals from the local people; a few had been killed.

39. "Politiek Verslag Sumatra over Feb. 1946," Medan, Mar. 16, 1946, Algemene Secretarie Batavia II, old. nr. 374, ARA.

40. BPSIM, *Sejarah Perjuangan,* p. 151.

41. He had been *wedana* (district head) until 1938, when the Dutch appointed him secretary of their newly formed Minangkabau Council. See ibid., p. 49.

42. Mr. M. St. Mohammad Rasjid was the son of an Indonesian official in the colonial administration. Born in Pariaman in 1911, he received government schooling up to the MULO in Padang, and then continued his studies on Java, obtaining a law degree in 1938. He practiced law for a short time in Sukabumi with Amir Sjarifuddin. The Japanese appointed him chief clerk of the high court in Jakarta until mid-1944, when he was brought back to West Sumatra with a group of trained officials who were Sumatran in origin. He became prosecutor of the high court in Padang and a member of the Hōkōkai.

43. On the membership and aims of the Volksfront, see Kahin, "Struggle for Independence," pp. 136–138.

44. Ibid., pp. 139–142. The fullest account of these events is found in Kementerian Penerangan, *Propinsi Sumatera Tengah,* pp. 112–121 and 478–482.

45. The two brothers reportedly participated in the 1927 uprising and were imprisoned by the Dutch. They had established a branch of the Pari after their release in the 1930s. For conflicting views on the nature of the Baso move-

ment, see Djamaluddin Tamin, "Sambutan pada peringatan 19 tahun hilang-
nja Tan Malaka," (Jakarta, 1968, Mimeographed), pp. 12–14; and BPSIM,
Sejarah Perjuangan, pp. 354–362.

46. Officials reportedly murdered at Baso included Landjumin Dt. Tem-
unggung, a high official under the Dutch, particularly at the time of the 1927
uprising, and the district head of Suliki and his assistant. Interviews with
Agussalim, Solok, July 17, 1976; Nasrun A.S., Jakarta, Oct. 4, 1976; and
Daranin St. Kayo, Maninjau, Aug. 14, 1976.

47. Interview with Abdul Halim, Jakarta, May 14, 1976. As commander
of Battalion 2 of the Banteng Division's Regiment 1, Abdul Halim led the
main military operations against Baso.

48. Without firm evidence regarding the prime instigator of the operation
to crush the Baso movement, the reasons behind the action cannot be fully
determined. Followers of Tan Malaka later accused Dahlan Djambek and
Bachtaruddin of responsibility, alleging that they were acting in behalf of the
Masyumi and the PKI. See Tamin, "Sambutan," p. 14.

49. He was appointed initially to the new and largely powerless position of
subgovernor of Central Sumatra and then to head a projected university in
Bukittinggi.

50. For details of these elections, see Audrey Kahin, "The Impact of the
Indonesian Independence Struggle on Minangkabau Society," in F. von Benda
Beckmann and Lynn L. Thomas, eds., *Minangkabau: Perspectives on Continuity and Change in West Sumatra* (Athens, Ohio: Ohio University Press,
1985).

51. Nefis [Netherlands Forces Intelligence Service] "Verkort Politiek Sit.
-Overzicht No. 7," Batavia, Mar. 17, 1947, pp. 10–11. The Dutch estimated
the strengths of the TRI and the lasykars in the Padang area at that time to be
5,000 TRI and 2,000 lasykars; "Overzicht Gecontroleerde Gebied Mid Sum,"
Jan. 1, 1947–July 21, 1947, p. 22, File 206–1, Sectie Krijgsgeschiedenis, Staf
van de Bevelhebber der Landstrijdkrachten, The Hague [hereafter *SK*].

52. Rasjid estimated that the ratio of supplies going to the TRI as against
the lasykars was between 100:5 and 100:8. Interview, Jakarta, May 18, 1976.

53. Many of the local Muhammadiyah leaders in West Sumatra followed
the national Muhammadiyah policy of eschewing political activity and con-
centrating on religious, social, and educational matters. St. Mangkuto was
one of the few who never followed this path of accommodation. For more
details on his background, see Kahin, "Struggle for Independence," p. 199.

54. Both Lengah and Rasjid had addressed the ulama meeting in Padang
Panjang and had defended themselves against the charges being brought
against them.

55. He demanded this of the chief justice. Interviews with (former Chief

Justice) Haroen Al Rasjid, Padang, June 16, 1976, and Colonel Ismael Lengah, Jakarta, Apr. 17, 1976.

56. The Lasymi was affiliated with Perti, and the Hulubalang with the adat MTKAAM.

57. According to Sjarief Usman, although thousands of men belonged to the Hizbullah, they had about 500 weapons, so only that number of Hizbullah soldiers could enter to Legiun Syahid.

58. Agus Salim Murai, the legion's highest Hizbullah officer, for example, demanded that the legion be incorporated into the TNI as a single regiment under his command. When this was denied, he refused to enter the TNI.

59. For details, see BPSIM, *Sejarah Perjuangan,* pp. 660–661.

60. Hidayat took up his position on November 18, 1948, when he accompanied Hatta to Sumatra. Colonel Lengah was relieved of his command in early December, and returned with Hatta on December 5, 1948. Interviews with Colonel Hidayat, Jakarta, Oct. 7, 1976, and Colonel Ismael Lengah, Jakarta, Apr. 17, 1976.

61. The elected nagari head was in charge of the People's Defense organization, with the local TNI commander as his deputy.

62. The leader of the BPNK was a member of the People's Defense organization in the village but was subordinate to the nagari head.

63. On January 2, 1949, Colonel Hidayat issued an order dividing Sumatra into five military territories, each headed by a military governor. Rasjid was appointed military governor of West Sumatra. Mahyuni, ed., "Peristiwa Situjuh, 15–1–49" (Situjuh Batur, 1972, Mimeographed), p. 10.

64. "Perhubungan Tentara, Pemerintah dan Rakjat," Instruction no. 8/GM, Jan. 11, 1949, in Bahagian Penerangan, Staf Gubernur Militer Daerah Sumatera Tengah, "Himpunan Instruksi Gubernur Militer Daerah Sumatera Barat" (typescript, n.d.), p. 9.

65. A full account of this incident appears in Sjamsir Djohary, "Peristiwa Situdjuh (15 January 1949)," M.A. Skripsi, IKIP Padang, 1971.

66. "Overzicht Situatie," Padang, Mar. 1, 1949, Mr. 263/geh/49, ARA, and "Badan Pengawal Negeri dan Kota [B.P.N.K.]," Instruction, no. 13/GM, Feb. 2, 1949 ("Himpunan Instruksi," pp. 18–22).

67. Document attached to "Overzicht Situatie," Padang, Feb. 7, 1949, Mr. 249/geh/49, ARA, and Instructions nos. 12, 19, 20, and 25 of Feb. 2, 7, and 22, and Mar. 5, 1949 ("Himpunan Instruksi," pp. 17–18, 35–42, and 58–60).

68. All these quotations are from "Overzicht Situatie," Padang, Mar. 1, 1949, Mr. 263/geh/49, ARA.

69. The Dutch described them as supporting establishment of "a free, independent government of Sumatra's West Coast on a democratic basis cooperating with the Netherlands in the spirit of the Linggadjati agreement."

"Overzicht Gecontroleerde Gebied Mid. Sum," p. 28, File 206–1 #154–155, *SK*.

70. "Politiek Verslag," Padang, Nov. 5, 1947, Mr. 203/geh/47, ARA.

71. The Dutch do not seem to have acted against open proponents of the Republican position unless there was evidence that they were providing active material support to the Republican side. "Overzicht Situatie," Padang, Mar. 16, 1949, Mr. 320/geh/49, ARA.

72. "Overzicht Situatie," Padang, Mar. 29, 1949, and July 4, 1949, Mr. 351/geh/49 and 639/geh/49, ARA.

73. The Dutch resident wrote: "We cannot close our eyes to the fact that in Bukittinggi there still exists a strongly Republican-inclined nucleus, that has the courage of its convictions and dares to express them, a quality which the wavering advocates of a loosening of political ties with Jogja lack." "Overzicht Situatie," Padang, June 1, 1949, Mr. 563/geh/49, ARA.

74. Interviews with Sjafruddin Prawiranegara, Jakarta, Sept. 30, 1976; Dahlan Ibrahim, Jakarta, Oct. 19, 1976.

PART 3

REGIONS OF
DUTCH DOMINANCE

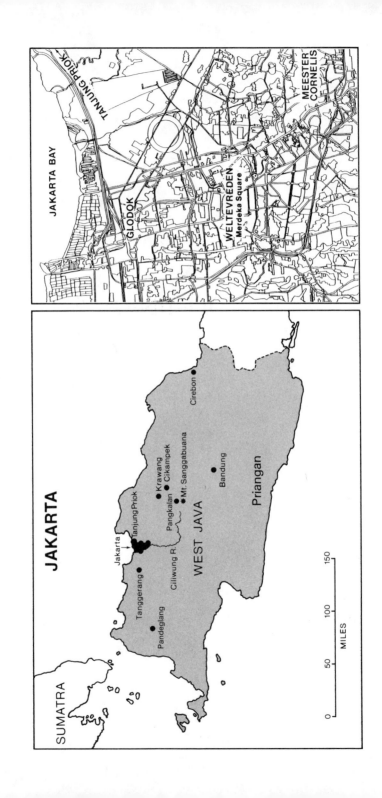

JAKARTA:
COOPERATION AND RESISTANCE
IN AN OCCUPIED CITY

Robert Cribb

In the study of modern Indonesia, the word Jakarta has become a kind of shorthand for central authority. The national revolution of 1945 to 1949, which began and ended with the establishment of a Republican government in Jakarta, did little to alter this image. The city was effective capital of the Indonesian Republic during the last months of 1945, formal capital until 1947, and capital of the Netherlands Indies until 1947. It was the headquarters of the Japanese military administration on Java until late 1945, and of the Allied military administration on Java from October 1945 to November 1946, as well as the designated capital of the Republic of the United States of Indonesia (Republik Indonesia Serikat, RIS) in 1949. Although the political heart of the Republic lay for most of the revolution in Central Java, central power was heavily and obtrusively present in Jakarta. The activities of various elites in Jakarta cast their shadows over regions far removed from the center, and it is easy to forget that Jakarta has a history of its own as a region and that the revolution was a time when the local contribution to events there was clearly visible.

The city's origins are traditionally traced to an armed trading post established in 1618 by Jan Pieterszoon Coen of the Dutch East Indies Company near the mouth of the Ciliwung, about forty-seven miles east of Banten, then the main political power in West Java.[1] Over the following centuries the trading post expanded south, merging with other small settlements along the Ciliwung, while the harbor shifted a few miles along the coast to Tanjung Priok. The city of Batavia became in its day the administrative, mercantile, and cultural center of the Dutch empire in Indonesia and a major center of European civilization in Southeast Asia.[2]

During its years of expansion, Batavia acquired a large and diverse population. By the twentieth century the old city where Coen originally built his fort was inhabited almost entirely by Chinese, the largest Chinese community on Java, who dominated medium-scale trade in the city. Inland and slightly uphill lived the Europeans and Eurasians—classified together under Dutch colonial law—in the leafy suburb of Weltevreden, where the most important government offices and business houses were also located. The oldest group of Indonesian inhabitants of the city were the Betawi, largely descendants of slaves brought from eastern Indonesia in the days of the East India Company to serve the Dutch city. They spoke their own dialect, Batavian Malay, and occupied a considerable area of land around the city. In the city, however, their numbers were diluted by large-scale immigration after the turn of the century, especially from the rest of Java.

Although Indonesians and Europeans inhabited the same city and depended on each other economically and socially, they were physically segregated in a kind of informal apartheid. The Indonesian *kampung* (neighborhoods) were tucked unobtrusively behind the European houses and commercial buildings which lined the main roads. "The suburb," wrote a British commentator of Weltevreden, "has been well planned, it is kept scrupulously clean, and while the natives in their bright coloured clothes, quietly making their way hither and thither, give the required picturesque touch to the life in the streets, the absence of the crowded native dwelling houses prevents the occurrence of those objectionable features which so often destroy the charm of the towns in the Orient."[3]

This physical segregation was matched by a social, cultural, and intellectual separation. Local Indonesians took little direct part in the administrative, commercial, military, and political life of the Dutch city. Education levels for the Betawi were low, for the Dutch ruled Jakarta more directly than other parts of Indonesia and had no need to build up a local elite as their agents, while the Betawi lacked their own traditional elite. A sizeable Indonesian educated elite also lived in Jakarta, coming almost entirely from other regions, and with few links to the other Indonesian inhabitants of the city. Its members enjoyed many of the privileges of an urban elite, but they also directly faced the racial discrimination which lay at the heart of the Dutch colonial system. This elite provided much of the leadership of the nationalist movement.

Despite its close associations with Dutch rule, therefore, Jakarta/ Batavia never came to represent simply the baleful, corrupting aspects of colonial society. At the outbreak of the revolution, it had an essentially neutral hue in nationalist eyes, in comparison with such areas as Ambon, in the South Moluccas, and the Minahasa, around the city of Menado in northern Sulawesi, which were seen as having gone over to the Dutch. Indonesian nationalism could and did shape its image of Jakarta in terms of the city's role in the revolutionary struggle. But the image was ambiguous: as the scene of the declaration of independence, Jakarta had symbolic significance, and its importance was reinforced by its status as the capital city of the Republic. On the other hand, Jakarta, scene of repeated negotiations, also became known as the city of diplomacy, a deprecatory description, at least in those circles that regarded negotiations as selling out to the Dutch.

It is not surprising that both these images of Jakarta's role refer to activities of the national elite in the city and ascribe to Jakarta the role of nothing more than an arena for events of national importance. The people of Jakarta, however, were more than passive onlookers. A local revolutionary movement grew out of the distinctive social and economic conditions of the region and developed an independence of thought and action that shaped the course of events in the city despite the power of the center. The story of the revolution in Jakarta, therefore, is less a story of local self-determination than of the changing relationship between the Republic, the Dutch, and local nationalists. The Dutch were eventually defeated and the local nationalists overshadowed and overwhelmed. In 1949, with the formal transfer of sovereignty, Jakarta came finally into the hands of the Republic.

Independence and the Takeover of Jakarta

Japan surrendered to the Allies on August 14, 1945. First reactions in Jakarta to the prospect of a return to Dutch rule were hesitant. Sukarno and Hatta did not declare independence until the 17th, and the older generation, uncomfortable as they may have been with the idea of renewed colonial rule, shrank for some time from supporting such a far-reaching act as a declaration of independence. Gradually, however, people from all levels of society in Jakarta, with the youth (*pemuda*) to the forefront, saw an opportunity to take part in deciding the future of their country. A pervasive atmosphere of action arose in the city. At first there was no clear sense of direction. No one knew what form the Dutch return would take or when it would come, and no one knew just how it could be met. But there was a compelling feeling that this was a wholly new situation, in which old rules did not apply and what had once been unthinkable could now be achieved.[4] In a rising tide of activity during the weeks after the proclamation, the pemuda daubed walls and monuments around the city with patriotic slogans (often in English for the benefit of international audiences) such as "Indonesia never again the life blood of any nation." They hauled the red and white national flag to the top of mastheads; seized public buildings from the diffident Japanese military administration and painted their walls with the words "Milik Republik Indonesia" (property of the Republic of Indonesia). Popular enthusiasm reached a peak in the massive rally at what is now Merdeka Square on September 19, when an estimated 200,000 people converged on the largest open space in central Jakarta to demonstrate their support for the Republic.

At the same time, people of Jakarta had begun to organize, to give form to the feeling that Indonesians had taken control of their own future. The Japanese had sought to mobilize and coordinate the Indonesians behind their war effort through a variety of mass organizations, and this experience of organized political activity was readily turned in 1945 toward the creation of nationalist action groups, both to fight the Dutch and to back up the fighters. The Japanese, moreover, had given young Indonesians military and paramilitary training in several organizations.[5] Two of these, the Peta (volunteer army) and the Heihō (auxiliary forces), which had received the best arms and training, were disbanded by the Japanese just after the surrender. Most of their members, however, reassembled in the BKR (People's Security Organization), but it was some weeks before the BKR became an effective military force. In the meantime, the paramilitary Barisan

Pelopor (Pioneer Corps) provided the guard at the declaration of independence and began to patrol the streets of the city.[6]

The more or less official armed forces, however, were soon far outnumbered by independent struggle groups *(badan perjuangan* later known as *lasykar)* which sprang up throughout the city. They were based especially in student hostels, under the leadership of educated pemuda, often with a strong ideological motivation, and in the kampung. There traditional, often ethnic, loyalties played an important role, and the neighborhood association, established by the Japanese as the smallest local unit of political control and mobilization, was a key element in translating will into organized action.[7]

In administration, as in military training, the nationalists benefited from changes made under the Japanese. As the war began to turn against them in 1943, the Japanese drained Java of Japanese manpower and appointed Indonesians to increasingly senior positions, giving them administrative experience not available under the Dutch. At the time of the Japanese surrender, Jakarta had an Indonesian deputy mayor, Soewirjo, a nationalist leader who was prominent in the circle that was later to become the PNI (Indonesian Nationalist Party). Below him was a hierarchy of Indonesian officials with training and experience in managing the affairs of the city. The Indonesians in the municipal administration were cautious, however, in considering an immediate takeover of local government. The Japanese had been instructed by the Allies to maintain the political and administrative status quo, and they had been careful not to flout this instruction openly. There appeared, in fact, to be a real risk that the Japanese might turn on the Indonesian nationalist movement and suppress it in order to demonstrate their good faith to the Allies. Thus it was not until September 7, 1945, that a self-appointed committee of Indonesian officials of the Jakarta municipal administration unilaterally transferred authority to Soewirjo and sent a delegation to the Japanese mayor of the city, Shigeo Hasegawa, asking him to hand over the government of the city peacefully. In line with Allied instructions, Hasegawa refused officially, but in fact he ceased to go to his office. The following weeks saw more and more individual officials as well as whole departments declare their allegiance to the Republic, and Soewirjo was formally elected head of the PNKD (Pemerintah Nasional Kota Djakarta, National Government of the City of Jakarta) on September 23, 1945. He was confirmed in his position on September 29, when Sukarno officially appointed him mayor of Jakarta. By October 1, the government of the city was effectively in Indonesian hands, and the PNKD, based in its city hall (Balai Agung) on the southern side of Merdeka Square, had begun the task of administering the city.[8]

All this activity at first attracted relatively little opposition. Although there were many Indonesians, particularly of the older generation, who initially had doubts about the Republic, very few felt inclined to take action on behalf of the Dutch, and as the Republic displayed greater strength and identity, positive commitment to it grew. The Japanese, for their part, despite Indonesian fears, were generally sympathetic to Indonesian nationalism, concerned only that a nationalist revolution might be directed against them or that the Allies might blame them for the establishment of the Republic. They restrained themselves from moving against the Republic in Jakarta, therefore, as long as it avoided either endangering or compromising them. The Allies were unable to oppose the Republic in Jakarta, for they had no armed forces there. With Java being transferred to Mountbatten's South East Asia Command only on August 15, 1945, Mountbatten had neither the troops nor the transport to organize a rapid reoccupation of the island. The Dutch prisoners of war and internees on Java, just emerging from their internment camps, concentrated their attention on physical survival and an improvement in living conditions, and were in any case not yet organized enough to present an effective challenge to the Republic.

The Republic Challenged

Except for the looting of Chinese shops in Glodok, an uneasy peace reigned in Jakarta for two to three weeks after the proclamation. By early September, however, Dutch internees from other parts of Java had begun to arrive in Jakarta in large numbers. Their attempt to return to their old houses and their old way of life were the first tangible signs of a Dutch resurgence. In every region the Dutch colonial system had its own distinctive characteristics. In Batavia, its racial aspects had been particularly strong, and they had been highlighted by sharp disparities in wealth and by the physical segregation in the city. The sense of deprivation felt by the people of Jakarta was interpreted racially, rather than socially. As the Dutch showed signs of demanding their old positions again, the scene was set for an outbreak of racial conflict.

In the second and third weeks of September, moreover, a new threat to the Republic appeared in the seas off Jakarta, and the uneasy calm disappeared. A flotilla of British and Dutch ships arrived in Tanjung Priok, the port of Jakarta, on September 15, carrying Ch.O. van der Plas as representative of the Netherlands Indies government. As representatives of the Allies, the British were there to accept the Japanese surrender and arrange for the repatriation of both the Japanese army on Java and the Allied prisoners of war and internees on the island. Lacking sufficient troops even to occupy Jakarta, the British stayed on their ships and worked primarily through the continuing Japanese military administration. The British had also expected to give general military cover to the returning Dutch administration, but as the strength of the Republic became clear, they retreated to a more narrow interpretation of their tasks and informed the Dutch that they were not prepared to fight a colonial war on behalf of the Netherlands.[9] When new contingents of British and British Indian troops arrived and began landing in Jakarta on September 28, 1945, therefore, they did so not under the banner of the returning Netherlands Indies government but as avowedly apolitical representatives of the Allies, entrusted with purely humanitarian and legal tasks.[10] On these grounds, and hoping to win international approval by being cooperative, Sukarno and the other Republican leaders urged the Indonesians of Jakarta to cooperate with the Allies. The Indonesians accepted British professions of neutrality, albeit with some doubts, and there was little resistance as the British disembarked in Tanjung Priok on the 28th. At the request of the British, van der Plas had not shifted his headquarters ashore on his arrival. Following the British landings, however, he took up residence first in the Hotel des Indes and then in an office building in the center of the city. He was joined at the beginning of October by Dr. H. J. van Mook, lieutenant governor-general of the Netherlands Indies, together with officials of the Netherlands Indies government-in-exile who had spent the war in Australia. Their arrival marked the beginning of the restoration of Dutch authority in Jakarta.

Distrusting Dutch political judgment and acutely aware that any provocative act by the Dutch was likely to result in British casualties, the British commander, Lt. Gen. Sir Philip Christison, tried to keep the Dutch presence as unobtrusive as possible by attempting to insist that the Dutch not expand their power in any field without his approval. Van Mook, however, disregarded these instructions and moved into the palace of the governor-general, while his skeleton staff of Dutch officials from Australia, supplemented by recruits from the Netherlands and former internees from Indonesia who had recuperated for a time in Australia, went about the business of reconstructing their administration. They requisitioned former government buildings under Allied authority, erased the words "Milik Republik Indonesia" and expanded the Dutch administrative structure in all fields.

The Battle for Jakarta

These signs of a resurgent Netherlands Indies encouraged former internees on the one hand and pemuda on the other to carry the struggle onto the streets of Jakarta. Armed vigilante groups of former internees and prisoners of war began to form soon after the Japanese surrendered. Ambonese soldiers of the Dutch colonial army were particularly active, gaining a reputation for indiscriminate harassment, intimidation, and shooting of Indonesians. The British suspected them of seeking to promote a breakdown of law and order in which the British would have to intervene. On the Republican side were the struggle groups, which had undergone many changes since they first emerged as serious political and military forces in early September. Some groups had merged into the formal defense structure of the Republic as units of the BKR, and more did so after it was transformed into the TKR (People's Security Army) on October 5. Others, often those with stronger ideological orientation, such as the left-wing API (Angkatan Pemuda Indonesia, Youth Force of Indonesia), remained firmly independent, both of the army and of the political parties which began to form only in late October. The Barisan Pelopor, for its part, having begun as a strong supporter of the government, drifted gradually away from it, becoming largely independent and changing its name to Barisan Banteng (Wild Buffalo Corps).

Although they were already engaged in running street battles with the Dutch vigilantes, the struggle groups offered no real resistance to the British forces as they landed. Within a few days, however, reports began to circulate that Dutch troops were also landing, disguised in British uniforms, and clashes began with the British as well. Fighting in Jakarta never reached the intensity of the battle of Surabaya, but it was persistent and costly for all sides. The heaviest fighting took place in local clashes between the struggle groups and the vigilantes. The warning cry *Bersiap!* (Get ready!), used to summon pemuda for battle with an approaching hostile force, was heard often enough to become a general term for the violent months of late 1945. The violence of this period included, however, individual and apparently random kidnappings and murders, often accompanied by torture, and it was the randomness of this terror, conducted by both sides, which gave late 1945 its particularly gruesome reputation and the conflict in Jakarta its strongly racial character.[11]

Despite the clashes that were taking place, the Republic's leaders still urged the people of Jakarta to remain calm and to avoid action. The leaders wanted to demonstrate to the world that the Republic was capable of maintaining law and order as an effective government, though their attitude was probably also influenced by humanitarian considerations and the potential political danger to themselves of strong revolutionary armed forces in the city, which might have ended up beyond their control. On November 19, Sjahrir, as prime minister, seeking to avoid a repetition of the events in Surabaya, ordered the TKR and the pemuda forces to evacuate the city. As Sjahrir must have expected, not all struggle groups obeyed him, but the order made it clear that those who continued to fight the Allies in Jakarta did so outside the framework of the Republic's strategy.

The British in Jakarta were suffering mounting casualties in the street violence of the bersiap period. Without any immediate prospect of relief, they decided that the city of Jakarta at least must be made safe. In Operation Pounce of December 27–29, 1945, they threw a cordon around the city, arrested known or suspected terrorists—a general term used in those days to refer to pemuda, bandits, and the Republican police force in Jakarta—took over public utilities, and impounded all cars in civilian hands.[12] Security for Europeans in Jakarta improved immediately, but acts of violence against Indonesians by Dutch and Ambonese soldiers and vigilantes continued. Shortly after Operation Pounce, Ambonese soldiers attempted to assassinate Prime Minister Sjahrir. Republicans also feared that the British might at any moment put Sukarno, Hatta, and other leaders on their arrest list. In secret and at short notice, therefore, it was decided that most of the government should move to Yogyakarta. On January 4, 1946, Jakarta woke to find that Sukarno, Hatta, and Amir Sjarifuddin had gone. Jakarta remained the capital in name, and Sjahrir and several ministries continued to be based there, but from that time on Yogya, and not Jakarta, was the political and administrative center of the Republic.

The Army and Lasykar in Krawang

The arrests of Operation Pounce were supplemented by further British action to break the power and organization of the pemuda in Jakarta, and large numbers of so-called extremists were held in the jails of Jakarta or imprisoned on the island of Onrust in Jakarta Bay. Many pemuda, however, were able to retreat to the relative safety of rural areas outside the demarcation line drawn by the British. There they consolidated and regrouped. The largest and best organized group in the area east of Jakarta was the 5th Regiment of the TKR, under the command of a former Peta officer, M. Muffreini Mukmin, at Cikampek. West of the city, at Tanggerang, was the 4th Regiment, under Singgih. In theory, both commanders were responsible to the commander of the Cirebon Division, but in fact each had a great deal of autonomy. Muffreini, in particular, took advantage of this autonomy to work out a modus vivendi with many lasykar operating in his area.

The lasykar were regarded as troublesome and disruptive by many of the Dutch-trained officers, who were rapidly gaining ascendance in the West Java command of the TKR. They competed with the army for weapons and supplies and refused to accept orders from the army, thereby offending against the notion of a strict military hierarchy capable of pursuing a coordinated strategic program. The lasykar, for their part, regarded the Dutch-trained officers as suspiciously Westernized and incapable of understanding the meaning of revolution.

This antipathy led to armed clashes between the two groups in other parts of West Java, but in Krawang, military leaders generally avoided a confrontation with the powerful local lasykar. This was partly because they could be less sure of victory and partly because leaders of both groups were willing to submerge their differences in their common opposition to Dutch military expansion.[13]

The lasykar of the area east of Jakarta were among the strongest in the Republic. The rural hinterland of Jakarta from the edge of the city as far east as the Citarum river consisted before the war largely of the "private domains"—tracts of land made over to private, generally non-Indonesian, landlords in the seventeenth, eighteenth, and nineteenth centuries. The landlords possessed many seigneurial rights and the restrictions placed on their activities by successive governments were often not enforced, with the result that the area was known as one of the most depressed on Java. In response, there grew up a strong tradition of rural unrest, expressed most often in the presence of gangs of brigands. On the outbreak of the revolution, the area was one of the first where the Japanese were disarmed and where Indonesians who had served the old order were removed from office and often killed. It was in this rural discontent that the lasykar found their principal support.[14]

There was, however, a general tactical confusion amongst the lasykar of the region. Their first inclination after the retreat from Jakarta was to launch a massive counterattack on the city. The idea of retreat did not sit comfortably with pemuda who had joined the revolution in order to prevent the return of Dutch power. Plans for a counterattack, however, were always postponed, often thanks to the urging of Muffreini, and the lasykar had to content themselves with what they saw as an eyeball-to-eyeball confrontation with the Allies across a demarcation line set by Allied patrols. Both the army and the lasykar organized a good deal of small-scale infiltration into Jakarta, using a network of generally unarmed nationalist ethnic, labor, and other organizations, especially in the port area of Tanjung Priok. The objects of infiltration were propaganda, sabotage, and general disruption of the Dutch administration. The infiltrators had a notable success in May 1947 when they were able to burn down the warehouse containing the cargo of the *Martin Behrmann,* an American ship captured by the Dutch while it was carrying a load of Republican rubber from Cirebon to Singapore in the face of a Dutch naval blockade of Java.[15]

Republican military theorists recognized early in the revolution that the Republic could wage a guerrilla war against the enemy far more effectively than a conventional war. The existence of the demarcation line around Jakarta, however, drew the Republican forces willy-nilly into a front-line strategy. Such a strategy, however, depended far more than guerrilla warfare on cooperation and coordination between various armed groups. Good personal relations between some army officers and lasykar commanders made informal cooperation possible, but the army's determination that it alone had ultimate responsibility for the military side of the revolution was an underlying source of tension between them. Tension increased between the two in November 1946 when the army began to implement a ceasefire with the Dutch as part of the Linggajati negotiations. In the same month unknown individuals kidnapped and killed a senior TRI (Army of the Indonesian Republic) officer involved in the truce negotiations and in attempts to persuade the lasykar to comply. In March and April 1947 the tension erupted into outright clashes between the TRI and lasykar groups in various places east of Jakarta. With their superior organization and generally superior arms, the TRI prevailed. Nevertheless, opposition in lasykar circles persisted, most maintaining the hardline position that the army's policy of accepting the truce and avoiding frontal clashes was soft on the Dutch.[16] In the months between March and July 1947, the TRI was able to consolidate its position to some extent and began at last to prepare for guerrilla war in the region. When the Dutch attack came, however, it was still far from ready, and effective Republican resistance around Jakarta collapsed rapidly.

The Balai Agung in Occupied Jakarta

Within Jakarta, meanwhile, the struggle was being carried on in rather different terms. The retreat from the city by Sukarno and Hatta at the beginning of 1946 was a hastily conceived operation. No one thought until considerably later to call it a *hijrah,* to equate it with Muhammad's temporary retreat from Mecca to Medina; rather, it was explained publicly in terms of the threat to the physical safety of the Republican leaders in Jakarta and the need to give leadership to the reconstruction effort in Central Java. It was, moreover, only one of a series of shifts by government departments and officials into the interior, a movement which had begun in October 1945 and was to continue well into 1946. It marked, however, a new phase in Republican liberation strategy, in which the creation of a functioning state apparatus was emphasized as a prerequisite for effective diplomatic and military action. The political energy which had gone at first into taking over the existing administrative structure now went into expanding it and making it work. Self-reliance and a consolidation of political strength were seen to be necessary. Public discipline was as much a part of the new strategic phase as of the old, and calls for discipline in the interests of the national struggle were only barely distinguishable from simple calls for political obedience, but the orientation toward national construction was new. Sukarno, addressing the people of Indonesia over Yogyakarta radio on the evening of his arrival, called 1946 a year of organization, coordination, and development and urged the pemuda to become "heroes of construction" rather than heroes of the battlefield.[17] This new emphasis did not assign an essential role to Jakarta, but it was a strategy with considerable relevance there.

Left behind in Jakarta when Sukarno and Hatta departed was the PNKD (National Government of the City of Jakarta), generally referred to by the people of Jakarta simple as the Balai Agung.[18] The leadership in Jakarta differed from that in most regions in not having strong local roots. Those who held positions in the Balai Agung did so by virtue of decisions they had made as members of the largely Dutch-trained Indonesian inelligentsia, a group that included very few Betawi. The Balai Agung, like the national elite in Yogya, was dominated by Javanese and Minangkabau. In the diverse immigrant society of Jakarta there was no traditional elite, and the Betawi produced very few national-level political leaders.[19] Soewirjo, a Javanese from Wonogiri who had first come to Jakarta to study at the law school, was elected to power by colleagues with similar backgrounds. His primary political base, therefore, lay in the Republican governmental apparatus in Jakarta. This structure in turn depended heavily on the political and material support of the central Republican government. The

Balai Agung lacked popular roots to begin with, and in the face of Dutch expansion never had the opportunity to consolidate its local power as a government; it was therefore the strategy of the central government which the Balai Agung had to implement.

It operated, moreover, within narrow limits. It was defenseless against Dutch military power in Jakarta and survived only because the British vetoed any attempt to remove it. In all their dealings in Jakarta, the British still maintained the polite fiction that they were not interfering in the internal political affairs of Indonesia, beyond carrying out their humanitarian tasks and insisting that the two sides meet to negotiate an agreement. Operation Pounce was intended officially to do no more than restore law, order, and stable government in the city, and it left the Republican establishment relatively intact. Thereafter, with Dutch-Indonesian negotiations under way, the British were not prepared to allow the arrest of Soewirjo and the abolition of the Balai Agung for fear that the negotiations would be jeopardized. This protection, however, had its price: the Balai Agung would be safe only as long as it did not disrupt law and order by extensive political agitation and made itself useful by contributing to stable government.

Thus, although the Republic intended the Balai Agung to be a gesture of commitment to its citizens in Jakarta, and maintained it at considerable expense to the treasury, there were strict limits on the extent to which the Balai Agung could act as a political agent for the Republic. It was a focus for the loyalty of the people of Jakarta, a sign that they had not been forgotten by Yogya, and an encouragement to continue with symbolic and emotionally important acts of nationalist defiance, such as shouting "Merdeka!" (Freedom!) in public places or erasing the blue stripes that Dutch sympathizers painted under the red and white Republican flags with which nationalists had decorated train carriages running in Jakarta. The Balai Agung provided a municipal government but was not geared to a more active role. It organized no anti-Dutch rallies and produced no strong anti-Dutch propaganda. And, although it had links with various underground and clandestine Republican organizations in Jakarta, it neither created a shadow administration that might have survived a Dutch purge nor infiltrated the Dutch administrative hierarchy in order to wreck or subvert it from within.[20]

The Balai Agung was, rather, a gesture to the world and to the

Dutch concerning the nature and aims of the Republic. Maintenance of a Republican administration in multiracial Jakarta constituted a statement that Indonesians could manage their own affairs, not only in the fastnesses of Central Java where they had no competition, but also at the very heart of the Dutch colonial empire. The political purpose of the Balai Agung, therefore, was best carried out by staying aloof from the Dutch, by maintaining a kind of apartheid under which each nationality was master in its own house. The British, however, were no more sympathetic to this esoteric view of the Balai Agung's political role than they were to more active alternatives. In Operation Pounce of December 1945, they had taken over the public utilities of Jakarta—water supply, gas, electricity, public works—as well as the police force, and they insisted that the Republic and the Dutch cooperate to run them. The British provided a head for each department to save either side from having to work under the command of the other, but this did not remove politics from the issue.

Under van Mook, the Netherlands Indies government was trying to transform Indonesia from a colonial society based on overt racial discrimination to a postcolonial meritocracy offering equal opportunities to all races. In practice it was expected that Europeans would continue to play a disproportionately large role, thanks to their greater training and skills, advantages which were the product of colonial inequalities. In theory, however, Indonesians would be able to advance as far as their abilities justified. In order to make this transformation credible, van Mook was not only willing but eager to accept skilled personnel from any quarter, including the Republic. He is even reported to have said that he would be glad to have Amir Sjarifuddin, then the Republic's minister of defense, as his director-general of economic affairs.[21] In any cooperative arrangement, therefore, the Dutch were keen to establish a single hierarchy based on technical skill, a hierarchy that they expected to dominate. The Republicans, by contrast, sought a system of parallel, equal hierarchies through which they would retain their integrity.

In practice the results were mixed: the police force, reorganized after Operation Pounce, consisted of two separate corps, Republican and Dutch, each with its own hierarchy and commander and united only by a single British officer at the head of the whole structure. In the public utilities, by contrast, there was a confused situation in which acceptance of Dutch technical expertise under British supervision was difficult at times to distinguish from subordination to Dutch control. In the course of 1946, the Dutch, by appealing to administrative rationality, were able to encroach steadily on the Republican domain. Individual buildings and departments in Jakarta were taken over one by one in a low key and unobtrusive manner. Dutch technicians assumed greater responsibilities where circumstances allowed. When the British finally withdrew from Jakarta on November 21, 1946, they handed over the positions they had occupied in the police and the public utilities to the Dutch. Without ever revising their commitment to preserve the Balai Agung, the British presided over a steady erosion of its position in Jakarta. The Balai Agung resisted as best it could with protests and the occasional strike, but it was largely powerless to stem the rising tide of Dutch authority.[22] On May 25, 1947, not long before the first Dutch attack, Republican officials in Jakarta formed a Nationalist Front in the city to oppose establishment of the state of Pasundan, which was announced by R. A. A. M. M. Soeria Kartalegawa in Bandung on May 4, 1947, at the instigation and with the assistance of local Dutch authorities.[23] They did this, however, only when propaganda for the Pasundan movement in Jakarta seemed to be winning a certain number of the city's Sundanese residents for Soeria Kartalegawa's cause. The Front itself concentrated on counter-propaganda and did not seek actively to build a mass base.

Economic Pressure and the End of the Balai Agung

Only from outside Jakarta was the Republic able to put effective pressure on the Dutch in the city. In May 1946 the Dutch introduced a postwar Netherlands Indies guilder to replace the Japanese occupation currency that had been circulating until then. Jakarta, however, depended for its food supply on the flow of rice and vegetables from the surrounding countryside, then under Republican control, so that when the Republic banned the new currency, the value of the new guilder sank and the Dutch were forced to tolerate the continued circulation of the Japanese money. This situation, economically damaging and politically embarrassing for the Dutch, lasted until the final months of 1946, when the army and lasykar around Jakarta cooperated in imposing a partly effective blockade against the flow of rice into the city. By this time, imported consumer goods were becoming increasingly available in Jakarta and, even without the blockade, the terms of trade between Jakarta and the interior were turning in favor of the Dutch. The Republic's own new currency, ORI, fell sharply in value, and only the continued blockade kept economic pressure on the Dutch. Realizing their vulnerability, the Dutch agreed, under the Linggajati Agreement of November 1946, to hand over their enclaves on Java to the Republic as part of a broader settlement. As the possibility of implementing Linggajati became steadily more remote in the course of 1947, however, the Dutch turned more and more to the idea of using military force to expand the enclaves into economically self-supporting regions.[24]

After the departure of the British in November 1946, the Dutch continued encroachment on the position of the Balai Agung. They were careful, however, to keep the Balai itself intact, for although the British were no longer present to veto any attempt to take it over, other considerations were important. At first, the Dutch had no wish to spoil the atmosphere of cooperation that surrounded the reaching of the Linggajati Agreement; later they did not want to risk appearing aggressive by removing the Balai Agung when they were considering more extensive plans for expansion. The Republicans of Jakarta for their part had to avoid acting provocatively, but they were no longer under pressure to cooperate and retreated into an increasingly penurious isolation in the city. From the last week of May 1947, it seemed increasingly improbable that a peaceful solution would be achieved. As the atmosphere darkened, the Republicans in the Balai Agung began to make preparations for an evacuation to the interior, and for strikes and sabotage to hamper whatever activity the Dutch might have in mind.[25] But the blow fell late in the evening of July 20, 1947, and well before the full attack began at dawn the following day, the Republican official presence in Jakarta was ended. Soewirjo and most of his senior subordinates were arrested, as were most of the Indonesian police force and a number of Republican officials present in Jakarta for the negotiations. Most of the remaining Republican buildings were also occupied. Jakarta was in Dutch hands.

Guerrilla Warfare in Krawang

The Dutch attack, though destructive and demoralizing, nonetheless left many army units and lasykar groups largely intact in the newly occupied environs of Jakarta, and these groups, once reorganized, began a rural guerrilla war against the Dutch. Within months of the Dutch attack, the Krawang area had regained its old reputation as a center of militant nationalism, and it remained so, in spite of Dutch pacification campaigns in late 1947. In addition to locally based armed groups, a cluster of Republican sabotage and intelligence organizations operated in the area, linked directly to Yogyakarta rather than with each other or with local units. The army and the lasykar also received indispensable financial support from Yogya, through both more or less official channels controlled by the ministries of defense and finance, and party connections. The Renville Agreement of January 1948 briefly checked the military campaign in the Jakarta region, for it was agreed that the Republic should withdraw its forces from occupied West Java. In fact, though many were withdrawn, a number of units were instructed to stay behind surreptitiously and unofficially to continue their military activities and to strengthen the Republic's political campaign in the area.

Many lasykar, too, refused to evacuate or disband, and several large units—the Bambu Runcing (Bamboo Spears), SP88 (Satuan Pemberontakan 88, Revolution Unit 88, originally an intelligence organization directly under the Ministry of Defense in Yogya), TII (Tentara Islam Indonesia, Islamic Army of Indonesia, the military wing of the Darul Islam movement to realize an Islamic state), and others—continued fighting, not only in disregard of official instructions from Yogyakarta, but also, and increasingly, with the attitude that they, rather than Yogya, represented the pure expression of Indonesian nationalism. The Renville Agreement, which in effect recognized Dutch authority in the territories occupied in the attack of July 1947, was bitterly felt, by those who had fought for the Republic in West Java, as a betrayal. The ideological affiliations of these alienated lasykar ranged from the Islamic fundamentalism of the Darul Islam to the national communism of the followers of Tan Malaka, and cooperation between them was limited largely to agreeing to keep out of each other's way. In January 1948, a few days after the signing of the

Renville Agreement which handed West Java to the Dutch, the Bambu Runcing, the SP88, and the TII in the Krawang area came together to form the Government of the Republic in West Java. This they claimed to be the true heir to the Republic declared by Sukarno and Hatta in August 1945.[26] They set up an extensive local administration in the Krawang area, with its headquarters in Pangkalan on the slopes of Mt. Sanggabuana. When the West Javanese Siliwangi Division returned to the area in early 1949 after the second Dutch military action, this government cooperated in establishing a network of territorial commands as the basis for further guerrilla war against the Dutch.[27] Conflict between the army and the lasykar, however, broke out again after the ceasefire arranged between the army and the Dutch in August 1949 and persisted well beyond the transfer of sovereignty which marked the end of the revolution in 1949.

The Republic's victory deprived the lasykar of their main political reason for existence. Some simply disbanded, some retreated into banditry. A few took on the far more difficult task of trying to change the nature of the independent Republic by armed struggle. The Bambu Runcing fought on in Krawang for a time before retreating toward the hills of Banten. The Darul Islam, though based to the southeast in the Priangan, also had its supporters in Krawang, but the area was generally brought under government control by the end of 1950.[28]

The Civilian Underground

Although the Dutch arrested Soewirjo in July 1947 and eventually expelled him, along with other senior Republicans, they invited the remaining Republican officials, numbering several thousand, to join Dutch service. In order to demonstrate the illegitimacy of the Dutch takeover, however, the Republic instructed its officials to remain inactive in the offices taken over by the Dutch. Most of them obeyed the order at first. But the Republic, crowded into a mere portion of Central and East Java and Banten, was in no condition to send large sums of money to Jakarta to support its officials there, as it had done before the Dutch attack. Many officials were willing to sell their furniture and clothes to avoid cooperating with the Dutch, but both furniture and patience were limited. During 1947, in the absence of financial support and even of clear political instructions from Yogya, there began a steady drift of Republican officials into Dutch employment. The Renville Agreement of January 1948, by recognizing Dutch control of the areas conquered the previous year, made the principle of non-cooperation somewhat pointless, for it gave the Dutch the legitimacy which the boycott sought to deny them. The Republic then gave its officials formal permission to seek employment with the Dutch. Nonetheless, many Republicans who had remained faithful to their instructions at considerable personal cost resented the fact that their sacrifices seemed to have been thrown away. The resentment was compounded when in early February 1948 Hatta announced, as a consequence of Renville, an amnesty for all who had gone to work for the Dutch.[29]

With the signing of the Renville Agreement, however, Yogya did develop a more coherent policy toward the occupied territories. On January 26, 1948, the Hatta government established a Cabinet Bureau for Occupied Territories, under the chairmanship of Soewirjo and with the general goal of coordinating Republican activities in areas under the Dutch, particularly East and West Java. In West Java it worked primarily through the remaining Republican officials in the region, who had ceased officially to be servants of the Republic once the agreement was signed. These officials were incorporated into what was called the Coordinator movement, an unofficial network of Republican officials, the aim of which was to preserve the fabric of the Republic's administrative structure in West Java for the eventual return of Republican government. The Coordinator movement received financial support from Yogya, largely the proceeds of covert sales of gold, opium, and plantation crops by the Republic in Jakarta and Singapore. The movement was strongest in rural areas, where Dutch power was weakest, but it found itself threatened there by the Siliwangi Division, whose own territorial command system expected to take over virtually all administrative responsibilities at the local level in the name of Nasution's concept of total people's defense. Tension developed at times between the two as each tried to establish and preserve its own authority. In Jakarta the Coordinator movement worked through the Republican delegation, which was based in Sukarno's old house at Pegangsaan Timur 56, where he and Hatta had declared independence, for the continuing negotiations with the

Dutch. The delegation had diplomatic immunity and safe communications facilities by virtue of its diplomatic role, and it was therefore an ideal coordinating point for Republican illegal activity in West Java,[30] though the Dutch soon discovered this fact and made use of the delegation in their attempts to gain intelligence about Republican plans.[31] The Coordinator movement apparently never succeeded in creating an extensive network in Jakarta itself.

The Federal Option

In the wake of their military attack of July 1947 the Dutch began to plan seriously for the creation of a federal state in West Java, later called Pasundan. Jakarta was included provisionally in plans for this projected state, although the city was supposed to be separated eventually as a federal capital territory under the direct control of the federal government. The Renville Agreement, however, provided for a plebiscite in the territories occupied by the Dutch in 1947 to decide their future status in the proposed Federal Republic of Indonesia.[32] Although no date was set for the vote, the Republican delegation in Jakarta soon became the coordinating center for the Republican campaign to win the plebiscite. In February 1948, Ali Budiardjo, a member of the delegation, formed the GPRI (Gerakan Plebisit Republik Indonesia, Republic of Indonesia Plebiscite Movement) to campaign for the Republic. The GPRI established branches both in Jakarta and the surrounding countryside and began an active political campaign to consolidate and expand the Republic's support. The movement put the Dutch momentarily on the defensive. In the event, the plebiscite was never held. The Dutch banned the GPRI in some areas, but it joined with other Republican organizations in West Java, particularly in the areas around Jakarta, to create a network which was able, despite the Dutch presence, to tighten the Republican's political control in the area.[33]

Jakarta and the northern coastal plain of West Java as far east as Cirebon were ideal political terrain for Republican resistance to Dutch sponsorship of the West Javanese state based on a supposed sense of nationalism among the Sundanese. The region, part Batavian Malay, part mixed Sundanese and Javanese, and part Javanese, and with a strong antifeudal tradition in many areas, was not likely to be enthusiastic about a state dominated by the feudal Sundanese of the Priangan. Republicans made up most of the indirectly elected delegation from Jakarta and the northern coastal plain to the Third West Java Conference in Bandung in February and March 1948—a conference that the Dutch planned as an alternative expression of popular will to the plebiscite. The delegation, led by Soejoso, a former Republican official in Jakarta, formed a strong caucus in the conference but could not prevent Pasundan's establishment. Initially, the Jakarta delegation had considerable influence in the provisional parliament of Pasundan, where it formed the principal backing of the first Pasundan cabinet of Adil Poeradiredja.[34] Without openly discarding their original intention to destroy the Dutch-sponsored state, the members of the delegation began to see the possibilities Pasundan offered, both for power and privilege for themselves and for destroying the greater enemy, the Dutch federal system, from within. Lacking a clear sense of direction, the Republican initiative in Pasundan soon became bogged down in the Byzantine world of Sundanese politics and lost much of its effectiveness.

The second Dutch military action of December 1948 barely affected Jakarta; the city was no more than the site of some of the constitutional negotiations that followed. In early 1950, after the transfer of power, the city was ruffled by an attempted coup organized in Bandung and Jakarta by R. P. P. Westerling, a Dutch counterinsurgency expert who had gained notoriety for his brutal tactics in southern Sulawesi in 1946. He was rumored to have links with the lasykar groups around Jakarta and the Darul Islam around Bandung, but his coup was essentially the work of outsiders and was soon crushed.[35] In other respects the transfer of power was orderly. No significant Jakarta group emerged in national politics as the product of shared revolutionary experience in the occupied city, and Jakarta slid with little effort back into its accustomed role as capital of the archipelago.

Conclusion

Jakarta began the revolution as a city of action. The Indonesians of the city mobilized early and on their own initiative against the Dutch, whom they resented as colonial masters, rather than against local indigenous elites seen as agents of colonialism. The nationalist rather than social orientation of the revolution in Jakarta fitted well with the attitudes of the dominant section of the national elite of the Republic, which sought to postpone extensive social reform until after the Dutch had been dealt with. The Republic, however, did not want to fight in Jakarta. For reasons of broader policy, its leaders discouraged the people of the city from acting, ordered Republican forces to leave the city, and used the Balai Agung as a statement of the Republic's claim to Jakarta rather than as a body to coordinate political or military struggle in the city. The Dutch, using their political and military power to bring the city almost completely under their control, destroyed the local revolutionary movement by mid-1947. Only in 1948 did the Republic begin seriously to attempt a political and military mobilization of the people of Jakarta, and then it was an effort directed almost entirely from outside. The remnants of Jakarta's mobilized youth of 1945, who carried on a militant struggle against the Dutch as lasykar in the areas around the city, were seen by the Republic's leaders as a dangerous embarrassment and were eventually crushed by the Republic.

Notes

I should like to thank Sidney Jones, Audrey Kahin, Ruth McVey, John Smail, and Ulf Sundhaussen for their helpful comments on earlier drafts of this paper, and to thank Shell Australia Ltd. for their financial support of my research.

1. Coen in fact built his fort on land that the Dutch East Indies Company had obtained in 1611 from the local ruler of the town of Jakatra, also on the Ciliwung, which was tributary to Banten. Jakatra itself was the name given to the older settlement of Sunda Kelapa to celebrate the defeat of a Portuguese fleet in Jakarta Bay in 1527. The present Jakarta municipal government dates the founding of the city to that year. See Abdurrachman Surjomihardjo, *Perkembangan kota Jakarta* (Jakarta: Dinas Museum dan Sejarah DKI, 1973), pp. 16–17.

2. On the sociology and geography of Jakarta, see Lance Castles, "The Ethnic Profile of Jakarta," *Indonesia* 1 (Apr. 1967): 153–204; James L. Cobban, "The City on Java: An Essay in Historical Geography," (Ph.D. dissertation, University of California, 1970); and Karl Helbig, *Am Rande des Pazifik: Stu-*

dien zur Lands- und Kulturkunde Südostasiens (Stuttgart: W. Kohlhammer, 1949), pp. 64–84 (a popular account based on his published doctoral dissertation, *Batavia, eine tropische Stadtlandschaftskunde im Rahmen der Insel Java* [Hamburg: University of Hamburg, 1931]).

3. Arnold Wright and Oliver T. Breakspear, eds., *Twentieth Century Impressions of Netherlands India: Its History, People, Commerce, Industries, and Resources* (London: Lloyd's Greater Britain Publishing Company, 1909), p. 442.

4. The patterns of thought and culture underlying the activism of the pemuda in the early stages of the revolution, together with the implications of pemuda involvement in national politics, have been thoroughly discussed in Benedict R. O'G. Anderson, *Java in a Time of Revolution: Occupation and Resistance, 1944–1946* (Ithaca: Cornell University Press, 1972).

5. On the political and military mobilization carried out by the Japanese, see George McT. Kahin, *Nationalism and Revolution in Indonesia* (Ithaca: Cornell University Press, 1952), pp. 103–111; and George S. Kanahele, "The Japanese Occupation of Indonesia: Prelude to Independence" (Ph.D. dissertation, Cornell University, 1967), pp. 47–48, 81–84, 116–154.

6. The Barisan Pelopor, or Suishintai, had been an armed youth wing of the Djawa Hōkōkai, the last of the mass organizations the Japanese had sponsored to mobilize the population in support of the war effort. Officially a nonmilitary organization, it was not affected by the order dissolving the Peta and Heihō. Its members were personally loyal to Sukarno and they gave his authority one of its few cutting edges in the capital during the weeks immediately following the proclamation.

7. On the neighborhood association, see Kanahele, "Japanese Occupation," pp. 142–145; and Kōichi Kishi, Shigetada Nishijima et al., eds. *Japanese Military Administration in Indonesia*, U.S. Department of Commerce, Joint Publications Research Service (Washington, D.C.: U.S. Government Printing Office, 1963), pp. 187–188.

8. On municipal organization in Jakarta under the Japanese and in the first weeks of independence, see Rochmani Santosa, "Djakarta Raya pada djaman Djepang (1942–1945)," paper given at the Second National History Seminar (Seminar Sedjarah Nasional II), vol. 6, no. 2 (Yogyakarta, 1970); The Liang Gie, *Sedjarah pemerintahan kota Djakarta* (Jakarta: Kotapradja Djakarta Raja, 1958), pp. 91, 106–107; *Republik Indonesia Kotapradja Djakarta Raya* (Jakarta: Kementerian Penerangan, 1953), pp. 74–76; and *Merderka* (Jakarta), Oct. 4, 1945.

9. The British occupation of Jakarta and general questions of British policy are discussed in Clifford William Squire, "Britain and the Transfer of Power in Indonesia 1945–46" (Ph.D. dissertation, University of London, 1977).

10. Small parties of sailors and marines had landed soon after the fleet arrived in order to protect the internment camps in Jakarta, but these landings

were deliberately kept low-key in order to avoid giving the impression that small parties were all that the British could field in Jakarta.

11. See Indonesia, Ministry of Foreign Affairs, *List of Material and Personal Outrages and Injuries Perpetrated against Indonesians by Dutch Soldiery in the City of Jakarta October–December 1945* (Jakarta, 1946); *Kotapradja Djakarta Raya*, pp. 548–550; *Merdeka*, Oct. 7, 1945–June 1, 1946, passim; *Ra'jat* (Jakarta), Nov. 3, 1945–July 9, 1946, passim; Rosihan Anwar, *Kisah-kisah Jakarta setelah proklamasi* (Jakarta: Pustaka Jaya, 1977); Johan Fabricius, *Hoe ik Indie terug vond* (The Hague: H. P. Leopold, 1947), p. 24; "Opgave van gekidnapte en/of vermoorde personen (Nederlandsche onderdanen)" [May 1946?]; Algemeen Rijksarchief [hereafter ARA], Archief Procureur-Generaal bij het Hoogerrechtshof van Nederlandsch-Indië [hereafter *Proc. Gen.*], dossier no. 480; and Troepencommando: "Kort verslag over November 1945," Centraal Archieven Depot, Ministerie van Defensie, The Hague [hereafter MvD], Asst. Adj. Gen. III A, ds. 224, Bundel IV, Geh. Ink. nr. 17.

12. Mountbatten to Cabinet Offices, Dec. 31, 1945, Public Records Office [hereafter PRO] file no. *FO* 371/53769; Noel Buckley [British correspondent in Jakarta], "British control Batavia," profile no. *WO* 208/1699; AFNEI (Allied Forces, Netherlands East Indies) to ALFSEA (Allied Land Forces, South East Asia), Dec. 30 and 31, 1945, *WO* 208/1699.

13. General questions of military organization and strategy and relations between the army and lasykar groups are dealt with in Ulf Sundhaussen, "The Political Orientations and Political Involvement of the Indonesian Officer Corps 1945–1966: The Siliwangi Division and the Army Headquarters," (Ph.D. dissertation, Monash University, 1971), pp. 77–119; and A. H. Nasution, *Sekitar perang kemerdekaan Indonesia, jilid 3: diplomasi sambil bertempur* (Bandung: Angkasa, 1977), pp. 195–198 and 426–470.

14. Detailed but patchy information on the lasykar and the TKR/TRI around Jakarta can be found in S. Z. Hadisutjipto, *Bara dan njala revolusi phisik di Djakarta* (Jakarta: Dinas Museum dan Sedjarah DKI Djakarta, 1971); Dinas Sejarah Militer Kodam V Jaya, *Sejarah perjuangan rakyat Jakarta, Tanggerang dan Bekasi dalam menegakkan kemerdekaan R.I.* (Jakarta: Virgo Sari, 1975); and *Sejarah pertumbuhan dan perkembangan Kodam V/Jaya: pengawal-penyelamat ibukota Republik Indonesia* (Jakarta: Komando Daerah Militer V Jayakarta, 1974).

15. *Nieuwsgier* (Jakarta), May 2, 1947; Rapport uitgevoerde werkzaamheden, d.d. 13–4–1948, opsteller onbekend, MvD, HKGS-NOI. [Hoofdkwartier Generaal Staf, Nederlandsch Oost Indië], Inv.nr. GG 57, 1949, Bundel 6323F, CMI [Centrale Militaire Inlichtingendienst] Document 5605 (pag. 18, vertaling 10).

16. One lasykar group, apparently tempted by unofficial Dutch promises

of service in the army of a new West Javanese federal state which the Dutch
were already considering, deserted to the Dutch, who used them, a little war-
ily, in their attack of July 1947 as "Her Majesty's Irregular Troops." On the
lasykar army, see Nasution, *Sekitar perang kemerdekaan Indonesia, jilid 4:
periode Linggajati* (Bandung: Angkasa, 1978), pp. 238–242; *Pikiran Rakyat*
(Bandung), Aug. 19, 1978; Sedjarah Militer Kodam VI Siliwangi, *Siliwangi
dari masa kemasa* (Jakarta: Fakta Mahjuna, 1968), pp. 186–190; and
J. A. A. van Doorn and W. J. Hendrix, *Ontsporing van geweld: over het
Nederlands/Indisch/Indonesisch conflict* (Rotterdam: Universitaire Pers Rotterdam, 1970), p. 90.

17. *Dokumentasi Republik Indonesia 1 Djanuari 1946–30 Djuni 1946*
(Yogyakarta: Kementerian Penerangan, 1950), p. 127.

18. On the Balai Agung in general, see *Kotapradja Djakarta Raya,* pp. 76–
82; The, *Sedjarah pemerintahan,* pp. 115–117; and *Minggoean Merdeka,*
(Jakarta), June 15, 1946. Something of the atmosphere of Jakarta as it was
felt by a civilian in this period can be gained from Mochtar Lubis, *A Road
with No End,* trans. Anthony H. Johns (London: Hutchinson, 1968).

19. Moehamad Hoesni Thamrin, who headed the prewar nationalist group
Kaum Betawi (Batavian group) and was a leader of national stature, died in
1941 without a political heir.

20. File: "Soewirjo," *Proc. Gen.,* dossier no. 818; Hoofdkwartier B Divisie,
"Nota betreffende de veiligheid van Batavia, 25 Mei 1946," MvD, HKGS-
NOI., Inv.nr. GG la, 1946, Bundel 49, stuk 106.

21. Interview with Dr. P. J. Koets, head of the cabinet of the lieutenant
governor-general and one of the chief political advisers to van Mook, Elle-
meet, Zeeland, Nov. 24, 1980.

22. On the various cooperative (and not so cooperative) arrangements, see
War Diary HQ 23 Ind. Div. "GS" branch, Java, Oct. 24, 1945, WO 172/7021
(PRO); "Samenwerking Batavia," n.d., Archief C. W. A. Abbenhuis (ARA);
"Verslag van het Algemeen Hoofd Tijdelijke Bestuursdienst Java over het tijd-
perk van Juli t/m December 1946," *Proc. Gen.* 894.6; *Ra'jat,* Jan. 5, 9, and
22, Apr. 14, 1946, Jan. 8, 1947; *Merdeka,* Feb. 18, 1946; *Minggoean Merdeka,* May 24 and 31, 1946; W. F. Wertheim, *Indonesie: van vorstenrijk tot
neo-kolonie* (Amsterdam: Boom, 1978), p. 129; and interview with M. Koois-
tra, military officer with responsibility for the Dutch civil police, The Hague,
Nov. 17, 1980.

23. Soeria Kartalegawa's state of Pasundan, which the Dutch never officially recognized, should not be confused with the Negara Pasundan established by the Dutch in occupied West Java in 1948 as part of their plan for a
federal Indonesia. Pasundan was also the official term in the Indonesian language for the prewar province of West Java.

24. On the question of currency, see Robert Cribb, "Political Dimensions of

the Currency Question 1945–1947," *Indonesia* 31 (Apr. 1981): 113–136.

25. File: "Soewirjo," Dagoverzicht van de plaats gehad hebbende gebeurtenissen, July 2, 1947, *Proc. Gen.* 147.1. On the Balai Agung in 1947 as perceived by a Dutch administrator, see J. E. Ysebaert [Hoofd Tijdelijke Bestuursdienst, Batavia] to L. M. Beel [Netherlands Prime Minister], May 21, 1947, in S. L. van der Wal, ed., *Officiele Bescheiden Betreffende de Nederlands-Indonesische Betrekkingen 1945–1950,* vol. 9 (The Hague: Martinus Nijhoff, 1981), p. 5.

26. See Samenvatting omtrent het wezen van het schijnbestuur "Pemerintah Republik Djawa Barat" (PRDB) Dec. 30, 1948, *Proc.Gen.* 138; "Politiek manifest van de Pemerintah Republik Djawa Barat" (PRDB), Aug. 17, 1948, MvD, HKGS-NOI., Inv.nr. GG 58, 1949, Bundel 6323G, CMI Document 5540 (pag. 11, vertaling 5).

27. See Abdul Haris Nasution, *Fundamentals of Guerrilla Warfare* (London: Pall Mall, 1965), for the theoretical background underpinning this activity.

28. See Herbert Feith, *The Decline of Constitutional Democracy in Indonesia* (Ithaca: Cornell University Press, 1962), pp. 55 and 81–82; and *Republik Indonesia Propinsi Djawa Barat* (Jakarta: Kementerian Penerangan, 1953), pp. 242–244 and 252.

29. *Merdeka,* Feb. 3, 1948.

30. It is striking that the Republicans habitually referred to such activity as "illegal" in much the same way as the Dutch resistance to the German occupation was known as the "illegaliteit," although in both cases it was the whole legality of the existing system that was being challenged.

31. Confidential interview, Rijswijk, the Netherlands, Nov. 26, 1980.

32. R.V.D. Mailbrief no. 1, February 1948, Bijlage 2, "Six additional principles for the negotiations towards a political settlement submitted by the Committee of Good Offices at the fourth meeting on 17th January" (ARA), Archief Algemene Secretarie te Batavia, Tweede Zending [hereafter Alg. Sec.II], dossier 666.

33. See Dienst der Algemene Recherche, "Overzicht: Republikeinse propaganda voor het (eventueel) te houden plebisciet," May 7, 1948, Alg.Sec.II, dossier 402.

34. See the documents gathered in Alg.Sec.II, 1066, especially "Overzicht van de 3e West Java Conferentie, gehouden te Bandoeng van 23 Februari t/m 5 Maart 1948."

35. See *Propinsi Djawa Barat,* pp. 228–232; also Kahin, *Nationalism and Revolution,* pp. 454–455. Westerling's own account stresses the local composition of his forces; see Raymond Paul Pierre Westerling, *Mijn memoires* (Antwerp and Amsterdam: P. Vink, n.d.), pp. 204–205.

SOUTH SULAWESI

SULAWESI SEA

MAKASSAR STRAIT

Menado

MINAHASA

MALUKU SEA

SOUTH
SULAWESI

LUWU

Palopo

Pare-
Pare

BONE

Makassar
GOWA

Bonthain

BANDA SEA

FLORES SEA

| 0 | 100 | 200 |

MILES

SOUTH SULAWESI:
PUPPETS AND PATRIOTS

Barbara S. Harvey

South Sulawesi during the Indonesian national revolution of 1945 to 1949 had the distinction of being the site of the most bitter resistance outside the Republic to the reimposition of Dutch rule and simultaneously the center of the most fully developed of the Dutch-sponsored federal states, NIT (Negara Indonesia Timur, East Indonesia State). In order to establish the NIT government in Makassar, which was the capital of South Sulawesi as well as of NIT, the Dutch resorted to a military pacification campaign from December 1946 until March 1947 that effectively ended significant armed resistance in South Sulawesi. The cruelty and suffering endured during these months constituted, for most of the people of South Sulawesi, their personal experience of the revolution.

As the Dutch were attempting to establish their control over South Sulawesi, the government of the Republic of Indonesia accepted, in the Linggajati Agreement, Dutch proposals for a federal United States of Indonesia. In this agreement, the Dutch recognized the de facto authority of the Republic only in Java and Sumatra. South Sulawesi was to be incorporated into a Great Eastern State which would be a component part of the projected federal United States of Indonesia. For a number of the nationalist leaders in Makassar who believed that armed resistance to the Dutch had little hope of success despite the enormous sacrifice of young lives, the Linggajati Agreement signaled Republican approval of their participation in the NIT organs then being established. For those nationalists still trying to carry on armed resistance in the countryside, however, and for those imprisoned or in exile, the agreement signified their abandonment by the Republic. Differing perceptions of Republican intentions thus intensified the contrast between the city-based collaborators with the Dutch and the reimposition of their rule, however disguised in federalist forms, and those Sulawesians still fighting in the countryside, or in Java, against the return of the Dutch.

Prelude to Revolution

The Dutch had exercised effective control in the interior of South Sulawesi only since 1910, when they subdued the area in a five-year military campaign. The city of Makassar, however, had been under their rule for more than two centuries, and had become a polyglot commercial center. From there, the Dutch had gradually extended their influence to the south, but local chiefs and rulers in these Makassarese districts, as in the Buginese heartland to the north, had continued to be the principal loci of authority. These local chiefs and rajas were the target of the Dutch in their military conquest of South Sulawesi from 1905 to 1910. Subsequently the Dutch constructed an elaborate system of direct and indirect rule, in which formally recognized kingdoms coexisted with the colonial civil service. Chiefs and rulers signed contracts swearing loyalty to the Dutch rulers and promising to carry out colonial orders and regulations. In return, they were permitted to exercise many of their traditional functions, particularly those involving religion and customary law. At the same time, the aristocracy became disassociated from several of their more oppressive functions, such as taxation and requisition of labor, which were taken over by village heads or colonial bureaucrats. Few Buginese or Makassarese, aristocrats or commoners, had the education necessary to join the civil service, which was the actual instrument of colonial rule, and was dominated by better-educated Minahasans and Javanese. Although the Buginese and Makassarese aristocrats lost virtually all of their political powers, they retained a considerable measure of economic power from their extensive landholdings and of traditional authority through their control of religious and community symbols. Thus, many of them kept their titles and perquisites, their wealth and their traditional prestige, without being compromised in the eyes of their subjects as tools of the colonial power.

Few competing leadership groups emerged in South Sulawesi society, for educational opportunities were severely restricted and there was little time for an intelligentsia to develop in the brief colonial period. Christian missionaries gained little foothold in the strongly Islamic Buginese and Makassarese areas, and thus there was no flowering of mission schools as in the Christian stronghold of Minahasa. As few young people from South Sulawesi went to the secondary schools, located in Java, few established ties with students from other parts of the archipelago. Nor did an Islamic counter-elite develop, for both the Islamic administrative hierarchy and the modernist Muhammadiyah movement were led by members of the aristocracy. Muhammadiyah schools did spread into the interior, and some young men from South Sulawesi attended Islamic schools in Java, but the numbers were few.

Buginese and Makassarese participated in only limited numbers in the nationalist movement. Local Dutch officials estimated in 1941 that the five nationalist groups existing in Makassar at that time (two of which advocated cooperation with the colonial government) had a total membership of only 588. Their presence in the interior was negligible.[1]

When they first occupied Eastern Indonesia in 1942, the Japanese did not encourage nationalist sentiment or political participation because they intended to retain the area under naval administration as a colony. They banned all political parties and merged all Islamic organizations into a single body, the Jamiyah Islamiyah. Initially, the authorities in the navy territories made almost no attempt to organize —or even to propagandize—the population. Until early in 1943 there was no propaganda section in the Navy Civil Administration in Makassar; no mass organization to mobilize support for the Japanese was ever established in Sulawesi; and a youth corps, the Seinendan, was set up there only in January 1944.[2]

Working with and through the local aristocracy, the Japanese formed district, municipal, and regional councils composed largely of chiefs and officials. There were apparently few or no Islamic representatives on these councils.[3] Although Buginese and Makassarese civil servants had greater opportunities to attain higher positions during the Japanese occupation, relatively few had the education or experience to take advantage of the opportunity. In general, the South Sulawesi aristocracy was spared the taint of collaboration with the Japanese because no forced laborers were recruited there, as was widely done on Java, and the village chiefs, not the rajas, were responsible for forced rice deliveries.

Only in early 1945, recognizing the inevitability of their defeat, did the Japanese increase Indonesian participation in government and in political organizations in an effort to gain support against the advance of Allied forces. In May 1945 they appointed one of the foremost local nationalists, Nadjamoeddin Daeng Malewa,[4] as the first Indonesian mayor of Makassar. Five local advisers were also brought into the Navy Civil Administration.[5] Then in June, the Japanese established a proto-nationalist organization, Sudara (Sumber Darah Rakyat, Nation Founding Friendship Association),[6] in Makassar in an attempt to bring together the various factions of the small nationalist elite in Makassar and the traditional aristocratic rulers of South Sulawesi. Although the most prestigious aristocrat in the area, Andi Mappanjukki, raja of Bone,[7] was named head of Sudara, the actual functioning of the organization was dominated by Dr. G. S. S. J. Ratulangie,[8] a Minahasan nationalist brought to Makassar in December 1943 as one of the first Indonesian advisers to the Japanese Navy Civil Administration. Several of the handful of local youths who had studied in Java joined Sudara and served to link the local nationalists and aristocrats with Dr. Ratulangie and the young Minahasans and Sumatrans he had brought with him.

The Japanese recruited some youths for their auxiliary corps, Heihō, but established nothing comparable to the Peta (the voluntary army on Java) until just a few months before their surrender. Then they set up the Bui Taisintai (a defense force) consisting of a single battalion of not more than 250 youths.[9] The young people in South Sulawesi thus had few opportunities to participate in mass organizations or to receive military training during the Japanese occupation.

Although the nationalist movement in South Sulawesi was weak, the tradition of resistance to the Dutch was strong. Memories of the Dutch conquest some forty years earlier were still vivid. The raja of Bone, Andi Mappanjukki, chairman of Sudara, had fought against and been exiled by the Dutch in 1906; he provided a living link to the earlier struggle against the imposition of Dutch control.

The Start of the Revolution in South Sulawesi

Not only was the nationalist movement in South Sulawesi less well prepared for independence than its counterparts in Java and Sumatra, but the Allies and Dutch authorities were also in a better position to resume control from the surrendering Japanese.

A week after the proclamation of Indonesian independence, the Sulawesi delegation that had participated in the discussions of the Independence Preparatory Committee in Jakarta returned to Makassar. The delegation, headed by Dr. Ratulangie, was welcomed on its return by a number of prominent local nationalists and Japanese officials in a brief display of nationalist unity and Japanese support.[10] Although the newly formed government of the Republic had appointed him governor of Sulawesi, Ratulangie was reluctant to set up a Republican administration in the province. He did not want to get into trouble with the Allies—or the Japanese—particularly since he was unsure of the support of either his fellow nationalists or the local aristocracy. Both he and the leader of the *pemuda* (young people), Manai Sophiaan,[11] had worked closely with the Japanese during the occupation, and, in view of Allied statements about collaborators, were apprehensive about their fate. Hesitant to take any action that might further incur the wrath of the Allies, they acted with extreme caution.[12]

In late August, former members of the Bui Taisintai and Heihō urged Ratulangie to declare Sulawesi part of the Republic and to make a show of force against the landing of Allied troops. Ratulangie, however, forbade the needless sacrifice of lives, and, rather than relying on the volatile, and unarmed, pemuda, tried instead to rally support for the Republic among the nationalists and the local aristocrats.[13] The nucleus of this support was found in Sudara, the staff of which apparently continued to function as a staff to Ratulangie, indeed almost as a provincial government apparatus although never formally proclaimed as such. Dr. Ratulangie's association with the raja of Bone in Sudara was of great importance in facilitating cooperation between the cosmopolitan nationalists of Makassar and the traditional aristocrats of the local kingdoms in support of the Republic and in opposition to the return of the Dutch.

The Dutch, however, made an early return to East Indonesia. Officals of the Netherlands Indies Civil Administration (NICA) accompanied Allied forces, including the advance guard of Australian troops which landed in Makassar on September 21, 1945. Within a few days, all of the approximately 460 Allied prisoners of war still interned in South Sulawesi were evacuated to Australia, and the 3,000 Dutch internees were resettled in Makassar.[14] Unlike the British forces in Java, who were constrained by fears for the safety of the large number of internees and prisoners of war who were virtual hostages of the Republic, the Australians in Sulawesi now had a relatively free hand to deal with the Japanese and local Republicans. Their principal objective was to institute a functioning administration that could ensure public order and obtain rice from the interior to feed the city of Makassar. To this end, they immediately installed prewar Dutch officials, a number of them just-released internees, as provisional officials of the Australian civil administration.[15]

Although some older Indonesian officials, mostly from the Ambonese and Minahasa Christian minorities, welcomed the Dutch and facilitated their taking over government offices in the city, other segments of the population resisted their return. The local nationalists and pro-Republican rajas initially hoped to cooperate with the Australians without accepting the Dutch and attempted to convince the Australians of the extent of local support for the Republic. On October 15, the principal chiefs of South Sulawesi, led by the rajas of Bone and Luwu, issued a statement of support for the Republic and its governor in Sulawesi, Dr. Ratulangie.[16]

The pemuda and much of the population in the interior openly wore red and white colors as symbols of support for the Republic and violently opposed the return of the Dutch. There were a number of incidents, described in Australian reports as "minor riots and disturbances," including attacks on police barracks, which the Australians regarded as "clearly intended as demonstrations against the Dutch by extremist elements."[17] Although it was the reappearance of Dutch officials and colonial police and troops that provoked these incidents, the Dutch and Australians used the increasing disorder to justify the presence of NICA and the reconstitution of KNIL (Royal Netherlands

Indies Army) units. By mid-October, four to five hundred KNIL soldiers, mostly Ambonese, were stationed in Makassar.[18]

Numerous small Republican youth groups arose spontaneously in Makassar and the interior. Formal and informal relationships among the different groups were fluid, and members moved from one to another as the situation changed or opportunity arose.[19] Their military effectiveness was limited by their lack of weapons. Only a few firearms were seized or received from sympathetic Japanese or Australian soldiers. Although Australian patrols reported rumors of Republican caches of arms and ammunition, no arsenals appear to have been discovered. In November the local Australian commander decreed that only police officials could carry firearms, and only police, village guards, and local chiefs or officials were permitted to own traditional knives and spears.[20]

By the end of October, an estimated twenty-five youth groups were active in Makassar. One of the most important was the PPNI (Pusat Pemuda Nasional Indonesia, Indonesian Nationalist Youth Center). Headed by Manai Sophiaan and closely associated with the older nationalist leadership, the PPNI was a loose federation of politically oriented youth groups and *lasykar* (militias).[21] On the night of October 28–29, PPNI members led an armed attack on Dutch police and government buildings in Makassar, capturing two radio stations and replacing the Dutch flag in front of the government office building with the red and white flag of the Republic. They also attacked police barracks and the hotel where NICA officers were staying. Unable to cope on their own, the Dutch appealed to the Australians and with their assistance routed the attackers. Before the day was over the pemuda were either in prison or had fled.[22]

Contending Forces

As the violence intensified, Ratulangie, on the day of the attack, transformed his staff into a PKR (Pusat Keselamatan Rakyat, Center for People's Security), a name probably deliberately modeled on the BKR (People's Security Body) established in Java in August. Although the ostensible purpose of the PKR was to safeguard the well-being of the population, its real objective, according to Ratulangie, was to compete with NICA and "demonstrate the ability of Indonesians to govern their country."[23]

Under the name of the PKR, Ratulangie issued a petition addressed to the Allies declaring that the people of Sulawesi wanted an independent and democratic Republic of Indonesia and wished to be "an inseparable part" of that Republic. Circulated during November, it was signed by 540 rajas, customary chiefs, and religious, political, and social leaders. The petition was presented to the Australian commander for forwarding to the United Nations.[24]

Ratulangie also attempted to take advantage of the Australian forces' dismay at the strength of pro-Republican sentiment and the inability of NICA to maintain law and order to develop a basis for cooperation with the Allied forces. The Australian commander, Brigadier F. O. Chilton, told Ratulangie in a meeting on November 2, that if Ratulangie and the other leaders showed a willingness to cooperate and could demonstrate their control over the people by ending lawlessness and interference with the collection and distribution of rice, Chilton would "consider further steps to bring about a greater share in civil affairs for Indonesians."[25] However, Dutch officials claimed that Ratulangie, in reporting on his discussions with Chilton to the rajas of Bone and Luwu on November 6, deliberately distorted Chilton's remarks, and they demanded that Ratulangie be deported. Although the Australian headquarters in Morotai refused to accede to Dutch demands for Ratulangie's deportation, the local Australian commander was now wary of further contact with him. On November 21, Chilton issued an instruction stating that NICA was "an integral part of the military administration" and forbidding any action in the name of the Republic.[26] Thereafter it was impossible for the local chiefs to cooperate with the Australians, as several had indicated they wished to do, without accepting NICA.

In the ensuing weeks, the Australian military government intensified its pressure on local rulers to cease their pro-Republican statements and actions and to prevent violence by supporters of the Republic. Several local rulers were removed from their positions; a number were arrested and imprisoned. Some of the chiefs and rulers resigned rather than accepted NICA. In many areas, the common people, unswayed by legal niceties, refused to accept NICA Dutchmen as Australians and revolted against chiefs who cooperated with them.[27]

The Dutch also used economic pressure. NICA controlled the distribution of cloth and food, both in short supply by the end of the Japanese occupation. They allowed no private trading in rice, all of which had to be delivered to and distributed by NICA. In order to ensure a supply of rice for the city, and at the urging of NICA officials, the Australian commander on October 20 agreed to send battalions to occupy key areas in Bone (part of the rice-growing heartland) and other parts of the interior. At the same time, Australian troops were instructed to assist NICA officials in administration of the countryside.

Occupation currency was no longer legal tender and had to be exchanged for NICA money at an unfavorable and unrealistic rate. There were few possibilities for employment outside the Dutch administration or the Dutch business community. These economic pressures weighed most heavily in the city of Makassar, with its concentration of prewar civil servants, and the city soon acquired the reputation of being a center of pro-Dutch sentiment. A NICA administration was functioning there by the end of 1945, manned by prewar Dutch and Indo-European officials and Indonesians who were promised good salaries and high positions. Among the latter was the erstwhile nationalist Nadjamoeddin Daeng Malewa, who, whether from jealousy over Ratulangie's appointment by the Republic as governor of Sulawesi or from mere opportunism, accepted in November 1945 a position as commercial consultant to NICA.[28]

More local rulers and chiefs who refused to cooperate with the Dutch were removed after the departure of the Australian forces and the transfer of NICA headquarters from Morotai to Makassar in February 1946. After a brief British interregnum, authority over the outer islands was officially transferred from the South East Asia Command to the Netherlands Indies government on July 14, 1946. The Dutch exiled Dr. Ratulangie to West Irian in April 1946, and Andi Mappanjukki and his son Andi Pangerang were also exiled in November 1946. In the course of the revolution, the Dutch replaced probably between a quarter and a half of the rajas, *hadat* (council) members, subordinate rulers, and village chiefs. By 1949, about half of those removed from office were dead, 40 percent had been imprisoned or exiled by the Dutch, and the remaining 10 percent had turned to agriculture or commerce.[29]

The Dutch found a ready supply of cooperative replacements

among rival branches of ruling families. The most prominent among them were appointed to a supreme council of chiefs, the Hadat Tinggi, which was later institutionalized as the Supreme Council of the Federation of South Sulawesi under NIT.[30]

Armed Resistance to the Dutch

After the failure of the attacks in Makassar on October 29, 1945, armed opposition to the Dutch moved in two directions—to the countryside of South Sulawesi and to Java. Young nationalists went to Java, initially to seek aid for the struggle in Sulawesi but later, after their hopes for their own area were thwarted, to fight against the Dutch in Java. Dr. Ratulangie sent several youths to contact the organization of Sulawesi youth in Jakarta, KRIS (Kebaktian Rakyat Indonesia Sulawesi, Loyalty of the Indonesian People of Sulawesi), which was headed by his daughter. He instructed them to report on the situation in Sulawesi and to request assistance from the Republic for the nationalist struggle in Sulawesi. Manai Sophiaan joined KRIS and served in the Sulawesi commissariat of the Republican ministry of the interior in Java. Two others, Andi Mattalatta and Saleh Lahade,[31] were given a mandate by the Republican army commander-in-chief, General Sudirman, to establish a division of the national army in Sulawesi. Working with the first secretary of KRIS, Qahhar Mudzakkar,[32] who had his own armed unit, they trained and sent to Sulawesi a number of expeditionary groups. About a thousand youths landed safely there and linked up with local guerrilla groups.

Resistance to the Dutch in South Sulawesi was strongest in areas where the local ruler was pro-Republican and worked with the revolutionary pemuda: Suppa (near Pare-Pare), Luwu, and Polongbangkeng (south of Makassar). The young datu (local ruler) of Suppa, Andi Abdullah Bau Massepe (a son of Andi Mappanjukki), along with his predecessor as datu, Andi Makkasau, established a branch of the PKR in Pare-Pare and were brutally killed by the Dutch in January 1947. The datu of Luwu, Andi Djemma, took a strongly pro-Republican stand. Fierce fighting broke out in Palopo, capital of Luwu, in January 1946 after Dutch-officered KNIL troops entered a mosque. This battle was described by General Nasution as "the largest battle of the guerrilla war."[33] In Polongbangkeng, the local ruler, Haji Padjonga Daeng Ngalle, declared the district part of the Republic and served as adviser to the most effective guerrilla force in South Sulawesi, Lapris (Lasykar Pemberontak Rakyat Indonesia Sulawesi, Fighting Militia of the Indonesian People of Sulawesi). Operating primarily in the area south of Makassar, Lapris was involved in more than a hundred armed actions between December 1945 and February 1947.[34]

On January 21, 1947, representatives of ten guerrilla groups met in the village of Pacekke (near Pare-Pare) with youths who had returned from Java, including Andi Mattalatta and Saleh Lahade. They planned to carry out their mandate from the Republican army commander to establish a division of the TNI (Indonesian National Army) in Sulawesi by commissioning three regiments of the Hasanuddin Division, one in each of the active Republican areas: Luwu, Polongbangkeng, and Pare-Pare. Only the third was actually commissioned, however, because Dutch military action made travel and communications difficult and dangerous, and relatively few guerrilla leaders were able to attend the meeting. Those present decided that it was impossible to continue the fight in Sulawesi; the cost in civilian as well as military lives was too high. Many of the pemuda decided to fight in Java instead, but of the nearly one thousand youths who had returned to South Sulawesi in the expeditionary groups only about a hundred escaped prison or death to return to Java.[35]

Dutch Policy in South Sulawesi: Military Pacification

The vehemence of pro-Republican resistance in South Sulawesi throughout 1945 and 1946 came as a surprise to the Dutch. It threatened their plans to experiment with a new relationship within which the old colonial tie could be preserved in a new form. In February 1946, Lt. Governor-General van Mook formally proposed the creation of a federal United States of Indonesia in a "commonwealth relationship" to the Kingdom of the Netherlands. The Dutch selected East Indonesia as the first area to become such a state. The Dutch were relatively strong militarily in this area, which contained both Ambon and Minahasa, traditionally major recruiting grounds for the KNIL. Further, the Dutch were correct in their assessment that the idea of a federal state would appeal to people in the outer islands, who were already somewhat fearful that the numerically preponderant Javanese would dominate politically an independent Indonesia. Discussions on the formation of the East Indonesia State (NIT) began at the Malino Conference in July 1946 and culminated in the proclamation of NIT in Den Pasar, Bali, on December 24, 1946.[36]

In time, NIT was to become the most fully developed and autonomous of the federal states. But before it could be established, the Dutch had to eliminate pro-Republican resistance in South Sulawesi, the most populous area in East Indonesia and the site of the new state's projected capital, Makassar. They took advantage of rivalries among the leading nationalists and among the aristocracy and, as noted above, they removed noncooperative chiefs and rulers. Gradually Dutch military and administrative control was extended into the interior. Then, from December 15, 1946, through February 15, 1947, they mounted a pacification campaign, which encompassed most of South Sulawesi. A young Dutch commando, Raymond "Turk" Westerling, claims to have drawn up operational plans for the military pacification of the whole island, which ended significant armed resistance within two months. He began by branding all acts of pro-Republican sympathy as terrorism and all persons sympathetic to the Republic as extremists. The Dutch could then claim that they were acting against mere bandits in the interest of protecting the common people. Although he himself was not directly responsible for all the killing and intimidation that occurred as Dutch control was reimposed in South Sulawesi, Westerling's tactics were followed, and his name is indelibly imprinted on the pacification campaign.[37]

The Dutch were careful to involve Indonesians in the decision to mount the campaign and in its implementation. They had the council of rajas issue a statement requesting elimination of the extremist groups that were disturbing law and order. When prominent women from Sulawesi petitioned Dutch civil and military officials about the severity of the tactics being used, a loyal civil servant, Sonda Daeng Mattajang, reported to the Den Pasar Conference that "those who are being killed are only terrorists and bandits."[38]

The way the pacification campaign was carried out in the countryside also involved Indonesians in the responsibility for the killings. The most usual technique, and the one recommended by Westerling, was to assemble villagers in a central area and ask them to point out the "extremists" among them. The commandos shot those so designated on the spot. If no information was volunteered, the commandos chose several villagers at random and shot them. The process continued until information, correct or not, was elicited.

Known guerrilla leaders were caught and publicly tortured and/or killed, with the intention of giving psychological impact to Dutch warnings against working with the extremists. Pro-Republican aristocrats, village leaders, *imam* (Moslem leaders), and Muhammadiyah activists are said to have been particular targets.

The precise number killed in the pacification campaign, whether the 40,000 claimed by the Republicans or the 3,000 admitted to by the Dutch, was of significance less in political terms than in psychological and social impact. The involvement of Indonesians in responsibility for the killings left as its legacy a desire for revenge and retribution, which underlay much of the brutality of the postrevolutionary rebellion of Qahhar Mudzakkar. In the villages, people who had lost family members because other villagers had pointed them out as terrorists—whether the charge was true or merely a means of self-protection—had cause for resentment and an *adat* (custom)-sanctioned desire for revenge. Those who had been imprisoned remembered who had betrayed them and longed for their day of freedom and chance for retribution. The rajas who sat on the council of rajas were blamed for having sanctioned the pacification campaign. NIT officials and parliamentarians were seen as accomplices in the terror. The pemuda hunted down as criminals believed that those of their elders who had participated in the formation and functioning of NIT had willingly signed their death warrants.[39]

Negara Indonesia Timur

Proclaimed in December 1946, in the midst of the Dutch pacification campaign, NIT was effectively accepted by the Republic in March 1947 with the signing of the Linggajati Agreement. This agreement recognized de facto Republic of Indonesia authority over only Java, Madura, and Sumatra. It further provided that the Republic, Borneo, and East Indonesia would be included as component parts of a United

States of Indonesia, which would be a member of a Netherlands-Indonesian Union.[40]

Why did recognized nationalists agree to cooperate with the Dutch in NIT? Mr. G. R. Pantouw, who had worked with Dr. Ratulangie in Sudara and the PKR before serving as minister of information in the first NIT cabinet, explained:

> I separated myself from the PKR: I saw that you can't expect anything from such a body. . . . I was with Nadjamoeddin, we both organized another political body to cooperate with the Dutch because resistance at that time was disappointing. . . . We cooperated in several ways with the NICA, especially in respect to economic affairs. We found people had suffered so much during bombardments and the Japanese occupation, we felt it no longer responsible to [resist the Dutch].
>
> Most people thought NIT a puppet government, but in fact it was our pressure. . . . We wanted to force the institution of Indonesia Timur because we could no longer tolerate the NICA as a governing body—that would be reinstitution of colonialism.
>
> At that time it was impossible in our eyes [to become a part of the Republic]. We had no military power, had nothing. To resist the Dutch you must have soldiers and weapons; we had neither. We had no weapons to resist effectively, and we regarded it as irresponsible to let the pemuda die for their ideals in such a way.[41]

Nadjamoeddin Daeng Malewa served as prime minister and minister for economic affairs in the first NIT cabinet, ceremonially installed in Batavia on January 13, 1947. The first session of the NIT parliament opened in Makassar on April 22, 1947; its members consisted of the fifty-five representatives to the Den Pasar Conference who had been chosen by NICA-appointed councils, fifteen representatives appointed directly by the lieutenant governor-general, and ten persons appointed by the NIT president, a profederalist Balinese nobleman named Anak Agung Gde Sukowati.[42]

Despite the careful selection of members of the parliament, it was soon apparent that there were many pro-Republicans among them, notably the first chairman, Tadjuddin Noor.[43] The two pro-Republican groups in parliament were the progressive faction, which included members from North and Central Sulawesi, Maluku, Bali, and Lombok, and the national faction, whose members were considered the spokesmen for the aristocratic rulers of South Sulawesi and Sumbawa. Both groups refused to participate in the initial cabinets and considered themselves noncooperators.[44]

The Nadjamoeddin cabinet supported the Dutch military action against the Republic in Java and Sumatra in July 1947, but Nadjamoeddin publicly and sharply criticized Dutch policy after he was humiliated at the United Nations when the Security Council refused to hear the delegation from NIT, of which he was a member. He was summarily dismissed by the Dutch from his position as NIT prime minister on September 20, 1947.[45]

A successor cabinet, under Dr. S. J. Warouw, affirmed its support of Dutch actions against the Republic and consequently was ousted by parliament on December 9, 1947. A nonparty Balinese aristocrat, Anak Agung Gde Agung, who was acceptable to all parliamentary factions, succeeded a week later in forming a cabinet that included for the first time representatives of the two pro-Republican groups. A year later this cabinet resigned in protest of the Dutch attack on the Republican capital of Yogyakarta, but the NIT president again called on Anak Agung Gde Agung to form a new cabinet. The second Anak Agung cabinet continued until December 1949, when Anak Agung became minister of the interior in the cabinet of the federal Republic of the United States of Indonesia (RIS). Interim cabinets continued until the formal dissolution of NIT on August 17, 1950.[46]

Despite the expression of of pro-Republican views in the NIT parliament and cabinet, the Dutch were able to retain a firm grip over East Indonesia, including South Sulawesi, during the revolution. Not only did they have overwhelming military force in the area, but they also retained control of the major source of revenue, the copra trade, in the hands of the Batavia government. In addition, a Dutchman, M. Hamelink, held the position of minister of finance in all NIT cabinets. The Dutch also relied on aristocratic elements, especially those appointed to replace pro-Republican chiefs and rulers and thus dependent on Dutch support, to buttress their rule.[47]

Within South Sulawesi itself, the Dutch established a temporary representative council in March 1946 to advise on the political and administrative organization to be set up in the area. Chaired by the commanding officer of NICA, who named thirteen of its forty-two members, it approved the selection of the representatives of the self-governing territories (fifteen representatives), the directly ruled area (nine), and the municipality of Makassar (six).[48]

Traditional forms of government were retained or resuscitated, with councils of subordinate chiefs advising the rulers. The former directly ruled areas were transformed into what were called neo-lands, which were indistinguishable from the older self-governing territories. In October 1948, the thirty self-governing territories and eight neo-lands were combined into the Federation of South Sulawesi, under the administrative authority of the council of rajas. Only in early 1949 were elections held for a South Sulawesi Council, which was to share administrative responsibility with the council of rajas.[49]

As a further protection for their positions, the aristocratic rulers in East Indonesia demanded the formation of a senate with veto power over the proposed NIT constitution. The Dutch met this demand in return for the rulers' agreement to renegotiate their contracts to replace the Dutch Government with NIT. The senate was established on May 28, 1949, with one representative from each of the thirteen NIT regions, the governments of ten of which were controlled by aristocratic elements.[50]

Although the Dutch, aided by compliant local aristocrats and their own military and financial strength, kept a tight grip on East Indonesia, they were unable to silence voices sympathetic to the Republic. Even though the NIT parliament was essentially an appointed temporary representative assembly until elections were held in late 1949, it provided a potent forum for the expression of pro-Republican sentiments. Its ousting in December 1947 of the Warouw cabinet, which had supported the July 1947 Dutch attack on the Republic, and the resignation of the Anak Agung cabinet in December 1948 convinced the Dutch of their inability to manipulate the other components of the projected federal state while they destroyed or crippled the Republic.

In the negotiations leading to the transfer of sovereignty in 1949, NIT representatives spearheaded the federalists' unwillingness to cooperate with the Dutch against the Republic. Their inability to use NIT, their model federal state, to further their objectives contributed to the Dutch decision to transfer sovereignty to Indonesia and abandon the colonial tie. Although the transfer of sovereignty in December 1949 was made formally to the federal Republic of the United States of Indonesia, demands for merger of the federal states into a unitary republic quickly spread, and by August 1950 all the federal states had merged into the unitary Republic of Indonesia.

Character of the Revolution in South Sulawesi

The national revolution in South Sulawesi had two distinct aspects, characterized here as puppet and patriot.[51] In part the distinction is chronological: most people in South Sulawesi initially resisted the reimposition of Dutch rule; only when that became impossible did significant numbers consent to work with the Dutch. In part the distinction is geographical: the Dutch took control of the city of Makassar relatively quickly and located their administrative and military headquarters for East Indonesia there; in the countryside guerrilla activity continued, at least sporadically, thoughout the revolution. To see the puppet-patriot distinction as a sharp dichotomy, however, is to ignore the significant role of pro-Republican noncooperators in the NIT parliament and cabinets in convincing the Dutch of the futility of their attempt to defeat the Indonesia national revolution. Nevertheless, the striking differences between the revolutionary experience in the countryside and in the city of Makassar underlay much of the turmoil which engulfed South Sulawesi during Qahhar Mudzakkar's rebellion from 1950 to 1965.

Makassar's emergence as the capital of NIT had two effects on the city. First, because NIT included all of eastern Indonesia, officials and parliamentarians came to Makassar from the whole eastern archipelago. Thus the cosmopolitan, multiethnic character of the city—and the contrast with the interior—was intensified. More important, the city became identified as a center of pro-Dutch sentiment and activity, and even those nationalists whose participation in the NIT parliament was as noncooperators were tinged with collaboration. In the countryside this collaboration was seen as particularly nasty, because of the ruthlessness of the military pacification campaign with which it was inevitably associated.

Resistance to the Dutch was more prolonged in the countryside than in the city, although the Dutch were able to eliminate all but sporadic guerrilla activity in little more than a year. For many Buginese and Makassarese, the city thus came to symbolize the puppet aspect of

South Sulawesi's history in the 1945 to 1949 revolution, while the interior, as the home of the resistance fighters, symbolized the patriot aspect.

Because of the early landing of Allied forces and Dutch administrators and the weakness of the local nationalist movement, no Republican government was proclaimed in Sulawesi. The activities of the nationalist and pro-Republican aristocrats within Sudara amounted to little more than spreading the news of the proclamation of independence. The attempt to cooperate with the Australian military authorities and at the same time to oppose the return of the Dutch was doomed to failure by the inclusion of NICA as part of the Australian military administration. Dutch officials were in place in South Sulawesi by the end of September 1945, and NICA was a functioning administration in most of the province by the end of the year. The Dutch thus remained the target of hostility, and the national revolution to gain independence remained the priority goal.

Despite the weakness of the nationalist movement in South Sulawesi, both in leadership and in organizational development, Republican symbols had wide currency from the outset of the revolution. Such practices as raising the red and white flag of the Republic, wearing red and white colors, and posting copies of the proclamation of independence were common in the interior as well as in Makassar. Although South Sulawesi was in many ways little touched by Dutch colonialism, and its pemuda lacked the ties other youths developed in schools in Java and the Netherlands, the widespread display of these Republican symbols clearly implied a sense of an Indonesian nation. Centuries of Buginese and Makassarese seafaring and migration throughout the archipelago may have created this consciousness at a deeper level. And memories of resistance to the Dutch conquest in the early years of the century undoubtedly intensified the determination to resist their return in 1945. Thus, although the nationalist movement in South Sulawesi was very weak, and although there were no Buginese or Makassarese prominent in the Republican government on Java, there was a strong commitment to the goals of the revolution.

There were, as we have noted, many people in South Sulawesi who cooperated with the Dutch or participated in the institutions of NIT. Some were prewar civil servants, many of them from the Minahasan and Ambonese Christian minorities. Some were Buginese and Makassarese who owed their positions to the Dutch. Dutch manipulation of the selection of rulers in a number of the kingdoms after the 1910 conquest provided a ready supply of disgruntled "outs" who could be substituted for an earlier selection if he should turn recalcitrant. Some cooperators appear to have been motivated by jealousy and opportunism. The resentment of the leading local nationalist, Nadjamoeddin, over the selection of the outsider Ratulangie as Republican governor of Sulawesi made him an easy subject for manipulation by the Dutch. Nevertheless, despite initial tensions between Ratulangie and the local rajas, Ratulangie, with Andi Mappanjukki's active assistance, did gain the support of most of the local rulers in the opening phase of the revolution. By the end of 1946, however, the Dutch had replaced virtually all of the prominent pro-Republican chiefs and rajas with others, more amenable to their return.

Some political leaders considered themselves nationalists but believed that resistance to the Dutch was futile and interpreted Republican acceptance of the Linggajati Agreement as a recognition of this fact so far as Sulawesi was concerned. Thus they convinced themselves that they could advance the national cause as sympathizers with the Republic within NIT institutions. And, indeed, the resignation of the NIT cabinet in 1948 in protest of the Dutch attack on Yogyakarta and the obvious sympathy for the Republic of the NIT representatives during the 1949 negotiations on the transfer of sovereignty helped to demonstrate to the Dutch the hopelessness of their effort to thwart the establishment of the Republic of Indonesia.

Within South Sulawesi itself, the presence of the Dutch and the focusing of attention on them meant that national revolution took precedence over social. In any case, the ruling aristocracy had not only retained its traditional prestige and influence but also was little compromised during the colonial period. Few of its members were sufficiently well educated to be effective officials, and they neither were, nor were seen to be, mere instruments of the colonial power. Indeed, the rulers of the most powerful and prestigious kingdoms had led the fight against the Dutch in 1905 to 1910 and did so again in 1945 to 1949.

Not only at the top level—not only at the level of the rajas of Bone and Luwu—did aristocrats take the lead in supporting the Republic. In many kingdoms, large and small, the traditional rulers and their sons and followers led the fight against the Dutch. These pro-Republican aristocrats and those associated with them were the targets of Dutch retaliation and found themselves replaced by other, usually lower ranking and less well educated, aristocrats who were prepared to cooperate with the Dutch.

Any social revolutionary impulses that may have existed in South Sulawesi were thus deflected from the aristocracy as a ruling class and were directed instead against particular rulers or officials who owed their positions to their cooperation with the Dutch. Although South Sulawesi at the time of the revolution was still a rigidly stratified society, the politically important divisions within it did not follow class lines. The principal division was between those who cooperated with the Dutch and those who did not.

This division cut across both class and ethnic lines. Thus, although many Christian Minahasans and Ambonese worked with the Dutch in the civil service and the KNIL, others, such as Dr. Ratulangie, were active supporters of the Republic. Of the four most famous martyrs of the revolution in South Sulawesi, one was Minahasan, one Javanese, one Buginese, and one Makassarese.[52]

The principal division may have been between those who cooperated with the Dutch and those who did not—between the puppets and the patriots—but it was perceived differently in the city and the countryside. The people in the countryside, the guerrilla fighters, and those in exile or prison, tended to see the division in stark terms: one either fought the Dutch or acquiesced in their return. The idea of noncooperation, to which the nationalists in the city who participated in the NIT parliament but not in its initial cabinets resorted to justify their actions, was, to the resisters, a too-subtle and ultimately meaningless distinction. For the most part, they discounted the impact of pro-Republican noncooperators in NIT on the Dutch in persuading them to abandon their attempt to recreate a colonial relationship through a federal system. Thus, although the noncooperators who participated in NIT did so as supporters of the Republic, and indeed served the Republic's interests, they were not seen by the resisting patriots as having made the sacrifices for the revolution of those who were killed or imprisoned for their opposition to the Dutch. The nationalism of the ethnically mixed and relatively well-educated politicans in the city seemed weaker than the nationalism of the ill-educated youth in the hinterland, a number of them from the aristocracy, many from Islamic schools and organizations, who had risked their lives for their principles.

The divisions within South Sulawesi left a legacy of bitterness and revenge. A number of pro-Dutch rulers and officials were removed, some killed, after the transfer of sovereignty and the dissolution of NIT. The years of turmoil in South Sulawesi from 1950 to 1965 provided ample opportunity to settle debts of honor or revenge. The division in this conflict, however, was again not primarily along class lines, and by the end of the postrevolutionary rebellion the traditional aristocracy, supported by the central government, was firmly entrenched.

The legacy of the years of revolution was felt not only within South Sulawesi, but also in relations between the region and the center. Despite national recognition of the martyrdom of Westerling's victims, South Sulawesi was tainted in the eyes of many by the collaboration implicit in the establishment of NIT, as well as by the participation of many of the area's aristocratic rulers in regional and local councils. Some people in South Sulawesi felt, too, that they were not regarded nationally as having participated in the revolution because the region was not recognized as part of the Republic until after the transfer of sovereignty. From their point of view, however, especially if they had fought in the jungle or suffered in jail, the Republic had abandoned Sulawesi to the Dutch by excluding the island from the area designated as Republican-controlled territory in the Linggajati Agreement.

Many South Sulawesians came to believe that, whatever their suffering in the cause of the revolution and however important the demonstration of pro-Republican sympathy within NIT, their contribution was viewed by national leaders as essentially marginal to the course of the struggle. The fighting and negotiating that determined the outcome of the revolution took place in Java, and it was those few pemuda from South Sulawesi, largely those who had fought in Java and who met the educational and other requirements for assimilation into the Java-based national institutions, who could enjoy the rewards of independence. The poorly educated youth of South Sulawesi, who had spent the revolution in prison or in the jungle, lacked paper qualifications and found themselves ill equipped to compete for civil and military positions, either with pemuda who had fought in Java or with officials who had retained their positions in NIT. Few in this group were recognized as revolutionary fighters, and few were accepted into the TNI. Many felt that, their usefulness finished, they had been discarded, unappreciated *("habis manis, sepah dibuang").*[53] This sentiment was a dark portent for the future.

Notes

This is a revised version of a paper presented at the Association for Asian Studies meeting in Toronto, March 13–15, 1981. I am grateful to Takashi Shiraishi, other members of the panel, and especially its chairman, Audrey Kahin, for their comments and suggestions, which have helped to focus my analysis. I am also grateful to George McT. Kahin for sharing with me research materials on South Sulawesi and the NIT that he collected in Indonesia during 1948 to 1949.

1. C. H. ter Laag, "Memorie van Overgave van den Resident van Celebes en Onderhoorigheden," 1937–1941, dossier 28318, pp. 1–5, Archives of the former Ministry of the Colonies, The Hague.

2. Kōichi Kishi, Shigetada Nishijima et al., eds., *Japanese Military Administration in Indonesia,* U.S. Department of Commerce, Joint Publications Research Service (Washington, D.C.: U.S. Government Printing Office, 1963), pp. 202, 242–244, and 258; George S. Kanahele, "The Japanese Occupation of Indonesia: Prelude to Independence" (Ph.D. dissertation, Cornell University, 1967), pp. 51–52, 86–87, and 152.

3. Kishi and Nishijima, *Japanese Military Administration,* pp. 157–158 and 172–176; Kanahele, "Japanese Occupation," pp. 112–115; Harry J. Benda, James K. Irikura, and Kōichi Kishi, *Japanese Military Administration in Indonesia: Selected Documents* (New Haven: Yale University Southeast Asia Studies, 1965), pp. 219–229.

4. Nadjamoeddin was born in Makassar about 1907, studied in Java, then worked in Makassar for the Department of Economic Affairs. Selected three times for the Makassar city council, he was a member of Parindra (Partai Indonesia Raya, Greater Indonesia Party) until 1939, when he formed his own party, Persatuan Selebes Selatan (South Celebes Union), which advocated cooperation with the Dutch. He was imprisoned on charges of embezzlement in 1940. After his release he worked closely with the Japanese.

5. Kanahele, "Japanese Occupation," p. 224.

6. The establishment of Sudara is noted in Kishi and Nishijima, *Japanese Military Administration,* p. 430. It seems to have been solely a Japanese initia-

tive. See Kanahele, "Japanese Occupation," pp. 176–180 and 225. Lists of members (not precisely identical) are given in Kanahele, "Japanese Occupation," pp. 225–226, and in "Konsep Buku Sedjarah Cor[ps] Has[anuddin]" [hereafter "Sedjarah CorHas"] (Panding, 1972, Mimeographed), p. 2.

7. Second son of the 34th raja of Gowa, Andi Mappanjukki's maternal grandparents had both been rajas of Bone. He was datu of the kingdom of Suppa and fought with his father and other nobles of Gowa against the Dutch in 1906. He was exiled to Selayar for two years but was installed as raja of Bone in 1931.

8. "Sam" Ratulangie was born in Tondano, Minahasa, in 1890 to a Dutch-educated school teacher. He supported himself as a journalist while studying for a doctorate in science at the University of Zurich. He taught in a technical school in Yogyakarta on his return to Indonesia, then moved to Bandung, where he was associated with a number of other nationalist intellectuals. He became head of a Minahasa association, then secretary of the Minahasa Council, and from 1927 to 1931 served as a member of the Volksraad (People's Council). The Japanese appointed him a member of the consultative council of the mass organization, Putera.

9. H. J. Koerts, "Rapport van de bestuursambtenaar Koerts over de situatie in Zuid-Celebes, 2 Nov. 1945," in S. L. van der Wal, ed., *Officiele Bescheiden Betreffende de Nederlands-Indonesische Betrekkingen 1945–1950* [hereafter *NIB*], vol. 1 (The Hague: Martinus Nijhoff, 1971), p. 517. Interview with Andi Mattalatta, Makassar, Feb. 17, 1972.

10. "Report on the Sulawesi Representatives' Journey to Java," Indies Collection of the Rijksinstituut voor Oorlogsdocumentatie (Amsterdam), doc. no. 00609–21; Indonesia, Kementerian Penerangan, *Republik Indonesia: Propinsi Sulawesi* (Jakarta, n.p., 1953), pp. 211–212.

11. Manai Sophiaan was born in Takalar, south of Makassar, in 1915; he attended high school in Yogyakarta and completed teachers college in Java. He taught in the nationalist Taman Siswa school in Makassar from 1937 until imprisoned by the Dutch in 1940. He had also worked as a journalist during those years, and from 1942 to 1945 was with the newspaper *Pewarta Selebes,* whose Japanese editor, Kondo Saburo, was a strong advocate of Indonesian independence.

12. Many Sulawesians interviewed blamed Sophiaan for his failure to obtain arms from the Japanese authorities in Makassar. On the other hand, a memo written by Dr. Ratulangie's secretary, W. S. J. Pondaag, in 1949 states that the local Japanese commander, far from offering help, informed Dr. Ratulangie that any attempt to seize power would be suppressed by force. Undated memorandum, "East Indonesia," p. 1.

13. "Sedjarah CorHas," pp. 7–9; interviews with Andi Mattalatta, Jakarta, Mar. 1, 1971, and Makassar, Feb. 17, 1972, and M. Saleh Lahade, Makassar, Sept. 21, 1971.

14. W. B. Russell, *The Second Fourteenth Battalion: A History of an Australian Infantry Battalion in the Second World War* (Sydney: Angus and Robertson, 1948), p. 312.

15. "Provisional proposals for reoccupation of Batavia without immediate liberation of the rest of Java, van de gedelegeerde bij het geallieered opperbevel in Zuid-Oost Azie (Van der Plas), 22 Sept. 1945," *NIB,* vol. 1, p. 151; Pondaag, "East Indonesia," p. 2. The prewar mayor of Makassar was reinstalled in 1945, according to the list of mayors in *Buku Kenangan 50 Tahun Berotonomi Daerah Kota Makassar* (Makassar, 1956), p. 23. See also H. Moh. Sanusi Dg. Mattata, *Luwu Dalam Revolusi* (Makassar, 1967, Mimeographed), pp. 196–197.

16. *Propinsi Sulawesi,* p. 224; "Sedjarah CorHas," p. 9.

17. Signs of sympathy for the Republic and hostility to the Dutch are described in many of the reports in the War Diary, HQ 21 Infantry Brigade, Australian War Memorial [hereafter AWM] files 8/2/21, 8/3/14, and 8/3/16.

18. I have found no exact information on the date when KNIL units were reconstituted, or when they were in place in Makassar. However, KNIL troops, described as recently released Ambonese internees, instigated shooting incidents in Makassar on October 2 and 15. Russell, *Second Fourteenth Battalion,* p. 313; Walcott to CONICA, Oct. 16, 1945, War Diary, HQ 21 Inf. Bde., AWM file 8/2/21. Four KNIL companies were reported in Makassar by mid-November in "Overzicht van chief commanding officer Nica te Morotai (DeRooy) betreffende de algemene situatie in Borneo en de Groote Oost over de periode 21 t/m 30 Nov. 1945," *NIB,* vol. 2, pp. 377–378. The arrival of 400–500 KNIL troops, no date given, is mentioned in *Propinsi Sulawesi,* pp. 217 and 222.

19. The most complete source of information on youth organizations and militias in South Sulawesi during the revolution is the compilation "Rangkaian Sedjarah: Kelasjkaran2, kesatuan2, dan Badan2 Perdjoangan Kemerdekaan Republik Indonesia di Daerah Sulawesi Selatan/Tenggara 1945–1949" [hereafter "Kelasjkaran"] (Makassar: Kantor Urusan Veteran, 1958); there is no overall pagination, but each group is given a consecutive register number. The data in this compilation were part of an effort to qualify those who had fought as guerrillas during the revolution for veteran's status and benefits. Both the lapse of time and the purpose for which the data were presented should be kept in mind in using this source to assess the strength and activities of the pemuda and guerrilla organizations in South Sulawesi.

20. "Routine Order no. 224, 19 Nov. 1945 (extract from GRO 273/45)," War Diary HQ 21 Inf. Bde., AWM file 8/3/14. "Weapons Carried by Natives in Country Districts," HQ Makassar Force, Ref. no. G363; War Diary HQ 21 Inf. Bde., AWM file 8/3/16. Reports on searches for weapons and Japanese guards are in these files and in file 8/2/21. The pro-Republican sympathies of individual Australians are mentioned in J. Tumbelaka, *Soelawesi ditengah gelombang masa* (Yogyakarta: Serie Seroean, 1947), p. 9; in an interview in Makassar, Dec. 7, 1971, Lt. Col. A. R. Malaka said that some weapons were given by or bought from Australian soldiers, but most of what few there were had been taken from the Dutch.

21. "Kelasjkaran," Register no. 58/III/1958. Manai Sophiaan, "Hari-hari Pertama Pendaratan NICA di Sulawesi Selatan," in Lahadjdji Patang, *Sulawesi dan Pahlawan2nya* (Jakarta: Yayasan Kesejahteran Generasi Muda Indonesia, 1977), p. 172. This book is said by its compiler to be based on accounts by participants in the revolution, interviews, and documentary sources. Unfortunately sources for particular items are rarely provided, which limits the book's usefulness.

22. War Diary, HQ 21 Inf. Bde., AWM files 8/2/21 and 8/3/16; DeRooy Report (Nov. 1–10, 1945) *NIB*, vol. 2, p. 35; *Propinsi Sulawesi*, pp. 225–226; "Sedjarah CorHas," pp. 10–11; " 'PPNI' Kelasjkaran," Register no. 58/III/1958.

23. "Notes on discussion between CO Makforce and Ratulangie 2 November 1945," War Diary, HQ 21 Inf. Bde., AWM file 8/2/21. On the PKR, see also Tumbelaka, *Soelawesi*, pp. 11 and 15–17.

24. The petition is reproduced in *Indonesian Nationalism and Revolution* (Clayton, Victoria: Monash University, 1971), pp. 46–50. Sanusi (*Luwu*, pp. 122–123) says that the petition was presented to the Australian commander on January 17, 1946, but that he denied the request to forward it to the UN because in meetings in December and January the rajas had agreed that changes in the situation in Sulawesi would have to await developments in Java.

25. "Report on Conference with Ratulangie in Bone, 6–7 November 1945," War Diary, HQ 21 Inf. Bde., AWM file 8/2/21.

26. "Instructions to all officers of Makforce 21 November 1945," Appendix I, War Diary, HQ 21 Inf. Bde., AWM file 8/2/21. The instruction is excerpted in Anthony J. S. Reid, *Indonesian National Revolution, 1945–50* (Melbourne: Longman, 1974), p. 45.

27. On the situation in Luwu, see Appendix A to "Preliminary Report on Surveillance Party of Sedang River 19–27 Nov. 45"; on Gowa: Appendix 1-B; on Bone: "Report on a visit to Watampone 28/29 Nov. by Capt. P. D. Connolly," all in War Diary HQ 21 Inf. Bde., AWM file 8/2/21. Reports on subse-

quent meetings, patrols, and intimidation are in files 8/2/21, 8/3/14, and 8/3/16. See also the second DeRooy report (Nov. 21–30, 1945), *NIB*, vol. 2, p. 222; H. A. Ninong (Ranrang Tua Wajo), "Riwayat Hidup Singkat" (Ujung Pandang, 1975, typescript), pp. 23–24; Pondaag, "East Indonesia," p. 3; and Jay Bigelow, "Report from South Celebes," *Asia and the Americas*, May 1946, p. 227.

28. "Notes of Interview, 20 Oct. 45," War Diary, HQ 21 Inf. Bde., AWM file 8/2/21. "Report on operations of Makforce 22 September–20 December 1945," in War Diary HQ 21 Inf. Bde., AWM file 8/2/21; second DeRooy report (Nov. 21–30, 1945), *NIB*, vol. 2, p. 225 and 232–235; "Memorandum van fd directeur van binnenlands bestuur (Van der Plas), 17 Nov. 1945," *NIB*, vol. 2, p. 109; "Nota van fd directeur van binnenlands bestuur (Van der Plas)" (undated), *NIB*, vol. 2, p. 116. The economic pressures on the Indonesian middle class are described in George McT. Kahin, *Nationalism and Revolution in Indonesia* (Ithaca: Cornell University Press, 1952), p. 353.

29. Estimates provided to George McT. Kahin in 1949 by Andi Burhanuddin, then chairman of the South Sulawesi Council and former *karaeng* of Pangkajene.

30. The Hadat Tinggi was established in late 1945 or early 1946 and formalized as the Supreme Council in November 1948. It carried out the functions of both the Supreme Council and the representative council of South Sulawesi until members were elected to the latter body in early 1949. A. Arthur Schiller, *The Formation of Federal Indonesia, 1945–1949* (The Hague and Bandung: Van Hoeve, 1955), p. 173; *Indonesia Timoer*, Nov. 13, 1948.

31. Andi Mattalatta was born in Barru, south of Pare-Pare, in 1922 to an aristocratic family from Gowa. His father declined to serve as local ruler under the Dutch. He attended school in Makassar, then became a teacher and athletic coach. Mohammad Saleh Lahade was also from Barru; his father was a school teacher. He attended a Dutch middle school in Yogyakarta and graduated from the agricultural high school in Bogor. This made him one of the most highly educated young men from South Sulawesi.

32. Also known as Kahar Muzakkar, a name he adopted from a famous teacher at the Muhammadiyah Islamic Teachers College he attended in Surakarta. Born in Luwu, he returned there to teach in a Muhammadiyah school in 1941. He was banished by the Council of Luwu in 1943, worked briefly for a Japanese firm in Makassar, then went into business in Surakarta. He remained in Java during the revolution but returned in 1950 to lead a rebellion that kept much of South Sulawesi in turmoil until his death in 1965.

33. A. H. Nasution, *Tentara Nasional Indonesia*, 3rd printing, vol. 1 (Jakarta: Seruling Masa, 1970), p. 228.

34. For a detailed account and full references, see Barbara S. Harvey, "Tra-

dition, Islam and Rebellion: South Sulawesi, 1950–1965" (Ph.D. dissertation, Cornell University, 1974), esp. pp. 145–153.

35. "Sedjarah CorHas," pp. 54–57; " 'Barisan Pemberontak Ganggawa,' Kelasjkaran," Register no. 64/III/1958. Interviews with Andi Mattalatta, Jakarta, Mar. 1, 1971, and Makassar, Feb. 17, 1972; M. Saleh Lahade, Sept. 21, 1971; A. R. Malaka, Makassar, Dec. 1, 1971; and M. Daeng Sibali, Makassar, Mar. 6, 1972.

36. A brief summary of these events is in Schiller, *Federal Indonesia,* pp. 21–23. Accounts of the proceedings are in W. A. van Goudoever, *Malino Maakt Historie* (Batavia: Regeerings Voorlichtings Dienst, 1946); D. J. van Wijnen, *Pangkalpinang* (Batavia: Regeerings Voorlichtings Dienst, 1946); W. A. van Goudoever, *Denpasar Bowt een Huis* (Batavia: Regeerings Voorlichtings Dienst, 1947); Algemeen Regeeringscommissariaat voor Borneo en de Groote Oost, *De Conferentie te Denpasar,* vols. 1 and 2 (Batavia: G. Kolff, n.d.); and *Propinsi Sulawesi,* pp. 75–121.

37. Raymond "Turk" Westerling, *Challenge to Terror* (London: William Kimber, 1952), pp. 88–123; Tweede Kamer der Staten-Generaal, Zitting 1968–69, *Nota Betreffende het Archiefonderzoek naar gegevens omtrent Excessen in Indonesie begaan door Nederlandse Militairen in de periode 1945–1950* (The Hague, 1969), Appendix 2, pp. 2 and 11. For Indonesian accounts of the campaign, see *Propinsi Sulawesi,* pp. 243–248, and Sjamsuddin Lubis, *Sulawesi Selatan,* vol. 1, *Sulawesi dan Pahlawan2nya,* pp. 115–130. Although these accounts describe the brutality of the reimposition of Dutch rule throughout South Sulawesi, the state of war declared on December 11, 1946, encompassed only the four districts of Makassar, Bonthain, Pare-Pare, and Mandar. *Staatsblad* 1946, no. 139.

38. Lubis, *Sulawesi Selatan,* vol. 1, pp. 96–97. The text of the women's petition is in document no. 03170, "Sedjarah Militer Angkatan Darat 1945–1960, Kronologi Bahan Sedjarah TNI KODAM XIV/Hasanuddin," File: "Peristiwa Penting Lainnja," Dinas Sejarah Militer, Bandung. An approximate translation is in Sanusi, *Luwu,* pp. 338–339. See also the account of one of the signers of the petition, H. A. Ninong, "Riwayat Hidup," p. 43.

39. The link between the killings, revenge, and rebellion was frequently mentioned in interviews in Makassar and Jakarta in 1971–1972. See also Husain Ibrahim, "Rivalitas, Dendam dan Pembaharuan dlm Masjarakat Sulawesi Selatan," *Ensensi,* I/5–6 (Aug. 1971), pp. 105–106.

40. The text of the agreement, in English, is in Charles Wolf, Jr., *The Indonesian Story* (New York: John Day, 1948), pp. 175–178. The disheartening effect of the signing of this agreement on the nationalists in areas excluded from the de facto Republic is mentioned in A. H. Nasution, *Tentara Nasional Indonesia,* vol. 2 (Jakarta: Seruling Masa, 1969), pp. 87–88.

41. Interview, Makassar, Oct. 23, 1971.

42. *Propinsi Sulawesi,* pp. 122–124 and 132; Van Goudoever, *Denpasar,* pp. 102–103; and *Conferentie Denpasar,* vol. 2, pp. 47–48.

43. Born in Borneo of Buginese parents, Noor was brought to Makassar with Dr. Ratulangie as an adviser to the Japanese Navy Civil Administration. He had been a member of the Putera Consultative Council in Java, but was excluded from the leadership of Sudara. He did, however, serve as head of the bureau of general affairs on Dr. Ratulangie's staff in the early months of the revolution. He is said to have established good relations with the local nationalists, despite rivalries with Nadjamoeddin and Ratulangie. Noor served as chairman of the NIT parliament for just over a month, resigning on May 27, 1947, when a progovernment member introduced a motion of no confidence.

44. Interview with Henk Rondonuwu, Makassar, June 9, 1971; George McT. Kahin's interview with Arnold Mononutu, Makassar, Mar. 19, 1949.

45. He was tried and convicted the following year on charges of corruption. He died while in jail. *Propinsi Sulawesi,* p. 135; Henri J. H. Alers, *Om een rode of groene Merdeka* (Eindhoven: Vulkaan, 1956), p. 149; reports of the trial are in *Indonesia Timoer* during November 1948. As minister for economic affairs, Nadjamoeddin had ample opportunity to engage in the sort of manipulation and corruption of which he was charged (diversion of textiles). He had been arrested in the 1930s on similar charges. Since the earlier charges were known to the Dutch when they appointed him, it seems likely that something other than corruption was the real reason for Nadjamoeddin's fall from grace. Mr. G. R. Pantouw has suggested that because Nadjamoeddin was a friend of Van Mook he was vulnerable to attacks from Dutch rightists; interview, Makassar, Oct. 23, 1971. Alers said that the NIT minister of justice, Mr. Soumokil, engineered Nadjamoeddin's downfall.

46. *Propinsi Sulawesi,* pp. 136–141 and 158–159.

47. Schiller, *Federal Indonesia,* pp. 251 and 272; Kahin, *Nationalism and Revolution,* p. 361; J.A.A. van Doorn and W. J. Hendrix, *Ontsporing van Geweld* (Rotterdam: Universitaire Pers Rotterdam, 1970), pp. 62–64.

48. Schiller, *Federal Indonesia,* pp. 124–125; *Staatsblad,* 1946, no. 72. Neither includes a list of members.

49. Schiller, *Federal Indonesia,* pp. 98, 104–106, and 173.

50. Kahin, *Nationalism and Revolution,* pp. 363–367; *Propinsi Sulawesi,* pp. 122–123.

51. I have used "patriot" as an approximate equivalent of the Indonesian word *pejoang,* literally fighter or struggler, which is commonly used in South Sulawesi to characterize the pro-Republican resistance.

52. They were: Wolter Mongisidi and Emmy Saelan (both of whom had been students in Makassar, participated in the October 28–29 attack, and

then joined Lapris), Andi Abdullah Bau Massepe (datu of Suppa and son of Andi Mappanjukki), and Ranggong Daeng Romo (Lapris military commander). *Propinsi Sulawesi,* pp. 366–369; Lubis, *Sulawesi Selatan,* pp. 92–93 and 114–127; Lahadji Patang, *Sulawesi,* pp. 119–120 and 155–167; Radik Djarwadi, *Surat dari Selmaut: Kisah Pahlawan Nasional Robert Wolter Mongisidi* (Surabaya: GRIP, [1960]); and H.M.R. Amin Daud, *Ranggong Dg. Romo* (Makassar: Jajasan Artja Pahlawan, [1971]).

53. The Indonesian phrase refers to the spitting out of chewed sugar cane when the sweetness is gone.

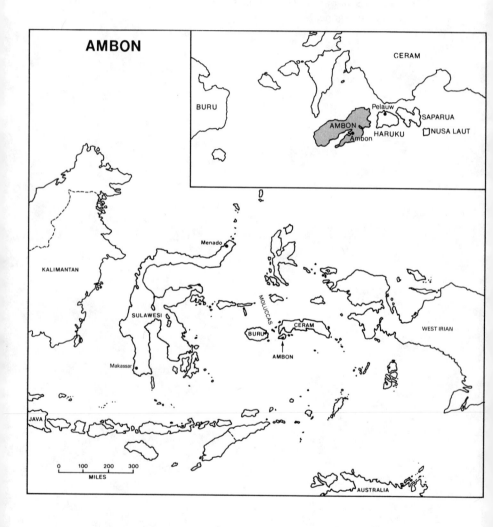

AMBON: NOT A REVOLUTION BUT A COUNTERREVOLUTION

Richard Chauvel

There was no revolution in Ambon in the various senses in which the term is usually understood in the Indonesian context. There was no physical struggle for the attainment of independence from the Dutch, nor was there a violent reordering of the Ambonese social order in the years that followed the capitulation of Japan. Rather, there was a fierce and bloody attempt by the RMS (Republik Maluku Selatan, Republic of the South Moluccas) to prevent Ambon from falling under the effective authority of the new Indonesian government just four months after the formal transfer of sovereignty from the Netherlands in December 1949. In what might be termed a preemptive counterrevolution, a powerful coalition of soldiers, members of the traditional elite, and civilian officials—the major beneficiaries of the colonial presence in Ambonese society—sought to sever their links with Indonesia and reverse the process of three decades of social change. The thrust of this process had undermined the authority of the traditional elite and isolated the soldiers and officials, all of whom feared that their influence would further decline if Indonesian authority was firmly established on Ambon.

The postwar years in Ambon have usually been viewed as a background to the RMS. The emphasis has been on separatism and regionalism rather than revolution—on the area's relations with the rest of Indonesia and with the colonial power rather than the sociopolitical development within the society. This study attempts to correct the balance and also draw attention to similarities between the underlying patterns of social change and political environment in Ambon and in other regions in the archipelago.

As befitted one of the oldest and most integrated parts of the Netherlands Indies, in Ambon the issue of Indonesian independence, and Ambon's participation in it, dominated local politics from the 1920s on. The issue became closely intertwined with the struggle for control of the society between an *adat* (custom)-based, Dutch-supported elite and an emerging group, part nationalist and part loyalist pro-Dutch, who based their leadership claims on education and occupational skills. The character of nationalist politics had its roots in the changing social structure and historical experience of the area. Unlike the situation in parts of Java, Sumatra, and Sulawesi, the political struggle for Indonesian independence was conducted within structures determined by the Dutch. After the initial Allied occupation in 1945, the Moluccas remained an area of uncontested Dutch military and political control. Local politics operated within the Dutch-created federal institutions and, much to the surprise of their creators and many Ambonese, the pro-Indonesia Ambonese nationalists beat their conservative opponents in the Dutch-sponsored elections, and dominated the local representative institutions. From that base, however, the nationalists were unable to extend their control over the society as a whole. In the first four months of 1950 they found themselves contending not only with their old loyalist opponents, but also with some 2,000 armed Ambonese soldiers of the former colonial army. Both groups felt betrayed and deserted by the departing Dutch.

The Historical and Social Setting

The Ambonese islands of the central Moluccas lie in that part of the eastern archipelago where the Malay and Melanesian worlds overlap, with the consequence that the region is ethnically and culturally extremely heterogeneous. Stemming from its role, first as an entrepot, then as a source of spices, Ambon's historical trading relations brought with them economic and political ideas together with two world religions, Islam and Christianity, that have dominated Ambonese society over four centuries. The small, lightly populated group of islands, where sago harvesting and fishing provided an easy if minimal subsistence, might have been left to their own devices if it had not been for the fact that the much-sought-after clove grew as plentifully there as the sago palm. To insure a reliable and cheap supply of cloves, both the Portuguese and Dutch considered it essential to establish political control over the area of clove production. Ambon experienced nearly 450 years of first trading contact with and later political domination by Europeans. The Ambonese Christian community was a product of the European contact just as the Moslem community was of the earlier trading relations with Javanese, Ternatenese, and Makassarese.

By the closing decade of Dutch rule, the population of the Ambonese islands was about 65.9 percent Protestant and 32.7 percent Moslem.[1] In Ambon town, apart from Moslem and Christian Ambonese, there were Chinese and Arabs, as well as Moslems from elsewhere in the archipelago. Outside the town, with a few exceptions, Moslem and Christian Ambonese lived in separate *negeri* (villages) each with its own *raja* (village head) and *seniri negeri* (village council). With the exception of Christian Nusa Laut, all the islands have both Moslem and Christian negeri. In the colonial period, members of the village council chose the raja from the raja families, though the Dutch resident had overriding powers of veto, appointment, and dismissal. From the beginning, the Dutch ruled the negeri through the raja. Above the village level, the only Ambonese in the administration were administrative assistants, drawn from the prominent raja families, who helped the lowest European officials.

The clove trade declined sharply from the late eighteenth century, and the consequent loss of profitability led the colonial government to abolish the monopoly in 1864. Subsequently, despite occasional good years, Ambonese villagers also found the clove trade generally unprofitable, and cultivation declined rapidly. All attempts to establish an alternative cash crop failed, and the Ambonese islands were left with a stagnant export economy and a sago-based subsistence economy under increasing population pressure.[2]

Concurrent with the abolition of the monopoly, the Dutch were expanding and consolidating their control over the archipelago during the later nineteenth century. This meant that the Dutch needed reliable and effective manpower for their army and for the lower levels of the expanding bureaucracy. For both purposes they recruited large numbers of Christian Ambonese. A Western style of education had gone

hand-in-hand with Christianity and schools had existed since Portuguese times, but educational opportunities increased in the closing
years of the century. In the following decades, thousands of Christian
Ambonese left their homeland to serve the Dutch in civilian and military capacities throughout the archipelago. Service as soldiers and
clerks transformed the Christian Ambonese colonial experience from
one of intense exploitation under the spice monopoly to one of relative
privilege. Many Christians considered they had a special relationship
with the Dutch because of their shared religion and their service, particularly military, in the pacification of the archipelago.

Moslem Ambonese did not participate in the late colonial enterprise. Dutch army authorities did not recruit them, as they did the
Christians, nor were there any educational facilities in Moslem villages until the 1920s. The Moslems for their part considered any
involvement with Dutch employment or education as akin to becoming a Christian. They were not, however, left unaffected by the
changes in the colonial world around them. The lifting of the clove
monopoly, together with improved communications, facilitated the
reestablishment of contact between Ambonese Moslems and their co-
religionists elsewhere in the archipelago and beyond, where they
encountered the outside world not as servants of the colonial power,
but as seamen, traders, and *haji* (those who have made the pilgrimage
to Mecca). Contact with the Moslem world brought new ideas into
the Ambonese negeri, and, over time, produced significant changes in
belief and practice.[3]

Thus the experiences of Christian and Moslem Ambonese differed
markedly in the late colonial period. Christian identification with the
Dutch contrasted with Moslem distrust and noninvolvement. The
Christians, with Dutch support and education, dominated Ambonese
society to such an extent that many non-Ambonese thought of Ambon
as a Christian area.

The Ambonese, particularly the Christians working outside the
homeland, were confronted with a dilemma by the growth of the
Indonesian nationalist movement. Because of their educational advantages, Christian Ambonese were among the first Indonesians to move,
as clerks, professionals, and soldiers, into the gray area between the
European elite and the mass of the indigenous population. They
quickly realized the opportunities offered through further education

and occupational advancement, and, with the Dutch patronage and support, they established one of the earliest voluntary organizations—the Ambonschstudiefonds (1909)—to provide scholarships, and at times schools, for promising Christian students.[4] By the late 1910s a few Ambonese, like their fellow Indonesian nationalists, began to realize the limitations of working within the system and that ultimately the only solution would be found in an Indonesia independent of the Netherlands. This was a particularly difficult position to adopt for the many Christian Ambonese who considered themselves superior to their fellow Indonesians and aspired to equality with the European.

The Ambonese nationalists founded a branch of Insulinde (the nationalist party on Java led by Douwes Dekker and Dr. Tjipto Mangoenkoesoemo) in 1917 in Ambon and Sarekat Ambon (Ambon Association) in 1920. These two organizations sought to promote broad objectives of socioeconomic development and demanded greater political participation for the indigenous people in managing their own affairs. Their greatest impact in Ambon itself was through their involvement in village disputes. Following the abolition of the clove monopoly in 1864, the rajas' financial position and authority had declined, and the increased mobility of the Ambonese villagers exposed their negeri to the outside world. Age-old conflicts concerning rival individual and family claims to negeri leadership could no longer be confined to the village. Urban, educated, and predominantly Christian, members of Insulinde and Sarekat Ambon from outside the negeri provided leadership to, and articulated the grievances of, both Christian and Moslem villagers, bypassing the raja and the lower levels of the Dutch administration. They thus posed a challenge to the Dutch-supported adat elite for the society's leadership, to which the Dutch and the rajas responded strongly. The Dutch first supported the right of the raja and the administration to exclude unwanted visitors from the negeri and, second, exiled the principal nationalist leaders from Ambon. A. J. Patty, the Sarekat Ambon leader, was exiled in October 1924, and his departure marked the end of a period of relatively unrestricted and successful political activity.[5] From then until the Japanese invasion, the nationalists were kept on the periphery of Ambonese society, isolated from the rural population.

Nevertheless, in the 1930s Sarekat Ambon was able to work quietly and effectively in the town of Ambon under a new leader, E. U.

Pupella,[6] who established a Taman Siswa-type school, Balai Pendidi-kan, and for several years published a weekly newspaper. Pupella gathered around himself a small group of supporters who came from both religious communities. Although the most prominent of them were Christian,[7] much of the organizational and financial support came from the Moslems. They had a strong awareness that, as Ambonese Indonesians, they had to seek a common bond outside religion and were convinced that Ambon's future was in an independent Indonesia, where Ambonese society would have to be radically transformed. In particular, Christians would have to reorient their occupational preferences for government, civil, and military service toward economic development at home. Like other members of Ambon's very small political elite, the nationalists had enjoyed varying degrees of Dutch education, but unlike most of their counterparts, they now had autonomous organizational experience—running their own schools and party without reliance on, and often in the face of opposition from, the administration.

Sarekat Ambon was not a mass movement, nor was the commitment to Indonesian independence widespread in Ambonese society, but it showed itself able at times to mobilize support amongst diverse groups—rural and urban, Moslem and Christian. This nationalist activity revealed that the Ambonese were not as loyal nor their society as stable as many of their own leaders and the Dutch liked to believe.

Shifting the Balance: The Japanese Years

Within just twenty-four hours, the Japanese armed forces brought to an end nearly 300 years of Dutch domination of the Ambonese islands. The Japanese attack, launched on January 31, 1942, quickly overcame the combined defenses of the KNIL (Royal Netherlands Indies Army) and an Australian battalion. While intending to retain eastern Indonesia as part of their empire, in the three and a half years of occupation the Japanese did much to shift the political balance between the adat elite and the nationalists. Within the existing administrative structure, the Japanese appointed Sarekat Ambon leaders to senior positions in the administration in place of or above the favored sons of the adat elite, with Pupella becoming head of the subregency of Ambon. At the negeri level, the majority of rajas retained their positions—indeed some developed cordial relations with the Japanese—but as a group they did not enjoy the unquestioned public support of the Japanese as they had of the Dutch.

Apart from the administration, the nationalists were influential in several other areas. The Japanese-sponsored newspaper, *Sinar Matahari*, was under nationalist editorship; the national school was permitted to remain in operation, and Taman Siswa principles were promoted in other schools. Although Sarekat Ambon was banned along with all other political organizations, the Japanese established a youth group, Seinendan,[8] with the objective of reviving the *pemuda* (youth) spirit extinguished by the Dutch. In contrast to the practice elsewhere in Indonesia, the Seinendan pemuda were given no military training, but nationalists in the administration did provide them with some political training. The experience of the nationalists in the wartime administration, however, was not an umixed blessing, for they were associated among the populace with severe material deprivation and harsh Japanese methods. At the end of the war they were unable to retain the authority the Japanese had vested in them.

The Japanese impact on Ambonese communal relations was just as fundamental, breaking the special relationship with the occupying power traditionally enjoyed by the Christian Ambonese. The Japanese suspected the Christians of pro-Dutch sympathies and tended to discriminate against them. This attitude was reflected in their earlier and more enthusiastic sponsorship of a Moslem organization than of its Christian counterpart. As a result, the two communities diverged markedly in their response to the change of colonial masters, with many Moslems welcoming the Japanese liberators, while Christians mourned the loss of their benefactor.[9]

Indonesia Merdeka! Ambon Merdeka?

The proclamation of Indonesia's independence on August 17, 1945, transformed what had up till then been an issue of discussion among a small group of politically aware Ambonese into a question of real and immediate importance for the whole society. In the months and years

that followed the proclamation, Ambon's place in the state struc-
ture(s) of the Indonesian archipelago was the dominant and all pervasive issue of contention among the Ambonese. It in turn was directly
related to the divisions and allegiances within the society and the
ongoing struggle for societal leadership—a struggle intensified by the
wartime experience and the growing prospect that the second Dutch
coming might only be temporary. Although Indonesia, and Ambon's
place in it, dominated local politics, Ambonese opinions with all their
differences had little or no impact on the principal decision makers in
the revolution—Indonesian or Dutch.

The first Dutchmen and Australians to return to Ambon, on September 22, 1945, a month after Japan's capitulation, noticed little
response there to Sukarno and Hatta's proclamation, let alone opposition to the reestablishment of colonial rule. The Allies were aware,
from their intelligence reports, that the Japanese had established
nationalist organizations, but they did not observe any activity.
Throughout the Ambonese islands the Allies were warmly welcomed.
Traditionally loyalist groups—those who felt they had suffered at the
hands of the Japanese because of their pro-Dutch sympathies—immediately reasserted their dominance. The Allies transferred the local
administration without incident from Pupella's provisional government into the trusted hands of members of one of Ambon's prominent
families, the Gaspersz. One of the first acts of the returning Dutch
officials was to remobilize the former colonial soldiers, who were soon
involved in clashes with interned Japanese troops, Javanese comrades-
in-arms, and civilian Ambonese. It was as if the old colonial image of
Ambon as the bastion of loyalty was being reconfirmed.

After the Allied return, the nationalists and others who had worked
with the Japanese assumed a very low profile, understandably anxious
about possible Dutch action against them, as well as wary of the
Ambonese soldiers. Pupella contemplated establishing a Republican
government, but decided against it because of the likely opposition
from the soldiers.[10] A number of pemuda organizations were formed
by members of the Seinendan, including the Persatuan Pemuda Indonesia (Indonesia Youth Association), established in February 1946
under Pupella's and Wim Reawaru's auspices, which represented their
first cautious attempt to establish a Republican movement.[11] Little

came of these predominantly Moslem groups before 1949 or of their reported plans for "illegal underground activities."[12]

Dutch Policy and Ambonese Preference

Politics in Ambon evolved in large part in response to the development of the Dutch federal strategy. The different political groups reacted to that strategy as it formed, and, more generally, to the ebb and flow of the military-diplomatic struggle between the Republic and the Dutch.

On February 10, 1946, a government declaration outlined Dutch ideas for the realization of the Queen's promises of 1942 in terms of an autonomous democratic Indonesia as equal partner in the Kingdom of the Netherlands. For the next six months conservative loyalist groups in Ambon held the initiative. The most concrete idea they proposed was formation of a Moluccan Commonwealth (Gemenebest Molukken), consisting of the northern Moluccas and New Guinea as well as the southern Moluccas. The then-dominant conservative elements in Ambon saw the Commonwealth as constituting a separate grouping within the Kingdom, along with the Netherlands, Indonesia, Surinam, and the Antilles, with very limited relations with Indonesia. Implicit in the idea was an awareness of Ambon's own economic weakness, yet the proposed Commonwealth would not be so large or populous as to preclude the Ambonese from playing an important role. It is unclear who first initiated the idea, but it enjoyed quite wide support among the rajas and the educated elite in Ambon and among emigrés in Java. The promoters of the Moluccan Commonwealth were motivated by concerns similar to those which later contributed to the RMS (Republik Maluku Selatan, Republic of the South Moluccas), but they were more aware of the problems of economic and political viability and accordingly sought a larger unit. The idea came to nothing, partly because the Sultan of Ternate did not respond favorably to the proposals made to him by an Ambonese negotiating team under Dr. Tahitu.[13] But most significantly, the Moluccan Commonwealth, particularly in its separatist guise, did not fit into Dutch plans for a state structure covering much of the eastern archipelago and based on smaller local units.

In late 1945 and early 1946, the Indies government had been only too pleased to hear the loud protestations of Ambonese loyalty, which in the hostile environment confronting them must have been music to their ears. However, as van Mook developed his strategy to combat the Republic by presenting an alternate Indonesia, also independent, but federally structured and more amenable to Dutch influence, the loyal Ambonese desire to remain part of the kingdom, separate from Indonesia, became more difficult to accommodate. The loyal Ambonese were needed in the federal State of East Indonesia (NIT) to help keep it amenable. As a separate part of the kingdom, Ambon would only be an administrative and economic burden and a possible source of conflict with Indonesia.

Public construction of the federal system was undertaken at two conferences in 1946. At the first of these, held at Malino in South Sulawesi from July 10 to 22, 1946, Dutch-appointed delegates assembled from Borneo and the "Great East." Ambonese representatives at the conference appeared to accept Dutch plans for the incorporation of Ambon into a federal Indonesia, but they did oppose the adoption of the Indonesian flag (red and white) and anthem ("Indonesia Raya") for the new state.[14]

By the time of Malino, it was evident that the idea of a Moluccan Commonwealth had been rejected by the north Moluccan sultans and ignored by the Dutch. Its demise coincided with the reemergence of Ambon's nationalist leadership into the public political arena. The core group around Pupella—not more than a dozen people who had worked together in the 1930s and cooperated with the Japanese—established PIM (Partai Indonesia Merdeka, Free Indonesia Party) on August 17, 1946, the first anniversary of the proclamation of independence. Its first public meeting attracted greater interest than any previous political gathering in Ambon and completely overshadowed the meetings held at the same time by representatives from the Malino conference to explain the conference and its results. Of the 1,500 who attended PIM's inaugural meeting, roughly three-quarters reportedly came from the Moslem community.[15] Pupella outlined the party's objective as the pursuit of an independent Indonesia through legal means, which meant participating in the federal institutions. PIM's leaders were Republicans, their ultimate objective was the realization of the 1945 proclamation. However, in Ambon there had to be a federal means to a unitary end. Because of the strong Republican and separatist minorities, only in federalism was there a compromise that could maintain Ambonese unity.[16] Under Pupella's undemonstrative and pragmatic leadership, PIM pursued a cooperative pro-federal policy carefully calculated to promote the Indonesia cause in an area under uncontested Dutch control and in which influential groups still clung to their colonial links. Pupella managed to maintain this policy despite the opposition of Reawaru and other leaders who were less inclined to tolerate the twists, turns, and compromises involved. The conflict between Pupella's pragmatism and Reawaru's open support of the Republic was to remain a constant source of tension within the PIM.

PIM had organized itself in good time to be ready for the Dutch-sponsored elections in early November 1946 for the DMS (Dewan Maluku Selatan, South Moluccan Council), which was to be Ambon's representative body at the lowest level of the NIT federal structure. An expanded version of the prewar Ambonraad (Ambon Council) which had covered only the Ambonese islands, the new council was to represent the entire newly designated territory of the South Moluccas. Pupella's party was permitted to campaign in the villages, and it established a rudimentary organization in some of them. It also supported candidates who were sympathetic to its cause, though many of them may have been nominally members of opposition groups. PIM's opponents—the rajas, the *pendeta* (Protestant pastors), and the veterans—had their own functional organizations of long standing, but for the campaign they formed an election committee. Members of the committee enjoyed the advantage of the use of government facilities as well as access and influence in the negeri as a result of their positions. In addition to the committee and the Free Indonesia Party, a number of independent candidates ran, such as Tahitu, and Albert Wairisal, who, politically, were willing to support Dutch plans for a federal Indonesia, but whose commitment to Indonesian nationalism made them sympathetic to PIM. None of the contenders had a comprehensive program to submit to the electors. Electoral appeals were made in symbolic terms, national flags and anthems, representing the respective commitments to the Dutch and the Republic. At both stages of the indirect election, voting was for individuals rather than organizations and, accordingly, personality and reputation were important factors.

The results were a remarkable victory for PIM. It won four of the seven seats from the town and island of Ambon. Dr. Tahitu also won a seat, so that the rajas gained only two. In the other Ambonese islands the Moslems voted en bloc for the progressive raja of Pelauw, A. B. Latuconsina. The remaining four seats went to independent candidates, who, like Tahitu in Ambon, were sympathetic to the nationalist cause. The result was a tribute to PIM's persuasive powers and organizational skill. The loyalists were scandalized. How could an institution purporting to represent the Ambonese include only two members of a group—the conservative rajas—who felt themselves to be the society's leaders? Salt was rubbed in the wounds of the loyalists when the DMS first met, for the non-Ambonese representatives—elected by village heads—aligned themselves with the Free Indonesia Party and independent intellectuals rather than with the conservative rajas.

The elections results say as much about the nature of the different political forces as about Ambonese political preferences. For all the old elite's traditional prestige and official support, its organizations suffered in comparison with the nationalist PIM because membership was based on function rather than political commitment. This meant that rajas or pastors did not necessarily agree with the political stance of the organization of which they were formally members. The old elite indubitably suffered from complacency and from the fact that they were unaccustomed to having to compete for support because, previously, the Dutch had successfully isolated the negeri populations from outside influences that could challenge their authority.

The results confirmed that the society was deeply divided and uncertain about its future and leadership. The half-year following the return of the Dutch had given abundant evidence that there were influential groups who wanted to perpetuate the colonial relationship. The DMS results revealed that there was also a constituency attracted to the nationalist cause and an organization capable of challenging the adat elite for social leadership. There were also indications that Ambon's most obvious division, between Moslems and Christians, was becoming politically significant. PIM's leadership was drawn from both Christian and Moslem communities, but much of its support was Moslem. Other than the rajas, very few Moslems had a vested interest in prolonging the colonial system. In the election a number of Moslem villages did demonstrate a distinct split between a conservative raja and a population supporting PIM.[17]

Ambon and the State of East Indonesia

One of the first acts of the newly established South Moluccan Council was to elect delegates for the second Dutch-sponsored conference of 1946, held at Den Pasar in December of that year. Three months later the council confirmed Ambon's place in the newly created State of East Indonesia when, by a majority of twenty-seven to three with three abstentions, it declared that the South Moluccas should remain in NIT "until the moment that the people decide, through the DMS, whether they wish to continue in NIT or not." The meeting climaxed two months of intense political activity which included a visit from NIT President Sukowati and a series of meetings held by local and emigré loyalists, the latter campaigning for the South Moluccas' immediate withdrawal. The debate itself was remarkable for its role reversals. The two conservative rajas in the council, Gaspersz and Pelu, men who had built careers on loyalty to the Dutch cause, argued the case for withdrawal of the South Moluccas from NIT and in so doing found themselves probably for the first time in their lives criticizing the government they had served faithfully for two decades, while Pupella was the main speaker in favor of NIT.[18]

In the year between the beginning of political activity in March 1946 and the DMS decision to remain in NIT, the apparent balance of power in Ambon had changed dramatically—from the effusive loyalty of an Ambon led by the old elite to an Ambon with fledgling democratic institutions dominated (more by skill than numbers) by the PIM leadership. Not surprisingly, the old elite felt themselves to be under-represented in the DMS and the new NIT parliament. They had expected the Republic to be dealt with by the Dutch in much the same way as Aceh and Lombok had been—with the help of Ambonese soldiers. What became incomprehensible to the rajas, soldiers, and veterans was that the Dutch government itself should be working toward a supposedly independent Indonesia. Dutch insistence on the inclusion of Ambon in federal Indonesia amounted to a rejection of their loyalty. A pillar of their world view had collapsed.

In response to the unfavorable election result, those groups that had cooperated with the committee in the elections—the rajas, the pastors, and the veterans—joined with a teachers' association and a Christian youth group to form a federation, GSS (Gabungan Lima [later Simbilan] Serangkai, Federation of Five [later Nine] Associations). This federation opposed independence under the current conditions and expressed a preference for a lasting Dutch administration in the South Moluccas. Ambonese could in the future assume administrative responsibility, but Ambon would remain within the Dutch Kingdom.

From the time it was established, the GSS federation was associated with the Jakarta-based PTB (Persatuan Timur Besar, Association of the Great East), which sought to promote the separation of Ambon, Menado, and Timor from Indonesia to form together a separate entity in the kingdom with similar status to that of Surinam. The PTB was led by emigré Ambonese and supported principally by Ambonese soldiers. The relationship between them and the conservative rajas of Ambon, who dominated the GSS, was uneasy despite the similarity of their goals. Traditionally distrustful of Ambonese politicians from Java, whether nationalist or loyalist, the rajas never supported attempts by the Jakarta-based association to mobilize support in Ambon itself, preferring to remain in control of their own home ground. Nevertheless, the PTB's connections with a number of Dutch politicians and military leaders associated with the Rijkseenheid (unity of the Realm) movement were largely responsible for the PTB's viability and its eventual participation as a "vital interest" at the Round Table Conference at The Hague. For those intimately involved, distinctions between GSS and PTB were clear, but for a broader public the similarity of objective meant that the two groups became synonymous.

In petitions to the Dutch government, the PTB claimed the right of self-determination for Ambon, Menado, and Timor under the Linggajati Agreement (Articles 3 and 4), and asserted that the PTB, rather than the South Moluccan Council represented the Ambonese people.[19] For the Dutch, however, more was at stake than sentiment and Ambonese preference. NIT was the oldest and the strongest of the federal states, but there was within it a fine balance between Republicans and those sympathetic to the Dutch cause. If Ambon, Menado, and Timor were given the chance to separate, the viability of the state would come into question.

The Middle Ground

The discussion thus far has centered around two political groupings: the nationalists organized in PIM at one end of the spectrum, and, at the other, a group variously described as conservative or loyalist, among whom the rajas, pastors, and soldiers were the most prominent, who were loosely associated in the GSS/PTB. In addition to these, during 1947, a number of individuals who had previously been involved in local politics began to emerge as a more discernible group. They thought of themselves, and were often designated in Dutch reports, as intellectuals, indicating that they had reached high levels in the Dutch Indies education system and had become professionals. They differed from the nationalists in the Free Indonesia Party (PIM) in that they had little or no history of political activity or commitment, but rather a sympathy for the national cause. Apart from one or two progressive rajas who could be counted among them, they had no status in the adat system. Not surprisingly, many of them had been deeply influenced by their Dutch education, and in some cases by being brought up in an Indies bureaucratic environment outside their homeland. Although life in colonial society had not been a wholly negative experience, they harbored ambitions for reforming and emancipating their own society, and envisaged a greater role for themselves and others of like background in its affairs.

J. A. Manusama, in 1950 a key figure in the RMS, became one of the most significant leaders of the group and provided it with some organizational skill and identity.[20] Manusama was the archetypal colonial Ambonese emigré—born, raised, and educated in a Dutch-speaking Indies environment outside Ambon—who arrived "home" in mid-1947 as head of the new government secondary school. He claimed to be sympathetic to an independent Indonesia while entertaining doubts about its viability because of the disparate ethnic groups making up its population. The violence of the revolution in Java led him to move to Makassar and then to Ambon. He was elected to represent his fellow Ambonese emigrés in the South Moluccan Council (DMS), where he played a progressive role, cooperating with PIM, and campaigning for an Ambonese to replace the council's Dutch chairman. He supported Pupella in his attempts to limit recruitment for the KNIL, realizing that the occupational preferences of Christian Ambonese would need to be redirected to economic development of their own islands. In February 1948 he founded the GDMS (Gerakan Demokrasi Maluku Selatan, Democratic Movement of the South Moluccas) which sought an autonomous and democratic South Moluccas within the State of East Indonesia and ultimately in an independent Indonesia. The commitment of the Democratic Movement's intellectuals to an independent Indonesia varied from Manusama's conditional support (of a federal Indonesia to keep the revolution confined to Java and Sumatra) to lack of concern on the part of others with the state's constitutional structure.

The Second Election

The test for Manusama and his Democratic Movement came at the end of 1948 with the second, this time direct, election for the South Moluccan Council. The conservative GSS had difficulty finding suitable candidates from its own membership and had to support some of the intellectuals of the Democratic Movement. The Movement's leaders themselves suffered from their belief that their professional and social standing was enough to guarantee their election, and their campaign lacked energy as their program lacked clarity. Within the nationalist PIM, tension still existed between Pupella's moderate and tactical support of the federal system and the agreements negotiated between the Republic and the Dutch, on the one hand, and a more overtly Republican group under Reawaru on the other. In its campaigning, PIM laid great stress on the attainment of independence on January 1, 1949, as promised in Linggajati. As that date approached and the likelihood of independence disappeared, opposition to Pupella's moderate stance grew stronger.

The election, which took place without incident just a few days before the Dutch launched their second "police" action of December

19, 1948, resulted in an overwhelming victory for PIM.[21] This served to confirm the party's dominance of the South Moluccan Council and to refute the conservatives' allegation that its previous success was due to clever manipulation of the indirect voting system. PIM gained one additional seat, and Pupella scored a personal success by topping the poll by a considerable margin, while the once powerful rajas were further humiliated, only D. J. Gaspersz being successful. Manusama's moderates suffered a similar fate: only the popularist and pro-Indonesia Albert Wairisal was elected. Yet electoral success had its limitations. The regional head of Ambon, M. A. Pelaupessij,[22] who was appointed by the NIT government, still held wide powers and, partly because of its proven ineffectiveness, the South Moluccan Council was not held in high regard by the general population. Pupella's success, ironically, contributed to his party's difficulties, for as a result of the election, he had to spend much of his time as a parliamentarian in Makassar. The two elections had left still-powerful groups in Ambonese society frustrated at their inability to establish themselves in what promised to be the future institutions of power.

Having failed in his election bids in both Ambon and Saparua, Manusama immediately joined other unsuccessful candidates to form a committee to re-examine the place of the South Moluccas in the State of East Indonesia with a view to possible withdrawal. Although this initiative may be seen as the first sign of a disenchantment that would lead Manusama and his fellows to play an active role in the creation of the Republic of the South Moluccas (RMS), Manusama's own commitment to the federal system was temporarily insured by his appointment as the South Moluccan representative in the provisional senate in Makassar.

Any further political moves by the committee were precluded by regional head Pelaupessij's ban on political gatherings, which remained in force until August 1949 and acted as a restraint on the endeavors of conservative and separatist groups to revive their political fortunes. Pelaupessij justified the ban on the grounds that initiatives by the committee would provoke PIM to take countermeasures, which, in the unsettled conditions arising from the Dutch attack on the Republic and given the volatile emotions of his compatriots, could disturb maintenance of law and order.

Soldiers and Pemuda: Politics Changes Venue

The opening of the Round Table Conference extended the battle about the constitutional future of the South Moluccas, and who should represent the region, to The Hague. All the Ambonese factions, including the separatist PTB, had representatives there in one capacity or another. For the duration of the conference the telegraph wires between Ambon and The Hague ran hot with claims, counterclaims, and pledges of allegiance from the rival groups at both ends.[23]

In Ambon itself, the departure of Pupella and Pelaupessij for The Hague, together with the lifting of the ban on meetings, had a catalytic effect on political activity. The ban's rationale proved to be a self-fulfilling prophecy. The temporary absence of Pelaupessij and Pupella and the prospective departure of the Dutch created an authority vacuum that the acting regional head J. H. Manuhutu could not fill.[24] The political contest, which had up till then had a parliamentary character, in the last months of 1949 went into the streets and villages. In addition to the change of venue, new participants entered the contest as increasing numbers of soldiers returned to Ambon to await the future being decided for them in The Hague. Together with the police, the soldiers started to take an active interest in politics, more often than not allying themselves with the separatist GSS/PTB. On the other side of the political spectrum, Wim Reawaru, the dominant figure in PIM in Pupella's absence, revived his pemuda groups, last active in 1945–1946. Most of the young people came from the large Moslem villages on Ambon and from among the Moslem harbor laborers. Attempting to promote the pemuda as alternative police and army units available to the regional head, Reawaru trained them in the streets of Ambon town, marching them up and down, armed with sharpened bamboo instead of rifles. Few actions could have been more provocative to the soldiers, concerned both for their safety and their future employment. Beginning in October, frequent clashes broke out throughout the islands between the two groups as each endeavored to broaden its support among the village populations.

The NIT minister of internal affairs instructed Manuhutu to restore order. He, however, lacked police or military forces on which he could rely and, as his own sympathies inclined towards PIM and the pemuda, he was unwilling to order the pro-PTB police to take action against the young people. In this tense atmosphere, elections were held for the NIT parliament in Makassar. PIM repeated its previous success, winning the two seats from the Ambonese islands. The ceremony marking the transfer of sovereignty from the Dutch took place without incident, although Manusama recalls that the ancestors signified their displeasure with a torrential downpour,[25] and during December signs appeared on the walls of the market in the town of Ambon: *Awas! Singa Maluku nanti makan merah-putih* ("Beware! The Moluccan lion will devour the Republic").[26]

The interlude of tranquillity came to an abrupt end on January 7, 1950, when a series of clashes began between police and pemuda. The situation further deteriorated ten days later with the arrival in Ambon of a contingent of soldiers from the elite special forces, the "baretten" or berets, who also clashed with the pemuda. In these clashes three pemuda were killed and fifteen people were wounded.[27]

In the highly charged atmosphere of early 1950, Ambonese soldiers, still theoretically under Dutch command, were awaiting the reorganization of the KNIL.[28] Many of the returned special forces were bitterly disappointed to find that the Dutch administration had done little reconstruction work while they had been risking their necks and making themselves possible targets for Republican revenge by doing Holland's dirty work in Java and Sulawesi.[29] Anxiety and resentment among the soldiers were reflected in the instability of their political preferences as the separatist GSS/PTB competed with PIM leader Reawaru for their support. On March 24–25 Reawaru's endeavors resulted in an ill-timed and ill-fated declaration by a group of the special forces to the effect that they considered themselves to be no longer under Dutch command.

The NIT government in Makassar was highly critical of Manuhutu's handling of the situation in Ambon and particularly his inability to control the pemuda, whom the government regarded as responsible for the incidents. The NIT's attitude reflected the strategic situation in which it found itself after the transfer of sovereignty and the departure of former Premier Anak Agung Gde Agung to become a member of the central government. In 1949 Anak Agung's administration had supported regional head Pelaupessij's attempts to contain separatist

groups, and it had vigorously opposed the PTB's campaign to win
Dutch support. However, as the conflict between the pemuda and the
soldiers developed, Makassar viewed the activity of the pemuda in
Ambon as a threat and certainly did not wish to alienate the soldiers
on whose support survival of the NIT was dependent. There was concurrently a further shift in the NIT away from supporting nationalists
toward cultivating those whose main fear was the Republic, be they
separatists or federalists. (It appears that the NIT government made
approaches to Manusama to persuade him to take over from Manuhutu.) The Dutch were no longer the problem; now the State of East
Indonesia felt it was fighting for its very survival against pressure,
both internally and from Java, for a unitary state. Within a month of
independence, as a consequence of Republican urging and in response
to the Westerling coup attempt in West Java, all but two of the federal
states had collapsed and agreed to form part of the unitary state of
Indonesia.

The NIT government's ability to survive pressures from the unitar-
ist movement was dependent on the twin-related issues of the fate of
the Indonesian KNIL soldiers (mostly Menadonese and Ambonese)
stationed in NIT, and whether Jakarta would indeed move former
Republican TNI (Indonesian National Army) troops into eastern
Indonesia. In December 1949 the Republican government agreed not
to transfer troops to eastern Indonesia without Makassar's prior consent. The only Republican presence in Makassar would be a liaison
mission under Lt. Colonel Mokoginta. However, the first months of
1950 were dominated by a struggle between Jakarta and Makassar on
this issue, and Jakarta's unilateral decision in early April to send the
Worang battalion (mostly Menadonese) to Makassar provoked a
coup, led by a Buginese ex-KNIL captian, Andi Abdul Azis.

In the early hours of April 5, Andi Azis, with his own company and
some KNIL soldiers, captured the military liaison mission and took
control of the main government installations in Makassar, declaring
that his forces would combat any attempt to land troops of the
Worang battalion. Azis' action was the first phase of a plan to proclaim a separate Republic of East Indonesia. Although the NIT disassociated itself from Azis' action, the plan was in fact devised and led
by senior members of its government, including President Sukowati,
Soumokil,[30] the Ambonese attorney general and former justice minis-

ter, and the Ambonese finance official and former Moluccan Commonwealth advocate R. J. Metekohy.[31] The Azis coup and its failure was, as we shall see, a crucial stage in the events which would lead to the proclamation of the RMS.[32]

Manusama's Initiative

During the first three months of 1950, Manusama, the former moderate leader of the Democratic Movement, had not been politically active. But about the end of March, concerned about the collapse of most of the federal states and the threat posed to the continuing existence of NIT by Republican troop movements and the unrest in Ambon itself, he realized that a clash between Republican troops and Ambonese KNIL in Ambon could only result in a blood bath in which the civilian population would be the victim. He decided to hold a mass meeting to demonstrate Ambonese support for the NIT government, which was by then at a critical stage in negotiations with Jakarta following the Azis coup.[33] The meeting was not held until April 18, two days after Dr. Soumokil had arrived from Makassar.[34] Manusama spoke eloquently in defense of federalism, on the evils of revolution, and the dishonesty of the Jakarta government, and declared that, were Makassar to fall, Ambon would become "the final defensive bastion."[35]

On April 21, NIT President Sukowati formally declared that the State of East Indonesia was in principle prepared to join a unitary state. Two days later a meeting at Tulehu organized by Manusama urged the DMS executive to break all constitutional and political relations with the federal government and NIT. Subsequent meetings culminated in a public gathering held on the night of April 24 where acting regional head Manuhutu finally abandoned his opposition to the movement and proclaimed the Republic of the South Moluccas (RMS).[36]

It is difficult to assess the degree of popular support enjoyed by the RMS. Manuhutu alleged that he was intimidated by the soldiers into making the declaration, and they certainly acted violently both before and after it was made. In the opinion of Manusama and Soumokil, Manuhutu and Wairisal had to be the ones to proclaim the RMS in order to give the outside world the impression that the proclamation was the deed of the legally constituted local authorities. Nationalist leaders were intimidated and detained, and shortly after the proclamation Wim Reawaru was killed by the special forces. Nevertheless, at least in the early days, there was enthusiasm expressed for the RMS. It seems likely, however, that this was indicative largely of the highly charged and emotional atmosphere, especially the soldiers' demonstrated intolerance of the opposition. As recently as November 1949, in the elections for the NIT parliament held in circumstances relatively free of intimidation, the people of the Ambonese islands had reaffirmed the strength of their pro-Republican feeling.[37]

The RMS was not the preferred constitutional structure of its two principal civilian promoters, Soumokil and Manusama. They had accepted an independent federal Indonesia and sought to defend it. When that failed, the RMS was the last bastion to which they retreated, without thought or planning as to the new state's structure, resources, or viability. The aim was to keep the Republic and its revolution out of Ambon. Manusama acknowledged no spiritual or organizational debt to the separatist GSS/PTB, yet much of his and Soumokil's success can be attributed to the support they mobilized from the rajas and lower ranking officials formerly associated with the GSS/PTB. Beyond doubt, however, the RMS received its most crucial support from the soldiers. The disturbances in March and the failure to secure a rapid incorporation of the soldiers into the Indonesian army, together with the rise and fall of Andi Azis in Makassar, convinced them they had no secure future in the armed forces of the Indonesian state. During April their paramount concern was to keep Republican troops out of Ambon, and Manusama, and later Soumokil, were able to provide the necessary political leadership to achieve that objective, at least temporarily. The soldiers for their part eliminated PIM, Reawaru, and his pemuda as a political force, and ensured that Manuhutu and his colleagues cooperated to provide the RMS with the desired constitutional facade.

The RMS

The government of the RMS controlled the Ambonese islands from April to December 1950. Throughout these months there were intensive negotiations between the Dutch and Indonesian governments for a peaceful solution. The potential results of the sincere endeavors on both sides were limited on the one hand by a Dutch obsession with the principle of self-determination and on the other by the untimely interventions of the Indonesian military authorities, which undermined Dr. Leimena's peace initiatives in May and September. However, while the efforts were being made in Jakarta and The Hague, the RMS leaders appear to have taken no single initiative to avoid the blood bath that took place. Their entire diplomatic effort was directed toward securing recognition and military support from the Netherlands, the United States, and Australia, and many on Ambon appear to have believed that help would be forthcoming.[38]

The TNI launched its attack on the Ambonese islands in September, but it was nearly three months later, and after great human and material sacrifice, that it finally occupied the town of Ambon. Some of the RMS leaders and armed forces retreated to the island of Ceram, where during the following twelve years they either were captured or made their way via Irian to the Netherlands. In 1955, twelve RMS civilian and military leaders were tried and sentenced to prison terms ranging from three to fifteen years. Soumokil was captured in 1962 and executed in 1966.

Aftermath

The RMS and its suppression was perhaps the worst possible way for Ambon to be incorporated into independent Indonesia. Ambonese society emerged deeply divided, with members having fought on both the Indonesian and RMS sides in a conflict that had many of the characteristics of a civil war. The already strained relations between the Moslem and Christian communities suffered further through the clear identification of the RMS civilian leadership and the soldiers as Christians and the fact that most of the soldiers' Ambonese victims were Moslems. The Ambon-based political elite was also severely weakened and in the following decades proved unable to maintain much semblance of regional autonomy. Those associated with the RMS were discredited. Ambon's nationalists, such as Pupella, had failed in their efforts to persuade their compatriots that their future prosperity and development was to be found in Indonesia. Pupella continued his political career in the 1950s but never regained the influence he had enjoyed in pre-RMS days.

After the suppression of the RMS, the processes of social change which it had attempted to contain were accelerated and given new form. The rajas were quickly deprived of one of their crucial colonial supports—their judicial powers—and increasing numbers of rajas were appointed from non-raja families. Government financial support for the rajas, a bone of contention in the last decades of Dutch rule, became merely a token gesture.

One of the most significant aftereffects of the RMS was the disappearance of the KNIL as a social group. It is as if the KNIL and its social problems were exported to the Netherlands, when some 4,000 soldiers with their families were transported to Holland. As a result, a relatively small number of the Ambonese belonging to the postwar KNIL transferred to the TNI. Ironically, a good number of them were former RMS soldiers who subsequently distinguished themselves in the campaign against the Darul Islam, the movement for an Islamic state. Ambonese still serve in the TNI, but they no longer form a privileged group as they did in Dutch times.

With respect to the relations between the two religious communities, the RMS was an attempt to maintain Christian dominance in Ambonese society. At the time, rumors propagated by Soumokil of forced conversions to Islam appealed to deep-rooted Christian fears of being overwhelmed by Indonesia's Moslem majority. In any case, the transfer of sovereignty would have meant the loss of the special relationship between the Christian community and the government. The suppression of the RMS meant that the departure of the Dutch personnel was more abrupt and absolute than it might otherwise have been, which left, for example, the Protestant Church dependent on its own resources, as it had been during the war. More generally, the utility of Christian Ambonese identification with things Dutch declined. The erosion of the Christian advantage in education, which began before the RMS, gained momentum with the rapid expansion of government education.

In these post-RMS developments, the coin was reversed for the Moslems. They no longer lived in a country ruled by Christians. For the first time, their religious and educational needs received direct encouragement and financial support from the government. The tensions created by the RMS and the subsequent increase in competition have not made for harmonious communal relations, but perhaps more complex and equal ones.

Notes

The author wishes to express his appreciation to the many Ambonese who gave their time most generously to elucidate the intricacies of their society. The author's research was supported in Indonesia by Lembaga Ilmu Pengetahuan Indonesia, the Arsip Nasional, and Universitas Pattimura, and in the Netherlands by the General State Archives, the Royal Institute of Linguistics and Anthropology, the Royal Institute for the Tropics, and the archives of the former Ministry of Overseas Territories and the Ministry of Defense. His sincere thanks are due the staff of these institutions for their encouragement and assistance.

1. *Volkstelling 1930,* vol. 1 (Batavia: Departement van Economische Zaken, 1936), p. 91. The figures are for "Ambonese" living in the *afdeeling* Amboina.

2. See R. H. Chauvel, "Stagnatie, exodus, en frustratie: Economische geschiedenis van Ambon van 1863 tot 1950," in *intermediair* (Amsterdam), Feb. 20, 1981.

3. See R. H. Chauvel, "Ambon's Other Half . . . ," *Review of Indonesian and Malayan Affairs* 14, 1 (1980): 53–67.

4. A. Th. Manusama, *Beknopt Geschiedenis der Vereeniging der Ambonschstudiefonds, 1909–1919* (Weltevreden: n.p., 1919).

5. Born in 1894 in Ambon, A. J. Patty, a Christian, failed to finish a medical training at Stovia. He worked as a clerk in private firms and as a journalist on Insulinde/NIP newspapers. He was a member of Insulinde/NIP in 1920. In 1919–1920 he campaigned among Ambonese soldiers. In 1922–1923 he established Sarekat Ambon in the Batavia Ambonese community before moving to Ambon in April 1923. Exiled from Ambon in October 1924, he was eventually sent to Boven Digul.

6. E. U. Pupella, born 1910 in Ambon, attended MULO in Makassar. He joined Sarekat Ambon there while working for Bataafse Petroleum Maatschappij. In 1933 he attended the Taman Siswa teachers training college in Yogyakarta. He returned to Ambon in 1934, became a leader of Sarekat Ambon, and was elected to the Ambonraad in 1938.

7. These included Pattimaipau, Tjokro, and Wim Reawaru, a Christian

(Adventist) who was an employee of the KPM shipping line. Reawaru became the most radical of Ambon's nationalist leaders.

8. *Sinar Matahari* (Ambon), Nov. 3, 1943.

9. "Sejarah Daerah Tematis Zaman Kebangkitan Nasional di Daerah Maluku" (Ambon: Proyek Penilitian dan Pencatatan Kebudayaan Daerah, 1977/ 1978), p. 122.

10. Interview with E. U. Pupella, Ambon, Feb. 2, 1975.

11. H. Luhukay, "Maluku dalam perlintasan suasana Orde Baru" (Ujung Pandang, typescript, 1967), p. 58.

12. Ibid., p. 61; Sejarah Militer XV/Pattimura, *Mengenal dari dekat Komando Daerah Militer XV/Pattimura* (Ambon: n.p., 1974), pp. 15 and 18–19.

13. "Politiek Verslag der Residentie Zuid-Molukken, 1–15 June 1946," RI. E81 (Ministry of Overseas Territories, The Hague). D. P. Tahitu, a Christian doctor in government service, worked with the Japanese administration. He had no political allegiances or experience before the war.

14. Ambonese attitudes toward Indonesia were strongly influenced by the experiences of Ambonese who had lived during the early revolution in the Republican or contested areas and who had been subject to attack and reprisals, often provoked by the behavior of Ambonese soldiers. Although there was no large-scale repatriation of Ambonese from Java and Sulawesi, the psychological influence of experiences in those regions on political thinking in Ambon was far greater than the actual numbers would indicate.

15. KNIL Hoofdkwartier, "Groote Oost en Borneo, sitrap no. 20, 31-8-46," Verbaal 31-12-47 LE 78 (Ministry of Overseas Territories, The Hague).

16. Interview with E. U. Pupella, Ambon, Jan. 20, 1979.

17. "Politiek Verslag der Residentie der Zuid-Molukken, October–November 1946" (Ministry of Overseas Territories); see also Chauvel, "Ambon's Other Half," pp. 70–75.

18. Nefis Buitenkantoor Amboina no. 49/geh Bijlage CIO-MIO no. 37 "Weekverslag 6 t/m 12 Maart 1947" (Nefis AA 23) Ministerie van Defensie, Centraal Archieven Depot (MvD), The Hague.

19. Petition, PTB to the Queen, dated May 8, 1947, in S. L. van der Wal, ed., *Officiele Bescheiden Betreffende de Nederlands-Indonesische Betrekkingen 1945–50*, vol. 8 (The Hague: Martinus Nijhoff, 1979), p. 580.

20. J. A. Manusama, a Christian of Ambonese and Eurasian parents, was born in Banjarmasin on August 17, 1910. He graduated in engineering at the Bandung THS in 1940, and was a secondary school teacher during and after the war.

21. "Politiek Verslag der Residentie der Zuid-Molukken, December 16–31, 1948" (Ministry of Overseas Territories).

22. M. A. Pelaupessij, a Christian and trained as a career official by the Dutch, was a trade consultant in Ambon in 1946 and appointed by the NIT as regional head (Kepala Daerah) in 1948.

23. E. I. van der Meulen, *De Ronde-tafelconferentie* (The Hague: Staatsuitgeverij, 1978).

24. J. H. Manuhutu, a Christian born in 1908, was a Dutch-trained career official. In 1946–1957 he was raja of Haria (Saparua) and was one of a handful of rajas who did not follow the loyalist GSS/PTB. He was a sympathizer but not a member of PIM.

25. Interview with J. A. Manusama, Capelle A/D I'ssel, Jan. 17, 1978.

26. KNIL/KL-WTIR no. 35, Makassar, December 21, 1949 (Secretariaat Landmacht Nieuw-Guinea, 1950, ZG 101, no. 79), MvD.

27. KNIL-WOMOT, no. 6, Feb. 16, 1950 (Landmacht NG, ZG 1, 79), MvD; and I. M. Djabir Sjah [Minister of Internal Affairs, NIT], "Het incident te Ambon," Jan. 26, 1950, Arsip Nasional, Ujung Pandang, no. 22/23.

28. Under the RTC agreements Indonesian soldiers in the KNIL had to choose between demobilization and transfer to the armed forces of RIS, a choice between simple subsistence in the village or joining the former enemy, complicated by uncertainties about pensions, pay, status, and security.

29. KNIL/KL-WOMOT, no. 12, Maart 30, 1950, bijlage C (HKGS-N.OI no. GG 81, ongenummerd 1950), MvD.

30. Soumokil was born, raised, and educated outside his homeland. Despite his lack of political experience he was appointed minister of justice in NIT. His career was threatened by his involvement in the execution of a convicted guerrilla leader, Mongisidi, for which the nationalists held him responsible. By early 1950 he had become such a political liability that he had lost his position in the federalist cabinet, but as attorney-general he fought hard to defend NIT.

31. R. J. Metekohy, a Christian, was a Dutch-trained civil servant. A delegate to Malino and Den Pasar, he became deputy minister of finance in the first NIT cabinet and an adviser to Ambonese military organizations in Makassar.

32. E. I. van der Meulen, *Dosier Ambon 1950* (The Hague: Staatsuitgeverij, 1981), p. 22.

33. Manusama's version of the RMS is contained in his *Om Recht en Vrijheid* (Utrecht: Libertas, 1952) and in a more extensive report, "Verslag betreffende de gebeurtenissen in de Zuid-Molukken na de sourvereiniteits-overdracht op 27 Desember 1949," September 1952, which has been partly published as the "Geheim verslag van Manusama" in T. Pollmann and J. Seleky, *Istori-Istori Maluku* (Amsterdam: De arbeiderspers, 1979), pp. 96–100.

34. He had left Makassar when his collaborators in the Azis Coup were

exploring the final possibilities to make an independence declaration and Soumokil's role was presumably to mobilize support for an independent East Indonesia in Menado and Ambon. While he was still in Menado he had learned, via an exchange of telegrams with Makassar, that the planned declaration would not go through. "Nederlands Indie, 1e & 2e Pol. actie," doos 045 (MvD).

35. Angkatan Darat Territorium VII, "Panitya Penjelesaian Pemeriksaan Terhadap Pemimpinan RMS" (Ambon, 1952). Following the meeting Manusama sent a telegram to Makassar urging the government to defend federalism and, if necessary, proclaim an independent republic. The telegram would suggest that he and Soumokil still entertained hopes for an eleventh-hour putsch (telegram exchange Soumokil-Hopster, 15/16 April, quoted in telegram PXOO [Schotborgh]-CGS [Buurman van Vreeden] nr. CS220 A, 16–4–50, "Nederlands Indie, 1e & 2e Pol. actie," doos 045), MvD.

36. The immediate circumstances of the proclamation have been the focus of bitter controversy as they touch on the RMS claims of legitimacy and popular support. Manusama and his followers maintain that the proclamation was the free and clearly expressed wish of the South Moluccan people. Manuhutu and Wairisal assert that they proclaimed the state under threat to their lives. Interviews with Manusama, Wairisal, and Manuhutu are published in Ben van Kaam, *The South Moluccans* (London: Hurst, 1980), pp. 107–114.

37. The events surrounding the proclamation did not spread beyond the Ambonese islands. There is no evidence suggesting support for the RMS from people living elsewhere in the South Moluccas.

38. Van der Meulen, *Dosier Ambon,* chs. 2 and 3.

OVERVIEW

Audrey R. Kahin

The preceding accounts have shown the diversity of the revolutionary experience in different parts of Indonesia and the intermingling of national and local concerns during the years in which, through a mixture of fighting and diplomacy, an independent Indonesian government displaced the colonial power and began to create a new nation state. The nature of the revolution in the far-flung regions of Indonesia was largely determined by local factors, though its course was also influenced by pressures from outside. The most decisive determinants were the relationship of the strongest political and social groups in the region to the local power-holders and the interaction of both with the Republican or colonial authorities at higher levels of government. The extent of the transformation that took place during these years depended in part on whether and how soon a local governmental authority emerged capable of channeling or containing the potentially explosive pressures for change that arose in the wake of the Japanese capitulation and the proclamation of an independent Republic of Indonesia. And the responsiveness of such a local authority either to Dutch attempts to reestablish their state or to efforts of the nascent Republican central government to exert its power was critically important in shaping the revolution's character.

Contrasting Character of Revolutionary Activity

The Tiga Daerah, Banten, and Aceh

The major periods of upheaval in the Tiga Daerah, Banten, and Aceh took place in the first six months after the declaration of independence. During these months all three regions were nominally under Republican control, but in none of them did the Republic's central leadership have the coercive power necessary to create an effective local apparatus responsive to its direction. As a result it reappointed most of the existing office holders once they had pledged their allegiance to the Republic. In both the Tiga Daerah area of Pekalongan and in Banten, however, the Republican government hesitated in confirming the new residents, and this hesitation intensified local suspicion toward them. In each case violence was sparked by the withdrawal of Japanese forces and widespread fears that the nominally Republican administration left in place was preparing to welcome back the Dutch.

A privileged segment in all three societies constituted the major pillar of the administration. These officials were isolated from their indigenous compatriots by the privileges they enjoyed and by the Western education and lifestyle many had adopted, an isolation that was intensified during the Japanese occupation. The Japanese had basically maintained the colonial structure in each region, but also looked to elements in the society that the Dutch had excluded, particularly Moslem groups, to mobilize popular support for Japan's war effort and assume certain judicial and advisory positions previously the prerogative of the Indonesian colonial elite. The major tasks left to the Dutch-trained officials were taxing and policing the society, and by August 1945 they had become exclusively identified with the extractive demands of the Japanese military administration and consequently the principal targets of blame for the deprivations suffered by the local people. The Japanese capitulation left this bureaucracy exposed to popular retribution unless they could call on a military force strong enough to protect them.

The character and strength of the armies in the regions and their capacity and willingness to protect the members of the administration were thus decisive in determining the course of the revolutions there.

In all three regions most Republican army officers came from backgrounds similar to those of the government officials. They could be expected to support them, and in the eyes of the rest of the society, were identified with them. For a variety of reasons, however, during the months of upheaval the newly formed regular army was not an effective security force in any of the regions: in the Tiga Daerah its strength was largely absorbed in confronting external rather than internal danger; in Banten it lacked both manpower and resources; and in Aceh the bulk of the young men, both trained soldiers and new recruits, had chosen to join nongovernment militias, allied with the social forces pressing for change.

The initial wave of revolution in all three areas shattered the fragile Republican-endorsed state structure. In all instances, once the Japanese withdrew, the village and district officials were the principal targets of the violence, those in the villages and rural areas being the most vulnerable to attack. The character of revolutionary violence, however, was markedly different in each of these three regions and this was partly due to the nature of the local groups that tried to assume leadership.

In both the Tiga Daerah and Banten, the most important revolutionary groups had histories of nationalist and anticolonial activity stretching back to the 1920s. In Banten the leadership—*ulama* (Islamic scholar), bandit, and Communist—that had spearheaded the 1926 rebellions again initially forged an alliance. In the Tiga Daerah many of the Communist leaders of the Popular Front, as well as the rural Islamic leaders, had also been active since the 1920s. But it was the bandit groups who were responsible for much of the violence, and they built up autonomous bases of power where the Popular Front's leaders exerted little control. In Aceh, the modernist Islamic PUSA (All-Aceh Ulama Association) that assumed leadership of the revolution also had a history of anticolonial activity, but, in contrast to leaders in the other areas, the PUSA leaders were strong enough that they did not need to come to terms with temporary allies possessing potentially divergent aims.

All three revolutions successfully changed the order at the village level, and at most district levels as well. The peasantry in Banten and the Tiga Daerah participated in creating the new order, electing their own leaders and forming representative councils, and, as a result, a variety of new local officials took over. In all three areas, the Islamic teachers were most frequently the heirs to the earlier administrative elite. They retained their new positions and were generally unaffected by whether or not, in the higher reaches of the residency government, revolutionary leaders too remained in power. And although the radical secular leaders did not succeed in retaining control of the residency level of the government in either the Tiga Daerah or Banten, neither was the colonial elite able to return. Thus in Banten, despite the fact that the dominance of the People's Council was short-lived, Kyai Chatib remained on as resident; and in the Tiga Daerah the central government failed in its attempts to appoint a resident from among the *priyayi* (Java's governing elite) so that there too eventually it had to name an Islamic nationalist to the post.

In Banten, the coalition of Communists, ulama, and bandits that formed the revolutionary People's Council disintegrated largely because the radical measures it tried to institute alienated its ulama support. Contributory factors were its inability or unwillingness to restrain the bandit groups in their campaign of kidnapping and killing in the countryside and internal ruptures between moderate PKI (Indonesian Communist Party) elements and the pro-Tan Malaka faction over the strategy to be pursued within the Indonesian national context. Even before the central Republican leadership openly opposed the council and encouraged the army to move against it, the coalition which formed the council had in effect fallen apart.

Similarly in the Tiga Daerah, strains between the radical Popular Front and the Moslem groups over the revolution's goals, coupled there too with the activities of the bandit groups, particularly in Tegal, helped forge an antiradical alliance between the Moslems and the local TKR (Republican armed forces), which then crushed the front and imprisoned its leaders before any direct intervention by the central government occurred.

In Aceh, in contrast, the young Moslem radical activists were not pursuing an aim inconsistent with that of the religious leaders or the mass of the population. It was the modernist Islamic leadership that largely orchestrated the course of events and headed a cohesive movement with wide acceptance throughout the society. Once it came to power as a result of the revolutionary upheaval and gained control of the military and civilian governmental apparatus, it had a clear view of the new order it wished to establish, and successfully worked to create a functioning pro-Republican, but autonomous, state consistent with Islamic teachings.

Although the success of the Acehnese leadership in consolidating the revolution there was clearly aided by its freedom from Republican or Dutch pressures, neither the proximity of the Tiga Daerah and Banten to the centers of Republican and Dutch power nor any action by the Dutch or by the Republic was the primary cause of the failure of the most radical secular groups in these areas to achieve their ultimate revolutionary goals. Rather, the reason for this failure lay in basic fissures within the alliances themselves, caused by the dissonance between the aims of the People's Council or the Popular Front and those of the peasantry and the ulama—whether conservative or progressive. The radicals' inability to control bandit groups further alienated the broad-based support that they had enjoyed in removal of the old colonial order.

East and West Sumatra

Both of these Sumatran regions were contested areas throughout the revolution. The presence within each of two competing governments so soon after the Japanese capitulation conditioned the pattern of violence there, with the Republic striving to affirm its authority and legitimacy against internal rivals asserting their own claims to head the revolution, and also against the Dutch who were attempting to recreate their state structure.

The external and internal struggles, then, ran concurrently. But while, in West Sumatra, the outside threat generally acted as a centripetal factor, enabling the local Republican authorities to undercut the legitimacy of their internal competitors, in East Sumatra the internally generated violence of early 1946 brought about the virtual disintegration of the fledgling Republican administration. By mid-1947, when the Dutch occupied extensive lowland areas and began to construct their federal state of East Sumatra, their major opponents were warlord chiefs who paid nominal allegiance to the Republican government but were in reality autonomous and capable of choosing whether or not to ally with it at any particular time.

In East and West Sumatra, the Dutch used British enclaves in the regional capitals of Medan and Padang as bases and springboards to rally support from former colonial officials in efforts to extend their control over the whole region. The position of the bureaucracy, which was pivotal to that effort, was affected by a basic difference in the character of colonial rule in the two regions. While the Dutch in West Sumatra had governed the region directly, with their administrators staffing the bureaucracy down to the district level, in East Sumatra they had preserved the sultans, whose domains embraced much of the region, and thus the indigenous Malay rulers, not the Dutch, had become the prime focus of popular hostility. Western influence in this part of Sumatra, in contrast to the situation in the rural areas of Banten and the Tiga Daerah, had spread far beyond the colonial bureaucracy, particularly in the urban centers that serviced the plantation economy, so that in general the government officials did not form a group isolated from the society around them.

As in Java, prewar bureaucrats were appointed to staff the new Republican administration in East Sumatra in 1945, and their ambiguous loyalties made them a weak foundation on which either side could build its authority. Their vacillation and reluctance to assert Republican claims intensified the popular impression that these officials were following, not leading, the revolution and increased the dissatisfaction of more openly nationalistic groups competing to stamp their impression on the new state. No such ambiguity characterized the position of the sultans, whose status, power, and wealth had been protected and enhanced under colonial rule. In early 1946 as news filtered through of the fate of the *uleebalang* (hereditary territorial rulers) in Aceh and as it was clear that the Dutch were not yet strong enough to reassert their control militarily, the indigenous rulers did make some efforts to compromise with the Republic. But there was little doubt that they would rally to the colonial power as soon as its military strength improved.

In West Sumatra the lack of a traditional hierarchical social order had led the Dutch to maintain the village as the key unit of their colonial administration, and it was primarily at this level that they had shaped and manipulated traditional forms of governance to serve their needs. Indigenous colonial officials above that level came, not necessarily from traditionally privileged families, but from those who had achieved the requisite level of education. During the occupation, the

Japanese governor in Padang drew extensively from social groups outside the bureaucracy to advise him and head residency-wide organizations. Thus, with the coming of independence, although former colonial officials staffed most of the intermediate levels of the new
Republican bureaucracy, the leaders at the residency level came from a
much broader spectrum of society, ranging from small traders, farmers, and teachers to traditional coastal aristocratic families. Their
commitment to both the Republic and its central leadership was much
deeper than in most other regions, in part because of personal and
family ties with the men of Minangkabau origin who held some of the
highest positions in the national Republican government.

From the beginning, then, the provincial government in the Minangkabau was a stronger and more cohesive body than that in East
Sumatra and more closely tied both to the national leadship and to the
local society. In neither region was the line of demarcation separating
the new Republican officials from the rest of the society as sharp as in
Banten, the Tiga Daerah, or Aceh. But in East Sumatra an even deeper
gap divided the wealthy ruling families of the sultanates from the
remainder of the population. No such uniquely privileged group
existed among the Minangkabau.

There was qualitative difference between the two regions in the
character of the armed forces on which the Republican officials could
rely. In the closing months of their occupation of East Sumatra, the
Japanese had set up a number of special military units in addition to
the Giyūgun (people's volunteer army) to combat the impending Allied
invasion. Before the local Republican leaders finally established the
TKR in mid-October 1945, many armed bands (*lasykar,* militia) had
sprung up in town and countryside, based either on these Japanese-
trained special units, or on radical youth groups, particularly in the
towns, who rallied around a Giyūgun military commander or a prewar nationalist leader. These lasykar commanders attracted follow-
ings on the basis of their courage and charisma, as well as ethnic allegiance, so that the bands were usually intensely loyal to their leaders,
but had few ties to the official Republican establishment in the region.

In contrast, in West Sumatra the Japanese set up no special units
and the Giyūgun was the only military organization they trained. In
August 1945 the Giyūgun officers were the first to organize a Republican army, and, although independent bands soon sprang up alongside,

their commanders had also served in the Giyūgun and thus ties between them already existed. The strongest lasykars were those of the Islamic parties, and Moslem ex-Giyūgun officers in the regular army provided a bridge between them and the residency civilian establishment. When upheavals occurred, the Republican officials could call on a reliable armed force to protect and maintain their authority vis-à-vis dissatisfied social and religious groups.

The distinctions between the situation in the two Sumatran regions extended to their fundamentally different societies. The almost complete ethnic homogeneity of West Sumatra stood in sharp contrast to the ethnic mosaic that made up the Dutch residency of East Sumatra, as did the village-owned lands in the Minangkabau to the dominant plantation economy of the east. West Sumatra's relatively egalitarian village-based order differed markedly from the glaring social and economic inequities of the east coast principalities and sultanates; as did its almost universal adherence to Islam from the Christian-Moslem divisions of the neighboring area.

Differences in the local revolutionary context—both of the state and the society—were of more importance in determining the course of the revolution than was the degree of outside pressure brought to bear on the two regions. Internecine violence became endemic in East Sumatra, while on the West coast it was sporadic and localized. The government in the West was able to contain internal opposition, but in the East it disintegrated before it. Revolts rocked both areas in early 1946, but their extent and outcome were very different. While in East Sumatra the revolutionaries eliminated many of the ruling families and rendered much of the fragile Republican apparatus impotent, in West Sumatra the official Republican army crushed incipient rebellions in both early 1946 and March of 1947.

The Dutch did employ much larger military forces in the east than in the west. But well before their first major action in July 1947 much of East Sumatra was already split among competing warlords who governed territorial fiefdoms, supported economically by local agriculture and plantation products and by trade across the Malacca Straits. On the other hand, in West Sumatra, by that same date the Republic had eliminated potential internal threats to its authority by a mixture of force and compromise. Its main priority already was to create a more cohesive political order, through which it could withstand the mounting external Dutch threat, and it based this on local participation in village-based security and taxation bodies.

Jakarta, South Sulawesi, and Ambon

The pattern of events in these three regions was dictated to a much larger degree by outside pressures, in particular by the fact that soon after the independence proclamation the Dutch were already in an ascendant position there. Each of them then became an important part of the Dutch overall strategy for regaining control of Indonesia and for competing with the Republic for the allegiance of its people. As capital of the prewar colonial state, Jakarta (Batavia) was the major center of diplomatic interaction between Dutch and Republican authorities. South Sulawesi and Ambon were areas of critical importance in the construction of a federal Indonesia, in that Makassar was to become the capital and Ambon the most trustworthy base of civilian and military manpower for the largest component of the federal structure—the East Indonesian State or NIT. Furthermore, early in the revolution, the Republican government acknowledged temporary Dutch authority in all three, explicitly in South Sulawesi and Ambon, and tacitly in Jakarta, and this undercut the possibility of Republican followers in these regions mounting any effective military challenge to Dutch power.

The extent of the intermingling of national and local politics in Jakarta makes it in many ways unique among the regions considered in this book. Not only did its indigenous inhabitants, the Betawi, have virtually no voice in the political and social developments in their city in the colonial period, but no other Indonesians in fact played any real role in its administration, as its bureaucracy was staffed almost totally with Dutch and Eurasian civil servants. In August 1945, then, there were few senior local officials on whom the Republic could call to create an Indonesian-staffed administration, and the men it appointed were mostly Western-educated professionals from other parts of the country, with little or no administrative experience and few ties to city's native population. The principal result of this was that, when, under overall British auspices, the Dutch began to introduce their own administrative apparatus into Jakarta, it paralleled that of the Republic, rather than competing for the allegiance of the same body of officials, and the two structures coexisted uneasily side by side until the British withdrawal opened the way for the eventual total dismantling of the Republican city government by the Dutch at the time of their First Military Action.

At no time did this feeble symbol of Republican authority have a military arm to protect itself. The evacuation of Republican armed forces from Jakarta in late 1945 to avoid clashes with British and Dutch troops tacitly conceded the former capital to these Western powers, whose own military forces were being steadily augmented during these months. The only challenges to the Dutch that remained were the bands of young irregular forces, uncontrolled, and indeed often disowned by the Republic's regular army leadership. Thus the effective state apparatus in Jakarta was never the Republic's, but that of the Dutch.

The initial weakness and early dismantling of the Republic's governmental apparatus in South Sulawesi followed a pattern somewhat similar to that in Jakarta, but in many ways the situation more closely resembled the one in East Sumatra. The moderate political nationalist appointed by the Republic as resident of South Sulawesi was as reluctant as Sumatra Governor Hasan to assert the Republic's authority in his region for fear that any such decisive action would provoke retaliation from the Japanese still officially in control, and the Australians and Dutch who were already poised to take over. Republican efforts to use the Australians as a counterweight to the Dutch were as ineffective as similar tactics with the British in other parts of the archipelago, and were overwhelmed by the reality of the greater authority and military power the Dutch were able to deploy in the region.

The revolutionary experience in South Sulawesi was distinguished from that in the other areas discussed by the way in which the Dutch used their military and governmental power and by the sultans' support of the Republic. In contrast to the fate of their counterparts in East Sumatra, the South Sulawesi sultans, because of their anticolonial stance, did not become a major target of the revolutionaries. The massive Dutch military forces were by far the prime focus of popular hatred, and the anticolonial struggle against them transcended in importance any goal of reordering the indigenous society. Makassar's concurrent role as capital of South Sulawesi and of the NIT (East Indonesia State) also meant that, while the Dutch employed brutal tactics against their opponents in the rural areas of South Sulawesi, they needed to compromise with the moderate nationalists in its capital in an effort to win their participation in, and support for, a federal Indonesia. These urban nationalists, then, had significant leverage on the Dutch, and could publicly defy them to an unusual degree in the Dutch-created political arena, with little chance of suffering real retribution. The revolutionaries in the countryside had no such alternative. There, the strength of the Dutch army and the Republic's de facto cession of the region to Netherlands authority in the Linggajati Agreement combined to undercut any chance of creating an organized Republican army to challenge Dutch power. The merciless Dutch campaign to eradicate guerrillas and their supporters from the rural areas took advantage of this military weakness. The decisive factors determining the course of the revolution in both Jakarta and South Sulawesi, then, were the dominance of Dutch military forces and the acquiescence of the Republic's central leadership in their retention of control.

In many ways the course of events in Ambon was the obverse of that in the other regions—a counterrevolution, not a revolution. Here it was the officials and soldiers staffing the structure of political authority who rebelled against the plans being worked out by their Dutch superiors both for the shape of the future state they would serve and for their own home region.

As one of the oldest areas of Dutch rule, Ambon, unlike most other regions of the archipelago, could indeed look back to more than 300 years of colonial governance, the impact of which had penetrated deeply into the society and shaped the forces within it, so that nearly two-thirds of its population was Christian. Thus a majority of the Ambonese had adopted Dutch religion and often other aspects of Dutch culture as well; and a Moslem minority—mostly rural or trading—identified with their fellows in other parts of the archipelago in their religion and culture. Yet the educated Christian elite also produced leaders who headed the nationalist or pro-independence parties, although the mass of their support was from the Moslem villages. And also, when the population at large was faced with clear alternatives in a reasonably free election, Dutch loyalist groups were rejected in favor of those promoting an independent Indonesia. However greatly this might have been influenced by the better organizing techniques of the nationalists, it does show that there was no simple dichotomy between pro-Dutch Christians and pro-Republican Moslems, for the parties espousing moderate nationalist aims through the NIT drew support from the Christian majority as well as the Moslem minority.[1]

The Christian Ambonese, however, were the most prominent indigenous components of the Dutch colonial civilian and particularly military apparatus throughout the archipelago, and it was these members of the colonial administration who throughout the revolution attempted to ensure that their Ambonese home islands would be maintained as a separate unit of the Netherlands kingdom. Ultimately, faced with the outcome of the Round Table Conference where they saw their rulers rebuff their loyalty and relinquish them to a minority status within the emerging independent Indonesia, they became temporarily the actors against, rather than victims of, the course of events in their region. In proclaiming their Republic of the South Moluccas and asserting their right to determine the state they would serve, the Ambonese soldiers and civilian officials defied the Dutch and the new Indonesian government, and even perhaps a majority of their own people. They did not prevail, for, without the support of their former masters, these colonial servants could not withstand the concentration of force the government of Indonesia eventually brought against them. But, as a group, they stood for a while against the tide that had engulfed their vacillating counterparts in other parts of Indonesia, who had attempted to bend with and adapt to the wind of change that swept over the archipelago during the five years of revolution.

Concluding Observations

We have seen how one of the critical factors that determined which of the regions would experience revolutionary violence was the degree of effective governmental authority. Thus in all four areas where insurgents overthrew the instruments of the state—the Tiga Daerah, Banten, Aceh, and East Sumatra—the local officials were in effect no more than symbols, lacking an adequate security force to protect them and unsure of which political authority they served. Of the Dutch-occupied areas, only in Ambon did a situation develop in 1950, where, with government authority divided and uncertain, dissidents felt able to challenge the established order, in this case through a counterrevolution launched by men seeking connections with a different state. None of the three other areas dealt with in this book experienced violent revolutionary change. In West Sumatra, where local Republicans were strong enough to shape the government, revolutionary outbreaks were sporadic and restricted; they were, however, sufficiently powerful to compel the authorities to respond positively to popular demands for replacing local officals and altering the administrative order. In South Sulawesi and Jakarta, where, with the aid of other Allied forces, the Dutch were soon able to reestablish their rule, they were strong enough to crush any rebellious activity with ease.

In the areas where the old order was destroyed, however, the extent to which the insurgents were successful in establishing and maintaining a new social and political order was influenced less by the countervailing strength of the national Republican or colonial authorities than by the character of the revolutionary forces themselves, the course of their political development over the previous decade, the quality of their leadership, and its interaction with other groups in the society. Only in Aceh (and in West Sumatra, where most of the innovations were introduced through less violent means) was it possible to maintain the changes instituted at all levels of the regional government, though it should be noted that in Banten, the Tiga Daerah, and East Sumatra, the changes brought about in the early months of independence were never completely reversed.

Violent outbreaks were generated in large part by the internal local tensions activated by colonial rule in general, and in particular by the hardship and suffering of the immediately preceding years under the Japanese occupation; and these outbreaks were often exacerbated by long-smouldering antagonisms among ethnic and religious groups. There was a clear distinction, however, between the character of violence in the towns and in the rural areas. Closer similarities existed between the course of events that followed the independence proclamation in Jakarta, Medan, and Makassar, for example, than between what occurred in any of these towns and its rural hinterland.

In most of the larger towns in these eight regions, the bands of *pemuda* (youth), particularly those who had received paramilitary training from the Japanese, were frequently the mobilizing force behind, as well as leaders of, the actions against the state authorities—

whether of the Republic or the Dutch.[2] In the early months of independence, these militant groups patrolled the city streets, fighting the Dutch and KNIL (Royal Netherlands Indies Army) forces, sometimes attacking and looting shops and businesses thought to be owned by Dutch sympathizers, and generally opposing the restrained policies of the regular Republican army when it withdrew to regions surrounding the cities. Also characteristic of these urban areas was the existence of a faction of older moderate Republican nationalists who felt able to tread a middle way and still envisage the possibility of following an evolutionary path to eventual independence. This group included members of the Republic's Balai Agung in Jakarta, as well as of the Dutch-sponsored councils in Makassar, Medan, and Ambon. Most of them came from the Western-educated upper strata of urban society, who in the 1930s, if they had returned to their home regions on completing their schooling, had stood on both sides of the struggle, and sometimes occupied a neutral area between, either serving in Dutch-sponsored representative bodies, or, if professionally trained—doctors, lawyers, teachers—becoming leaders of the local nationalist organizations, cooperative and noncooperative. This educated elite had been the mainstay of the small prewar nationalist movements in Ambon and South Sulawesi, as well as Medan and Jakarta. In the postwar period in Makassar, Ambon, and Medan, a number of its members chose to participate in Dutch-sponsored assemblies in an effort to provide a legal opposition which could help secure Indonesian independence by working within the federal system.

Usually, however, no such middle ground existed in the countryside. There the situation was far more polarized and compromise was rarely an option. The conditions of the revolution were such that it was primarily in the rural areas, not in the cities and towns, that major political, social, and sometimes economic changes were effected, and they were frequently brought about by violent means. As local officials were seized, killed, or fled to the towns, alterations of the social order were often introduced. In such regions as Banten, the Tiga Daerah, and Aceh it was generally peasants who precipitated the revolutionary activity—usually by rioting to seize food supplies and destroy the structure of the administration as Japanese control collapsed. Although in Aceh youth groups played a major role in leading the subsequent violence, this does not appear to have been the case in either the Tiga Daerah or in Banten. The wellsprings for radical and revolutionary activity in Banten were the Communist, Islamic, and bandit groups that had headed earlier rebellions against the Dutch. And in the Tiga Daerah too, the prewar socialist and Communist leadership, together with bandits and traditionalist Moslems took over the revolutionary movements initiated by the peasants to overturn the old order.

Although in Aceh and in other rural areas of Sumatra and Sulawesi young people were often in the forefront of the struggle, these rural pemuda, as well as the revolutionary leaders they followed, differed in terms of background, ideology, and aims from their urban counterparts. Certainly in West Sumatra and Aceh the majority of the rural insurgents—young and middle-aged—had been trained in Islamic schools and belonged to Islamic organizations. In the closing decades of Dutch rule, their elders and teachers had stood outside colonial society, so they had fewer ambivalent feelings than their Western-educated brothers and sisters toward the colonial administration. In comparison with South Sulawesi where most of the fighters were "ill educated youth" coming from both the aristocracy and from Islamic schools and organizations, these Sumatra revolutionaries had often received a relatively good education in the modernist religious schools. In East Sumatra, graduates of Islamic schools formed only one component of the postwar revolutionary elite but they were the foundation of the PUSA in Aceh, and they provided a substantial proportion of the political and military leaders in West Sumatra. In South Sulawesi, in contrast, they rarely achieved roles of leadership during the revolution, usually spending the years in prison or the jungle, and emerging from the struggle ill-equipped to compete with their Western-educated brothers who had participated in the KRIS (nationalist organization for Sulawesi people) on Java or in the Dutch-sponsored assemblies of the NIT in Makassar.

It could be argued that the violence that broke out in many of the rural areas was essentially a series of agrarian revolts, mounted coincidentally with a national independence struggle, wherein "peasant goals . . . were not intrinsically different from previous peasant aims in rebellions or riots."[3] Such a contention would seem reinforced by the fact that in the Tiga Daerah and Banten, after the removal of the old order, the regional revolutionary leaders were unable to mobilize the peasantry to support more radical revolutionary action. But such an argument ignores the fact that, although their aims did not coincide with those of the radical secular groups, these peasant insurgents in fact had aims that reached far beyond local parochial concerns and were genuinely revolutionary.

As in Vietnam, in the early days of Indonesian independence "salvation from the foreigner was taken by the peasantry to include salvation from hunger, tenantry, and taxes."[4] But in addition, it is clear that more generally it meant reordering Indonesian society in accordance with indigenous political, social, and religious criteria. And in some instances, the opportunity provided by the breakdown of state power permitted the people in the countryside to sustain the momentum of their initial rebellious activity and focus it effectively on changing the political order of which they were a part.[5] But only in a few areas, such as Aceh, and to some extent East Sumatra, did this involve any fundamental and permanent change in the economic order as well. In the other regions, once Japanese food stocks had been seized and the symbols of government destroyed, the peasants focused their principal attention on choosing replacements for the old colonial officials rather than making any basic alterations in the economic structure. To achieve their goal, they were willing to ally with those local elites that embodied traditional values and had not benefited from the presence of the colonial power. And overwhelmingly in most rural areas of Indonesia these were the Islamic teachers and leaders who during the colonial period had remained aloof from, and antagonistic toward, the Dutch administration.

A common and enduring characteristic of the new order evident in at least four of the regions was the role of Islamic religious teachers elected to positions of local authority. As prominent figures in schools and villages, they had frequently become the principal local symbol of opposition to Dutch colonialism, embodying for much of the peasantry the distinguishing qualities of the new Indonesia that would supplant the Netherlands Indies. The strength of this expectation opened the way for religious leaders to establish a fundamentally Islamic state in Aceh, form a strong religious component in the government of Banten, and achieve heavy representation in the lower levels of the government in West Sumatra and the Tiga Daerah. Even during their brief period of ascendancy, the Communist councils in the Tiga Daerah and Banten had to countenance coexistence with an elected or otherwise popularly chosen administration heavily influenced by Islamic teachers.

The fact that they shared a single, all-embracing goal—an independent Indonesia—is one major characteristic that distinguishes these local uprisings from the general category of agrarian revolt. Because the people in the rural areas of Indonesia were struggling against an *ancien régime* that was colonial rather than indigenous, events at the local level were tied closely with those at the national level. The revolutionary leaders in all regions emphasized their ties to the national revolution, and the slogans and symbols of the prewar nationalist movement—the red and white flag, the Indonesian language, and the Indonesia Raya anthem—were an integral part of the revolution, not only for the political leaders, but for the entire population.

Thus, the nationalist leadership in urban and rural areas was strengthened to the extent that it could isolate and emphasize the character of the Indonesian nation that would be realized through the removal of foreign rule and the governmental system it had imposed. In further defining the new nation, however, it called on traditional and religious myths of the ideal society, which in general were rooted in the concept of egalitarianism.[6] The sources of this egalitarianism, at least in the countryside, were traced not to Western socialist thought, but to traditional indigenous ideals of *sama rata sama rasa* (on the same level, feeling as one)[7] or to the "profound moral egalitarianism" of Islam.[8]

As for the Republic's central government, its very weakness during this period served to strengthen the loyalty of the local revolutionaries to its leadership. For because of its inability to exert its authority by force, it had to rely on the *idea* of an independent Indonesia that had gained strength and force over the previous three decades. Thus it was not a central state dragooning the regions into compliance with its own vision, but one whose weakness left it no alternative but to permit them the scope to provide substance to this idea in conformity with their local perceptions.

In this pattern of revolutionary power, there was, however, a discrepancy between a shared goal of independence and diverse views of the form that independence would take. The strength of anti-Dutch nationalism was certainly tempered in some of the non-Javanese regions by a fear of the potential of a "Javanese imperialism" that could threaten the indigenous societies and moral order after Dutch power had been removed. Many non-Javanese, while strongly nationalistic, would, given the option, have supported a federal state free of the Dutch, in preference to the unitary state proposed by the Republic. Building on this disagreement, the Dutch tried to counter the national struggle for independence with their proposals for a federal Indonesia, and many peoples outside Java were attracted by the prospect of a federal order in which their regions could retain substantial autonomy vis-à-vis any central government on Java. If the Dutch had been sincere in granting the federal states genuine independence, they would probably have been more successful, but their efforts to manipulate local leaders and undermine adherence to the goal of independence discredited the idea of federalism to such an extent that, after the transfer of sovereignty, the concept was no longer politically viable, and advocacy of such a system was frequently viewed as tantamount to treason.

In essence, we have been concerned with a series of largely autonomous regional revolutions in pursuit of a common formal goal—an independent Indonesia—whose contemplated content and character varied in accordance with both the traditions and changing social dynamics of each region. But virtually all of the major actors, whether leaders or participants, whatever their immediate goals, saw their activities, erroneously or not, as coinciding with, and an integral part of, a country-wide revolutionary process through which an Indonesia, independent of Western power and in tune with what they perceived as indigenous Indonesian cultural and religious values, would emerge.

The national leaders moved, as revolutionary leaders usually do, to compromise with residual elements of the previous order, which, in this anticolonial revolution, involved making concessions to the withdrawing colonial power and co-opting indigenous members of the old colonial order. As this process worked itself out in the series of negotiations that ended with the transfer of sovereignty from the Dutch, increasing numbers of the staunchest revolutionaries in the regions felt themselves betrayed. Well before 1950, seeds of later upheaval were planted as disillusionment with the national Republican leadership began to set in, and they grew apace once full independence was achieved. The idea of national independence was strong enough to keep most revolutionaries loyal until this aim was realized and until, soon thereafter, the actions of the new state, now impinging directly on their regions, made clear to them how far their local visions of independent Indonesia differed from its reality.

Notes

1. That a large Christian community was not necessarily the base for solid pro-Dutch support even in eastern Indonesia is also seen in the fascinating account of events in Halmahera during the period, which appears in James Haire, *The Character and Theological Struggle of the Church in Halmahera, Indonesia, 1941–1979* (Frankfurt am Main: Verlag Peter D. Lang, 1981), especially pp. 24–52.

2. On the *pemuda,* see Benedict R. O'G. Anderson, *Java in a Time of Revolution* (Ithaca: Cornell University Press, 1972), especially ch. 2, pp. 16–34.

3. Theda Skocpol, *States and Social Revolutions* (Cambridge: Cambridge University Press, 1979), p. 117.

4. David Marr, *Vietnamese Anti-Colonialism, 1885–1925* (Berkeley: University of California Press, 1971), p. 277.

5. These situations had something in common with Theda Skocpol's description of that in the French, Russian, and Chinese revolutions, when "the revolutionary political crisis of the autocratic state . . . interacted with the structurally given insurrectionary potential of the peasantry to produce the full-blown social-revolutionary situation that neither cause alone could have produced. It was the breakdown of the concerted repressive capacity of a previously unified and centralized state that finally created conditions directly or ultimately favorable to *widespread* and *irreversible* peasant revolts." Skocpol, *States and Social Revolutions,* p. 114.

6. Such a radical vision, in Jim Scott's words, "nearly always implies a society of brotherhood in which there will be no rich and no poor, in which no distinctions of rank and status (save those between believers and non-believers) will exist." James C. Scott, "Protest and Profanation: Agrarian Revolt and the Little Tradition," pt. 2, *Theory and Society* 4 (1977): 225.

7. As Takashi Shiraishi has pointed out, this phrase was not, in fact, a traditional part of Javanese culture, but was first coined in 1918 by Mas Marco Kartodikromo. It "immediately gained wide currency in the pergerakan [early nationalist movement] with Kiyai Haji Sirah of Banyumas in 1918 already depicting the golden age that would be realized with the coming of the Ratu Adil [Just King] as sama rata sama rasa." "Disputes between Tjipto Mangoenkoesoemo and Soetatmo Soeriokoesoemo: Satria vs. Pandita," *Indonesia*

32 (Oct. 1981): 94. The Minangkabau have a saying expressing the same egalitarianism ideal for their society, *tagak samo tinggi, duduak samo randah* (to stand equally high, and to sit equally low).

8. Clive S. Kessler, *Islam and Politics in a Malay State: Kelantan 1838–1969* (Ithaca: Cornell University Press, 1978), p. 244.

GLOSSARY
OF FOREIGN TERMS, ABBREVIATIONS,
AND ACRONYMS

(If a term is particularly applicable to one region, this is indicated in parentheses.)

abangan	nominally Moslem
adat	custom, customary law
afdeeling	subresidency administrative region under the Dutch
AMRI (Angkatan Muda Republik Indonesia)	Younger Generation of the Republic of Indonesia (Tiga Daerah)
API (Angkatan Pemuda Indonesia)	Youth Force of Indonesia
badan perjuangan	struggle organization
Balai Agung	City Hall (Jakarta)
Bambu Runcing	lit., sharpened bamboo [spears]; armed force of the "Indonesian People's Republic" in West Java
bapak	father
Barisan Banteng	Wild Buffalo Corps
Barisan Merah	Red Corps (PKI, East Sumatra)
Barisan Pelopor	Pioneer Corps
Barisan Rakyat	People's Corps (Aceh)
bengkok	a usufruct of village land used by officials (Tiga Daerah)
bersiap	to be ready, vigilant (used to characterize the early period of the revolution)
BFO (Bijeenkomst voor Federaal Overleg)	Federal Consultative Assembly

BHL (Barisan Harimau Liar)   Wild Tiger Corps (East Sumatra)
BKR (Badan Keamanan Rakyat)   People's Security Body
BPI (Badan Pemuda Indonesia)   Indonesian Youth League (Aceh)
BPK (Barisan Penjaga Keamanan)   Security Guard Corps (Aceh)
BP-KNIP (Badan Pekerja Komite   Working Committee of the Central
    Nasional Indonesia Pusat)   Indonesian National Committee
BPNK (Badan Pengawal Nagari dan   Body for Guarding the Villages and
    Kota)   Towns (West Sumatra)
BPPI (Balai Penerangan Pemuda   Indonesian Youth Information Office
    Indonesia)   (West Sumatra)
BPRI (Badan Pemberontak Republik   Insurgent Corps of the Indonesian
    Indonesia)   Republic (Banten)
Budi Utomo   High Endeavor (early nationalist
                                             association on Java)
bupati   administrative head of *kabupaten*
                                             or regency
bung   brother, egalitarian form of address

camat   subdistrict head, below *wedana*

daerah   region
Daerah Modal Revolusi   Region of Capital for the Revolution
                                             (Aceh)
Darul Islam   lit., home of Islam (movement to
                                             realize Islamic state)
datu   local ruler (South Sulawesi)
dayah   traditional Islamic boarding school
                                             (Aceh)
Dewan Rakyat   People's Council (Banten)
DMS (Dewan Maluku Selatan)   South Moluccan Council

FDR (Front Demokrasi Rakyat)   People's Democratic Front
fuku shūchōkan   [Japanese] assistant resident

GBP3D (Gabungan Badan   Federation of Resistance
    Perjuangan Tiga Daerah)   Organizations of the Three
                                             Regions
GDMS (Gerakan Demokrasi Maluku   Democratic Movement of the South
    Selatan)   Moluccas
Gemenebest Molukken   Moluccan Commonwealth

Gerindo (Gerakan Rakyat Indonesia)	Indonesian People's Movement (prewar)
Giyūgun	people's volunteer army on Sumatra established by Japanese
GPRI (Gerakan Plebisit Republik Indonesia)	Republic of Indonesia Plebiscite Movement
GSS (Gabungan Simbilan Serangkai)	Federation of Nine Associations (Ambon)
gunchō	subdistrict level administrators under Japanese
guru	teacher
Hadat Tinggi	Supreme Council of Chiefs (South Sulawesi)
haj	pilgrimage to Mecca
hawa nafsu	passion
Heihō	Indonesian auxiliary forces under Japanese
hijrah	Mohammad's retreat from Mecca to Medina
Hizbullah	Army of Allah (militia attached to Masyumi party)
Hōkōkai	service association under Japanese
Hulubalang	militia of the adat party, MTKAAM (West Sumatra)
imam	Moslem leader
ISDV (Indische Sociaal-Democratische Vereniging)	Indies Social Democratic Association
jago	fighting cock
jawara	bandit (Banten)
kabupaten	regency, administrative division above district, under a bupati
kafir	unbeliever
kampung	village, or town neighborhood
kecamatan	administrative division, subdistrict level, under a camat
kedaulatan rakyat	people's sovereignty

Kenpeitai — Japanese military police

kewedanaan — district, administrative division, under a *wedana*

KNI, KNIP (Komite Nasional Indonesia Pusat) — Indonesian National Committee, Central Indonesian National Committee

KNIL (Koninklijk Nederlandsch Indisch Leger) — Royal Netherlands Indies Army

Komite Revolusioner Indonesia (KRI) — Indonesian Revolutionary Committee (Banten)

KRIS (Kebaktian Rakyat Indonesia Sulawesi) — Loyalty of the Indonesian People of Sulawesi (Sulawesi organization on Java)

kromo — high Javanese

Kyai (K) — title of respect for orthodox Moslem scholar or teacher

Lapris (Lasykar Pemberontak Rakyat Indonesia Sulawesi) — Fighting Militia of the Indonesian People of Sulawesi

lasykar (laskar) — militia

Lasymi (Lasykar Muslimat) — militia of the Moslem party Perti (West Sumatra)

Legiun Penggempur — Stormtroop Legion

Legiun Syahid — Legion of Martyrs

lenggaong — semi-bandits (Tiga Daerah)

lurah — village headman

madrasah — modernist Islamic school (Aceh)

Mahkamah Syariah — Islamic courts

Markas Besar Rakyat Umum — People's General Headquarters (Pidie, Aceh)

Markas Umum Perjuangan dan Pertahanan Rakyat — General Headquarters for the People's Struggle and Defense (Aceh)

Masyumi (Majelis Syuro Muslimin Indonesia) — Council of Indonesian Moslems (modernist Moslem political party)

Merah-Putih — Red and White, the Indonesian Republic's flag

merantau — to leave one's home area

merdeka	freedom
Mr.	Meester (academic title of the holder of a law degree)
MTKAAM (Majelis Tinggi Kerapatan Adat Alam Minangkabau)	High Consultative Council of Adat of the Minangkabau World (West Sumatra)
Muhammadiyah	modernist Islamic social and education association
MULO (Meer Uitgebreid Lager Onderwijs)	advanced primary schools under the Dutch
Murba	political party founded in 1948 with allegiance to Tan Malaka and national Communists
nagari	extended village (West Sumatra)
Naga Terbang	Flying Dragon (militia, East Sumatra)
Nefis	Netherlands Forces Intelligence Service
negeri	village (Ambon)
ngoko	low Javanese
NICA	Netherlands Indies Civil Administration
NIT (Negara Indonesia Timur)	East Indonesia State
NST (Negara Sumatera Timur)	East Sumatra State
NU (Nahdatul Ulama)	Council of Moslem Scholars
ori (Oeang Republik Indonesia)	Republic of Indonesia currency
panglima	commander
pangreh praja	"rulers of the realm" administrative corps on Java
Pari (Partai Republik Indonesia)	Republic of Indonesia Party
Parindra (Partij Indonesia Raya)	Greater Indonesia Party (prewar)
Parsi (Partai Sosialis Indonesia)	Indonesian Socialist Party (briefly in 1945)
Partindo (Partij Indonesia)	Indonesian Party (prewar)
patih	chief minister of regent
pemuda	youth, young people
Pemuda Ansor	youth group of prewar NU

pemuda rakyat	poor, nonelite youth
pendeta	clergyman, priest (Christian)
penghulu	head of religious officials at regency level (Java); lineage head (West Sumatra)
perang sabil	holy war
pergerakan	early nationalist movement
perjuangan	struggle
Permi (Persatuan Muslimin Indonesia)	Moslem Union of Indonesia (prewar party in West Sumatra)
Persatuan Pemuda Indonesia	Indonesia Youth Association (Ambon)
Persatuan Perjuangan (PP)	Struggle Union
Persi (Persatuan Sopir Indonesia)	Indonesian Drivers' Union
Perti (Persatuan Tarbiah Islamiah)	Islamic Education Association, conservative religious party (West Sumatra)
Pesindo (Pemuda Sosialis Indonesia)	Indonesian Socialist Youth
Peta (Pembela Tanah Air)	Defenders of the Fatherland (volunteer army on Java under Japanese)
PIM (Partai Indonesia Merdeka)	Free Indonesia Party (Ambon)
PKI (Partai Komunis Indonesia)	Indonesian Communist Party
PKR (Pusat Keselamatan Rakyat)	Center for People's Security (South Sulawesi)
PMI (Pemuda Muslim Indonesia)	Youth affiliate of the PSII
PNI (Partai Nasional Indonesia)	Indonesian Nationalist Party
PNI Baru (Pendidikan Nasional Indonesia)	New PNI, Indonesian National Education [Movement] (prewar cadre party of Hatta and Sjahrir)
PNKD (Pemerintah Nasional Kota [D]Jakarta)	National Government of the City of Jakarta
PPNI (Pusat Pemuda Nasional Indonesia)	Indonesian Nationalist Youth Center (South Sulawesi)
PRI (Pemuda Republik Indonesia)	Indonesian Youth League
priyayi	member of Java's governing elite
PSII (Partai Sarekat Islam Indonesia)	Indonesian Islamic Union Party
PTB (Persatuan Timur Besar)	Association of the Great East
PUSA (Persatuan Ulama2 Seluruh Aceh)	All-Aceh Ulama Association

Putera (Pusat Tentara Rakyat)	Center of People's Power (under Japanese)
raja	village head (Ambon); elsewhere, ruler
RIS (Republik Indonesia Serikat)	Republic of the United States of Indonesia
R.M. (Raden Mas)	*priyayi* title
RMS (Republik Maluku Selatan)	Republic of the South Moluccas
rōmusha	forced labor (under Japanese)
Sabillilah	Path of Allah (Moslem militia)
santri	strict, or devout Moslem, also pupil in *pesantren* (religious boarding school)
Sarekat Ambon	Ambon Association
Sarekat Islam (SI)	Islamic League (first nationalist political organization)
Sarekat Rakyat	People's Alliance
saudara	brother, form of address
Seinendan	Youth Corps (under Japanese)
seniri negeri	village council (Ambon)
Shū sangikai	residency advisory council (under Japanese)
Sudara (Sumber Darah Rakyat)	Nation Founding Friendship Association (South Sulawesi)
suku	ethnic group
Sumatra Thawalib	Students of Sumatra (groups of modernist Islamic schools initially in West Sumatra)
surau	Moslem house of prayer and education
Taman Siswa	lit., Garden of Pupils: nationalist school system founded by Ki Hadjar Dewantoro
tani	small peasant, peasant farmer
Temi (Tentara Merah)	Red Army (PKI militia in West Sumatra)
Tentara Marsose	Territorial Army (East Sumatra)

Tentara Perjuangan Rakyat	People's Struggle Army
TII (Tentara Islam Indonesia)	Islamic Army of Indonesia
TKR (Tentara Keamanan Rakyat, Tentara Keselamatan Rakyat)	People's Security Army, People's Salvation Army (name of official Republican armed forces from October 1945–January 1946)
TNI (Tentara Nasional Indonesia)	Indonesian National Army (name of official Republican armed forces after May 1947)
TRI (Tentara Republik Indonesia)	Army of the Indonesian Republic (name of official Republican armed forces, January 1946–May 1947)
ulama	Islamic scholar
uleebalang	hereditary territorial ruler (Aceh)
Volksfront	People's Front
Volksraad	People's Council (prewar)
wakaf (waqaf)	religious obligation
wayang	traditional Javanese drama, particularly shadow plays
wedana	district head
zakat	religious tax

CONTRIBUTORS

Richard Chauvel has recently completed a Ph.D. at Sydney University and is currently a research fellow at the Australian Institute of Multicultural Affairs in Sydney.

Robert Cribb lectures in Indonesian politics and history at Griffith University in Brisbane, Australia. He received his B.A. from University of Queensland and his Ph.D. from the School of Oriental and African Studies in London, with a dissertation on the role of Jakarta in the Indonesian revolution, 1945–1949. He has published articles in the fields of Indonesian political history and marine biology.

Barbara Sillars Harvey received a B.A. from George Washington University and an M.A. from Radcliffe College, both in international relations. From 1955 to 1968 she was with the U.S. Information Agency, serving in Washington, Seoul, Korea, and Surabaya, Indonesia. In 1974 she received a Ph.D. from Cornell University in government and then lectured in politics at Monash University in Melbourne, Australia. She joined the U.S. Department of State in 1978, serving in Singapore and then as desk officer for Vietnam and later Korea. She was appointed American consul in Surabaya in August 1984. Her monograph, *Permesta: Half a Rebellion,* published by the Cornell Modern Indonesia Project in 1977, was translated into Indonesian and published in Jakarta in 1984.

Audrey Richey Kahin is editor of *Indonesia* (Cornell University), the major scholarly journal devoted to that country, and of the Cornell Modern Indonesia Project's monograph series. She received her B.A. from Nottingham University in England and her Ph.D. in Southeast Asian history from Cornell University. She has spent substantial periods of travel and research in Indonesia and other parts of Southeast Asia, with her prime focus on the Minangkabau region of West Sumatra. Among her publications are articles on the Indonesian revolution, Minangkabau society, and the nationalist movement. She is co-editor of *Interpreting Indonesia's Politics* (1982).

Anton Lucas received a M.A. in Asian studies from the University of Hawaii in 1972 and a Ph.D. from the Australian National University in 1980. He is currently a lecturer in Indonesian studies in the School of Social Sciences, Flinders University of South Australia. His publications include "Social Revolution in Pemalang, Central Java, 1945," *Indonesia* 24 (October 1977); "Masalah wawancara dengan Informan Pelaku Sejarah di Jawa," in *Aspek Manusia dalam Penelitian Masyarakat,* edited by Koentjaraningrat and Donald K. Emmerson (1982); and "Jago, Kyai Guru: Three Life Histories from Tegal," in *Other Javas Away from the Kraton* (1983).

Eric Eugene Morris, prior to undertaking his Ph.D. studies at Cornell University, received his B.A. in political science and history from Baylor University and his M.A. in Southeast Asian studies from Yale University. He conducted fieldwork for his dissertation in Indonesia from December 1974 to July 1977. Since 1979 he has been working for the Office of the United Nations High Commissioner for Refugees in Jakarta, Indonesia, Geneva, Switzerland, and currently in Bangkok, Thailand.

Michael van Langenberg received his B.A. and Ph.D. from the University of Sydney and is currently senior lecturer in Indonesian and Malayan studies at the University of Sydney. His recent publications include "North Sumatra Under Dutch Colonial Rule: Aspects of Structural Change," in the *Review of Indonesian and Malayan Affairs;* "North Sumatra 1942–1945: The Onset of a National Revolution," in *Southeast Asia Under Japanese Occupation,* edited by Alfred McCoy (1980); and "Class and Ethnic Conflict in Indonesia's Decolonization Process: A Study of East Sumatra," in *Indonesia* (April 1982).

Michael C. Williams was educated at University College, London, where he obtained a B.Sc. in international relations, and the School of Oriental and African Studies, London, where he obtained an M.Sc. in the politics of Southeast Asia. He has recently submitted a Ph.D. thesis on "Communism, Religion and Revolt in Banten in the Early Twentieth Century" at the University of London. He was lecturer in politics at the University of East Anglia between 1978 and 1980, and for the past four years has been head of Asia research at the International Secretariat of Amnesty International. He has recently been appointed senior political writer with the BBC Far Eastern Service. He is the author of *Sickle and Crescent: The Communist Revolt of 1926 in Banten* (1982) and has contributed articles to *New Left Review* and *The World Today.* He is also a regular contributor to *The Economist.* He is an editor of the journal *Communist Affairs.*

INDEX

Abas, Mr. Abdul, 120, 129
Abdulhadi, Kyai, 63
Abdulhalim, Kyai, 72, 73, 79 n. 25
Abdullah Arif, 88
Abdullah Bau Massepe, Andi, 216
Abu Sudja'i, K. H., 31, 35–36
Aceh: history of revolution in, 83–110,
    266–269, 276, 277, 278, 279, 280;
    sultanate of, 2; War, 83–84, 105 n. 2;
    view of Islam in, 160
Adiwinata, Joesoep, 73
Administrative officials. *See* Local offi-
    cials
Afif, Haji, 72
Ahmad Hasballah Indrapuri, Teungku,
    91
Ali, Hasan, 95
Ali, Mohammed (Mamak), 68, 72
Alirachman, 66, 68, 71
Allied forces: in Indonesia, 7, 8, 13, 179,
    181–182, 214, 224, 244; landings, 93,
    185, 211–212. *See also* Australian
    forces; British forces
Ambon, history of revolution in, 11, 217,
    237–264, 273, 275–276, 278
Ambonese: killed in Tiga Daerah, 30;
    officials in South Sulawesi, 212, 226;
    soldiers, 186, 188, 213, 256. *See also*
    KNIL
Ambonraad, 247
Ambonschstudiefonds, 241
Amin, Teuku M., 96
Amir, Dr. Mohammad, 120, 122, 129
Amir Sjarifuddin, 33, 34, 43, 173 n. 42,
    188, 193; negotiates Renville, 9;

resigns as prime minister, 15; role in
    Madiun, 17–18; visits Sumatra, 157
AMRI (Younger Generation of the Repub-
    lic of Indonesia), 29
Anak Agung Gde Agung, 221, 222, 255
Angling, Jaro, 68
Anticolonialism, in Banten, 55, 71–72
Antilles, 245
Anyer, 60
API (Youth Force of Indonesia), 186
Arif, Teuku Nya', 90, 92, 94, 96; biogra-
    phy, 107 n. 26, 108 n. 33
Aristocracy. *See also* Rajas (Ambon); Sul-
    tans; *Uleebalang*
—East Sumatra: prewar, 115–116, 117–
    118; in revolution, 124–125, 134–135,
    139 n. 18, 270
—South Sulawesi: compared with East
    Sumatra, 274; under Japanese, 209–
    210; prewar, 208–209; in revolution,
    211–212, 214, 215–219, 221–222,
    224, 225–227
—West Sumatra: 271
Armana, Haji, 72, 74
Army, Republican. *See also* BKR; Mili-
    tary training; TKR; TNI; TRI
—active in Krawang, 196
—compared in different regions, 266–
    267, 271–272, 277–278
—East Sumatra: participation in trade,
    126–128, 140 n. 28; role, 135. *See*
    also Warlords
—formed, 16
—Tiga Daerah, 38
—West Sumatra, 159–160

Arsad, Tb. Mohammed, 60
Asaat, Mr., 154
Asj'ari, K. Hasjim, 35, 50 n. 42
Asnawi, Kyai, 66, 79 n. 28
Australia, 9, 259
Australian forces: in Indonesia, 7, 212–
  213, 214, 215, 224, 242, 244;
  weapons seized, 213
Azis, Andi Abdul, 11, 256–257, 258,
  264 n. 34

Bachtaruddin, 156, 158
Badan perjuangan (struggle organiza-
  tions), 16, 28, 183
Bagan Siapiapi, 127
Bakri, Semaun, 73
Balai Agung, 184, 190–195, 201
Bali, 218, 220. *See also* Den Pasar Con-
  ference
Bambu Runcing movement, 75–76, 196–
  197
Banda Aceh. *See* Kutaraja
Bandits, role in revolution, 267–
  269, 279. See also *Jawara; Leng-
  gaong*
Bandung, 11, 194, 200
Bangka, 10
Bangun, Pajung, 121
Banten: history of revolution in, 54–81,
  266–269, 276, 277, 278–279, 280; in
  1926–1927 rebellion, 4, 56, 57
Banteng Division (West Sumatra), 159–
  160, 161, 162–163
Banyumas, 24, 42
Barisan Banteng (Jakarta), 186
Barisan Pelopor (Pioneer Corps): Jakarta,
  182–183, 186, 202 n. 6; Tiga Daerah,
  26, 35, 49 n. 32
Baso movement, 157, 173–174 nn. 45–
  48; legacy, 168
Bassaif, Achmad, 68, 71
Batak Christian Association, 117
Batavia. *See* Jakarta
Bedjo, 121, 127, 129
Belgium, 9
Bengkulu, 149
Bersiap period, 187; effect in Ambon,
  262 n. 14
Besar Martokoesoemo, Mr., 28–29, 30–
  31, 37, 42, 47 nn. 16, 17
Betawi, 180, 191, 273. *See also* Jakarta

Beureu'eh, Teungku M. Daud, 87, 91, 94,
  98; biography, 106 n. 13
BFO (Federal Consultative Assembly), 11
BHL (Wild Tigers), 121, 124
BKR (People's Security Organization), 16;
  Jakarta, 182, 186; West Sumatra, 151,
  172 n. 30. *See also* TKR; TNI; TRI
Blockade: Dutch, 127, 190; Republican,
  195
Bone, 210, 215
Bone, raja of, 210–212, 214, 225–226.
  See also Aristocracy (South Sulawesi);
  Mappanjukki, Andi
Boven Digul. *See* Digul, Boven
BPI (Indonesian Youth League), 91
BPNK (Body for Guarding the Villages
  and Towns), 163, 165–166, 175 n. 62
BPPI (Indonesian Youth Information
  Office), 150, 152, 172 n. 30
BPRI (Insurgent Corps of the Indonesian
  Republic), 74–75
Brebes, 23, 29–31, 33, 42, 44–45
Brigade B (East Sumatra), 127, 129, 130
British forces: in Java, 7, 14, 30, 36,
  185–187, 192–194, 195, 202 n. 10; in
  Sumatra, 124, 151. *See also* Allied
  forces
Budiardjo, Ali, 199
Budi Utomo, 116
Buginese, 208, 224, 226
Bui Taisintai, 210, 211
Bukittinggi, 145, 148, 151, 157, 164,
  176 n. 73
Bureaucracy. *See* Local officials

Cash crops: Aceh, 85; Ambon, 239
Central Republican Government: degree
  of influence, 98, 269; opposition to, in
  regions, 69, 257; policies, national,
  13–14, 41, 256; policies toward
  regions, 70, 72–74, 102–104, 196,
  198, 201, 207–208, 227; strength,
  276–277, 281
Central Sulawesi, 220
Ceram, 259
Chaeruddin, Entol, 59
Chaerul Saleh, 75–76, 81 n. 53
Chatib, Kyai Achmad: under Japanese,
  58–59; in 1926, 57; as resident, 63, 64,
  66–68, 71, 72, 75, 76, 81 n. 53, 268;
  and restoration of sultanate, 73, 80 n. 41

Chilton, Brig. F. O., 214
Chinese: actions against, 12, 30, 64, 65,
    184; in East Sumatra, 114, 115, 126,
    132–133, 135; in Jakarta, 180
Christianity, role in Ambon, 238–242
Christians: in East Sumatra, 272; and
    Moslems, in Ambon, 238–242, 243,
    248, 259–261, 275–276; participation
    in NIT, 224; in Sulawesi, 209, 226. *See
    also* Protestants
Christison, Lt. Gen. Sir Philip, 186
Chusnun, Mohammed, 74, 75
Cikampek, 188
Cilegon, uprising of 1888, 56, 64–65
Ciliwung, 179
Cinangka incident, 60–61
Ciomas, 64, 71
Cirebon, 190
Cloves, 239, 240
Coen, Jan Pieterszoon, 179–180, 201 n.
    1
Commerce. *See* Trade
Committee for the Preparation of Indone-
    sian Independence, 7
Communists. *See also* Musso; Pari; PKI;
    Tan Malaka
—Banten, leaders of revolution, 61, 63,
    65–68, 72, 76–77
—prewar role of, 3–5
—role in revolution, 12, 17–18, 267–
    269, 279, 280
—Tiga Daerah: and Moslems, 49 n. 31;
    prewar, 25; in revolution, 24, 33–34
—West Sumatra, prewar, 147
Coordinator movement, 198–199
Cumbo, Teuku Muhamad Daud, 93
Currency: Jakarta, 194–195; South Sula-
    wesi, 215

Darul Islam, 196–197, 200, 260
Daud, Sultan Muhammad, 84
Daud Syah, Teuku Chi' Muhamad, 96
Dekker, Douwes, 241
Den Pasar Conference, 218, 220, 249
Dewan Rakyat. *See* People's Council
Digul, Boven (West Irian), 25, 57, 120
Digulists: Banten, 58–59, 62, 68; East
    Sumatra, 120; Tiga Daerah, 33, 37
Diplomacy, vs. armed struggle, 14
Djajadiningrat, Hilman, 64, 69, 71
Djamaluddin Tamin, 58

Djambek, Dahlan, 150–151, 157, 159–
    160; biography, 171 n. 24, 172 n. 28
Djambek, Syekh Djamil, 150
Djamil, Mohammad, 156–157, 158,
    174 n. 49
Djemma, Andi, 216
DMS (South Moluccan Council), 249–
    250, 253, 257; elections for, 247–248,
    252–253
Duding, Mad, 64
Dutch
—colonial rule: in Aceh, 84–86; in
    Ambon, 238–242; in Banten, 56, 57; in
    East Sumatra, 114–118; history of, 2–
    3; in Jakarta, 180–181; in South Sula-
    wesi, 208–209; in Tiga Daerah, 24–25;
    in West Sumatra, 146–148
—forces: in East and West Sumatra, 269–
    270, 272–273; in Jakarta, South Sula-
    wesi, and Ambon, 273, 275. *See also*
    First Dutch attack; Linggajati Agree-
    ment; Renville Agreement; Second
    Dutch attack
—power during revolution, 212–213,
    215, 221, 276–277, 278; in Aceh, 98;
    in Ambon, 244; in Jakarta, 184–185,
    185–189, 192–194, 197–198, 201; in
    South Sulawesi, 207, 214, 217–219

East Indonesia, 6–7
East Indonesia, state of. *See* NIT
East Sumatra, history of revolution in,
    113–143, 269–273, 276, 277, 279,
    280
East Sumatran State. *See* NST
Education, Western, 278, 279; in Aceh,
    86; in Ambon, 240, 241, 243, 251; in
    Jakarta, 180; in South Sulawesi, 208–
    209; in Tiga Daerah, 36; in West Suma-
    tra, 152
Elections: Dutch-sponsored, 247–249,
    250, 252–253, 255, 275–276; in revo-
    lutionary areas, 32, 158–159, 280–281
Emed, Tb., 72
Emergency Government of the Republic
    of Indonesia. *See* PDRI
Ethnicity
—ethnic groups: in East Sumatra, 114–
    116; in Jakarta, 180–181; in South
    Sulawesi, 208
—as factor in revolutionary violence: in

East Sumatra, 126, 122, 123–126, 128, 129–130, 134–135; in Jakarta, 183, 184–185; in South Sulawesi, 226; in Tiga Daerah, 30–31; in West Java, 199–200

Eurasians, 12, 30–31, 37, 180, 215, 273

FDR (People's Democratic Front), 16, 17

Federal Consultative Assembly, 165

Federalism, 247, 257

Federal State of Indonesia: attitudes toward, 98–99, 250, 282; collapse, 256; plans for, 10, 207, 217–218, 273, 275–276. *See also* NIT, NST, RIS

Federal strategy, effect of in Ambon, 245–247

Federation of South Sulawesi, 222

First Dutch Attack (1947), 9, 98; East Sumatra, 126; effect on NIT, 221; Jakarta, 195, 274; Tiga Daerah, 45; West Sumatra, 145, 151

Food distribution, 25–26, 47 nn. 10, 15, 67, 215

Forced labor, 6, 26, 89, 210

Free Indonesia Party (Ambon). *See* PIM

Gaspersz family, 244, 249, 253

GBP3D (Federation of Resistance Organizations), Tiga Daerah, 33–34, 38–39

Gerindo (Indonesian People's Movement), 117–118

Giyūgun (People's Volunteer Army), 6, 16, 271–272; in Aceh, 89–90; in East Sumatra, 121; in East and West Sumatra, 271–272; in West Sumatra, 149–150, 151, 152, 160, 163, 171 n. 20. *See also* Japanese occupation; Military training; Peta

Goedhart, Governor, 84–85

Government of the Republic in West Java, 197

GPRI (RI Plebiscite Movement), 199. *See also* Plebiscite

GSS (Federation of Nine Associations), Ambon, 250–252, 255

Hadat Tinggi (Supreme Council of Chiefs), 216, 218, 222, 232 n. 30. *See also* Aristocracy; Sultans

Hague, The, 11, 18, 250, 254

Halim, Abdul, 163, 174 n. 47

Hamelink, M., 221

Hamka (H. A. Malik Karim Amrullah), 120, 169 n. 6

Hardiwinangun, R. T., 70, 80 n. 35

Hardjowardojo, Suhardjo, 163

Hasan, Mr. Teuku Mohammad, 120, 122, 155–156, 274

Hasan Kreueng Kale, Teungku, 91

Hasanuddin Division, 217

Hasegawa, Shigeo, 183

Hasjmy, A., 87, 91, 104, 108 n. 31; biography, 107 n. 28

Hassan, Kyai Abuya, 71, 79 n. 25

Hatta, Mohammad: arrested by Dutch, 5, 10; under Japanese, 6; prewar, 4–5, 147, 154; pushes rationalization program, 17, 162–163; and the regions, 41, 43–44, 69–70, 73, 145, 161; returns to Yogyakarta, 10–11; settles conflict in Tapanuli, 129; as vice-president, 7, 13–14, 15, 17, 23, 198; withdraws from Jakarta, 188, 190–191

Heihō, 6, 72, 182, 210, 211

Hidayat, Col., 163, 175 n. 60

Hidayat (Banten), 58

Hilman, Tb., 66, 68, 72

Hitam, Burhanuddin Tuanku Nan, 157. *See also* Baso movement

Hizbullah: in East Sumatra, 124; in Tiga Daerah, 35; in West Sumatra, 160–162, 174–175 nn. 57, 58

Hizbul Wathan, 152

Hōkōkai, 149, 151, 153

Hulubalang, 162, 174 n. 56

Hurgronje, Snouck, 84, 89

Husin al Mujahid, Teungku Amir, 88, 95–96

Husin Yusuf, 96

Ibrahim, Dahlan, 150, 163; biography, 171 n. 26

Idris, K. H. Iskandar, 36–38, 39, 51 n. 51

Illegal PKI, 33–34, 49 n. 35. *See also* Communists; Musso; PKI

India, 9

Indian troops, 185. *See also* British forces

Insulinde, 116, 241

ISDV (Indies Social Democratic Association), 3

Iskak Tjokroadisoerjo, Mr., 29

Islam, role of: 26–27, 279, 280–281; in
  Aceh, 86–88, 97–98, 104–105; in
  Ambon, 238–239, 240–242, 275; in
  South Sulawesi, 209. *See also* Islamic
  leaders; Schools, Islamic; Moslems
Islamic leaders
—Aceh: aims, 100–103; under Japanese,
  88–89; prewar, 83–84; in revolution,
  90–92, 96
—Banten: attitude to Republic, 73–74,
  77; under Japanese, 59; prewar, 56, 57;
  relation to sultanate, 77 n. 3; in revolution, 61, 63, 64–65, 67–68
—prewar, 3–4, 5
—in revolution, 267–269
—South Sulawesi, 219
—Tiga Daerah: become local officials,
  32, 49 n. 30, 50 n. 41; under Japanese, 26, 59; prewar, 46 n. 9; in revolution, 31, 34–36
—West Sumatra, 154, 159–160
Islamic state, 91–92, 99–101, 105
Islamic teachers, 280–281

Ja'far Sidik, Teungku, 91
Jakarta (Batavia), 2, 11, 19, 179–181,
  201 n. 1; history of revolution in, 179–
  205, 273–274, 277, 278
Jamiyah Islamiyah, 209
Japanese
—occupation: in Aceh, 88–90; in
  Ambon, 242–243; background, 6–7; in
  Banten, 57–60; in East Indonesia,
  209–211; in East Sumatra, 118–122;
  effect of, 266, 277–278; in Jakarta,
  180, 182–184; in Tiga Daerah, 25–27;
  in West Sumatra, 148–150, 152, 153
—troops: in Banten, 60–61, 63; clashes in
  Ambon, 244; in Tiga Daerah, 28–29
—weapons, seized in South Sulawesi,
  213, 229 n. 12
Java: Ambonese soldiers in, 255; under
  Japanese occupation, 6–7
Javanese: attitude toward, 166, 218,
  281–282; in East Sumatra, 114, 116,
  124, 135; in Jakarta, 191; in South
  Sulawesi, 208, 226; traders, in Ambon,
  239
Jawara (bandits), in Banten, 56, 57, 59–
  60, 61, 63, 66, 68, 72, 75–77, 80 n.
  40

Joes, Haji, 66
Jusuf, Mr., 58

Kaigun Bukanfu Daisangka (Japanese
  Navy Counter-Intelligence), 58–59, 74
Kalimantan, 7
Kamid, Jaro, 59, 63, 66, 68, 72, 74
Kamidjaja, 33–34, 38, 39, 40; biography,
  49 n. 34, 53 n. 69
Karangcegak, 25
Karis, Jaro, 59
Karo, 114, 115–116, 124
Kartalegawa, R. A. A. M. M. Soeria,
  194, 204 n. 23
Kasman Singodimedjo, 70
Kenpeitai, 28–29, 58, 61
KNI (Indonesian National Committee): in
  Aceh, 94; in Banten, 66, 72; in Tiga
  Daerah, 32; in West Sumatra, 151,
  153, 155, 156, 158
KNIL (Royal Netherlands Indies Army),
  11, 48 n. 23, 242, 278; in Ambon,
  255–257; fate of, 260, 263 n. 28; in
  Jakarta, 186; in South Sulawesi, 216,
  230 n. 18; recruitment, 217, 252
KNIP (Central Indonesian National Com-
  mittee), 7, 9, 70
Kototinggi, 166
Krawang, 75, 188–190, 196–197
KRI (Indonesian Revolutionary Commit-
  tee), 68
KRIS (Loyalty of the Indonesian People of
  Sulawesi), 216, 279
Kusumuningrat, Iskandar, 71
Kutaraja (Banda Aceh), 94, 95
Kutil, 31–32; biography, 48 n. 27

Labuhan Bilik, 115, 127, 140 nn. 22, 27,
  172 n. 23
Lahade, Saleh, 216, 217
Lammeulo, 93, 94
Land: distribution, 124; ownership, 85,
  89, 208–209; rights, 117–118
Language: Aceh, 104; Tiga Daerah, 40
Lapris (Fighting Militia of the Indonesian
  People of Sulawesi), 217
Lasykar (militia), 16; activity in Kra-
  wang, 188–190, 196–197; in Banten,
  66, 75; in East Sumatra, 121, 124–
  125, 126–128; in East and West Suma-
  tra, 271–272; in Jakarta, 183, 186–

187, 201, 203 n. 16; in South Sulawesi, 213; in West Sumatra, 152, 160–
162, 162–163, 174 n. 51. *See also*
Army; *Pemuda;* Warlords
Law, in Aceh: administration of, 85–86,
89; Islamic, 86, 87, 88–89, 101–102,
107 n. 23
Leadership: in Aceh, 90–92, 95; in
Ambon, 248–249, 251–252; in Banten, 56, 66, 70–71; in East Sumatra,
120–122, 128–130; in Jakarta, 191–
192; in South Sulawesi, 216–217, 224–
226; in West Sumatra, 154–155. *See
also* Islamic leaders
Legiun Penggempur (Stormtroop Legion),
129, 130
Leimena, Dr., 259
Lengah, Ismael, 150–151, 160–161, 163;
biography, 171 n. 27, 172 n. 28, 175
n. 60
Lenggaong (bandits), 31–32
Linggajati Agreement: attitudes toward,
75, 161; effect of, 19, 190, 225, 227;
provisions of, 8–9, 195, 207, 219, 250,
252
Local officials
—in Aceh. *See Uleebalang*
—in Ambon, 237, 240, 243, 251, 276
—background, 13
—in Banten: under Japanese, 59; prewar,
56, 57; in revolution, 63–65, 67, 69,
72, 75
—in East Sumatra, 124–125
—in Jakarta, 183, 197–198, 201, 273
—in NIT, 224
—regional differences among, 266–267,
270–271, 277–278
—in South Sulawesi: under Japanese,
209–210; prewar, 208–209; in revolution, 212, 215, 227
—in Tiga Daerah: under Japanese,
26–27; prewar, 24–25; in revolution,
23, 30–31, 32–33, 38, 40–42, 44–
46
—in West Sumatra, 155–156, 165, 173
n. 38
Lombok, 220, 249
Lubis, Marzuki, 120
Lumbantobing, Abu Bakar, 140 n. 28
Luwu, 216–217
Luwu, raja of, 212, 214, 225–226

Madiun rebellion, 17–18
Madrasah. See Schools, Islamic
Magelang affair, 42, 52 n. 63
Mahroezzar, 140 n. 28
Makasau, Andi, 216
Makassar, 207; capital of NIT, 218, 220,
222, 223, 253, 255; under Japanese,
210; prewar, 208–209; in revolution,
19, 211–213, 215; site of Azis coup,
11, 258
Makassarese, 226, 239
Malao, Liberty, 121, 129, 140 n. 34
Malays, in East Sumatra, 114–116, 124–
125, 131–132, 133, 134–135, 143 n.
48
Malino Conference, 218, 246
Maluku, 220. *See also* Moluccas; South
Moluccas
Mamat, Tje, 57–58, 62, 65–68, 71
Mancak, 64
Mangoenkoesoemo, Dr. Tjipto, 241
Mansjur, Entol Mohammed, 74
Manuhutu, J. H., 254, 255–256, 258;
biography, 263 n. 24
Manusama, J. A., 251–253, 255, 256,
257–258, 264 n. 35; biography, 262
n. 20
Mappanjukki, Andi, 210, 215, 225; biog-
raphy, 229 n. 7
March 3 affair, 159–162, 168
Martadilaga, Jusuf, 76
Martin Behrmann, 189–190
Marxists, 3–4, 5, 42–43. *See also* Com-
munists; Pari; PKI
Masyumi party, 15, 31, 154, 172 n. 36;
in Tiga Daerah, 35; in West Sumatra,
158, 161
Mattalatta, Andi, 216, 217; biography,
232 n. 31
Medan, 19, 116, 124, 270, 277, 278
Melik, Sayuti. *See* Sayuti Melik
Menado, 250, 251
Menadonese, 30, 256
Menes, 60, 64
Metekohy, R. J., 257; biography, 263 n.
31
Midjaja, K. *See* Kamidjaja
Military training, under Japanese, 6, 119,
182–183, 210. *See also* Giyūgun; Japa-
nese occupation; Peta
Minahasa, 209, 217

Minahasans: in NIT, 224; in South Sulawesi, 208, 212, 226
Minangkabau: form of government, 153, 172 n. 33; representation at center, 154, 191, 271; society and culture, 145, 146, 149, 166, 167–168; state, 165–166
Moeklas, Haji, 46 n. 9
Mokoginta, Lt. Col., 256
Moluccan Commonwealth, 245–246
Moluccas, 238. *See also* South Moluccas
Mook, Lt. Gov. Gen. H. J. van. *See* van Mook, H. J.
Morotai, 214
Moslems: in Ambon, 243, 246, 248–249, 254; in Tiga Daerah, 34–36, 38–39, 49 n. 31, 268; vis à vis Christians, 259–261
Mountbatten, Admiral Lord Louis, 6, 184
Mudzakkar, Qahhar, 216, 219, 223; biography, 232 n. 32
Muhammadiyah: in East Sumatra, 117; in South Sulawesi, 209, 219; in Tiga Daerah, 34–36, 37, 51 n. 46; in West Sumatra, 152, 174 n. 53, 160
Mujahidin, 94–95, 108 n. 31
Mukmin, M. Muffreini, 188–189
Mu'min, Haji, 63
Murba, 75
Musso, 17–18, 33
Muzakkar, Kahar. *See* Mudzakkar, Qahhar

Nadjamoeddin Daeng Malewa, 210, 215, 225; biography, 228 n. 4, 234 n. 45; prime minister in NIT, 220–221
Naga Terbang (Flying Dragon), 121, 126, 139 n. 17
Nainggolan, Dr. F. J., 129
Napindo, 126, 130
Nasution, A. H., 17, 73, 163, 198, 216–217
Natadiredja, 65
National Front (Medan), 131
Nationalist Front (Jakarta), 194
Nationalist groups: in Ambon, 238, 240–242, 244; prewar, 3–5
Natsir, Mohammad, 154, 161
Navy Civil Administration (Japanese), 209–210

Netherlands, the, 8, 9. *See also* Dutch
New Guinea, West. *See* West Irian
Newspapers: Ambon, 242, 243; East Sumatra, 142 n. 44; Tiga Daerah, 43
NICA (Netherlands Indies Civil Administration), 14, 155; in East Indonesia, 212–213, 215, 221–222; in Java, 30–31, 48 n. 23
NIT (East Indonesia State): attitude of, in 1950, 255–257; capital in Makassar, 207; history of, 10, 11, 218, 219–223, 273, 274, 276, 279; noncooperators in, 223; place of Ambon in 246, 247, 249–251, 253, 254; role, in South Sulawesi, 219, 224, 225, 226–228
Noer, Mohammed, 72
Noor, Tadjuddin, 220
North Sulawesi, 220
NST (East Sumatra State), 10, 11, 129, 131, 133, 134
Nur el Ibrahimy, Teungku, 99

Office of Religious Affairs (Aceh), 101
Operation Pounce, 187–188, 192–193
Opium, 128, 198

Pabuaran, 64
Pacekke, 217
Padang, 19; under British, 151; under Dutch, 159–160, 165, 270; Sukarno in, 149
Padang Sidempuan, 129
Padjonga Daeng Ngalle, Haji, 217
Padri movement, 146
Palembang, 58
Palm oil, 99, 114, 126–128
Palopo, 216
Pandeglang, 64, 68, 71
Pane, Timur, 121, 126–127, 129; biography, 139 n. 22
Pangerang, Andi, 215
Pangkalan, 197
Pangreh praja. See Local officials
Pantouw, Mr. G. R., 220
Pare-Pare, 216–217
Pari (Republic of Indonesia Party), 4, 57–58, 65–66, 157. *See also* Tan Malaka
Parindra (Greater Indonesia Party), 117
Partindo (Indonesia Party), 117
Pasundan (est. by Kartalegawa), 194, 204 n. 23

Pasundan, Federal State of, 10, 11, 199–200, 204 n. 23
Patty, A. J., 241; biography, 261 n. 5
Payakumbuh, 164
PDRI (Emergency Government of the Indonesian Republic), 10, 18, 145, 164
Peasantry: in revolution, 267–268, 278–281; role in Aceh, 85, 93–95; role in Banten, 60–61, 63–65, 66; role in Tiga Daerah, 25, 27, 40–41. *See also* Rural areas; Villages
Pekajangan, 35–36
Pekalongan, residency of, 23, 24, 29, 63; town of, 38–39
Pelaupessij, M. A., 253, 254, 255
Pelauw, raja of, 248
Pelu, 249
Pemalang, 23, 29–31, 33–34, 45–46
Pematang Siantar, 116
Pemuda (youth)
—composition of, 16, 277–279; in Aceh, 90–92, 93, 96; in Ambon, 243, 244, 254–256; in Banten, 58, 61
—in East Sumatra: in early revolution, 121, 122–123; groups among, 124, 125, 128, 130; under Japanese, 118–119; opposed to Chinese, 132; role, 135–136
—in Jakarta, 182–183, 186–188, 201, 202 n. 4
—in South Sulawesi: in early revolution, 211, 212–213, 230 n. 19; hunted down, 219; under Japanese, 210; role, in Java, 216, 217; role, in South Sulawesi, 224, 227–228
—in West Sumatra, 151–152, 163
Pemuda PUSA (PUSA Youth), 88
Penang, 99, 115, 126–127
Pendidikan Nasional Indonesia. *See* PNI Baru
People's Council (Banten), 65–71, 268
People's Defense organizations (West Sumatra), 163, 165–166, 175 n. 61. *See also* BPNK; Regional Defense Council
People's General Headquarters (Aceh), 94–95, 108 n. 34
Perjuangan (armed struggle) vs. diplomacy, 14
Permi (Moslem Union of Indonesia), 147–148

Persatuan Pemuda Indonesia (Indonesia Youth Association), Ambon, 244
Persi (Drivers' Union), 57, 58
Pesindo (Indonesian Socialist Youth): in Aceh, 91, 93, 94–95, 108 n. 31; in East Sumatra, 124, 126, 128; in Tiga Daerah, 34
Peta (Defenders of the Fatherland), 6, 16; in Banten, 58–61, 63, 67, 72; in Jakarta, 182; in Tiga Daerah, 26–27, 36, 51 n. 47. *See also* Giyūgun; Military training
Pidie, 85, 89, 93, 94–95
PIM (Free Indonesia Party): in elections, 247–249, 252–253; eliminated, 258; established, 246–247; led by Reawaru, 254
PKI (Indonesian Communist Party), 3–5, 17–18; in Banten, 56, 62, 65–68; in East Sumatra, 117, 124; in Tiga Daerah, 25. *See also* Communists; Illegal PKI
PKR (Center for People's Security), South Sulawesi, 213–214, 217
Plantation: crops, exported, 126–128, 198; economy, in East Sumatra, 114, 115, 116, 119, 135; workers, 124
Plebiscite, 9, 199. *See also* GPRI
PNI (Indonesian Nationalist Party), 4, 15, 33, 117
PNI Baru (New PNI), 4, 33, 147
PNKD (National Government of the City of Jakarta), 183–184. *See also* Balai Agung
Poeradiredja, Adil, 200
Poh An-tui, 133
Polongbankeng, 216–217
Popular Front (Tiga Daerah), 268. *See also* GBP3D
Portuguese, 239
PP (Struggle Union), 15, 69, 157; in Banten, 58; in Tiga Daerah, 45. *See also* Tan Malaka; Volksfront
PPNI (Indonesian Nationalist Youth Center), South Sulawesi, 213
PRI (Indonesian Youth League): in Aceh, 91, 93; in West Sumatra, 150, 152
Priangan, 56, 73–74, 197, 200
Priyayi. See Local officials
Protestants, 239, 247–248, 250–251, 260. *See also* Christians

PSII (Indonesian Islamic Union Party), 35, 147
PTB (Association of the Great East), 250–251, 254
Pupella, E. U.: biography, 261 n. 6; heads PIM, 246–247, 252–254; under Japanese 243; loses power, 259–260; prewar, 242; replaced by Dutch, 244; supports NIT, 249
Puradisastra, 68
PUSA (All-Aceh Ulama Association): controls Aceh's trade, 99; under Japanese, 89; prewar, 86–87; in revolution, 90, 94, 95, 267, 269, 279
Putera (Center of People's Power), 26
Putih, Raham Tuanku nan, 157. *See also* Baso movement

Rajas, in Ambon (village heads): deprived of power, 260; under Japanese, 243; in elections, 247–249, 253; postwar actions, 237, 241, 245, 249–251, 258; prewar, 239, 241–242. *See also* Aristocracy; Local officials; Sultans
Rankasbitung, 62, 68, 70
Rasjid, Mr. St. Mohammad: biography, 173 n. 42; as military governor, 164; as resident, 153, 156, 158, 159
"Rationalization" program, 17, 19, 162–163
Ratulangie, Dr. G. S. S. J.: biography, 229 n. 8; exiled, 215; under Japanese, 210; as Republican governor, 211, 213–214, 220, 225, 226; sends *pemuda* to Jakarta, 216;
Reawaru, Wim, 244, 247, 252, 254–255, 258; biography, 262 n. 7
Rebellion, 1926/1927: 4; in Banten, 56, 57, 58, 64–65; in Tiga Daerah, 25; in West Sumatra, 147
Regional Defense Council (West Sumatra), 153, 163, 172 n. 34
Regionalism (Banten), 56, 71–72
Renville Agreement: consequences of, in Jakarta, 198; provisions of, 9, 15, 196–197, 199; reaction to, 16, 74, 75
Republican Central Government. *See* Central Republican Government
Riau, 159
Rice: deficiencies, 60; deliveries under Japanese, 6, 25–26, 47 n. 47, 89, 210;

exports, 127; land in Pidie, 95; situation, in South Sulawesi, 212, 215; and sugar, 25
Rifai, Achmad, 72
Rijkseenheid movement, 250
RIS (Republic of the United States of Indonesia), 179, 221
RMS (Republic of the South Moluccas): Manusama in, 251, 253; proclamation of, 11, 257–258, 264 n. 36, 276; rule, 237, 258–259; similarity to Moluccan Commonwealth, 245; support for, 257–258, 264 n. 37; suppression of, 259–261
Roem, Mohamad, 10
Roem–van Royen agreement, 10, 18, 167
Roesad Dt. Perpatih Baringek, 156, 158
Round Table Conference, 10–11, 250, 254, 263 n. 28, 276
Rubber: exports, 99, 126–128, 190; plantations, 15, 114
Rural areas. *See also* Peasantry; Villages
—character of revolution in, 12, 19, 29, 60–61, 94–95, 277, 278–281
—Dutch pacification of, 218–219
—war against Dutch in: East Sumatra, 131; Jakarta, 189, 196–197; South Sulawesi, 216–217, 223, 226–228; West Java, 198; West Sumatra, 166

Saalah J. St. Mangkuto, 160–161
Sabang Island, 93
Sabilillah, 160–162
Sadeli, Achmad, 64, 67
Saldi, Haji, 64
Salim, H. Agus, 154
Salim Nonong, 63
Saparua, 253
Saragiras, 121
Sardjio, 38–40; biography, 51 n. 52, 53 n. 70
Sarekat Ambon, 241–242, 243
Sarekat Islam, 3–4, 25, 35, 116
Sarwono S. Soetardjo, 121
Sastradikaria, Raden, 64
Sayuti Melik, 37, 51 n. 49
Schools, Islamic, 279; in Aceh, 86–88, 103, 106 n. 14; in Ambon, 242; in South Sulawesi, 208, 209, 227; in West Sumatra, 87, 146–148, 152, 158
SEAC. *See* South East Asia Command

Second Dutch Attack (1948): 10, 164, 197, 200; in Banten, 75; in East Sumatra, 127; effect in Aceh, 103; effect in Ambon, 252, 253; NIT attitude toward, 221; in West Sumatra, 145, 151, 163, 164–165
Seinendan, 209, 243, 244
Semarang, 36, 42
Serang, 64, 70, 77 n. 2
Seulimeum, Teungku Abdul Wahab, 94–95
Shū sangikai, 149
Siliwangi Division, 17, 73, 74, 75, 163, 197, 198
Simalungan, 114, 115–116
Singapore, trade with Republic, 99, 115, 126–127, 135, 190, 198
Singgih, 188
Sinting, H., 58
Siregar, Dr. Gindo, 129
Siregar, Mohammed Arif, 58
Siregar, Mohammad Jakub, 120–121
Sisal, 114, 126
Sitompul, Hopman, 120
Situjuh Batur, 165
Sjafei, Mohammad, 149, 151, 156; biography, 170 n. 17
Sjafruddin Prawiranegara, 10, 18, 103–104, 164
Sjahrir, Sutan, 4–5, 13, 15, 23, 42, 43, 44, 69, 70, 154, 187, 188
Sja'maun, Kyai, 59, 67–68, 73; biography, 79 n. 25
Sjihab, H. Abdul Rahman, 120
Slawi, 29, 37
Social revolution: 12–13, 15; in Aceh, 93–98, 104; attitude of central government toward, 69; attitude toward in Jakarta, 55, 60–64, 75–76; in East Sumatra, 122, 123–126, 157; in South Sulawesi, 225–226; in Tiga Daerah, 23, 29–31, 35, 39–41, 43, 44, 45
Soebagio Mangunrahardjo, 42
Soejoso, 200
Soekrawardi, Raden, 60, 69; biography, 78 n. 16
Soemitro Kolopaking, 44–45, 53 n. 70
Soepangat, 31
Soeprapto, R. M., 37–38, 53 n. 70
Soewignjo, 37

Soewirjo, 183–184, 191–192, 198; arrested, 195, 197
Soldiers, Ambonese: 237, 240, 244, 249, 250, 254–256, 258, 259, 260
Soleiman, Agus, 68, 72
Soleiman Gunungsari, 63, 66, 68, 72, 74, 75
Sonda Daeng Mattajang, 218
Sophiaan, Manai, 211, 213, 216; biography, 229 nn. 11–12
Soumokil, 256, 257, 258, 259; biography, 263 n. 30; role in Azis coup, 264 nn. 34, 35
South East Asia Command, 6, 184, 215
South Moluccan Council. *See* DMS
South Moluccas, 254
South Moluccas, Republic of. *See* RMS
South Sulawesi, history of revolution in, 207–235, 273, 274–275, 277–279
SP88 (Revolution Unit 88), 196–197
Struggle groups. See *Badan perjuangan; Lasykar*
Sudara (Nation Founding Friendship Association), 210, 211, 228 n. 6
Sudarsono, Major, 76
Sudibja, Mas, 73
Sudirman, General, 10, 16, 216
Sugar, 15, 24–25, 27, 30
Suhaimi, Kyai, 65
Sukanda Bratamenggala, 73; biography, 80 n. 43
Sukarno: arrested by Dutch, 10; under Japanese, 6; as president, 7, 15, 16, 41, 43, 103, 181, 185; prewar, 4–5, 149; and regions, 39, 43, 44, 69–70, 91; returns to Yogya, 10–11; withdraws from Jakarta, 188, 190–191
Sukowati, Anak Agung Gde, 220, 249, 256, 257
Suleiman, Chatib, 147, 149, 153, 156, 158, 163, 165; biography, 169 n. 10, 170 n. 18, 172 n. 35
Sultanate: in Aceh, 83–84; in Banten, 56, 77 n. 3, 80 n. 41. *See also* Aristocracy
Sultans of North Moluccas, 246
Sumatra: division of, 104, 137 n. 1, 175 n. 63; Japanese occupation of, 6–7
Sumatra Thawalib, 117, 146–147
Sumbawa, 221
Sundanese, 194, 199–200
Supeno, 42, 52 n. 64

Suppa, 216–217
Surabaya, 8, 33, 187
Surawijaja, Tb. Entik, 64
Surinam, 245, 250
Sutalaksana, 73, 78 n. 13
Syammaun Gaharu, 96, 108 nn. 34, 39; biography, 108 n. 32
Syatori, Kyai, 31

Tahir, Ahmad, 120
Tahitu, Dr., 245, 247–248
Talang, 31
Taman Siswa, 108 n. 32, 117, 120, 242, 243
Tanggerang, 188
Tanjung Priok, 179, 185, 189–190
Tan Malaka: and Banten, 58, 59, 62, 268; and the PP, 14–15; prewar, 4, 57; and West Sumatra, 154, 157, 165
Tapanuli, 126–128
Tebu-ireng, 35
Tegal: after 1945, 44–45; prewar, 23, 24, 25; social revolution in, 29–32, 33; transfer of arms in, 28
Teluk Bayur, 151
Temi (Indonesian Red Army), 156, 162
Ternaja, Entol, 70, 78 n. 13
Ternate: sultan of, 245; trade, 239
Tiga Daerah, history of revolution in, 23–53, 266–269, 276–280
TII (Islamic Army of Indonesia), 196–197. *See also* Darul Islam
Timor, 250, 251
Tirtasujatna, Raden T. R., 62–63
Tje Mamat. *See* Mamat, Tje
TKR (People's Security Army), 16; in Aceh, 93; in Banten, 67, 68, 71, 79 n. 29, 80 n. 37; in Jakarta, 186, 187; in Krawang, 188–190; in Tiga Daerah, 30, 36–39, 44, 268. *See also* BKR, TNI, TRI
TNI (Indonesian National Army), 17–18; and Ambon, 259, 260; in Banten, 74, 75; to East Indonesia, 256; in East Sumatra, 129, 135–136, 141 n. 31; and South Sulawesi, 217, 228; in West Sumatra, 163, 164, 165. *See also* BKR, TKR, TRI
Toba, 124, 135
Tomo, Bung, 74

TPR (People's Struggle Army), 96
Trade: in Aceh, 85, 99; in Ambon, 238–239, 240; in East Sumatra, 115, 126–128, 135, 140 nn. 22, 23, 28, 272; in South Sulawesi, 221
Traders, 146
Traditional elite. *See* Aristocracy
TRI (Army of the Indonesian Republic), 16, 190; in Banten, 73; in West Sumatra, 152, 157, 160, 161, 174 n. 51. *See also* BKR, TKR, TNI
Tulehu, 257

Ujung Pandang. *See* Makassar
Ulama. See Islamic leaders
Uleebalang: as local officials, 90, 92; under Japanese, 88–89; overthrown, 93, 94, 95, 96, 108 n. 40; prewar, 83, 84–86
Umar, Mohammad Saleh, 120, 121
Unions: in Banten, 57; in Tiga Daerah, 46 n. 7
United Nations, 214, 221; Good Offices Committee, 9
United States, 9, 13, 14, 259
Urban areas, 165–166, 223, 226–227, 277–278
Urip Sumohardjo, 16
Usman, Sjarief, 150, 162; biography, 171 n. 25

van der Plas, Ch. O., 80 n. 35, 185
van Mook, H. J., 8, 185–186, 193, 217, 246
van Royen, J. H., 10
Villages, 267–268; in Ambon, 239, 241, 248, 275; in East Sumatra, 134; in Tiga Daerah, 29, 32; in West Sumatra, 158–159, 163, 270–271. *See also* Peasantry; Rural areas
VOC (Dutch East India Company), 2, 179–180
Volksfront, 15, 141 n. 33, 156–158, 159. *See also* PP; Tan Malaka

Wadut, 64
Wairisal, Albert, 247, 253, 257
Wali al-Fatah, 45, 53 n. 71
Warlords, 126–130, 272
Warouw, Dr. S. J., 221, 222
Warungunung, 63

Westerling, R.P.P. "Turk," 11, 200, 218–
  219, 227, 233 n. 37, 256
West Irian, 7, 11, 215
West Java, 196–197, 198
West Kalimantan, 11
West Sumatra, history of revolution in,
  145–176, 269–273, 277, 279, 280; in
  1926–1927 rebellion, 4
Widarta, Subandi, 33–34; biography, 49
  n. 35, 53 n. 69
Wiriaatmadja, Raden Djumhana, 63
Wonosobo, 45
Worang, 256

Xarim MS, Abdul, 117, 120, 121
Xarim, Nip, 121

Yamin, Mohammad, 154, 157
Yano Kenzo, 149, 170 n. 15, 171 n. 20
Yogyakarta, 10, 55, 188
Yogyakarta government. *See* Central
  Republican Government
Yoshizumi, Tomegoro, 58–59
Youth. *See Pemuda*

Zainuddin, Natar, 120, 121

Production Notes

This book was designed by Roger Eggers.
Composition and paging were done on the
Quadex Composing System and typesetting on
the Compugraphic 8400 by the design and
production staff of University of Hawaii Press.

The text and display typeface is Sabon.

Offset presswork and binding were done by
Vail-Ballou Press, Inc. Text paper is Writers R
Offset, basis 50.